Illinois Central College
Learning Resource Center

Linguistic speculations

LINGUISTIC SPECULATIONS

FRED W. HOUSEHOLDER, 1913 -

Research Professor in Linguistics
and Classical Studies
Indiana University

CAMBRIDGE

AT THE UNIVERSITY PRESS

1971

Published by the Syndics of the Cambridge University Press
Bentley House, 200 Euston Road, London N.W.1
American Branch: 32 East 57th Street, New York, N.Y.10022

Library of Congress Catalogue Card Number: 78-145 601

ISBN: 0 521 07986 1

Printed in Great Britain by
Alden & Mowbray Ltd at the Alden Press, Oxford

Contents

Preface

In 1964 the idea came to me of writing this book. Over the years I had formed a number of opinions about linguistic questions, questions which I considered (and consider) interesting and important, and opinions which are at least unpopular and perhaps novel, though, in general, I belong to the school which doubts the possibility of genuine novelty. Instead of writing these ideas up as journal articles and shipping them off to editors one by one, I thought I might do better to combine them into a book. There are several reasons for this. The individual essays which form the chapters of this book cover a wide range of topics, and together present (I hope) a coherent linguistic philosophy (not a new metatheory), implicitly much of the time, explicitly now and again. The style in which I prefer to write is not one which is currently in fashion for linguistic journals; I can get away with it in reviews, but only the late Uriel Weinreich ever really cared for it in articles. In style I do not include merely the literary shape, the choice of words and the structure of paragraphs, but also the tone or spirit and the type of argument.

In 1965 (just about the time I started this book) an article of mine appeared in the first issue of *Journal of Linguistics*.[1] In this, I asked a number of questions about the phonological theory which had two years earlier been launched (or better, perhaps, fired) at a complacent linguistic establishment, and which is now the new orthodoxy. I thought I asked my questions in an amiable and friendly manner, but the response, which appeared in the next issue,[2] was frightening in its lack of courtesy or of any attempt at that effort to understand without which communication must always fail. And (so far as I can tell) none of my questions was answered, and my puzzlement by certain arguments evoked repetition of the same arguments. It reminded me somewhat of the cliché rustic who believes that by shouting loud enough he can make the monolingual foreigner understand him. Since then one of my questions has received a partial answer from the work of a former student. I had asked what it meant to say that phonemes were merely convenient

[1] *Journal of Linguistics* 1:13–34 (1965).   [2] *Journal of Linguistics* 1:47–138 (1965).

ad hoc abbreviations for particular sets of features, which alone had
status in the system. The answer is rather an analogy:[1] phonemes are
statusless abbreviations for sets of phonological features in just the same
sense that words or morphemes are abbreviations for sets of semantic-
syntactic features, and just as numbers are abbreviations for the iterated
act of counting ("another and another and . . ."). In short, phonemes,
morphemes and numerals are *ad hoc* abbreviations not of the linguist-
analyst, but of the language and its speakers. And, however low their
status, they are the devices that make language psychologically possible
('chunking', the experts sometimes call it). The theory has since been
much revised (in details, not in basic principles) and the official text[2] is
now available. This is just one of a number of important books which
appeared after my own was finished in draft. In the main, these have
caused me to make only minor modifications; almost none of the topics
which interest me here are considered (at the moment) as worthy of
attention by our bright young linguists, and their main current concerns
(which may be cued by the names 'English transformational rules',
'deep structure', 'generative semantics', and 'lexicalism') are hardly
mentioned here. It is not that I find these matters without interest, but
rather that they are so subtly technical that it is very difficult to write
clearly about them.

And that is what I hope to do in this book. Given the sympathetic
effort to understand which I spoke of earlier, my readers, whether
linguists or laymen, neo-rationalists or neo-positivists, should be able to
grasp what I'm trying to say in any given chapter, whether they then
agree with it or disagree violently. Violent disagreement, I have found, is
an excellent stimulant of thought. Many of these chapters started from
such a reaction to a published article or to a remark by some student or
colleague.

Naturally I am writing this book for my fellow-linguists, in each chapter introducing at least one new or unpopular proposal for consideration.
Nevertheless I have tried manfully to keep the use of unexplained technical terms to a minimum. I hope that non-linguists will not all be repelled
by the language, the manner of argumentation, or the tone.

What are the qualities of the Chomskyan revolution which have

---

[1] See Gerald Sanders' unpublished 1967 dissertation, 'Some General Grammatical
Processes in English' (available from University Microfilms; also from the Linguistic
Circle of Indiana University, Lindley Hall, I.U., Bloomington, Ind.).

[2] A. N. Chomsky and M. Halle, *The Sound Pattern of English*, New York, Harper
and Row, 1968.

proved most attractive to the young? When it all began, around 1956 or so, the outright rejection of those linguists who were then most highly respected was undoubtedly very appealing; after one has had Bloomfield and Bloch, Trager and Smith held up as ideals year after year, it is refreshing to hear that they were all utterly wrong and can safely be ignored. But more recent students have never read these giants of the forties and fifties (in many cases, I was surprised to learn, they have not even heard of them), and know their names only from contemptuous discussions by Postal or Chomsky, so that this appeal is no longer valid. A little bit later, between 1958 and 1962, more or less, there was the appeal of belonging to an élite repressed by the authorities, working in underground cells to prepare the day of freedom for mankind. This, too, is now gone, since Chomskyism became the established orthodoxy between 1962 and 1964. What remains is the style of argument, from second-order implied premises that are assumed to be obvious to the initiate, with footnoted references only to unpublished papers and oral communication (completely neglecting the old-fashioned principle of priority which demands that proposals be attributed to their first publisher; there is, in fact, an implication that these proposals are so brilliant they couldn't possibly have been published before), with the subtle machinery of claims, strong claims and metatheoretical considerations. This still has appeal, and is presumably going to be the normal form of linguistic discourse for the next decade or so.

And in certain respects this is a fine and healthy thing. We should always be willing to search out and reconsider our fondest beliefs, our oldest traditions, the words of wisdom passed on to us from our gurus. This is, in fact, what I am attempting in the present book; some of the traditions I pick up are from the age of the Indo-Europeanists, some from the Prague school, some from the American phonemicists, and some (now hoary in an amazingly short time) from Chomsky and his immediate pupils. Some are actively taught now, others are actively rejected, but all can bear one more consideration. The principal method of discussion is a careful consideration of the consequences, for any given tradition, of accepting it and of rejecting it. If it is true, what else must be? If it is false, what can be inferred? In doing this I may seem to some to be firmly committed to a positivist or operationalist or empiricist view of things, and opposed to a rationalist or idealist view. In a sense, this is so, but no more so (I hope) than it is of any scientist who believes in the possibility of increasing the total of scientific knowledge. Certainly if there can be no detectable consequences of the truth or falsity of a proposition, it is hard to attach much importance to it. And no process or device which offers some hope of helping us to find relevant particular truths should be rejected as unworthy.

In considering the published statements of others I have tried consistently to read for understanding, not for polemic. In reading for polemic one takes advantage of the enormous ambiguity of language by looking for a grammatically possible interpretation of each sentence which will make it inconsistent with itself, obviously false or ridiculously tautological. Many scholars have developed wonderful skill at this, and the technique is much admired by the young. I hope I have never done it myself, but I can recognize it. In reading for understanding, on the other hand, one proceeds from the assumption that the writer would not intentionally contradict himself, tell lies or talk in circles, and is intelligent enough to fall into such errors by accident fairly seldom. One then attempts to find interpretations which are free of these faults and appropriate to the context in which they occur. It is surprising how difficult this is sometimes; people do indeed say things which at first glance are wildly different from what they mean or else appear quite incomprehensible. But goodwill and honest effort can get us through most such passages. This goodwill is only what any scholar has a right to expect from us, whatever his era or dogma.

My strongest disagreement with current dogma is on a point which seems to me of relatively little importance to linguistic research, but one upon which Chomsky and others place great emphasis, the hypothesis that human language capability cannot be explained by postulating an enlarged brain with more interconnection which is, otherwise, of the same general type as that found in other intelligent mammals, but requires some unique and complicated arrangement, different not merely in size but in some more essential way. One often feels in reading discussions of this point that Chomsky is on the brink of postulating a pre-existing immortal soul. The arguments about the awesome complexity and novel nature of the devices needed to explain language acquisition strike me as totally unconvincing (though I may be regarded as stupid for not being convinced). The complexity of the machinery needed to explain sense perception, in particular seeing, is well-known; this part of the brain's activities certainly involves elaborate pre-programming for special purposes. But the great success of man in evolution has always been attributed by others to increasing generalization without much specialized pre-programming, and I think that, so far, this view has much more to commend it.

The great contributions of the Chomskyan revolution are seen differently by different men at different times. The first one, for me, was the provision of a device for writing explicit grammars, in such a way that gaps and defects would be relatively easy to detect. And I still think this is one of the most important. But there are two others that seem nearly as great to me; the emphasis on explanation, on offering reasons other than whim or intuition for linguistic decisions, and the restoration of validity (even if only limited validity) to introspective evidence. I do not share the common view that the performance–competence dichotomy and the theory of the three adequacies or the new emphasis on linguistic universals are major contributions. These are often useful, but not really wholly novel.

This book is not a complete account of the present state of linguistics. The field is changing with such swiftness today that any attempt at such an account would risk being out of date even before I could commit it to paper. The reasons for this situation are many, but we might profitably speak of a few of them. (1) After a longish period of almost linear growth, the number of linguists since about 1955 seems to be increasing exponentially. (2) Naturally, a large part of this increase consists of young linguists, many of them bright young linguists, and most of *them* ambitious bright young linguists. So the race for glory is on; some of these young men and women feel that if they don't succeed in making a startling new discovery or proposal within two or three years, the opportunity will be lost forever. (3) These young men, in the first instance, talk only or chiefly to each other, exchanging xeroxes and dittoed copies for a long time before communicating their paradoxes to the outside world. (Their findings are not always cast as paradoxes, but since this brings the greatest glory it is a favored form: "There is no such thing as linguistic change"; "All languages are really identical"; "The fundamental form of a language is Morse code"; and so on.) (4) But with all this fervor and activity the science cannot possibly stand still or go in circles; real progress must be made. And this state of affairs will most probably continue until the young men of 1960 or 1965 have become the holders of power, or until bright young men stop being attracted into linguistics in any appreciable numbers. (5) Papers, published and unpublished, are now appearing on my desk at a rate about three times greater than I can read them. I can barely keep up with the titles and authors. At present I am in the peculiar position of having read a dozen or more articles and monographs which will not be published for another year or two, but *not* having read some of the articles and books published in the last year or two. And I am not the only one. (6) In particular, the fundamental rules (or metarules) for the form of grammars, the restrictions on rules, the details of phonological and syntactic and semantic features, even the nature of explanation – none of this is likely to be settled for a decade, at least.

At any rate, for these reasons and for others related to these in one way or another, neither I nor anyone else can claim to give a firm account of modern linguistics which will remain firm.

Most of this book grows out of arguments with my students or younger colleagues. A second stimulus is the naive (or not-so-naive) questions raised by non-linguistic colleagues, particularly psychologists, philosophers, computer experts and mathematicians. Questions which people in the field would never in the world raise (simply because the progression of steps leading to membership in the field is such as to prevent these questions from ever coming to mind) readily come to the lips of our non-linguistic colleagues. And our natural reaction of impatience with ignorance deserves to be checked occasionally so that we may be sure if the question *is* meaningless and irrelevant. A third source of inspiration comes from reading. Every year or two an article appears that seems to be so utterly wrongheaded, to disregard so completely the clear knowledge won by earlier generations, that it demands examination. Simple error does sometimes occur, of course, particularly now that periodicals are proliferating and editors overworked. But the most irritating kind of article is not the one which demonstrates that Latin is directly descended from Eskimo or that higher pitch is manifested by lower frequency of vibration, though one hopes that innocent children will not be led astray. The real gadfly effect comes from articles which blithely proceed from scratch to investigate matters which have been well and truly investigated in the past, with many solid results, quite as if these earlier researches had never been done. Now, as a matter of private education it is undeniably far better to make one's own discoveries (if possible) than to learn about them at second hand. But to behave in this way in public is another matter, and when it happens one is stimulated (once one has recovered from blind rage) to reflect again on these maettrs and verify that the sound conclusions are indeed sound.

So one common characteristic of most of the following chapters is that they are, in part at least, provoked by some irritant of this sort – except for passages that are inserted to establish a common basis of knowledge on which a later argument may rest. A second common feature is an attempt (not always successful) to make the task of the non-professional reader pleasant and not unduly burdensome. It is nice to pretend that linguistics is similar to quantum mechanics and relativity theory in its need for prerequisite knowledge and skill, but it isn't really so. An intelligent and literate man, whether he be philosopher or engineer, literary critic or astronomer, should be able to think about the problems of linguistics and follow arguments about such of them as are not concerned with technicalities quite as well as any graduate student who knows all the in jokes and the out scholars. So I have consciously aimed at comprehensibility. I am quite aware that a lifetime of communicating with my colleagues in one or more special jargons may well be thought to have disqualified me permanently for achieving this goal, but I may plead in extenuation that I have also communicated with many other sorts of people about many other topics in a considerable range of vernacular styles. My ordinary language may not be shiny bright, but it is not entirely covered with rust.

I have read almost every major book in the field from 1920 to the present day, most of the articles in such older journals as the *Bulletin de la Société de Linguistic, Indogermanische Forschungen, Glotta*, etc., from about 1930 to 1940; and in *Language, Word, Lingua, International Journal of American Linguistics* and other more modern periodicals I have read virtually every word from 1935 (or from the first issue) up to 18 months ago or so. This, incidentally, makes my problem of indebtedness acute (not that I have much faith in originality anyway), so that whoever believes I have been influenced by him is probably right. For critical help with my manuscripts, I am chiefly indebted to George Grace, Robert Dyer, Rulon Wells, J. M. E. Moravcsik, Reginald E. Allen, Dwight L. Bolinger, John Lyons, Bengt Sigurd, Lester Rice and (above all) James McCawley and Frances Karttunen.

Finally I must say a few words about misunderstanding and failure of communication. I have always rated clarity high among stylistic virtues, second only (I suppose) to the duty of avoiding dullness, and I formerly supposed that a high degree of success in communication was within my grasp – or anyone's. I now know better. Nothing can be so clearly and carefully expressed that it cannot be utterly misinterpreted. Possibly certain formal propositions of mathematics are exceptions to this rule, but I'm not even sure of this. What I am sure of is that you who read this book will miss my meaning again and again. Still, as all writers must, I hope that you will correctly understand and like some bits, and that you will neither praise me excessively for things I did not intend nor condemn me roundly for something I really did say.[1]

F.W.H.

March 1971

[1] An earlier version of this preface was given as a lecture at Western Kentucky University. Versions of chapters 1, 3, 6, 7, 13, 15 and 16 have also been given as lectures, at Indiana University and elsewhere. Chapter 1 was published in the first issue of *Language Sciences* (1968).

I *The ultimate goals*

What is linguistics? What good is it? What is a linguist? What does he hope to learn? Why become a linguist?

Questions like these can be asked and answered from a number of points of view. One may ask them to be answered autobiographically: "Why did *you* become a linguist? What good is it to you? What did you expect or get from it?" Here one is usually looking into the operations of chance and emotion. When I was in high school, our house burned down with all its furnishings and books; one of the new things we acquired as a result was a Webster's Unabridged Dictionary with an introduction and list of Indo-European roots; this fascinated me, and I resolved to study as many languages as I could. I took a series of degrees in Greek (and Latin), as the most relevant field available. By chance there was a war, and by chance I heard of an Army establishment concerned with grammars and dictionaries. I decided to apply for a job, in the hope of maybe being assigned there later if drafted. By chance I got the job. The place was, of course, full of young linguists. And so the story goes on, with a succession of coincidences and marginal motivations. Nowadays this would be a little unusual, perhaps, when dozens of universities offer degrees in linguistics. But these answers are not enough. Why did Indo-European ring a bell? And what was the bell? Here we need the services of a psychologist for one kind of answer and an expert rhetorician for the other kind. Certainly the only answer I could have given at the time I graduated from college is unsatisfactory: "Languages offer a fascinating puzzle; it's fun to examine them and compare them, more fun than math, even, because it's more surprising." I had, of course, already been influenced by Jespersen, but I don't think any of the explicit questions he posed altered my ultimate goals very much. So we must abandon this line of attack; the answers given by different linguists will obviously be wildly different unless we *can* find a reliable analyst to discern the identities concealed in the differences.

We should not fail to notice that the kind of random motivations that might be effective in 1970 are likely to be quite different from those which worked in 1930. Etymologies are much less freely tossed at the young nowadays, whereas trees and labeled bracketings[1] are more in evidence. The doctrine which strongly attracted me, that the variety of language was so great that complete understanding could never be attained, has yielded ground to a feeling that languages are so simple and uniform that perfect explanations are now only a few years off – a feeling that seems to stimulate our young linguists to feverish activity lest all the truth be known before they can sign their names to it. If I had believed this in my graduate school days, it would probably have steered me permanently out of linguistics. The belief (whether true or false) which is attractive to one kind of temperament may be wholly off-putting to another.

Another way of asking or answering is in terms of definition or usage: what do people generally say linguistics is? or what do *linguists* say makes a man a linguist? Hunting through the literature one may find all kinds of answers: "Linguistics is the scientific study of language (and languages)" or "A linguist is a man who is concerned with describing (*or* discovering the structure of *or* writing grammars of) languages." The first of these answers is not very satisfactory, since 'scientific' is a word which communicates very little except vague feelings of approval (for most people) or disapproval (for some), and 'language' as an abstract non-pluralizable noun is also in urgent need of explanation. If we say that 'language' means that which is characteristic of all or most natural languages, then we seem to be restricting linguistics to the search for universals and defining properties, plus (perhaps) the discovery and proof of theorems deriving universals *from* defining properties and from the neurological and physiological characteristics of man. This is an important and laudable goal toward which a little progress has been made, but there are few older linguists who would have been willing to regard this as their principal, central, or only true goal. The current idea[2] that the goal of linguistics is to explain "the behavior of the speaker who, on the basis of a finite and accidental experience with language, can produce or understand an indefinite number of new sentences", may seem at first sight to be different, but on closer inspection it boils down to the same thing, since this "behavior of the speaker" is admittedly a universal, and surely one from which many other important universals must follow. Conceivably it is even the essential defining property.

---

[1] If technical terms puzzle you, look in the index for explanations and cross-references.
[2] E.g. A. N. Chomsky in *Syntactic Structures* 2.2; developed more fully elsewhere.

It is possible to interpret this description of the language-learner's behavior as a directive for the linguist in more than one way. The most obvious would be a search for a built-in linguistic analysis algorithm (or 'mechanical discovery procedure'): if all persons dealing with the same language arrive at the same implicit grammar of that language, maybe it is because they all use the same algorithm. The objective of most linguists from 1930 to 1956, to find some such algorithm, would seem to follow quite reasonably from this explanatory goal, although their motivation was, ostensibly, different. Recent linguists, however, apparently deny the existence or even the possibility of such an algorithm, and postulate instead[1] a built-in evaluation procedure; the language learner forms hypotheses about the structure of what he hears in the form of paired alternative 'rules'; both of which (one supposes) are entertained simultaneously for a time until the evaluation algorithm is able to plump for one or the other. The retained 'rule' is then shortly paired with another alternative 'rule' and the evaluation algorithm again chooses. Then whole sets of rules are paired and evaluated, and eventually (perhaps; this is not clear to me) complete alternative grammars are so compared according to the built-in algorithm. The linguist's primary task is to determine what this comparison algorithm is (no algorithm has been postulated for the rule-forming and rule-pairing activity), and show that all other characteristics of human speech are direct or indirect consequences of the nature of this algorithm.

In order to account for linguistic change either some defects in the algorithm or some changes in the nature of the 'finite and accidental' samples from which the rules are unconsciously derived have to be assumed, but such defects or deviations must be supposed to affect only what are known as 'low level' or 'late' rules. The suggestion which sometimes used to be made, that all linguistic change consists in adding rules, would lead, of course, to the absurdity that languages inevitably become more complicated; and, if we assumed a million-year development of human language with an average of only one new rule added every century, all present-day languages should have something over 10,000 rules (this does not include purely lexical rules, of course). It would further imply complete preservation of all earlier stages of every language. This would be wonderful for the historical linguist, if true.

---

[1] If our understanding of their remarks is correct. Of course the combination of an evaluation procedure with a rule-forming device is itself an algorithm, merely a less specific one than the linguists of the forties had in mind. For an improved notion see James D. McCawley's review of *Current Trends* in *Language* 44:560 (1968).

But obviously (as is generally agreed) rules are deleted, revised, and substituted as well as added – and, indeed, whole blocks of rules may be rearranged or replaced – and infinite reconstructability is not a reality.

We have mentioned two possible inferences from the language-learning axiom, mainly because these represent points of view actively taken (or taken for granted) by many linguists. But these are not the only possible ones, and even these two allow of some variation. A third view might go like this: what is built into all human beings (and is perhaps especially lively in very young ones) is (a) an automatic generalizer, a tendency to assume that even a single instance allows the formulation of a general rule and to formulate some such rule however insufficient the data, along with (b) a similarity-seeking drive, which forces, at every new experience, an exhaustive memory search for all previous experiences which could be said to resemble it in any way. Ultimately there must also be a discriminator or difference-seeking drive, but this seems to be acquired or taught, in the main, rather than instinctive. In a sense, of course, the similarity-seeker and the generalizer may be thought of as two sides of the same device; still, they are not identical. The similarity-seeker says "This utterance is like earlier utterances A, B, C, ... in two different ways, k and q"; the generalizer says "If k, then q", or "If q, then k". Meanings of words certainly seem to be acquired in this manner, where k represents the word form and q the criteria postulated for its use.[1] A new occurrence of k without q leads first (one may suppose) to a rapid rechecking of all instances of k in memory for a different set of criteria, q', and, failing that, to a disjunctive hypothesis: "If k, then either q or q'." In ordinary language, we either formulate a new basic meaning (or better, perhaps, expectancy set) or assume homophony (that k *sounds* just like k', but is *really* a different word), but instinctively prefer the former. The question, however, may be raised whether there is anything specifically linguistic about all this; isn't this, in fact, the way we acquire all our opinions about the world and ourselves, our knowledge and our superstitions (though not, perhaps, our values)? There is, of course, a second way, namely direct verbal instruction, which undoubtedly plays a strong part in early vocabulary acquisition, but probably has only a minor role in grammar formation.

But are there devices peculiarly designed for language-learning and

---

[1] Our automatic generalizer does not, of course, formulate an explicit definition; most of us would have a hard time defining words we use fluently every day. See below, ch. 5.

irrelevant to other activities? Some linguists and psychologists believe that there are, but so far no one has demonstrated their existence or convincingly specified their nature. Suppose we take an old-fashioned view for a moment and assume that discrimination and identification of speech sounds are important aspects of language-learning. In a sense there can be little doubt that a kind of algorithm is involved, but it does not seem to be exclusively linguistic: When a rule "If k then q" meets a counterinstance, one hypothesis may be "This is not really an occurrence of k, but of something different, k'", and as this hypothesis is tested again and again the list of distinctions is gradually built up. There can be little doubt that many of the procedures of phonemic analysis (which we will discuss later) are merely explicit formulations of such activity. This particular instance will illustrate only the use of contrasting pairs; the identification of sounds in non-contrasting order positions (e.g. one initial and another word-final) as instances of the same phoneme requires something different, perhaps the establishment of the relevance of order: "*nap* and *pan* are different words". But there may well be languages (Chinese, for instance) where such identification is irrelevant and never in fact made. The identification of sounds in analogous positions "c in *cim* is the same as k in *kam*" may also not be made unless it is relevant to the morphophonemics (i.e. automatic changes in declension or conjugation), e.g. if *cim* means 'I eat', *kam* 'I drink', *bim* 'you eat', *bam* 'you drink', etc. Economy of inventory, for its own sake, does not seem to be a built-in need of human minds; there appears to be no strong drive to reduce the number of relevant phonological distinctions.

What else can we say about the language-learning device? An extreme assumption sometimes made is that from different accidental samples of language different speakers build identical grammars. This seems to be false; in many cases two different rules may have the same effect in 98% of all cases, and each speaker may write off the other 2% as slips of the tongue or simple errors (a hypothesis which very young children do not readily adopt, apparently, but which adults often prefer). Take the case of the distribution of the so-called subjective and objective forms of personal pronouns, for instance:

(1) The simplest rule is "if the pronoun immediately precedes the first element of the verb (i.e. the first auxiliary, if there is one, otherwise the verb stem) or, in questions, immediately follows the first auxiliary (or form of *be* with which there is no auxiliary), then use the subjective

form (*I, he, we,* etc.); everywhere else use the objective form (*me, him, us,* etc.)". This gives such phrases as 'I did it', 'I came', 'Did he go?' 'Where am I?' and 'You saw me', 'Come with me', 'Between you and me', 'He's disguised as me', 'I speak of him who knows', 'He's better than me', 'He's better than I am', 'It is me', 'You know us boys', etc., but also 'John and I did it', 'Me and John did it', 'Will he and you come?' 'Will you and him come?' 'Us boys did it', 'They spoke to the officers (John and me)'.

(2) If, to the same rule, a provision is added that the pronoun (to be subjective) must constitute the whole subject, then we get 'John and me did it', 'Will him and you come?' with everything else unchanged.

(3) If, instead, we alter "immediately precedes" of rule 1 to read "immediately precedes or is linked by *and* or *or* to, or constitutes the determiner of a N(oun) P(hrase) which immediately precedes", and "immediately follows" to "immediately follows or is linked by *and* or *or* to, or constitutes the determiner of an NP which immediately follows", we will get 'I and John did it', 'We boys did it' and 'Will you and he come?'

(4) Rule 3 is rather complex; a simpler alteration would be to add a third alternative to the condition of rule 1: "or if it immediately precedes or follows *and* or *or* or immediately precedes as determiner a plural noun". This yields the same forms as (3), plus 'Between you and I' and 'You know we boys'.

(5) A kind of hyperurbanism yields a complete reversal of the first rule: if the pronoun is the entire object of a verb or preposition, use *me* etc., otherwise *I* etc. This yields 'Between you and I', 'I'll take he and you', 'They spoke to the officers (John and I)', 'I speak to he who knows', 'You know we boys', as well as 'I and John did it', 'Will you and he come', etc.

(6) The book rule, of course, is none of these, but "If the Latin equivalent would require *ego, tu, is, ille,* etc. rather than *me, mihi, te,* etc., then use the subjective forms, otherwise the objective forms." This is the simplest statement of the rule, but requires a knowledge of Latin. For those ignorant of Latin no easy formulation is possible, but to rule 1 we could add alteration 3 and the following disjunctions to the condition: "or occurs as all or part of an NP predicate after *be, become* (in the sense 'come to be'), and similar 'linking' verbs, or after *as* or *than* where the NP which provides the base of the comparison is the subject". This will lead to the following changes from the list of exam-

ples under (1): 'It is I', 'He's disguised as I', 'I and John did it', 'Will you and he come?' and also such things as 'In his last incarnation, Pythagoras became I', 'Would you like to be I?', etc.[1] I am fairly sure that the rule I followed in normal conversation as a child was rule 1, or possibly rule 1 with modification 2. Nowadays, in writing, I would use rule 1 with modification 3, while avoiding as much as possible sentences like 'I and John did it'. We all know many people who use modification 4 or rule 5; probably these rules represent the statistically predominant usage of middle-class Americans. But the interesting fact is that it takes many hours of listening to determine which rule(s) a given speaker is using, since the output is the same most of the time.

Word-meanings provide many similar instances. Here the difficulty of detecting discrepancies is far greater; two speakers may communicate successfully for many years before either discovers that they do not have the same interpretation of word k, or make the same distinction between k_1 and k_2. All that is necessary is that there be two independently variable features which, in ordinary life, nearly always co-occur. Most stools, for instance, are backless, long-legged, and have small round tops. For speaker A, the attribute 'backless' may be criterial, and for B 'small round tops'; they may, nevertheless, go along for years calling the same items 'stool' until one day they stop in a bar which is provided with seats having long legs, small round tops, and backs. Speaker B may refer to these as stools, to be challenged by A, who says they're chairs (or perhaps seats), not stools. If such a confrontation occurs between an adult A and a child B, it normally leads to B's revising his criteria, but if A and B are adults it often leads to an argument or even a quarrel, or a bet to be settled by asking the next person C or (occasionally) by looking in Webster or the O.E.D. In this case Webster doesn't help; though he specifies "without a back", he hedges with "usually" and gives no clue as to what items *with* backs are eligible to be called stools.

But more often than not A and B go through life without ever having such a confrontation; perhaps without explicitly formulating *any* criteria. And this must be the case, not only for individual words, but also for grammatical patterns (syntax, constructions) and co-occurrence preferences (usage, "can one speak of an X of Y", etc.) as well. Linguistic change, no doubt, is partly powered by this phenomenon.

[1] See for a different discussion of this facet of English, E. Klima, 'Relatedness between Grammatical Systems', *Language* 40:1–20 (1964).

If there is a language-learning algorithm, we must not forget that part of its efficacy in children depends upon the phenomenon of *correcting*; adults smile indulgently and say "You mean X, don't you" or "That's not a Y" or "We say Q, not P," and similar remarks. In some cases this clearly leads to some part (perhaps very minor) of the grammar being directly taught *to* the child rather than derived *by* him.

Let us now, for the moment, leave our examination of the consequences of defining 'linguist' or 'linguistics' on the basis of the language-learning assumption and consider other definitions. For many years, certainly, the most popular informal definition, used, e.g. when a linguist wanted to identify his field to a layman who had never heard of it, went like this: "A linguist is a man who writes grammars (*or* descriptions) of languages"; or "Linguistics is the art and science concerned with rules for best discovering and describing the structure of a (strange) language." If you were fussy, you might add the adjective "descriptive" and say that there were also studies (or a study) called historical and comparative linguistics, and a specialist in this field could be defined as "a man who writes etymologies and laws of correspondence and development", while the science is "that concerned with discovering and describing etymologies and laws of correspondence or development". If you were pushed to make a definition which included both of these aspects, you might take refuge in something vague like "linguistics deals with all formal aspects of language and languages", and then go on to mention terms like diachronic, synchronic and panchronic as well as descriptive, comparative, historical and perhaps a few more. The question which was very seldom asked in those days was "Why?" That is, why does anyone want to describe the structure of languages or write etymologies? The answer usually would be in terms of personal taste and preference. Some people enjoy golf, others enjoy brain surgery, and others enjoy linguistics. Most of us thought the question stopped there, that once this point had been reached, any further investigation was up to the psychologists. And part of it surely is, namely the part that asks "Why is Joe Blow interested in linguistics instead of nuclear physics?" But there is another part which might run like this, "Why should an interest in linguistics be considered of any more consequence or relevance than an interest in contract bridge or National League earned-run averages for the past 50 years?" Linguists are not alone in being uncertain about the answer to that question; I have encountered the same discomfort in mathematicians, chemists, biologists and historians (not to mention musicians). The most obvious way of disposing of the ordinary anti-egghead heckler is to point to practical and profitable applications, but no academic feels comfortable with such a defense. Many mathematicians of my acquaintance stoutly denied that the practical applications of mathematics were relevant to the question, and favored an esthetic basis: "mathematics is beautiful, like music, and its beauty is its justification".

I used to use the same defense for linguistics, but there are two dangers here: (1) you may get back to competition with the expert on baseball statistics; (2) you may be pushed (like some musicians and painters) into an anti-intellectualist or sensationalist position, claiming that only feeling has value or something equally silly. So we tend to fall back on the type of answer physicists are more likely to give: "The study of linguistics increases our knowledge and understanding of the universe." It is agreed that understanding the universe is something good in itself, needing no further justification, or else we will again get entangled with the notions of practical utility and profit which we have been trying to avoid. But we must still probe a little: in what ways does linguistics contribute to this understanding? What aspects of the universe do we hope to understand better because of it? This amounts to a classification question; what is the place of linguistics among the sciences? Most of us in the past have tended to put it down near anthropology and sociology, as concerned with a cultural and social phenomenon, language, or else with mathematics and logic as the study of a class of formal systems, languages. We often quarreled a bit among ourselves about this, but on the whole the emphasis on linguistic form as the primary object of the linguist's attention was acceptable to most of us, and this form was generally felt to fall in a different category from forms of dance, of folktale, of social organization, of warfare, and the like. After all, a careful study of Sioux syntax is not likely to contribute much to our knowledge of Sioux behavior and *Weltanschauung*, though there have been a few who followed Baudouin de Courtenay and Whorf in thinking it does contribute a little. But then, does a detailed choreographic analysis of a Sioux war-dance (if there is such a thing) contribute anything of this sort either? A fundamental opposition may develop between those who are interested in the ways in which all languages are alike and those who are more interested in the ways in which they can be different. For many years it was almost an article of faith that there was no way in which languages could *not* differ (provided they satisfied some simple definition, usually involving communication, speaking, cultural transmission and infinite potentiality);[1] many linguists were eager to show that in language X there was no noun-verb contrast, or at least were willing to believe that such a language could be found. But now it is clear (for instance) that every language in fact has some sort of noun-verb contrast, and that it is an inescapable necessity of the nature of the language that it must have such a contrast. What is not universal is the way in which the difference is marked. Even here, the possibilities are finite.

There is one other plausible niche for linguistics, the one which seems to follow from Chomsky's basic proposition – as a branch of psychology. If the central task of linguistics is to explain how we learn to speak, then linguistics belongs to the psychology of learning. If this is so, then we can justify our interest in the particular details of this or that language only at the level of the collector of baseball statistics. But probably this is true of every field: some parts of it, some objects of interest, contribute to a fundamental goal; other parts, other objects, may fascinate the specialist without any such relevance. Most of the time we do not know; even batting averages may some day turn out to increase our understanding of man and the universe.

Let us briefly come back to the question mentioned above: "Why do you want to describe languages?" Two groups of people have a definite pragmatic answer to this (other than "So I can get a job teaching linguistics" which is a possible answer for any academic specialty), the cultural anthropologists and the missionaries. The missionaries' answer is "To speed the day when the Bible will be available in every human tongue", and this is a goal which, for them, is beyond question. Some of the anthropologists have a similar reply: "To improve my preparation for fieldwork." This answer implies two premises: "Fieldwork is better done in the native language" and "Knowing linguistics helps one learn languages better and faster." Most anthropologists are willing to grant the second, even if a few of them have reservations about the first; and most missionaries are convinced. The number of linguists associated with or trained at one of the numerous Summer Institutes of Linguistics in this and other countries is probably equal to the total of all other American linguists. Why are these people convinced that linguistics is

---

[1] Sapir in *Language* (p. 2 in the original, p. 4 in the reprint): 'Speech...varies without assignable limit as we pass from social group to social group.' See also Martin Joos in *Readings in Linguistics* 1, p. 228.

a good thing? Mainly because it offers them three techniques for discovering the structure of a new language: phonemic analysis, morphemic
analysis and IC (immediate constituent) analysis. In spite of Chomsky's
firm conviction that all of these methods are worthless[1] (even though
some discovery procedures may be possible which are totally unlike
these), the practitioners of them believe that they have benefited enor-
mously over the past twenty or thirty years. Certainly good grammars
were written before these methods came along, but everyone in the
field seems to believe that the proportion of bad grammars has dropped
since their introduction. However, if the ultimate goal of linguistics is
merely to devise and improve discovery procedures (which we will discuss in some detail in later chapters), then it can no longer pretend to be a
science; it is merely research and development with a practical orienta-
tion. It must, in this case, be either narrowly empirical, a trial-and-
error sort of art, or derive its theoretical basis from some (other)
science. So if the methods of phonemic, morphemic and IC analysis (not
to mention other less fully developed procedures such as semantic
feature analysis or Pike's matrix analysis, which we will discuss in a
later chapter) have any general validity at all, it must be because they
either conform to or at least do not conflict with the unconscious in-
ductive steps by which we all learn our native languages. And now we
have come back, though indirectly, to Chomsky's most general view,
that the nub of the problem of languages lies in the child's language-
learning process, though not to his more specific proposition, that this
process can only be explained if the child's brain has a genetically
built-in evaluation procedure for choosing between grammatical rules,
and (at least relatively) useless for anything else.

There is, of course, another way of viewing the goal of linguistics
which seems somehow purer and less indirect; is there a minimum set of
axioms or assumptions from which all observed characteristics of natural
languages may be deduced, and no unobserved (given infinite time)
characteristics? If so, what is it? Some of these axioms will surely turn
out to be psychological-neurological, concerned with the nature and
limitations of the brain – how much can be apprehended at once, how
much can be stored in the short-term memory, how larger constructs are
organized, and so on. For instance, the general fact of two levels of
structure, phonological and morphological (in one terminology), and

---

[1] Expressed in *Syntactic Structures*, ch. 6, but also elsewhere. See also C. F. Hockett,
The State of the Art, ch. 2, C11–12, pp. 40–1.

not one or three,[1] is almost certainly deducible from some such axioms, though no one has yet published the proof. So, in the end, all notions of the proper goal of linguistics are related. But there will always be differences of taste and temperament which incline one linguist more toward the collection of data, and description and comparison of individual languages, but lead another to concentrate on formal proofs of abstract propositions. And for either one to claim that he alone is a real linguist, while the other fellow is an ignoramus or a pseudo-scientist, seems rather short-sighted.

[1] Some linguists, like S. Lamb, do speak of more than two levels or strata, but even for them the crucial break is between these two, and any others are directly linked to only one of these, as we shall see in ch. 8 below.

2 Remembering and talking

Psychologists and laymen distinguish various kinds and degrees of memory: active and passive memory (recall and recognition); short-term and long-term memory; accurate and defective (or total and partial) memory; instant and delayed memory; and many more. We know very little about any of them; most experiments have been concerned with short-term memory of lists of nonsense syllables, letters, words, numbers, patterns, colors, etc. But it is clear (to me, at any rate) that all memory involves associating or linking, and is in a way already a kind of language, or at least, symbolic. This linking or pairing is shown in the design of some psychological experiments by organization of the lists as lists of 'paired associates', such that presentation of one member of each pair should elicit the other. Of the experiments discussed in a special issue of the *Journal of Verbal Learning and Verbal Behavior* devoted entirely to memory (2, 1 July 1963) about half used paired associates. An ordinary list, e.g. a telephone number or a sequence of letters of the alphabet, can be considered as a chain of pairs; i.e. BQZYAAL (or 2709225) is made up of the linked pairs BQ (27), QZ (70), ZY (09), YA (92), AA (22), and AL (25). But here the matter is complicated because other items on the list must have some influence as well; i.e. there are also pairs B–Z (2–0), Q–Y (7–9), Z–A (0–2), Y–A (9–2), A–L (2–5), B––Y (2––9), Q––A (7––2), Z––A (0––2), Y––L (9––5), and so on. When you memorize a part in a play, the opening word or 'chunk' of your line is paired with the end of the cue speech of the last speaker, but from then on within the speech we have the list situation, each new chunk conditioned (in some measure) by everything that has gone before.

In what ways may kinds or operations of memory (excluding habits – e.g. rules and skills – from our notion of memory) differ? Some obvious ways were mentioned in our opening sentence: (1) We know (or at least believe) that there is a difference between our remembering the beginning of a short sentence all the way to the end and our remembering a sentence of similar length some years after last hearing (or saying) it. Maybe there are other temporal classes as well: possibly our memories of yesterday's conversation are different from either of these. Or are they all simply one kind of memory marked by a gradual decay? Nobody seems to be sure yet, but both long and short memories are linguistically important: without one we couldn't complete a sentence, without the other we couldn't speak or understand at all, since our control of language is built of our linguistic memories. (2) There are various ways we can behave when *first* we hear (or see) the thing-to-be-remembered, and also when later we call up (or try to call up) the memory. (3) The element of intention or deliberateness provides a criterion at both ends of the memory span: we may, like the actor, try to memorize something to be remembered later, and we may later rack our brains to remember something, whether memorized or not. But we also remember many things (including sentences and words) without trying either at the moment of hearing (or reading) or at the time of recollection. The effort connected with the initial act may include a self-specification of the conditions under which recall is to take place – something like post-hypnotic suggestion. Probably, also, we should distinguish between wanting and trying. (4) At the time of learning there may be single or repeated stimuli (whether by accident or design); e.g. the actor may read his lines over and over again or the TV watcher or radio listener may hear the same commercial repeatedly. At the remembering end this factor seems less relevant, but at any rate we can consider the situation of a teacher who has learned the names of every member of his class, and now frequently needs to remember them as he calls upon different students in turn. Every such repetition is simultaneously an ending and a beginning: it is a repeated remembering, but also a reinforcement of the memory.

The three dichotomies numbered (2) to (4) above form a 2^3 or eight-celled matrix of possibilities, and it may be interesting to see if all eight cells are filled. But first we might take up two other oppositions (mentioned in our first sentence) which clearly apply only at the terminal or remembering end, both of which have to do with completeness or perfection. (5) One kind of defective memory is surely recognition: we know the word or sentence when we hear it, but cannot ourselves produce it on any kind of cue. But this is just one kind, and an examination of all the kinds known (with some consideration of their causes) should teach us more about memory than almost anything else. Unfortunately, as far as I can discover, very few experiments have been made in this area, so we will have to content ourselves with an anecdotal treatment of the subject. (6) Superficially, at least, what are commonly called slips of the tongue seem often to be indistinguishable from errors of memory. I mean here the kind of slip which does not involve interference phenomena; but even the interference types (metatheses, in which sounds or letters or words are interchanged, as in 'door' for 'road' or 'queer dean' for 'dear queen' – the spoonerism – haplologies, in which one of two identical elements is omitted, as in 'leisurely' for 'leisurelily' or 'Jones'' for 'Jones's', etc.) might be laid to short-term memory in some cases.

Let us take the case of remembering a name: "Who was that fellow we rented the cabin from three years ago?" Let's say his name was actually George Stimpson. The extreme cases are three: (1) We come up with the name George Stimpson almost immediately; (2) we fail to come up with anything at all; (3) we come up with a totally incorrect name, say Henry Brown, and have the same firm confidence in our recollection that we do when we remember perfectly (as in the first case). Accompanying any of these three *verbal* memories (or non-memories) there may be any amount of associated memories of matters other than the name: "He drove out to see us on July 5th"; "He had a German accent"; etc. These, too, are expressed in words; nevertheless we all feel that there is a real difference between remembering a truth (or a proposition) and remembering a particular linguistic expression of that proposition. But in what ways can we fall short of perfect recollection of the name without reaching total oblivion? Here there ought to be research, but I can't find any in the literature, so I will again fall back on my own defective memory. (a) We may remember the name correctly, but have no faith in our own memory: "George Stimpson? No, that just doesn't sound right, somehow." (b) We may forget the last name and remember the first: George Brown or George blank, say; (c) conversely, Henry Stimpson or blank Stimpson; (d) we may substitute a very similar name, John or Joe or Gordon or Roger for George, Simpson or Sampson or Timkins for Stimpson; (e) we may substitute a roughly similar name of some famous person or someone else known to us: Wally Simpson, say; (f) we may not come up with any *name* at all, but be able to specify some things about it – first name monosyllabic, last dissyllabic; first name begins with G or J or contains an R or an O, last name begins with S or T, contains an M or P, ends in -son, etc. And some of these memories may be wrong, of course: we may think of initial D instead of G, or F instead of S, and so on. Whether or not there is any system to these defective memories can only be answered by research, but off hand it seems probable that, in some cases at least, there will be a measure of partial similarity. But I think it is worth saying here that the partially correct memories that seem to occur most often to me and my immediate circle are (1) rhythmical memories – number of syllables and position of accent; (2) alliterative memories – the initial consonant(s) or pre-stress consonant(s), (3) rhyme memories – the stressed vowel, the final consonant(s), vowel plus consonant(s).[1] With names this is usually contaminated by the partial limitation of tentative answers to those stored in a bin labeled "Names", or somehow so tagged; i.e. we may come up with Joe Simpson, but never with Dorge Fimpson (or, at any rate, hardly ever), unless our memory is further marked as "new name", "never heard it before" or the like. If the word we are searching for is the name of a tropical plant, then this restriction is off, except as providing a source for the "something like" item: "I can't remember the name, but it's something like 'wisteria'." A memory like this is nearly always clear cut as to its being only "something like", *perhaps* because it is essentially a recollection of having said or thought "That name is something like 'wisteria'." With minor modifications to allow for partial differences in the sound systems, this seems to be the way our memory works with all vocabulary items in a language we are just beginning to learn; after we acquire some mastery of the language our memory for ordinary words begins to operate more like that in our native language, i.e. a multiplicity of semantic and perhaps syntactic associations may cross-cut and interfere with pure graphic or phonological memory. It is not unusual, even in one's own language, to remember

---

[1] Shortly after writing this passage I was trying to remember the name of a former student. At first I had the feeling that it began with a C+l cluster, and was one syllable in length; was it Blythe? or perhaps Clyde? I tested a number of other names fitting this general pattern without success. A day or two later as I was walking across the campus, the correct name suddenly popped in: Blair. A month afterwards I confidently gave a scholar's name to a student as being George X. Only after unexplained failure to find the name in standard bibliographies did any doubt arise. In this case I never did think of the right name, but accidentally ran across it in reading: Roger. The two names can almost be derived from each other by interchanging /r/ and /j/, yet this example doesn't properly involve metathesis, or alliteration, rhythm or rhyme, but only a loose sort of assonance.

For much more information on this aspect of linguistic memory, see the article 'Verbal Evocation' by Dwight L. Bolinger, originally published in *Lingua* 10:113–27 (1961), reprinted in *Forms of English* (edited by J. Abe and J. Kanekigo, Harvard University Press, 1965) pp. 253–65. See also V. Fromkin, 'Speculations on performance models', *Journal of Linguistics* 4:4768 (1968), and Roger Brown and David McNeil, 'The "tip of the tongue" phenomenon', *Journal of Verbal Learning and Verbal Behavior* 5:335–7 (1966).

that one knows a given word 'perfectly well' but can't think what it means or even the general area in which it is used, and conversely one may know very well that a word exists to fill a certain semantic spot, but be totally unable to recall it. Words first encountered in reading are, by many people, strongly associated with position on the page: "I can't remember that to save my life, but I know I saw it on the left-hand page about ten lines down from the top." For words first encountered by ear there seems to be no equivalent association, except, perhaps, with the person from whom they were heard or the place where they were heard. Words encountered in reading are also often accompanied by a vivid mental image of the lower-case roman printed form (capitals are included only as initials of proper names), and errors of memory here seem to be most frequently either metatheses of letters, or errors in double versus single or in silent letters. Similarity in shape of letters seems to play almost no role, except perhaps in cases where there is also a phonological similarity, as in the case of b and p or m and n. One often has a feeling about a word just written or typed that it "doesn't look right"; sometimes the feeling is sound, sometimes not. But context-restrictions often rule out such errors; neither Sinpson nor Simbson is a likely mistake for Simpson, though Simson might be. This does not, of course, by any means exhaust the ways in which our phonological memory can be wrong in one part or way but not in others, but most of the others (like some of these) are not purely or not at all phonological, as when Mr Stimpson is misrecollected as Mr Grant (via phonological association with Simpson and a middle-name association with U. S. Grant). Another point worth remembering is that partial and erroneous memories are often succeeded by complete correct ones; a few seconds, minutes or hours after coming up with Sampson or Grant we'll suddenly say "No! I remember; it's George Stimpson!" And this confident second memory is nearly always right.

All this suggests that our memory bears little obvious resemblance to the storage component of a computer with a simple table look-up program. Computers *do* make mistakes, of course, but in a straight-forward look-up operation of this sort mistakes are rare and much more restricted in their variety.

All acts of memory seem to be, as we speculated earlier, paired-associate look-ups: given item A of a pair (which may contain or be in some sense composed of several other pairs), determine item B of the same pair. The equivalent computer problem is, then, given a dictionary-like list in storage, each entry of which contains a series of items – an identification number, a spelling, a set of syntactic class-markers, a set of semantic class-markers, a list of probable co-occurring words, a list of spellings of synonyms and antonyms, etc. – write a program which will accept any combination of one or more of these stored items, and, after searching, tell you either (a) which entry (or entries) contains that combination, or (b) that no entry contains it. It could also be written to locate those entries which contain all but one of the specified items, or all but two, or (in some cases) items whose values differ by less than a specified amount from those being sought. By introducing devices to stop the search short of complete success, a program could be written, of course, which would fail to recover an entry which was in fact present. A program which, when asked to retrieve 'Simpson' given certain specified items stored with it, prints out "It begins with S" and then blocks, could surely be written, and, in general, the idea of a human memory-simulating program seems like a fruitful one; but ordinary retrieval programs don't work that way. Nor is it easy to program a computer so that it first gives some partially correct information about a look-up item and then, after a lapse of some minutes, while actually engaged in doing another job, suddenly blurts out the correct answer.

Let us turn back to our cubic matrix based on notions of *effort*, *repetition* and replacement of either at the *beginning* of the experience or at the *end*, in the moment of remembering. The cube, with +Effort at left, +Repetition at the front, and Beginning at the top, would look like this:

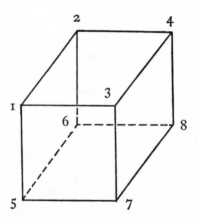

And three sections of this matrix look like this:

+Eff.	*−Eff.*		*+Eff.*	*−Eff.*			*Beg.*	*End*
Beg. 1,2	3,4		+Rep. 1,5	3,7		+Rep.	1,3	5,7
End 5,6	7,8		−Rep. 2,6	4,8		−Rep.	2,4	6,8

Can we exemplify all eight cells? Cell 1 is repeated effort at the beginning. This is any ordinary situation of memorizing lists, poems, parts in plays, etc. Cell 2 is a single effort at the beginning. This is the situation of looking hard or making a mental note to remember; it probably does involve a little rapid sub-vocal repetition, but many psychological experiments are carefully designed to reduce the possibility of repetition. Cell 3 is repetition at the beginning but without effort to memorize; this might be a situation in which a radio station plays a popular record or an annoying commercial over and over again. Cell 4 is the normal unrepeated, unmemorized encounter with verbal material. How the memory operates with this, no one knows, but the short-term memory is nearly always in this mode. Some of it may also be in some way available to long-term memory, but the theory sometimes proposed that every word we have ever heard or read is stored away somewhere if we only knew how to get at it is surely exaggerated. Cell 5, effort and repetition at the time of recall, probably only occurs as an intermediate stage, e.g. rehearsing a play. In a sense, if the effort to remember any-thing is successful, there will be *one* repetition; this is not intended to count as a repetition in the present scheme, however. Cell 6, effort without repetition, is the ordinary situation of someone trying to remember something (e.g. a name). Cell 7, repetition without effort, may be the situation of an actor in a long run of a successful play; though perhaps the interval between repetitions is too great to qualify them as 'repetitions' in our sense. If that is so, cell 7 may be empty, except for things like the popular song or linguistic problem that keeps running through your head until it drives you crazy. With most people, however, it's the melody, not the words, which behaves this way. Cell 8 is pure spontaneous memory; some word or phrase or sentence just pops into your head under the stimulus of some chance encounter, even though you don't care at all.

Since the end and the beginning are independent events, the sixteen combinations of 1 to 4 with 5-8 should all be considered possible, although many of them would no doubt be a little unusual. The exam-ples given for 1 and 5 separately will combine; 1 and 6; 1 and one of the

B

examples of 7; 1 and 8 combined would be the spontaneous memory of some line you had once memorized. 2 with 5 is odd, partly because 5 is;[1] 2 and 6 is natural; 2 and 7 implausible; 2 and 8 possible; 3 and 5 seems unlikely; 3 and 6 is possible; 3 and 7 odd; 3 and 8 the normal combination; 4 and 5 is probably rare; 4 and 6 common (e.g. remembering a name one merely chanced to hear once); 4 and 7 far-fetched; 4 and 8 probably quite common though often unrecognized. This combination – no effort, no repetition at any time – is presumably one basis of our linguistic competence, though perhaps 3-8, with repeated exposures, is more important, if we allow the repetitions to be widely scattered in time. There are several problems here. (1) Memory of this sort, without any conscious associations, is not recognized as being memory; it's merely "happening to think (of)" or "happening to say" something. (2) Research is difficult, because any kind of experimental arrangement will automatically shift the situation from 4-8 or 3-8 to 1-5 or 2-5. (3) Our ignorance is almost complete. Is it true that everything we've ever heard or said or read or thought is stored permanently in our brain? If not, how much is? For how long? How and in what form? (At a conservative estimate, by the time a normal educated reader-speaker of English reaches the age of 25, at least a few billion running words – said, read, heard or thought – have passed through his consciousness, more than can be found in some small libraries.) How is it so difficult to tap this store deliberately when it just pours out involuntarily? Once again we can report a few introspective anecdotal observations: We are apparently able to recognize (at least sometimes) a word we have encountered only once before, even after a lapse of some years; we can usually match it with the right kind of context (and context of situation); if we have met it three or four times, we may use it spontaneously, even if we don't know what it means; we are usually incapable of saying how much of the context we put it in is remembered, and how much is newly created. What difference is there between letting your mind wander or daydreaming and thinking? Is thinking perhaps a series of successive mind-wanderings, the chains being restarted in some manner whenever the wanderings get too far off the track?

The recent theory that the storage of all this linguistic material is in the form of a dictionary (in which each entry is elaborately labeled as to

---

[1] Dwight L. Bolinger suggests "telling oneself [e.g. on Sunday] to put the trash out Monday morning, then on Monday morning trying to remember what one was supposed to do, and after remembering, repeating the formula to make it safer next time".

class membership of all kinds, semantic, syntactic and phonological) and a generative grammar (i.e. a sentence-building device) of some kind which includes a transformational component (in which rearrangements and modifications are made) will explain a great deal of what goes on, but still not everything. How is it arranged? Certainly it is not alphabetical. But there must be many rapid access paths leading to any given word w, the most important ones (for speaking ability) being those via paradigmatic and syntagmatic association, i.e. by way of all the words we have ever heard in the same frames in which we have heard w, or those which have formed part of some context of w. These, in turn, are linked to others in some way.

One fact which suggests that what we have stored is more like a concordance than a dictionary is the frequency with which we call up, not single words, but whole sentences and long phrases. A great deal has been made of the speaker's ability to produce and understand sentences which he has never heard before; unquestionably we have this ability, but the occasions on which we are called upon to use it *to the full* are probably infrequent. Mostly we improvise like the guslars of Yugoslavia (or, if you prefer, Homer), in centos;[1] sentences and paragraphs patched up from older sentences and paragraphs, with an occasional daring substitution of a single word here or there. When we write artistic prose or verse (original, not translated), a kind of subconscious censor tries to prevent repetitions of bits more than three or four words in length, but a concordance of one man's spoken output for a year or two or even of a voluminous writer's (Erle Stanley Gardner's? John Creasey's?) written output might be instructive. Until we get this, we can have no exact idea of the relative proportions of originality and repetition. Items which can only be stored and used as units, i.e. idioms or clichés, are not in question here, of course. Speakers who expose themselves relatively little to bombardment from outside (via large-scale reading) will probably be much more self-repetitious. Most of us are acquainted with (if not related to) such people, whose entire repertory seems to be exhausted within a year or two. But until we can get complete concordances of the entire input and output of one speaker for a sufficient period of time, or at least something which can be regarded as a valid sample of input and output, all statements about originality or repetitiousness

---

[1] Markov approximations and centos are discussed in ch. 15, below. For more evidence bearing on re-use of longish phrases, see H. A. Whitaker, 'On the representation of language in the human brain', *Working Papers in Phonetics* 12, U.C.L.A. 1969, especially the sections on 'ictal speech'.

must be regarded as anecdotal only (including, of course, what I have said here).

A further point about the nature of linguistic competence. If we are not to be caught in an infinite regress, we cannot suppose that speaking is a kind of translation (as is often done); we think some profound thought (in an unknown form) and then 'code' it or translate it from that unknown form into English. If this were so, then it is difficult to imagine what the underlying form of thought could be but another language – one, alas, inaccessible to study, but about which we could ask again how thoughts are put into form. I know that many respectable scholars disagree about this, but I can't for the life of me see why. Consequently we must suppose that (excluding various pictorial images and vague feelings, beliefs or expectations) thoughts are created *along with* their linguistic shape. (This is not to deny that we often feel we have something to say but can't quite decide how to say it, but only to suggest that this feeling requires explanation.) One possible mechanism for this is the constant random recombination in our brains of linguistic bits and pieces of all sizes, possibly in a way somewhat similar to a fairly high order (fourth or fifth, most likely) Markov approximation.[1] Before speaking or giving conscious attention to the thought, a kind of editing device takes over, trimming off excrescences, substituting individual words, checking details like government and concord, and in general making sure that we have a well-formed sentence. A really original thought could result when some other association than the merely syntagmatic one (i.e. what follows what) of ordinary Markov chains was responsible for one or more juxtapositions. This other kind of association might be any of several: resemblance of sound, link through some non-verbal memory (e.g. link of identity or similarity of place, of time, or coincident emotions, etc.). We probably give ourselves much undeserved credit for originality; we feel somehow that we're creating absolutely novel sentences. And some of them indeed may be novel, but not as many (or as novel) as we think. Here again, more research is needed.[2]

One point which seems obvious to us by introspection: the rate at which linguistic material flows in the brain is far faster than any feasible

---

[1] See p. 297.

[2] Throughout this chapter we are restricting ourselves to verbal memory; in particular, the occasional use of *memory* as equivalent to 'habitual skill', e.g. in 'I remember how to ride a bicycle', is here excluded. Since speaking involves such skills, it is obvious that they might be of interest to linguists; but not to us in this chapter.

speaking rate; often, as we speak, we can be aware of whole sentences passing through our thoughts in between two successive uttered words. Many potential linkages of phrases may be subconsciously rejected before one comes to our conscious attention, and many may be consciously considered for each one uttered, although all three processes (subconscious chaining and editing, conscious verbal thinking, speaking) may be, to all intents and purposes, continuous. To return to memory for a moment, it seems probable again that the chance of any particular bit figuring in our thoughts or dreams is higher if that bit has impinged on us more recently. So among other factors involved is a principle (very loose, of course) of last in, first out. This is one of the factors that makes it possible for us to stick to the subject in speaking or writing – or to leave it only when we want to. In speaking, the presence (and sometimes the words) of our interlocutor; in writing, the presence before our eyes of what we have already written are other factors contributing to the same result.

Can we from all this form any clear notions of how we speak? Most probably we do not first think thoughts in some unknown subconscious semantic or sememic language (though a few people claim to have such intuitions) and then translate them into English. Certainly we do not plan the complete syntactic structure of a sentence before we start to speak (at least not always), since it is sometimes the case that we are in the embarrassing position of not being able to finish our sentences without going back and starting over or hoping that our listeners will not be confused by an anacoluthon.[1] Because of the great variety of ways in which we may partially forget linguistic (and non-linguistic) material, it is clear that the model of a tape-recorded dictionary subordinated to a syntactical program is not adequate. On the whole a picture of millions of nodes linked by billions of connections of a number of different kinds (phonological, orthographic, experiential, semantic, syntactic – commutational or paradigmatic and sequential or syntagmatic, etc.), the connections having various degrees of probability (depending somehow on frequency and recency of prior use), with special links joined with the mechanisms of overt speech and leading to a syntactic editing and revising program, seems to correspond roughly with the evidence, but clearly all this must still be regarded as an elaborate metaphor. Before we as linguists can derive much benefit, the psychologists must find the answers to thousands of questions which have hardly even been posed as yet.

---

[1] *Anacoluthon* is the technical term for finishing a sentence which is not quite the same as the one you started – the two halves don't fit together grammatically.

3   *What must a language be like?*

Every science must, from time to time, make an effort to delimit its scope in some way, to indicate what things or events fall within its province and what ones do not. This question has concerned linguists for some time, and has often engendered fairly fruitless disputes with psychologists or others who wanted to specify a different domain from that preferred by the linguist. In this chapter we will examine first, a number of candidates for consideration as languages or texts (specimens or evidences of a language) and the reasons linguists offer for accepting or rejecting them, and then a number of defining criteria which have been proposed. The importance of this task becomes more obvious in recent years with the emphasis on universals of language, and the possible conclusions that may be drawn from a given universal. The distinction between formal and substantive universals which Chomsky makes in *Aspects* (27–30), will not occupy us much here; most of the candidates for formal universals (as, for instance, those discussed in the Texas Conference volume edited by Bach and Harms called *Universals of Language*) are very abstract and require elaborate chains of reasoning to define, while some seem blindingly trivial. But this does not mean that all the candidates proposed at Dobbs Ferry[1] some years earlier were substantive universals. We will, however, be concerned with a different, three-way distinction among universals: (1) universals due to the fact (if it is a fact) that all human language goes back in line of cultural transmission to a single origin; (2) universals which are conditioned by the structure of the human anatomy, in particular of the brain, and are handed on in the germ plasm – (a) physiological, (b) neurological; (3) universals which are implicit in the nature of language, defining characteristics or necessary consequences of defining characteristics. Universals (1) and (2) are universals of *human* language; the third class are universals of any possible language used by any kind of

[1] *Universals of Language*, ed. by Joseph H. Greenberg, Cambridge, Mass., M.I.T. Press, 1963; 2nd ed. 1966. My threefold division here corresponds (independently) to J. M. E. Moravcsik's in *Foundation of Language* 3:224 (1967); 1 = his 'accidental' more or less, 2 = his 'synthetic non-trivial' and 3 = his 'analytic'.

creatures anywhere in the universe. It seems necessary to examine this third class (however trivial) very carefully before going on to the cultural (accidental) and physiological-neurological universals.

What are some categories of things or events which might be taken for languages or texts of languages? Perhaps we should first dispose of things about which no argument is ever likely to arise, things which all hands will agree are non-linguistic – roads, buildings, bridges and other products of human activity, mountains, trees, planets and other natural objects, for instance. All these we would, I think, dismiss for one of two reasons: (a) they are not purposeful at all, or else (b) their primary purposes are not communicative. Almost all artifacts (and even some natural objects) are capable of communicating in some degree or manner, but only secondarily. A further intuitive reaction is that these objects are not sufficiently varied or patterned to be linguistic; somehow language presupposes variety and pattern as well as purpose and communication.

Very well, then what about music? Here we find several classes of events. Consider a symphony. It has plenty of variety and pattern, as well as some purposefulness and even a kind of attempt to communicate. But it may be performed in many different places by many different orchestras for different audiences and long after the death of the composer. The same thing may be said of a play; but in a play the characters are also ostensibly communicating with each other. Is this the case with the performers in an orchestra? If so, they would be miming another type of music, spontaneous solo improvisation in which performers alternate. Such styles exist (as in the cutting matches of old-time jazz), though more usually with the goal of winning a victory rather than exchanging messages. And there are literary (folklore) parallels to this, too. But the literary uses of language do not impress us, intuitively, as being primary. Are there any pure musical events which would match our prejudiced notions of a primary use of language? There are, of course, instances of whistle talk or drum talk in various cultures in Africa and America, but these are all clearly secondary, coded representations (normally restricted in various ways) of genuine linguistic material. And virtually everything we have said about music here could also be said about the dance.

Superficially very like linguistic material is the type of religious performance called glossolalia, which is found in several parts of the world, but is best known from certain fundamentalist sects in the United States. These materials have a clear phonological structure (which normally agrees well with some sub-set of the phonology of the performer's native language), and often sound as if they really ought to mean something.[1] They resemble a symphony in the absence of complex correlations of the performance with subsequent behavior of the listeners, but are normally improvised.

A much more frequent proposal for 'language' status is one of the various communication systems used by birds, mammals or insects (chiefly), e.g. baboons or honeybees. Most linguists would reject the baboon system without much hesitation on the ground, primarily, that it contains only a small number of distinct messages, and no new ones are possible. A linguist's language cannot be so restricted; if it should turn out to be finite (and all our sentiments shrink from this idea) at least the number of distinct messages should be far greater than any ordinary number – on the order of 10^{100} at least, not just 10^6 (millions) or 10^9 (American billions) or 10^{12} (British billions). But the bee candidate at least purports to satisfy this requirement: every message contains a component indicating distance (which may comprise only a few distinct steps) and one for direction which, being an analog message (i.e. direction is indicated by pointing), could indicate any one of an infinite number of directions. We may argue that the bee nervous system is incapable of infinitely fine discriminations of direction, but even so, it seems quite likely that the number of discriminable directions would be quite large in comparison with the number of baboon calls, say. And yet most linguists feel better about baboon calls than about bee dances. Why? Partly because of the analog nature of bee dancing; nothing of importance in human language has this feature. But mainly, I think, because of the enormous restriction on subject matter. Would a man be judged normal, who, at first hearing, spoke perfect English, but all of whose utterances were of the form "This is X feet long", where X could take any English value corresponding to a cardinal number? Would he be thought to speak English? Particularly if the *only* utterance by another to which he responded at all was "How long is this?" And the bee's performance is not as digitalized as this.

A favorite speculation of science-fiction has to do with identifying something or other as a long and detailed message from another intelligent being (or race). Suppose we keep a record of the fluctuations in

---

[1] Dr Eugene Nida reported on this subject to the Linguistic Society of America several years ago, and played a number of tapes. See also J. R. Jaquith, 'Toward a typology of formal communicative behaviors: Glossolalia', *Anthropological Linguistics* 9, 8:1–8 (1967).

the radiant emission (of light or radio waves, for example) from some far-off heavenly body. What would we look for in this record to encourage us? At least two things: first, recurrent regularities which cannot be explained by any known astro-physical facts, and then a limited number (in the range 10 to 500, more or less) of distinct recurrent patterns into which the record is more or less exhaustively divisible. And, if both these were found, we might look for larger scale recurrent regularities, now considerably more varied (1,000 or more groupings at the very least), and, if we found them, express optimism that the fluctuations might contain a real message.

Consider another case (once proposed by Max Zorn in a conversation): suppose a linguist-archeologist from Mars comes upon a narrow beach covered with bird-tracks. How can he decide that this is not an inscription conveying some message? Again much the same criteria would be applied: search for recurrent patterns and patterns of patterns. Clearly there are cases of this sort which would be indeterminate: some forms of writing and certain types of linear decorations may resemble each other very closely, particularly in small documents. Even more difficult would be the case of a musical score (let us imagine one which is completely free of all verbal instructions or other alphabetic symbols). Here we would find unquestioned patterns and recurrent second-order patterns as well. Possibly the variety would be too great and the recurrences too few in a sufficiently long sample, but the decision would surely not be easy. And indeed, as we saw, a composition does have many of the characteristics of a message.

It is quite common to speak of the various code systems ('machine languages', 'compilers', 'assemblers', 'programming languages', etc.) by which computer programmers direct the sequencing and nature of computer operations as *languages*. And they certainly have more of the properties (including grammars and rules) of ordinary languages than the other cases we have been examining. Indeed, I think we might all agree that a computer program *is* a text. But the text does not seem to qualify as a sample of a real language for the same reasons that a string of pure mathematical expressions does not. (1) Such texts are all uniquely renderable in English (or some other natural language), and are subject to the interpretation that they are merely coded forms of English (or another natural language), just as a specimen of Morse or a ciphered document would be. (2) Allowing that skilled programmers and mathematicians may manipulate their symbols directly, the range of subject-matter which can be handled is extremely narrow, less so than for bee-dances no doubt, but still incapable of getting a glass of water – let alone embodying a novel.

I think this is a fair sample of the kinds of object which most linguists would tend to exclude from the subject matter of their science. How do they go about it? What are some of the definitions which they have proposed? And do they all avoid universals of type 1 (cultural) and type 2 (genetic)? Here are a few samples.

(1) Language is a purely human and non-instinctive method of com-municating ideas, emotions, and desires by means of a system of voluntarily produced symbols (Sapir, *Language* 8 (Harvest Book edition)).

(2) A language is a system of arbitrary vocal symbols by means of which a social group co-operates (Bloch and Trager, *Outline of Linguistic Analysis* 5 (1.1); cf. Sturtevant, *Introduction to Linguistic Science* 2).

(3) A language [is a] symbol system ... based on pure or arbitrary convention ... infinitely extendable and modifiable according to the changing needs and conditions of the speakers (R. H. Robins, *General Linguistics* 13–14 (1.3.2)).

(4) Language is human ... a verbal systematic symbolism ... a means of transmitting information ... a form of social behaviour ... [with a] high degree of convention (J. Whatmough, *Language*, 8–16).

(5) Human languages are unlimited ... (an unlimited set of discrete signals) ... [have] great structural complexity ... structure on at least two levels ... (the learning task is considerable) ... are open-ended ... allow for the transmission of information (R. W. Langacker, *Language and its Structure*, 20–1).

While this is not an exhaustive set of definitions,[1] it is certainly a representative one. The criteria used here, many of the words used here, recur; few criteria not found here occur elsewhere. We will just add those mentioned by Hockett:[2] (a) symbol system, (b) open or productive, (c) with displacement, (d) with duality of patterning and (e) transmitted by tradition. Of these five, only (c) does not occur in the definitions

---

[1] The mathematical sense in which 'a language' is a collection of sentences or utterances is sometimes met today (e.g. D. T. Langendoen, *The Study of Syntax* 1), but linguists usually apply the term to the underlying system.

[2] E.g. in 'The origin of speech', *Scientific American* 203:88–96, or 'The problem of universals in language', in *Universals of Language*, ed. J. H. Greenberg, Cambridge, Mass., M.I.T. Press, 1966, pp. 1–29, or (with R. Ascher) 'The Human Revolution', in *Current Anthropology* 5:139 (1964), or *Course in Modern Linguistics*, New York, Macmillan, 1958, pp. 574–80.

already quoted. We will also confine ourselves to primary systems, excluding codes and transcriptions.

Let us briefly inspect each of these points to see (a) if it is necessarily true of any imaginable, even non-human, language; (b) if it is not a necessary consequence of (or necessary condition for) some more fundamental feature. The separate points seem to be: (1) human; (2) non-instinctive, traditional, conventional; (3) arbitrary; (4) communicative, transmitting information (5) social, cooperative; (6) systematic; (7) symbolic; (8) open, productive, infinitely extendable and modifiable; (9) verbal, vocal; (10) allowing displacement; (11) with dual patterning.

1. The property 'human' can be interpreted in two ways, and in either case it is inappropriate. If it means 'belonging to *homo sapiens*', it is not what we want, since we are willing to conceive of genetically distinct intelligent beings in some other universe; and if it is given a more general sense, it cannot be basic, since language itself is presumably one of the proofs of 'humanness'. Indeed many (like Hockett, cited above) believe it is the one essential defining trait of humanness.

2. 'Conventional' perhaps says a little more than 'non-instinctive' or 'traditional', since it implies more directly that 'arbitrariness of the sign' (criterion 3) which has impressed many linguists, and reflects the obvious fact that we may change languages (stop using English and use Russian, for example). But, essentially, all three terms say that particular languages must be learnt, cannot be transmitted by the genes (though there may conceivably be species-wide linguistic features which are so transmitted). Suppose we try to imagine a world where this is not so, where proficiency in a language is inherited, and babies talk as well (after a few days practice, perhaps) as graybeards. Since it is inherited, it cannot change[1] during a single lifetime, new things cannot receive new names, and our eighth property cannot be retained. I think most of us would not hesitate; we must keep infinite capacity for change and expansion (criterion 8) hence we must keep 'traditional' or 'conventional'. But since this property is a consequence of another, it cannot be basic.

3. Is arbitrariness also a consequence? A language would be non-arbitrary (in the only sense with which we are concerned) if, for all situations, events, objects, or desires, there existed a single algorithm

---

[1] Except perhaps very slowly, by some gene-carried device for testing and accepting innovations produced by other individuals in response to mutations. But how the innovations can then be transmitted is hard to see.

which would derive the linguistic expression of these situations, etc., from their observable traits or parts. But this clearly implies a one-to-oneness that we would be most unwilling to allow; the same events[1] ought to be capable of eliciting a variety of appropriate linguistic responses, though this does not seem to be a direct consequence of any other proposed property. Perhaps our algorithm could give some variety by randomly different selection of parts or traits; but this still seems unsatisfactory, since it scarcely allows error and cannot well allow falsehood. Falsehood was once suggested by Sturtevant[2] as a criterion for language (though he really meant criterion (10), displacement), and so we might add: (12) some expressions in a language must be capable of being false. To return, though, to our non-arbitrary algorithm; can it still be a non-arbitrary language if we allow the output which is automatically elicited by other aspects of the situation to be altered by the user's desire? Evidently not. And a truly non-arbitrary language could not change (except as the world changes), whereas property (8), as most linguists understand it, would make linguistic change a *necessary* feature of language. Furthermore, if we use 'distinct' in the sense 'not intertranslatable by any simple algorithm', most linguists would wish the definition of language to be such that an automatic consequence would be:

(8'): The number of distinct possible languages is greater than any pre-assigned limit.

This is not the same as Sapir's claim (*Language*, p. 4) that languages "vary without assignable limit" on the *kind* of variation – i.e. by one interpretation, may differ as much as you please in any way you please. Obviously, until we have an accurate specification of what a thing has to be if it is to deserve the name 'language', we cannot say what the limits are in particular, but every requirement of the definition and every logical consequence of it provides some "assignable limit", as does the structure of the user's anatomy and, in particular, his brain. Arbitrariness, then, seems to be a necessary consequence of the capability of unpredictable change, which seems, in turn, a legitimate interpretation

[1] Someone may wish to argue that since situations *always* differ in some way, the unpredictable variety of linguistic expressions which I am suggesting here could be correlated with these differences and made predictable. I am skeptical of the hypothesis that there is only one possible linguistic response to a given situation (namely the one that actually occurs), except in the sense that in general the only event which could possibly take place is the one which does take place. True, but beside the point.

[2] *Introduction to Linguistic Science*, New Haven, Yale University Press, 1947, p. 48.

of criterion (8), just as cultural transmission is: hence no part or interpretation of criteria (2) and (3) can belong to our definition.

4 (and 5). The first question about the 'communicative' test is whether and how (if at all) it differs from the 'social cooperation' test. It is difficult to see how any amount of cooperation could be achieved without some communication; the converse, however, is different. One important form of communication is communication with oneself, i.e. thinking. This activity varies, but for most people it takes up more time than any other use of language. Whether or not *all* thought uses language, most of us agree that much human thought does. Is it an essential feature of language? Perhaps we can imagine a race of beings who cannot use language (either silently or as talking to themselves) except in the presence of others, and then only in a perceptible way. It seems odd, like creatures who are alive only in the daylight, but possible, except perhaps for the genetically lethal consequences which might ensue. So use for thinking, though a natural consequence of other features, cannot be a defining characteristic of language. The remaining half of communication does seem to be indistinguishable from social cooperation, if one interprets these terms broadly. If a set or system of things or behaviour patterns *cannot* be used for some kind of cooperation with particular beings (not just "to whom it may concern") of one's own or another species, then it does not qualify as a language. Furthermore, this cannot be deduced from any other property of language on our list; hence either some form of (4) or (5), or some new criterion from which (4) and (5) can be deduced, is an essential feature of anything which we would be willing to call 'language'. In fact, this (if restricted in some way) is almost the only feature (other than (10), displacement, which obviously depends upon this feature) by which one could rule out a symphony as a text of some language. The test would have to lie in the possibility of a variety of correlatable responses; a symphony, though it is social and cooperative, cannot easily make us buy a loaf of bread and a dozen eggs, nor can it be addressed (by its composer? or the performers?) to a particular individual.

6. How systematic must a collection of entities be before we call it truly systematic? The difficulty is that utter chaos, complete randomness, absence of all pattern or system is extremely rare in nature and difficult to achieve by artifice. Suppose we tried to concoct a set of message-symbols (of any size you please) such that there were *no* partial similarities of form alone or of form and meaning together, other than those

shared by *all* members of the set. Even when the size of set is kept small – three or four members, say – the task is difficult: message no. 1 is signalled by scratching one's head; no. 2 by whistling *Dixie*; no. 3 by presenting a rose; no. 4 by sniffing loudly. Here already we have partial similarities between 1 and 3, 2 and 4, caused by the use of different senses. Let's try a set of four *visual* signs: (1) as before, (2) pulling one's ear, (3) rubbing one's chin, (4) tapping one's nose. This is better, but (1) and (4) share the feature 'fingertips used' and (1), (2), (3), but not (4) share 'friction involved'. If we get rid of this defect by involving the fingertips and friction in all the signs, we may ultimately get four which satisfy the requirement. But now try increasing the number from four to forty or four hundred or four thousand. Suppose we use a set of pure tones of identical loudness but differing in pitch. Can we make them all discordant? Possibly, but some pairs will seem to be more nearly harmonic than others, and if any pair is inharmonic in the same way and to the same extent as some other, we will have a regularity again. If we decide to make them differ by consecutive prime numbers in frequency, this in itself will be a regularity. In short, it is impossible to devise or find a totally unstructured set of symbols, a set without *any* partial similarities, if the set is to contain more than a handful of members. Suppose we could devise a set which appeared, at first glance, so chaotic and irregular as to defy analysis, and the set were then imposed on a group of intelligent beings. If these beings had a memory anything like human memory, the set would intensify its regularities and lose many irregularities within one or two generations.[1] It is often argued that this is an unpredictable peculiarity of the human brain; this is a factual question which cannot be settled until we have access to intelligences from other worlds, but since it certainly tends to promote survival, I am inclined to say that a necessary feature of *any* brain of equivalent power will be a tendency to economize effort by reducing unknowns to combinations of knowns and by being biased to look for similarities and patterns. So, while we conclude that system will indeed be a characteristic of any language, we will regard this fact not as basic, but as derived necessarily from the structure of any brain capable of using language, assuming (what may be false) that brain structure is distinguishable from language competence.

7. It is the case that everything we would be willing to call 'language'

---

[1] See incidentally the experiment reported by Erwin A. Esper in *Language* 42:575–80 (1966).

is, consists of, or contains symbols or signs of some sort. Is this characteristic irreducible? If criterion (3), arbitrariness, were basic, then
symbolism would be a necessary consequence; but we concluded that
(3) is a necessary consequence of (8), infinite variability and productivity.
But (7) also seems to be a consequence of (4) or (5) or some equivalent,
communication or cooperation; perhaps (4-5) and (8) *together* entail (7).
Suppose there are beings on some other world who can feel instantly all
the perceptions and emotions of any one (or more) other members of
their species. This might enable some sort of cooperation without any
symbolism, but there would be, apparently, no system involved, and
nothing which could be infinitely extended or which we would feel
inclined to call 'language'. Suppose some other extra-galactic creatures
could project dream-like scenes of all kinds for purposes of cooperation;
unless these scenes could be identified as 'future' or 'past', i.e. expectations, wishes, commands and predictions or narrative reports, there
would be hopeless ambiguity. But if some mark is added to achieve this
distinction, it is clearly a symbol of some kind. Indeed the dream-scenes
themselves must be counted as symbolic – though iconic and not wholly
arbitrary. Hence it seems clear that (4-5) alone entails 'symbolic' while
the addition of (8) makes it 'arbitrarily symbolic'.

8. The feature of openness or productivity, the capacity for change
and expansion, may include two different features: (8a) all kinds of new
messages may be concocted with the old resources, and (8b) the old
resources themselves may be modified or replaced. Would we exclude
from the category of language an otherwise copious and language-like
communication system which remained forever unchanged? Not, I
think, if we consider nothing more; but if its failure to change is due to
a built-in inability to change, then I suspect that many of us would have
qualms. What could cause this inability? Only some defect in the organism
using the 'language', and the defect would just about have to be that
the system is transmitted by heredity instead of tradition (criterion 2). But,
as we have already implied, it requires a considerable effort of faith to
believe that anything as complete as our requirement (8a) suggests could
ever be hereditary. Perhaps we should try to make (8a) a bit more precise:

Any two events that can be discriminated must be describable by some
'speaker' of the 'language' so that some other 'speaker', receiving these
descriptions, can correctly identify and discriminate the events

That's a little clumsy, but it should rule out such things as types of
insect communication which are restricted to announcing and locating

sources of food. This, then, suggests that (8b) is an automatic consequence of (8a) when new events become discriminable for whatever cause. But why should that ever require a change in the *system*? Only indirectly, we may suppose: the first step would be changes in frequency of certain kinds of messages; then, if those changes cause what had previously been simpler or more regular types of messages[1] to become less frequent, a new rule might be derived from the pattern of the now more frequent messages to make them also simpler or more regular. This hypothesis, if sound, would imply two interesting consequences: (1) linguistic change is, ultimately, externally caused; (2) any theory of constant rates of linguistic change presupposes a theory of constant rates of non-linguistic change. It should be the case that an isolated community without influence from other cultures and with a strong conservative tendency must exhibit a relatively slow rate of linguistic change. It cannot (except briefly, perhaps) show a zero rate, because (a) the composition of the community must change: new members are being born, old ones are dying, physical objects are decaying or being destroyed by natural forces; (b) each individual in the community is different each day by the sum of that day's experiences. Perhaps we can also add: (c) tension or hostility between generations tends to fix and regularize accidental or random deviations.

So we must reaffirm the basic nature of criterion (8), which we may now limit to (8a). Nothing can be called a language if it does not admit of indefinite expansion in the number of distinct messages.

9. The requirement that language must be verbal (Whatmough) or vocal (Bloch and Trager) seems unnecessary, and indeed wrong, except as an empirical generalization about known languages. If 'verbal' means that a language must have units of a certain sort, then it belongs to criterion (11). And, whatever it may have been for her teacher, Helen Keller's first[2] language cannot be called vocal, yet seems (from all

---

[1] This assumes that in every language there are *necessarily* some messages which are more regular or simpler than others and one of the conditioners of language change is frequency of occurrence. 'More regular' here has the sense 'conforming to a more general rule', i.e. one that is more economically formulable, involves less extensive lexical marking, fewer exceptions, etc.

[2] Strictly speaking, her second, since she had already acquired some ordinary English before her illness (which was before her second birthday). But (a) how much auditory-articulatory memory of this remained reverberating in her brain is unknown; (b) there is little reason to suppose that she converted all finger-palm signals into auditory-articulatory form – indeed it seems almost impossible that she could have done so. Reliable evidence about the language competence of congenitally deaf persons is very difficult to find.

accounts) to have been a language. As a historical fact, all known systems of communication on earth can be derived, by successive stages, from vocal systems. Reasons for this have often been suggested: vocal systems do not require mutual visibility; the hands are often not free when at work or engaged in fighting or hunting, but the mouth is busy only part of the time while eating; outside of the hands, only the tongue (and, in part, the lips) have the necessary freedom and dexterity.[1] But all this depends on granting feature 1 ('human') in the sense 'restricted to *homo sapiens*'. If we can believe that there might be other organisms with different anatomy and different senses, then their language perhaps would not be basically auditory or vocal. The possibility (which most of us believe) that human beings are genetically predisposed to learning vocal language in childhood is irrelevant to this point.

10. Hockett's feature 'displacement' is essentially the one proposed by Sturtevant (see p. 30, n. 2), and says that a criterial feature of any true language is that communications expressed by its means may refer to events which are separated in time or place from both speaker and hearer. It is alleged that this is not true of some forms of animal communication (though bee communication would be 'language' in this sense). For our purposes, this is merely a small part of what we mean by criterion (8). Reports, promises, predictions, and the like are necessary capabilities of any language, because *every* possible variety of communication must be within the range of any language. Hence we cannot count this as a distinct criterion.

11. Dual patterning, that is, the existence of two kinds or sizes of 'recurrent sames', one (morpheme or word) which is a recurrent same of form and meaning (or function) simultaneously, while the smaller one (sound or phone) is a recurrent same of form only, is rated rather high by Hockett. Is this an independent feature? Or is it perhaps, in some manner, a consequence of (7) (symbolism) and (8) (infinite productivity) taken together? Would it be possible to achieve (8) without this dualism? The problem seems to be linked up with the number and scope of minimal semantic features or elements that could be manipulated by the language user. In 'substance', whether phonological, graphological, musical, or what-not, it is easy enough to get along with a single pair of basic elements (a dot and a dash, perhaps), and a hundred are ample. But there does not seem to be any natural and obvious way to build up

[1] See, for instance, Peter Marler, 'Animal Communication Signals', *Science* 157:773 (1967).

all *meanings* from some very small number. There are numerous schemes (even Leibnitz was interested) concocted from various motives, but all alike are in large part clearly imposed from outside, not discovered, and the number of basic elements generally comes closer to 1,000 than to ten.

If we approach the problem as we did above in discussing feature (7) (symbolism), we come to a similar conclusion. We must suppose that all meaningful primes[1] ('morphemes' or the like) are substantially distinct and unanalyzable. But how can this be? How can there be 1,000 or more entities in any medium, no two of which resemble each other in any way not shared by all the thousand? It is no doubt a feature of the human brain to search always for similarities and for differences, but (as we saw in discussing the eighth criterion above) this is a prerequisite for anything one would wish to call 'language'. Consequently, any imaginable language-using beings in outer space must share this trait. What remains before authentic 'dual patterning' is reached? Apparently the main thing involved is the establishment of discrete scales of discriminable parts or qualities, with a very small number of steps (often only two, far below what could in fact be discriminated in many cases), and the ignoring of *some* discriminable qualities as irrelevant. It is possible, for instance, that the internal structure of simple Chinese characters[2] does not show a great reduction in number of features; but there *is some*, and there is a considerable range of acceptable rendering for each stroke of each character. It looks very much as if (11) is, then, a necessary consequence of (8) (and of (7), itself also a consequence of (8)).

12. The possibility of truth-value was suggested above (in our discussion of criterion (3)) as another feature of language. The effect of this is not very great. Even rudimentary call systems which include a 'danger cry' will allow for this cry to be false, i.e. uttered when there is in fact no danger. There can be no communication (fourth criterion) without this; in other words, (12) is a necessary consequence of (4).

What remains of our proposed defining criteria, and are they necessary and sufficient? Only two criteria are left:

---

[1] Semantic *features* as primes are excluded from this argument; what we are talking about is symbols which are minimal in both senses, i.e. not analyzable either into semantic features of any kind or into phonological features or segments. Of course there is no such thing in real life.

[2] All we need to know about Chinese characters is (a) that there are over 2,000 of them, (b) each corresponds basically to a one-syllable form with a distinct meaning, (c) they can be analyzed in terms of their component strokes.

Languages mediate communication (4-5) and in each language there are distinct messages corresponding to all discriminable events (8a).[1]

All the other proposed criteria, including the systematic nature of the correspondence, have been seen to be consequences of these two and of a property of any imaginable language-using brain – that it is constantly generalizing, comparing and identifying.

It is possible to argue that the definition implied by these criteria is circular, including the definiendum in some disguised form.[2] The problem words here are 'communication', 'message' and 'discriminable'; can they be defined in such a way as to avoid circularity? I think so. Communication (in the normal, interpersonal sense) takes place whenever an action or artifact of one individual which is primarily intended to be observed by another, *is* so observed. (Maximally successful communication, of course, is possible only when the observer and communicator share a whole range of experiences, many of which relate directly to communication. A speech in Russian conveys little to an Eskimo.) This is broad enough to take in music, dancing and various forms of non-linguistic entertainment, and will *not* include a variety of non-communicative uses of language (thinking, etc., mentioned above), but will cover most uses, including (say) novels or poems. The main uncertainty here is whether to incorporate the idea of transfer of 'knowledge' or 'information'. If we do, then literature is excluded again (along with music and art), but the infinity-of-messages criterion is easier to handle. And I'm not sure it can be done without allowing 'knowledge' as an undefined term.

What is meant by 'message' in (8a)? Suppose we say 'a single communication event'. Then the only arguable difficulty is 'single', and an element of arbitrariness on this point does not seem to be harmful. But 'corresponding' cannot be arbitrary (i.e. there must be no doubt which message corresponds to which event); if it were, almost any kind of communicative behavior could qualify as language. A communication event can be allowed to 'correspond' to another event in the sense required by (8a) only if the performer (i.e. speaker) intends such

---

[1] This is a minimal requirement. Of course there will necessarily be messages corresponding to other sorts of things, too – e.g. to all the discriminable ways in which a 'speaker' might influence a 'hearer' without physical contact. In a sense, all messages are commands, and it is wrong to reduce commands or questions to assertions. Rather we should reduce assertions and questions to commands: 'Believe X' and 'Tell me Y'.

[2] Of course I can escape by claiming to aim *not* at a definition but at a logical ordering of features or attributes.

correspondence and the observer accepts it. This is perhaps contrary to Augustine's views on Bible exegesis (that all theologically sound interpretations are correct) and to many critics' opinions about literary works, but it seems necessary for our purposes.

The difficulty raised by 'discriminable' lies in the questions "By whom?" and "How?" If we say "by us" or "by human beings", are we not smuggling back criterion 1, 'human'? And if we say "By the users of the communication system under consideration" we are faced with the counterquestion "How do we know these creatures can discriminate anything except precisely what they communicate?" Maybe bees are totally unable to discriminate between any two things or items unless one or both are food-sources, directions to food-sources or distances of food-sources. One answer to this might be to devise tests similar to those used by psychologists in discovering that (e.g.) rats or doves can distinguish (or be taught to distinguish) red triangles from gray, or large squares from small, or triangles from circles, etc. But then isn't the teaching in this case a kind of language teaching? "Red triangles *mean* food, large squares *mean* water, etc." It's a bispecific 'language' to be sure, in which humans communicate with rats, but does that alter the case? Possibly observed cases of natural discriminatory behaviour on the part of numerous birds and animals can be called 'symbolic' (e.g. "That twig is suitable for nest-building", "This tree is too far from the river for dam-building", etc.), but they are not communicative. Some psychological experiments show that human beings can discriminate more finely (e.g. in colours or musical tones) than the *normal* resources of the language allow, though they cannot remember such sub-linguistic distinctions as well. If we call on the resources of modern science to provide objective methods of discrimination, we may be faulted on the ground that modern science was created by language users. Still, I am willing to grant this weakness and postulate objectively discriminable events. But there may be such events which cannot be discriminated by the beings in question (or not without artificial aids of some kind); thus, for example, two stars, one of which is a powerful radio source, the other a source of X-rays, might cause us trouble without artificial aids. So we would have to say (1) objectively distinguishable, provided that (2) their distinction is within the sensory capacity of the organisms being tested, and (3) there must be no obvious upper bound on the number of events and kinds of events which are discriminable at any given time by the organism. Without the third provision, an inventory of only two messages might satisfy this definition for an organism capable of distinguishing only two 'events'. Among the discriminations that would most help in avoiding an upper bound are those of time (before, after, longer, shorter) and space (closer, farther, right, left, above, below, in front, behind, etc.); indeed it is unlikely that a species deficient in these discriminations could possibly have a language in the sense intended here.

A question can also be raised about the status of languages with only one surviving speaker (or even with two) and languages spoken only by bilinguals (i.e. nobody's first *and* only language). In both cases it may be possible to find many events for which the speakers cannot produce matching utterances. The common-sense response to this is that the *language* is not defective, but merely the particular speaker's *control* over it, and (in the case of the single speaker) the lack of a recipient is not a defect of the language but an irrelevant accident. Alternatively we might say that these are not fully languages, but could be made into languages by such-and-such additions – most trivially by adding new words to the lexicon, occasionally by adding also new rules for phrase or sentence-formation (as in the case of a language which not only lacks all cardinal numbers above three, but also the rules for producing sentences reporting on addition, subtraction, division or multiplication, if those rules could not be automatically included as features in the lexicon). In the case of the single speaker we could solve the problem by training a second speaker.

Suppose we do not try so manfully to avoid mentioning 'meaning' or 'reference'. Is our task then easier? (This amounts to reinstating criterion (7) 'symbolic' and deciding that it is not a consequence of (8) 'productive' plus (4) 'communication', but illicitly *implicit* in (4).) Communication would then be 'meaningful behavior' – or perhaps 'intentionally meaningful behavior' – and a message (again) a 'single instance of communication'. But this doesn't really make things easier; meaningfulness is an automatic property of anything attended to. In spite of the difficulties with (4) and (8a) alone, I strongly prefer that view; I am convinced, too, that it is historically sound. Communication was well developed in our ancestors before it acquired linguistic character; language was not a totally novel kind of behavior, but merely a development from non-language which resulted automatically as the inventory of signals approached and passed a certain upper bound (after which, of course, it exploded).

Are we satisfied with language as 'indefinitely expansible communicativity'? Can we derive from this definition all other properties which we wish, all proposed universals? Let us consider a few.

We hinted above that the universal vocal character (9) of language might be inferable from a joint consideration of the essential nature of language and human physiology. Actually, however, considerations of survival value[1] have to be brought in, too; communication at a distance, by night, in forests or tall grass is only possible with acoustic signals, and is desirable for survival. Given this fact, it is only with the vocal tract that a suitable variety of audible signals can be produced. (This is not to say that another organ *could* not have evolved to do the job as well.)

We have already argued that 'dual patterning' is a necessary consequence of our basic definition. What about the size of the phonological inventory: at least twelve and not over a hundred distinctive sound units, distinguished from one another by at least four or five and not over fifteen or twenty distinctive sound features? A smaller inventory (even one feature, two units) is perfectly feasible. The average length of messages would have to be noticeably greater, of course, but why not? Economy is not a design feature of language. But some kind and some measure of it are obviously advantageous to survival: if it takes fifteen minutes to say "Help!", you may never finish saying it. Redundancy is also universal among human languages, and again some measure of it is obviously of survival value: if your call for help is going to be misunderstood as merely a cheery "Hello!", you may not survive to enunciate more carefully in the future. A language totally lacking in redundancy would be one in which (a) all possible combinations of features, sounds, elements, etc. were distinctively grammatical and meaningful, and consequently (b) corresponding to each utterance there was a very large number of minimally contrasting utterances – something like $(2^n)^m$, where n is the number of binary distinctive features utilized in the language, and m is the number of segments in the given utterance. It is easy enough to make artificial languages of this sort, and easy enough also to see how impractical they would be, in spite of their economy.

In natural languages not all phonemes occur with equal frequency in running speech, and Zipf argued for his 'principle of least effort' as a logical explanation of the facts. In terms of binary features this appears to correspond to three facts instead of one: (1) the two values of certain

---

[1] Survival value affects both genetic success and cultural success, so that it provides no help in disentangling the innate from the learned. Phonological capability, however, is clearly innate.

features do not occur (relevantly) with equal frequency (e.g. distinctively voiceless segments might be more frequent than voiced ones); (2) not all individual oppositions are utilized with equal frequency (i.e. occur as relevant; e.g. the presence or absence of voicing may be beside the point most of the time), and (3) certain combinations of relevant features are less common than others (e.g. a voiced palatal affricate may occur only rarely). And, in all cases, the more frequent item or combination is, in some way, the simpler, or less complex, according to Zipf. Much the same sort of thing could be said about distribution among languages of the world, incidentally. The same principle applied to word-length emphasizes that, while uncommon items may be long or short, extremely frequent ones tend to be relatively short. While the exact formulation of the principle may be debatable, the facts (in general) are not. Somehow or other, then, among human beings, at any rate (whatever may be the case on other planets), both economy of some sort and redundancy of some sort must operate together to yield the range of inventories which are found. If redundancy allows every message to be understood when it is half-finished, economy (i.e. the impatience of listeners) will chop speakers off before they finish – until their grammar is altered to reduce the redundancy; if excessive economy forces the listener to ask to have the message repeated three or four times, the grammar will be modified to increase redundancy. But how these forces will allow 50 but not 150 phonemes – or 80, but not 120 – is not yet clear. I think, however, that once redundancy and economy are properly defined for language users, it should be possible to derive from acceptable axioms notions of optimum, maximum and minimum inventories of phonemes and of optimum and maximum lengths of word-like units. These things can certainly not be derived from the defining characteristics of a language by themselves, though maybe it can be shown that any language-users anywhere must be sufficiently like humans for analogous values to hold.

Finally, a word or two about syntactic structure. It has often been suggested that what is called the 'deep structure' of all languages is the same; in other words, that the most important form classes (e.g. 'noun' and 'verb-adjective') and the basic syntactic relations (say 'predication', 'modification', 'conjunction') and illocutions – i.e. statuses, moods – ('assertion', 'question', 'command') are everywhere the same.[1] We

---

[1] For some important observations on this point and the point discussed in ch. 1 about an inborn language faculty, see John Lyons in *Psycholinguistics Papers*, edited by J. Lyons and R. J. Wales, Edinburgh, Edinburgh University Press, 1966, pp. 129–32.

may, then, raise the question: "Insofar as this is true, to what extent is it an accidental – or biological – fact about human languages only, to what extent a necessary consequence of the defining features?" Put otherwise, "Is this a fact about human beings or a fact about language?" And how does it mean any more than to say "Anything that can be expressed in one language can be expressed in any other"? The illocutionary force can, of course, be shifted into the vocabulary by using explicit performatives: 'I wish you to tell me the name of this person' for 'Who is this?', and 'I wish you to come here' or 'I command you to come here' for 'Come here!' So far as I know, either this is not done on earth, or (at any rate) it is never done without special syntactic consequences which make the categories retain their relevance. Other categories may be relevant or more fundamental than these just mentioned: for instance it may be that 'description' or 'identification' if added to the illocutions will enable 'predication' to be defined as 'assertion of truth of description' and 'modification' as 'mere description'. Or still other notions may prove to be more basic. But can we envisage beings who communicate purposefully without *any* such categories? How?

4   *Sounds*

A great deal of information about ways in which human oral-nasal sounds are used for speech can be stated in a fairly simple way, and several inventions of the past half-century (of which the sound spectrograph is perhaps the most important) have helped increasingly adept experimenters to discover a good deal more than was known for sure in the days of Professor Higgins. In this chapter, therefore, I shall eschew technical jargon except where it is most necessary, and explain it (or refer you to explanations) whenever I do use it.

We have seen that there are a number of reasons (other than the obvious reason of monogenesis of human speech) why human beings should exploit the modulation of sounds carried mainly on outbreathed air as raw material for language. Freedom of hands and eyes to be otherwise busy and variety of possible modulations together seem (to many of us) more than sufficient.

We should consider voicing as part of the carrier[1] rather than one of the modulations; this is the only proposed 'feature' which can be entirely suppressed (in virtually all languages) to yield a distinct style of speech, whisper. Whisper friction must, then, be considered an alternative carrier; in all languages, however, voiced outbreathed air is the basic carrier,[2] or, to put it somewhat more technically, tonal sound produced by vibrations of the vocal bands (also called vocal cords, vocal folds) which, in turn, are induced by forcible expiration. Unmodulated this would be a steady low-pitched hum with open lips, something like a loud buzzing or a prolonged hesitation sound (*uh*). Similarly the basic whisper carrier is a kind of loud breathing noise, something like the 'roar

---

[1] This notion appears, e.g. in H. Dudley, 'The Carrier Nature of Speech', *Bell System Technical Journal* 19:495–515 (1940).

[2] In English, for instance, it is rare for more than 25% of a string to be voiceless; in some Oceanic and Australian languages voicelessness occurs only adjacent to pauses – in other words it is a boundary signal. Some Northwest American Indian languages give an impression of unusually high devoicing; a small sample of Upper Chehalis, for instance, shows almost 50% voiceless segments. It is quite likely that a calculation based on duration of voicelessness rather than number of voiceless segments would give a slightly different ratio, since voiceless segments (in general) tend to be short.

of the sea' one hears in a sea-shell. Either of these carriers may be modulated in a large number of ways, the voiced buzz in perhaps one or two more than the whisper. Let us consider some of these ways one by one and in combination.

1. The most basic modulation is the simple off-on switch. Since there are two things going on, expiration and voice, there are two kinds of switch-off possible. If one stops the outgoing air by closing the mouth (and nose; but one must consider that this is normally closed by the soft palate, the velum) either at the lips or further back with some part of the tongue, one gets the kind of modulation called a 'stop' or 'mute'. If one stops the vocal vibration, either (a) by opening the glottis (i.e. the space between the vocal bands) wide, or (b) by closing it tight, one gets the modulation called 'voicelessness', which is not to be considered (in type (a)) as identical with whisper: indeed a similar modulation can be applied to whisper, apparently (in part at least) by increasing the sub-laryngal pressure – i.e. breathing out faster and harder. If both the air-stream and the vibrations are stopped simultaneously, we have the class of sounds called voiceless stops; in the case of voiceless mechanism (b), if this is the only stoppage of the air stream we have a 'glottal stop', which can be considered a voiceless stop of a degenerate sort. A third possible kind of switch-off is the simple reversal of direction – stop breathing out and start breathing in – which occurs all the time in our non-speech activity. This never functions as a major speech-signal, though it may serve as a kind of punctuation on occasion. But, in general, speakers are like singers and wind-instrument players, looking upon the taking of a breath as a disagreeable necessity which they would gladly do without. The whisper and voicing mechanisms *can* be man-oeuvered while breathing in, but this is rarely made use of in any systematic way. Perhaps the commonest items of this sort in American culture are the in-breathed voiced *yeah* or *ayuh* or the like which is most common in parts of New England[1] and the quick voiceless in-breathing through clenched teeth which serves to mark such emotions as fright or surprise. Neither one can be considered an integrated part of American English.

2. We mentioned the fact that the normal carrier issues from the mouth, i.e. the nasal cavity is shut off by the raising of the velum or soft palate. The opening of this passage, then, constitutes another kind of

---

[1] Similar items are reported also from dialects of various European languages, Scandinavian especially.

modulation. Since the velum is not very agile, this modulation tends to run alongside several modulations by other devices. If the nose is opened when the mouth is closed, we get the 'nasal consonants'; if both exits for the voice are available at the same time, we have the 'nasalized' sounds (which are mostly vowels).

3. Acoustically speaking, sounds may be loosely divided into two types: tones and noises. The voiced carrier sound is an example of a tone; the whisper carrier is a noise. Tones (except for rare and irrelevant 'pure' tones, which have all their power at a single frequency) are characterized by a spectrum (i.e. pattern of distribution of power among the frequencies) which has power only at certain frequencies that are integral multiples of the fundamental, and no power at other frequencies. In a manner of speaking a tone contains not only (let us say) a particular C natural, but also the C an octave above (and two, three, four, etc., octaves above, also), the G above that, the E two octaves above, and so on, eventually including tones which are in between notes of the musical scale. A noise, on the other hand, tends to contain power everywhere in a whole range (or several ranges) of frequencies, not only (say) C, D, E, and F, but all possible pitches between C and D, D and E, and E and F; its spectrum is more continuous than periodic. Noises may, of course, have distinct and identifiable pitch if one portion of their spectrum is considerably stronger than the rest. Sticks of wood hit together make noises; sticks of wood carefully selected and graded can make a xylophone on which tunes can be played. This is by no means an adequate account of tones and noises, but it will serve as background for our present purposes.

Besides the whisper noise itself, we can make a considerable variety of other noises with our mouths, some of which are rarely used for speech, others frequently. The two commonest types are (1) continuous noises made by forcing air (a) through narrow passages (called friction noises or fricatives, a name which might seem more suitable, say, for the sound made by grinding your teeth together) and sometimes also (b) *past* openings of larger cavities (much as a flute-player blows air *across* the mouth hole, or as a child might blow across the neck of a bottle; these fricatives are sometimes referred to as sibilants, but they are rarely correctly described);[1] and (2) very brief noises caused by sudden

---

[1] Perhaps a few more words about these sounds are in order. (1) In all of them there are two sources of noise simultaneously present: the ordinary fricative constriction noise and the small-cavity eddy noise. The latter may be experimentally eliminated from an ordinary s (as in *sauce*) or š (as in *shush*) either by pulling the lower lip well

release of air under pressure (less often release of a partial vacuum), analogous to pulling the cork from a champagne bottle or opening a vacuum-packed can. In the pressure case, these are called explosions or releases – in certain rare cases, also glottalized stops or ejectives and egressive clicks; they are called implosives, ingressive clicks and sometimes labiovelars in the partial vacuum case. Let us postpone consideration of the various popping noises and consider here the fricatives and sibilants.

If such a noise is produced at a time when the carrier sound is turned off (by having the glottis wide open, as a rule), it tends to be articulated with some force, producing some characteristic noise spectrum which is usually quite audible (in the case of sibilants, very loud indeed). These noises are voiceless fricatives. When, however, the carrier is on, the noise itself is only faintly audible (or quite inaudible), and what is heard is primarily a modification of the spectrum of the carrier combined with a considerable reduction in perceived loudness (if the carrier is the voiced hum, there is also often a drop in pitch). These sounds are called voiced fricatives; and we can usually keep this name even when they are whispered.

back over the lower teeth and under the tongue-tip or by placing a stiff piece of paper or a filing card in the same position; it may be added to a θ (as in *thin, fifth*) by pulling out the lower lip so as to make a space between the lower teeth and lip and directing the air-stream into it with the tongue. When the eddy noise is removed from a s or š, it sounds much like a θ, and like it, is much reduced in loudness. Another way of eliminating the eddy noise component is by breathing in instead of out; the stream of air which strikes the edge of the cavity must be rather narrow. Fricatives like f, θ, and x (or German *ach*, for instance) sound much the same on inbreathing as on outbreathing; sibilants are radically altered. (2) Besides the hissing and hushing sounds of English (and closely similar sounds in other languages), two other kinds of sound sometimes also make use of this mechanism. The palatal fricative [ç] as in German *ich* very often adds a substantial eddy component; this is true in many varieties of Standard German, for instance. The lateral fricative [ɬ] (also called 'voiceless l', though it sometimes has a true voiced fricative counterpart) which is made by forcing air out between the side of the tongue and the upper molars, frequently adds an eddy component induced by the small cavity between the back teeth and the cheek. Without it, the sound is somewhat θ-like or f-like to English ears; with it the sound becomes more š-like. (3) No eddy mechanism can be added to a f made with outbreathed air, simply because there is no possibility of making a cavity outside the lower lip (except prosthetically, by holding a partly open envelope there, say), although the inbreathed variant, *with* cavity mechanism, is a naturally occurring interjection or audible gesture of fear or the like. None can be added to a velar x (at least I can't manage it), because there is no way to manipulate the tongue into forming a small enough cavity in the right location. (4) Most of the difference between a s and a š can be attributed simply to the size of the eddy cavity – small for a s, larger for a š. (Terms like 'slit', 'groove', etc., which occur in the literature are either irrelevant or secondary). A second relevant factor is the lower front teeth: the air stream must strike them for a š, need not for a s.

4. The voiced carrier is a tone, and hence has a fundamental frequency or pitch. Pitch is related to frequency of vibration, i.e. to number of pulses per second, in a logarithmic or exponential way: double the number of vibrations per second and you will raise the pitch by an octave. But what's the difference between speaking and singing? Singing voice is presumably a third kind of carrier, not just a free variant of speaking voice, at least in the vast majority of human cultures. Let us take the most essential case: what's the difference between singing in a monotone and speaking in a monotone? If you doubt that there is one, make the experiment. It is quite easy to talk on a fixed pitch and to sing on the same fixed pitch (without such irrelevant embellishments as vibrato) in such a way that observers will agree unanimously which is which. I'm afraid we must admit that not enough research has yet been done to justify a confident answer to this question, but a few tentative observations are perhaps warranted. (a) At the end of a spoken monotone, simultaneous with the drop in amplitude there is a rapid drop in pitch. This is normally absent from song, though individual singers may introduce it deliberately to produce a spoken effect. (b) The vocal cords in speaking are caused to vibrate in the manner most economical of effort and breath, and the resulting tone, as a consequence, is nearly always accompanied by some audible friction noise; in singing the level of effort is higher, and friction noise much less noticeable. It may well be that the actual manner of vibration is different in the two cases, but more research is needed. (c) A sung pitch is maintained with greater accuracy, less random deviation. (d) Sung tones tend to be accompanied by opening of the velum (nasalization) and wider opening of the mouth (added lip-rounding in many cases); both of these features alter the spectrum appreciably. Once we drop the monotone requirement we acquire many more differences – nature and variety of melodies, restriction to a scale or set of harmonically related pitches, tendency to use (on the average) lower pitches in speech than in song, greater regularity of rhythm in song than in speech (this may operate even in monotone productions), and so on.

But voice does always have pitch, and varying this pitch is a possible modulation. Whisper, too, may be said to have a pitch, but this pitch is not separately available for modulation since the means of modulation (changing of oral cavity size as in whistling) is already pre-empted by the devices of spectrum modulation (see page 49). In other words, variation in the pitch of a whisper is largely (not entirely) an automatic consequence of other modulations. In voiced speech, too, some changes in pitch are automatically caused by other modulations.[1] We have mentioned that imposing fricativeness on voice often causes a slight drop in pitch; in many cases glottalization of a vowel, that is, the constriction of the vocal cords to interrupt the voice, causes a sharp and considerable antecedent drop in pitch. But in general, variations in pitch can be controlled independently of all other modulations of the voiced carrier, except that various psychological causes, emotions such as anger or excitement, may reduce the amount of voluntary control. Again we need research, but some variations in pitch seem to be universally dependent on emotional states for physiological, not linguistic, reasons. Most languages, however, have modified and adapted these natural variations to make conventional indicators of grammatical categories (assertion, question, command, etc.) which can, in some way, be related to states of mind (confidence, doubt, dominance, etc.). Many languages, however, use some pitch or frequency modulation (FM) like other modulations to mark the difference between different words. Such languages are customarily called tone languages, and are of several types: (1) words are distinguished by different *kinds* of tone (as in Chinese: rising, falling, level, etc.); (2) words are distinguished by different *positions* of a single tone of one or two types (many languages in Africa and America: on first, last, next-to-last, etc. syllable or vowel of a word); (3) words are distinguished by *each syllable* having one of three, four or rarely five levels of tone. At least in the first type, there is some evidence to show that some tones originated from automatic pitch changes caused by other modulations. Generally speaking, although a race of beings equipped with absolute pitch discrimination and perfect voice control could easily develop a language in which fundamental pitch modulation was the only kind used, ordinary human beings have mainly used only such broad relative variations as 'higher', 'lower', 'the same', 'rising', 'falling' and combinations of these.

Although, in general, whispering would not seem to allow any such modulation, the fact that most pitch modulations are redundantly accompanied by other modulations (duration, amplitude, spectrum change) – in addition to the general redundancy of language – allows intelligible whispering in all known languages. The converse change, use

[1] High vowels seem to raise the pitch, for instance. See Lehiste and Peterson, 'Some basic considerations in the analysis of intonation', *JASA* 33, 419–25 (1961); P. Ladefoged, *A Phonetic Study of West African Languages*, Cambridge, Cambridge University Press (1964), p. 91.

of the tonal (and timing and amplitude) modulations alone (on drums, musical instruments of various kinds, or whistled) as a *limited* substitute for speech is especially natural (perhaps) for tone languages, but is also attested for some non-tone languages. I vividly remember a Chatauqua act (therefore very likely also a vaudeville act) of my childhood in which a violinist played an intelligible dialog of some five or ten speeches between a girl and her mother, after merely suggesting the background in words.

5. The alternative to FM in radio is AM, and the *amplitude* or loudness (psychologically evaluated in terms of the physical effort needed to produce it) is a very obvious variable used for modulation in speech. Both carriers can easily be modulated, though the available objective range is vastly greater for the voiced one. Here again we find three somewhat different ways in which this is utilized. (a) As in the case of pitch, amplitude is automatically decreased by such modulations as those used to produce fricatives – except perhaps the sibilants. Sibilants are often quite loud; the loudness, however, is greatest in a quite different pitch range from the carrier pitch. One conspicuous example of amplitude diminution is voiced *h*, i.e. the kind that we use in words like *ahead*: in this case the amplitude drop is the principal audible clue. (b) Amplitude variation (generally with simultaneous frequency variation, rise in pitch co-occurring with increase in loudness) is often used to mark the unity of such linguistic entities as words or phrases. In some languages pairs of words may be distinguished solely by the point in each where the greatest loudness is. Languages are sometimes said to have independent 'stress accent' and 'tone accent', but the examples are ambiguous and generally involve also duration (see pp. 55–7). (c) Many languages make use of amplitude variations (again, in the main, conjoined with frequency variations) to mark portions of a sentence as 'central', 'emphatic', 'contrastive', 'pre-terminal', etc. In other words, the sentence-intonation system usually includes some amplitude modulation.

6. The most striking modulation, the one that seems to our ears the most varied, is in the spectrum, that is the way different simultaneous component pitches of a tone or pitch-bands of a noise differ in relative loudness. This alone distinguishes different vowel sounds from one another, and automatic variations in the spectrum accompany most of the other modulations, and therefore contribute to the recognition of virtually all the sounds of language. But, in the latter case, they are of little

concern to the speaker (except, perhaps, in the case of the ventriloquist intent on creating the acoustic effect of a *p* without moving his lips), whereas, in the former, they provide the means by which the speaker controls his output. When we speak, we necessarily listen to ourselves, and what we hear is used (on occasion) to guide us in altering or editing what we say as we say it. This feedback or self-correction mechanism is of most importance for vowels (where the tongue has few fixed positions to be sensed directly) and for pitch and loudness.

It has become customary to describe acoustic spectra in terms of regions of peak strength, or 'formants'. Four or five such regions can easily be identified for most sounds, but three are virtually always adequate for unique specification, and two or even one often enough.

The voiced carrier tone is a complex tone with relatively strong harmonics all the way up to five or six thousand Hz (Hertz) – formerly called cps (cycles per second).[1] In practical terms, this means that a wide range of tone qualities or 'colors' or 'timbres' can be produced from the human voice, particularly if this voice is low-pitched. (As the fundamental pitch rises, of course, the distance between adjacent harmonics also increases; a fundamental of 1,000 Hz means consecutive stretches 1,000 cycles wide where there is no power, hence no possibility of spectral modification. In the range between 50 and 5,050 Hz, a fundamental of 100 Hz will have 50 harmonics available for shaping, one of 1,000 Hz will have only 5.) The whisper carrier is weak at the lower end of the spectrum, but has a stretch of continuous power from about 800 Hz to 3,000 Hz and beyond. Given the amount of redundancy present in most languages, this is usually enough for intelligible speech. This is almost precisely the range within which the second region of peaking (called formant two, F_2) occurs, and this region is the most important for identification of both vowels and consonants. (See figure 4.1.)

[1] Those whose knowledge of the physics of sound is weak might profit from such books as Denes and Pinson's *The Speech Chain*, Baltimore, Md., Bell Telephone Laboratories, 1963; M. Joos's *Acoustic Phonetics*, Linguistic Society of America, Language Monograph No. 23, 1948; B. Malmberg's *Phonetics*, New York, Dover, 1963; P. Ladefoged's *Elements of Acoustic Phonetics*, University of Chicago Press, 1962; Ilse Lehiste (ed.), *Readings in Acoustic Phonetics*, MIT Press, 1967. Excellent also are two articles in *The Proceedings of the Fourth International Congress of Phonetic Sciences*, edited by A. Sovijärvi and P. Aalto, The Hague, Mouton, 1962: Gunnar Fant's *Sound Spectrograph*, pp. 14–33; and B. Lindblom's *Accuracy and Limitations of Sona-Graph Measurements*, pp. 188–202. There are other valuable articles in the same book, but these two are especially useful. On general phonetics there are many books; most recently *Linguistic Phonetics* by P. Ladefoged (*Working Papers in Phonetics* 6, U.C.L.A., 1967), and David Abercrombie, *Elements of General Phonetics*, Edinburgh, Edinburgh University Press, 1967.

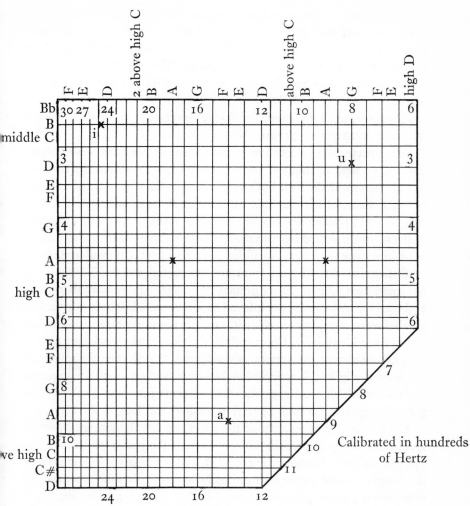

Fig. 4.1   Formant chart as devised by Martin Joos. i, u, a are placed at unambiguous positions; the other two crosses represent an intermediate front vowel (not far from the vowel of English *bet*) and a back rounded one higher than English *awe*, about where some speakers say *Oh!*

The ranges of F_1 (about 150–1,000 Hz) and F_2 (about 1,000–3,000 Hz) and the extent of their mutual independence are such as to permit a very large number of discriminable vowels and vowel-like sounds; however, because the tongue finds no resting-places and the speaker must depend on feedback to guarantee control, and because the greater

C

the number of distinct vowels, the greater the danger of error and misunderstanding, few languages use as many as a dozen steady-state vowels (i.e. vowels without distinctive change of spectrum during their production; pure vowels, non-diphthongs). The use of diphthongs or distinctively gliding vowels eases the burden on speaker and listener somewhat, so that the total of pure and glided vowels may well rise above 20. However, small inventories of simple vowels (3, 5 and 7 are especially frequent sizes) are the normal thing.

Pure spectrum modification is not incompatible with *some* tongue contact, or with opening of the velum. With open velum, so that the sound passes out through both nose and mouth, all spectra are spread out in a characteristic way that we identify as 'nasalized vowels'. With tongue-tip in contact and one or both sides open, we get a modification of the spectrum called lateralization. Though almost as many lateralized as plain or nasalized vowel qualities can be produced, it is often difficult to distinguish them by ear from non-lateralized vowels. No language has more than four liquid continuant laterals (few have more than one), and they are almost never employed as full vowels, but only adjacent to (i.e. before or after) vowels, since it is mainly the shift or transition which makes them identifiable. Conversely, if the sides of the tongue are placed in firm contact with the upper teeth and gums, the effect on the spectrum is relatively slight; this articulation, however, is often found accompanying vowels which are 'tense' in other respects (i.e. have easily distinguishable spectra far from neutral in quality) and long in duration.

The primary manipulators of the spectrum are the tongue, lips and jaw, which are only partially independent. If the jaw is wide open, the lips cannot easily be narrowly rounded, and if the jaw is nearly closed, the tongue cannot easily be maximally lowered. Roughly speaking, a more open mouth passage means a higher F_1 value, a further back point of narrowing (between tongue and palate) means a lower F_2 value, and the addition of lip-rounding means lower F_2 and F_3 values and general weakening of higher frequencies. If one remembers approximate values for the corner vowels in men's speech, it is fairly easy to interpolate for the others: i, $F_1 = 250$, $F_2 = 2{,}500$; u, $F_1 = 300$, $F_2 = 800$; a, $F_1 = 900$, $F_2 = 1{,}400$. These values, being at corners, can vary quite a bit, but the figures given are not abnormal. So if you find a vowel with an $F_1 = 450$ and $F_2 = 1{,}800$, the odds are that it will be some sort of [e], whereas $F_1 = 450$ and $F_2 = 900$ will surely be an [o]. F_2 values around 1,300 or 1,400 will be a bit ambiguous often, since they may be either front rounded or back rounded vowels; fortunately, few languages have both, and those few don't have many of either type.

Labialization may also be added (as a modulation of a modulation) to many consonants, where it particularly affects the beginning of the following vowel and (less) the end of the preceding vowel. The consonant itself, if it has a distinctive spectrum (as is the case, e.g. with a sibilant), may show recognizable modification, lowering the power in the 2 kHz–3 kHz neighborhood by about 300 or 400 cycles, and reducing its total amplitude a little. Retroflexion (or tongue retraction) provides a somewhat similar second-degree modulation. This is accomplished by keeping the front of the tongue near the back edge of the hard palate, normally with some hollowing of the part just behind the tip (which is often pointed straight up or curled back slightly). It is difficult to articulate a large variety of vowels in this position, so languages which have retroflex vowels generally don't have many. American English has one or two of frequent occurrence (the vowels of *bird* and the unstressed syllable of *rubber*), plus one or two others which alternate with sequences gliding from normal to retroflexed (the syllabics of *hard* and *lord* or *ford*; some speakers may have others). The effect of retroflexion is one of the most striking to see on spectrograms: F_3 is pulled down as much as a thousand Hz, while F_2 generally rises a little so that the two are only a few semitones apart. This resembles somewhat the effect of rounding, and indeed some front rounded vowels of French or German strike the naive American ear as r-like. Retroflexion of consonants is usually regarded as either a distinct position (as for apical – tongue-tip – stops in Indic and Dravidian languages, or a cluster-forming element, r, as in American English.

The reverse of labialization, in one sense, is spreading or delabialization of vowels which are normally rounded. It should be remembered that vowels articulated in the front of the mouth, vowels like [i] or [e], are normally unrounded; if rounding is added to them we get a type of vowel which we feel is characteristically French (though most of the languages of Northern Europe, including German, Norwegian, Finnish and Hungarian, have such vowels), I suppose because of the kiss-like articulation. The vowels made in the back of the mouth, on the other hand, are normally rounded ([o], [u]); by taking rounding away from them, i.e. by spreading our lips, we can make another kind of vowel which is often referred to as back unrounded or central. The American English vowel of *rub* or *but* is one such vowel, but some languages (especially in the Turkic family, and some Southeast Asian languages) have several. The high vowel of this variety (not greatly different from that in English *good*) shades gradually into a voiced velar fricative (like the gamma of Modern Greek before back vowels), a sort of tiger's growl.

Even more opposite to both rounding and spreading is, perhaps, palatalization (sometimes referred to by the Jakobsonian name 'sharping'), a feature normally attributed to consonants rather than vowels. This is accomplished by pressing most of the front half of the tongue (not the tip, which tends to be down by the lower teeth) against or close to the hard palate. Since this is essentially the position of an [i] or a palatal consonant [y] or IPA [j], in many languages palatalized consonants are indeed interpreted as sequences of consonant plus y. Sometimes the apicals or dorsals (ty or ky) develop noisy sibilant releases (like ch in *church*), becoming one sort of 'affricates'.

Though these phenomena (labialization, retroflexion, delabialization, palatalization) are spoken of as if they were secondary modulations of some basic sound, this is true only (if at all) from an articulatory point of view. Acoustically we just have different spectra.

Spectral variations that are automatic consequences of other modulations (e.g. closing the mouth at some point) can also be specified, though not always easily. It is likely that we generally hear these phenomena in terms of an imaginary movement of our own tongue, lips, etc. (which may also be true, in part, of the vowels). Any complete closure has a value approaching zero for F_1. If F_2 is low (below 1,200 or so) the closure is labial. If the difference between F_3 and F_2 is very small (less than 500), the closure is on the hard or soft palate somewhere, whatever part of the tongue is making the closure. But these conditions are not all both necessary and sufficient; F_1 may appear to be very low for fricatives as well as stops; labial F_2 may not seem to be lower than 2,000 adjacent to a high front vowel; $F_3 - F_2$ may be as much as 800 cycles for a front velar in some environments.

Noise, unless very faint, is always recognizable on spectrograms, as is silence or the cessation (and resumption) of voicing. The shift of the tongue to and from the position for a lateral usually leaves a very distinct trace. All pitch modulations are plainly visible, unless the spectrum has no high-frequency components.

We can say that a spectrogram shows all the clues that the speech hearer uses (except where they are too weak to register; our ears are more sensitive than Sona-Graph paper), but that the hearer's brain processes many of these clues in a way not represented on the spectrogram. No mechanical device has been able to interpret the cues in the sound wave as successfully as the brain.

7. There are at least three ways in which timing of some sort may provide a usable modulation of the carrier: (a) two independent modulations may be synchronized to varying degrees, with the start of one delayed one, two, three or more centiseconds after the start of the other; (b) a particular modulation may be held for varying durations; (c) the rate at which certain changes (especially those in pitch and loudness) take place may be faster or slower. In this section we will consider synchronization modulation.

This possibility arises most commonly with the turning off and on again of the voicing carrier, but is also relevant to the timing of double stops – i.e. clicks, ejectives, implosives and similar sounds, of the addition or deletion of nasality, and of the release of some stops (in particular those in which a considerable area of the tongue touches the roof of the mouth). A recent article[1] attempts to show that all contrasts of the aspirated-unaspirated, tense-lax or voiced-voiceless types (but not, e.g. glottalized-unglottalized) can be specified by the length of time between release of consonant articulation and beginning of voicing.

Clicks (in some cases) have the rare distinction of being almost as independent of the carrier as finger-snapping – hence so-called 'voiced' and 'nasalized' clicks, in which the voicing or nasality in no way modifies the sound of the clicks, but is merely a bit of background music for it. But when voice (with or without nasality) is turned off for a click, there can be various degrees of delay between the turning off (or on) and the articulation of the click.

In the case of ordinary glottalized stops (ejectives), which are made by compressing the air between the glottis (tightly closed vocal cords or folds) and the oral closure so that release may produce a click-like noise, one relevant delay is that during which the pressure is increased. The longer the delay, the louder the pop. A second delay is that between release of the oral closure and onset of voicing. If both delays are very brief, the sound is indistinguishable from a plain stop; if both are long we have a loud pop followed by a brief silence before the following vowel begins abruptly.

[1] Leigh Lisker and A. S. Abramson, 'A Cross-language Study of Voicing in Initial Stops: Acoustical Measurements', *Word* 20:384–422 (1964). But cf. Chin W. Kim, 'On the Autonomy of the Tensity Feature in Stop Classification', *Word* 21:339–59 (1965).

Both pre-nasalized and post-nasalized stops occur in languages of the world; both depend on delays. If the nasality is turned off before the stop is released we have pre-nasalized stops (which might also be called post-stopped nasals), sounds like nd, mb, and the like; if the nasality is not turned on till after the stop has begun, the result is post-nasalized stops or pre-stopped nasals – dn, bm, etc. Very similar are what might be called pre-lateralized and post-lateralized stops (apical or laminal only), but are more naturally considered post-stopped and pre-stopped l's, the former (a rare type) sounding like ld clusters, the latter like dl. Here again it is variation in the degree of coincidence between complete tongue closure and lateral opening or between central closure and lateral closure that produces the effects.

The dl-type is often called a voiced lateral affricate, which leads us naturally into the whole class of affricates; these are sounds where a closure spread over a considerable area is not opened simultaneously and with equal abruptness over the whole area, but sharply at one point (central, except for the dl types just mentioned and the corresponding voiceless [ɬ] or [ɮ] sounds), and more gradually elsewhere. This is normally a least-effort proposition; the nature of the closure is such that it would be extremely difficult and demand great care in articulation to break it cleanly all at once.

In theory one might also expect possible contrasts between vowels nasalized for varying portions of their length; in fact, perhaps because of the slight degree of agility possessed by the velum or because of the difficulty of discriminating nasal from non-nasal quality in the case of most vowels, no language seems to make use of this device systematically. What occurs is a contrast between phonemically nasalized vowels and phonemically non-nasal vowels adjacent to nasal consonants, where anticipation or lag causes part of the vowel to be phonetically nasalized. But a third degree ('absolutely unnasalized') in the same environment does not appear to be common.

8. Time may be involved more directly, whether as uncommon brevity or uncommon length, in the production of almost any type of modulation. As an automatic consequence of certain modulations, features of duration may acquire the status of clues; in vowels, for instance, the more open ones are, on the average, distinctly longer than the i's and u's. The phenomenon of greater vowel length before voiced consonants than voiceless is not by any means limited to English. Release noises, by their very nature, are extremely brief bursts; this

is true of ordinary stops, aspirated stops, glottalized stops and most clicks. A tap or flap (these are *sometimes* distinguished by direction of tongue movement, out for tap, in for flap), which is made by a ballistic movement (i.e. not under continuous control; one is, so to speak, bouncing the tongue off the palate), is necessarily a very short stop. A trill is a rapid succession of taps (of tongue tip or uvula), also in a sense ballistic (more like a blind rattling in the wind; the tongue exerts a constant pressure, but the exhaled air keeps pushing it away momentarily); though each tap is a very short stop, the general effect is of something continuous and often fairly long. It's rather like the vocal cord vibration slowed down.

But deliberate variations in length play a role in many languages, perhaps in all. (a) As part of the expressive or affective system of a language, prolongation of vowels, of consonants and of pauses frequently plays an important role, either alone or in association with variations of pitch or amplitude (or both). (b) A quantity feature may be applied to consonants or to vowels or (as is often the case) to both simultaneously. So in many languages there are contrasts like *aato* vs. *atto*. We usually write long consonants by simply doubling them; with vowels this is less common, other devices being the IPA symbol of length (a·to or a:to) and various diacritics (āto, áto, âto), though the latter have the disadvantage of being also used for other purposes. Significant clipping or shortening of vowels seems to be less widespread, except as a coincident feature with another (often glottalization or destressing – i.e. stress on a preceding or following vowel).

A few languages (e.g. Estonian) are said to have three degrees of length; such a situation can usually be reinterpreted as two binary contrasts – one (perhaps) in length of vowels, another in the nature of following consonants or syllables. At any rate, there are nearly always other clues; no speaker has to keep his eye on a stopwatch to avoid misunderstanding or mispronunciation.

Duration of vowels and consonants is intimately tied up with rhythm, just as amplitude is; this topic will rate a separate paragraph below (10).

9. Certain continuous changes may be made either rapidly or slowly. So, in pitch, if the tone rises an octave, it may do this very rapidly or very slowly; in changes of vowel quality also (say from an a to an i) we may move quickly or slowly, abruptly or smoothly. And, in releasing stops, we may do so sharply and cleanly or slowly and gradually as for affricates (discussed already under 7). Generally speaking this contrast of

rate of change is universally reinterpreted as a contrast between continuity and discontinuity; rapid changes in pitch tend to be regarded as two consecutive different pitches, whereas slow ones are conceived to be single changing pitches; rapid changes of vowel quality are regarded as two consecutive, heterosyllabic vowels, whereas gradual changes are regarded as monosyllabic diphthongs. This won't quite work for stops; a rapid shift from stop to vowel articulation is indeed regarded as a discrete sequence, but a slower changing is regarded as involving a different kind of consonant, an affricate (which is in a way a consonantal analog of diphthongs), and, in turn, is occasionally regarded as a discrete sequence of a stop followed by a fricative.

10. The phenomena of 7, 8 and 9 all involve time, and their effects (separately or in combination) are closely related to the phenomenon which we know as rhythm. A definition of rhythm which is crystal clear and wholly satisfactory is hard to get, but everybody agrees that it has something to do with approximate equality of successive spans of some kind. The main uncertainties have to do (a) with the degree of approximation to equality (how equal is equal enough?), and (b) with the proper way to measure the successive spans. Both doubts can and should be settled by experiment.

The *function* of speech rhythm, however, is clear: it provides the kind of organization of the speech chain needed to make speed possible. At very slow rates (one or two syllables per second, say) rhythm is quite irrelevant and useless and almost unnoticeable if present; when speeds rise above ten syllables per second or thereabouts, rhythm becomes increasingly necessary, unavoidable and obvious. The relation of this to distinctive characteristics of particular languages is indirect. In English or German it is linked to stress and vowel reduction, in languages like the Polynesian we note regular syllable-timed rhythm and many open syllables, in still others we find a system of vowel and consonant length, and so on. It also conditions the nature of the verse which is likely to be composed in any given language, so that English may come very close to German verse-forms, but not to Polynesian (or Chinese, or Ancient Greek).

11. In several earlier sections we have mentioned glottalized sounds and clicks. The oddity about them is that, unlike other types of sound which somehow modulate the outbreathed voiced carrier or the outbreathed whisper carrier, these are partially independent of the carrier. Clicks are of two types, ingressive and egressive. Ingressive clicks are the

more common type (a kiss, a cluck to a horse, the ts-ts or tsk-tsk – with silent k – of disapproval, the popping click of Makeba's *Click Song* are all ingressive), made by a double closure of the mouth, a sucking action, and release of the front closure. The back closure is nearly always the back (dorsum) of the tongue against the velum, though it may be much further forward for the bilabial ('kiss') click. This necessarily interrupts the passage of air through the mouth, but the nose is free, and any number of clicks may be articulated while producing a continuous and uninterrupted [ŋ] (velar nasal). Indeed one or two can be produced with the velum closed but the cords still vibrating; until, that is, the pressure between glottis and tongue becomes too great. Egressive clicks are made with the same two oral closures as ingressive ones, but with a squeezing of the tongue to force air out over the front closure. These are much less common (perhaps non-occurrent in natural language); a bilabial egressive click (sometimes with two or three vibrations of the lips) is occasionally produced in youthful high spirits, sometimes as a bottle-uncorking imitation. With the lips an audible bottle-opening sound may be produced without either sucking or squeezing with the tongue; this is because the rapid lowering of the jaw to open the mouth sufficiently decreases the air pressure to make an ingressive click. Much the same is true of the Makeba-type click where the tongue is pulled away from the palate, like a rubber suction-cup from the wall. The independence of voicing, particularly if the velum is lowered, is the same as for ingressive clicks.

Like clicks, glottalized stops are either ingressive or egressive, and are produced with double closure. In this case the inner closure is at the glottis, so the front closure may even be (though it rarely is) at the velum. Here, however, it is the egressive type that is most common; the whole larynx is raised, compressing the air behind the front closure, which is released a brief moment before the glottis is opened (the longer the delay, as a rule, the stronger the explosion and the easier the stop is to identify). In theory, the vocal cords could be in vibration while the compression is going on; in fact, however, this does not happen, and egressive glottalized stops (also called ejectives) are always voiceless. The reverse mechanism, in which the air in the mouth is rarefied by lowering the whole larynx before releasing the outer closure, can also be manipulated either with or without voicing; in this case, however, the stops are usually voiced (often called implosives), although occasionally voiceless ones turn up.

Because of the role of the glottis in these sounds, they are obviously not like clicks in being independent of the carrier, although their manner of production and their acoustic effect are similar.

Pike (in his *Phonetics*)[1] discusses a number of other carrier-independent sounds which can be made with tongue, lips or teeth, but so far no language has been found which makes use of them.

12. To sum up, then: in speech a basic carrier sound (voice or whisper) is either simply modulated (pitch-change, amplitude-change, spectrum-change, nasal opening, glottal closure, devoicing, oral closure, oral fricative stricture), or multiply modulated (any combination of two, three or all of the first four; closure or fricative stricture with either glottal closure or opening – though fricative stricture is not often combined with gottal closure) or the modulations are themselves modulated (by duration, rate of change of shifts in synchronization) or sounds independently produced are simultaneous with some other modulation (glottal opening, glottal closure, nasal opening). The variety thus made possible is so great that no language uses more than a fraction of the possibilities. Only two devices (oral closure and nasal opening) seem to be universal – though perhaps independent spectrum change is too – but two others are very widespread (fricative stricture and devoicing). Pitch and amplitude changes are nearly always, in whole or in part, reserved for various binding and connotational functions, as are some time phenomena in many languages.

[1] Ann Arbor, University of Michigan Press, 1944, pp. 32–41, 99–106.

5 Sameness, similarity, analogy, rules and features

All higher animals show some concern with deciding whether something (say A) is the same as or similar to or analogous to something (B), but human beings seem to be concerned in such operations on a grand scale, making such decisions much of the time at the rate of dozens or hundreds per second. There are at least two slightly different ways in which we use the word 'same'. In one way, particularly when we're talking about physical objects, which are concrete individuals, sameness suggests some sort of continuity. The chair I'm sitting in today is the same as the one I was sitting in last Friday *if* an observer *might* have kept it under continuous observation throughout the interval. This raises all sorts of philosophical problems, but for plain people like linguists it should be clear enough. Negatively speaking, this chair is not the same if an observer could have seen the janitor push it out of my office on Saturday and replace it with one from the next office. In courtroom trials, at least as conducted on television, witnesses consider that an object is the same if they can locate (and identify as 'same'!) a small mark which they placed on the object at some previous time. Whether a chair is still the same or not after a broken leg or two legs, or two legs and the seat, or three legs and the seat and the back, etc., are replaced is of interest to philosophers, but not to us.

When we say that the song you are humming now is the same as one you hummed yesterday, we have a different kind of sameness. Expressions like "the same book" or "the same record" may be ambiguous, meaning either "the same physical object, with local continuity, i.e. the same copy (the philosopher's 'token')" or "a different copy or exemplar with the 'same' contents (the philosopher's 'type')".[1] With

[1] For those who are not familar with this contrast, a *token* is an individual, unique instance or occurrence (e.g. of a word) corresponding or belonging to a *type* which may have many other tokens. So if I say "book" now, that particular token is gone forever, but the type 'book' is unaffected and will live to have many more tokens. Modern recording makes things a bit tricky; when we play the same disc over again, can we be said to be producing an entirely new token? In this chapter I have been somewhat influenced by D. L. Bolinger, 'Identity, Similarity and Difference', *Litera* 1:5–16 (1954).

linguistic material it is virtually always this second kind of sameness, not the first (physical-continuity) one with which we are concerned. Indeed the possibility of approximating physical sameness in speech by some sort of recording device is a very recent development; a hundred years ago it was barely dreamt of. And when we do use a tape-recorder nowadays, we hardly ever say "Is that the same word we were listening to yesterday?" More common is something like "I'll play that passage for you again." Of course "again" is a close relative of "the same", used for actions and events, of which physical continuity cannot be supposed. So "He sang the song again", "He sang the same song" and "He sang the same song again" all mean nearly the same thing.

If someone sings the 'same' words, to the 'same' tune, we'll say he's singing the same song; if he makes little mistakes here and there, we'll still allow that it's the same song in most cases, but if either words or music are entirely changed, it is no longer the same. With regard to speech, similarly, we may say "He said the same thing", "The meaning was the same", "The words were the same, but the tone of voice was not", "The way he said it was the same". Ordinary people say all of those but linguists (and some others) may also say "The intonation was the same", "The rhythm was the same", and perhaps a few other such remarks. Anything as complex as the average utterance is not likely to recur without detectable difference of some kind; one of our jobs is to find out how much different in what ways two speech 'sames' may be. This seems to differ somewhat from answering the same question about tunes; for one thing, different listeners may disagree about tunes, but we will all generally agree about words (if not about meanings or tones of voice). At the borderline there will no doubt be cases where we will say "These are very similar, but not the same", so perhaps in our efforts to find out what 'same' means, we may also learn what similarity is. Difference, too; any two things which are said to be similar are necessarily also different (at least in location or time, or else there would only be one), and any two things which we are willing to specify as different, must also be similar. Chalk and cheese, or day and night, or black and white are similar; we are not likely to say that parcheesi is different from a microphone, or yellow paper from meteorology. Still it would not be fair to say that 'different' means the same thing as 'similar', because if someone asks "In what way?" the answers will seldom overlap. There are at least two dimensions to every comparison.

Every linguistic comparison, every recognition of some linguistic form as the same as (or as different-though-similar to) something else requires the cooperation of memory. But it is not, as a rule, the memory of another specific utterance or token. The standard reference form in our brain is already abstracted from all heard, said or possible utterances of it. In the same way, when we recognize, either as class-member or individual, some object or event, we do so, as a rule, not by comparing it with some other particular individual memory, but with some kind of standard or least-common-denominator reference pattern. So both the forms and the meanings of our speech, as stored in our brains, are cut down by omission of all particularizing features, all irrelevancies; furthermore, by a continued application of the comparison process, the relevancies – of form, at any rate, and most probably also of meaning – are arranged and systematized very neatly. Of course, we do also remember particulars (e.g. the physical appearance and voice of individual persons) by some sort of unanalyzed Gestalt storage. We cannot (unless specially trained for police work) give a useful description of someone whom we can recognize on sight from any one of a number of directions and distances. I can think of no good parallel to this with linguistic material; our ability to identify voices is safely regarded as non-linguistic. But most of our memories of ordinary things – tables, chairs, even houses and cars (other than our own) – are quite remarkably devoid of personality, generalized and systematized.

How does one systematize, consciously or unconsciously? The only candidate so far proposed for this job is analogy. An analogy is a sameness of similarities and differences. If I have noted that A is like B, C is like D, E is like F, ... and then go on to compare the A-B similarity to (let us say) the E-F similarity, and conclude that they are the same, I am said to have established a proportion or analogy – A:B = E:F, which, just as in mathematics, is also stateable as A:E = B:F, i.e. the similarity (or difference) between A and E is the same as that between B and F. If we add more pairs to the analogy, the two forms become different: A:B = E:F = P:Q = R:S = L:M and A:E:P:R:L = B:F:Q:S:M.

What are the essential ingredients of a proportion? A mathematical proportion $2:4 = 3:6$ by convention leaves unspecified the condition 'in ratio' or 'in respect to multiplication or division'. Otherwise we should have other kinds of arithmetical analogies, e.g. $2:4 = 3:9$ ($= 4:16$) (in respect to power or root), or $2:4 = 3:5$ ($=4:6$) (in respect to addition or subtraction). In color, two shades of blue could differ in saturation just as two shades of red. Two pairs of musical tones could be proportional either as regards frequency or pitch (here frequency is by ratio, but pitch is taken as scalar, by difference) or else in amplitude or loudness. Most of our everyday cause-effect reasoning is proportional: the billiard player sends instructions to his muscles for sending the ball in the right direction at the right speed as the rapid output of an analog computer relating this shot to a previous number of shots. Of course our calculations may be incorrect and (in some cases) our proportions may be false because we have falsely assumed that A resembles B in a given way. But experience nearly always cures us of these; the ones that we wrongly cling to are our superstitions.

Intelligence tests make great use of proportions, straining to make them as obscure as possible and carefully refraining from specifying the respect, sphere or condition to be considered; and yet most of them yield to semantic cracking quite readily, even the ones constructed of apparently purely linear and geometrically irregular figures. These examples are not perfect; it is hard to find sets classified by three or more binary contrasts, and when they are, the analysis is often given directly by the language, as in small red circle:small red square = large green circle:large green square..., small red circle:small green circle = large red square:large green square..., and small red circle:large red circle = small green square:large green square..., etc. Almost analogous are sets of kinship terms, where sex is perfectly binary and generation is basically binary (perhaps): father:mother = brother:sister = uncle:aunt = son: daughter, and father/mother:son/daughter = uncle/aunt:nephew/ niece ... But the usual case is to find less neatness and less binarity.

Obviously such proportions may involve form alone, form and function, meaning alone, meaning and form, or even form, syntactic function (including constituency) and meaning, all three. Let us think about how they could apply to form alone (or rather with the functional restriction "to be a word of English") so as to make possible a simple rule for answering the question "Does this word sound the same as that word?" (which is often equivalent to "Is this the same word as that?" but not always). This is a question to which our response has become automatic by the time we are two years old or so, so consequently, we would never in the world think of asking it. But we invariably know, provided only we have been able to hear without distortion. The explanation of how we do it, clearly adumbrated by the old Icelandic theorist known as *The First Grammarian*,[1] was explicitly developed in

---

[1] See Einar Haugen, *The First Grammatical Treatise*, *Language* Monograph No. 25, 1950.

Europe and America during the thirties, by scholars who are nowadays often referred to as taxonomic phonemicists. A word like *bet*, let us say, is first opposed to things like *abet*, *you bet*, etc. and to those like *better*, *bet them*, etc., and *Bret*, *bent*, *best*, etc., by an analogy or analogies whose terms are *nothing*:*something*. Then it is successively opposed to pet, vet, get, debt, jet; to bait, to bit, bat, but, *[but], bot; to beck, *bep, *betch, Beth, Bess, and bed. *And there are no more*, except ones into which one of these (or more) could be inserted as a middle term; i.e. *beg* is not on this list because it is first and most closely opposed to *bed*, which *is* on the list. Indeed the list might be shortened. If, for instance, we say that *jet* is more directly opposed to *debt* and *get* (which are on the list),or *bot* more directly opposed to *but*, and so on, we might delete them from the list.

But these are details which we shall take up in a later chapter. Here let us just spell out more fully some of these analogies.

(1) bet:pet = bad:pad = big:pig = bug:pug = burr:purr = bend:pend = buff:puff = ... = din:tin = dun:ton = dip:tip = dart:tart = dim:Tim = ...zoo:sue = zinc:sink = ... = vat:fat = very:ferry = Vee:fee = ... = gull:cull = gosh:cosh = ...etc. and with one slight difference = bed:bet = bad:bat = rib:rip = gab:gap = mend:meant = rug:ruck = ... = need:neat = bud:but = bid:bit = card:cart = ...mid:mit = lose:loose = his:hiss... = halve:half = leave:leaf = ...lug:luck = large:larch = ... etc. These analogies may be summed up as = voiced:voiceless (or −voiceless : +voiceless, or −tense : +tense, or something similar), and named collectively the voice correlation or the tenseness correlation or the like. The first set are distinguished from the last set as 'initial' from 'final', i.e. the first set go *voiced initial*:*voiceless initial* ... and the last set *voiced final*:*voiceless final*. (2) bet:vet = berry:very = best:vest = ... = den:Zen (or possibly den:then) = ... pat:fat = chip:ship = ... (shifting to finals) = dub:dove = ... = cup:cuff = hoop:hoof (for some people anyway) = blade:blaze (or ride:writhe) = ... etc. = (in summary) stop:fricative (or −fricative: +fricative). Here again there might well be some argument about details, but in the main, these proportions seem natural and proper. (3) bet:get = bat:gat = bun:gun = ... = pat:cat = pick:kick = pot:cot = ... (shifting from 'initial' to 'final') ... = tub:tug = rub:rug = ... = tip:tick = tap:tack = nip:nick = ... = rum:rung = hum:hung = ham:hang = rim:ring... etc. Here we can immediately sum up as labial:velar; we will see later how it has been carried even farther. (4) bet:debt = bin:din = bowl:dole = ... =

... = pat:tat = pin:tin = pone:tone = ... = me:knee = met:net = mat:gnat = mick:nick = ... = fin:thin, etc. or fin:sin, etc. ... = (finals) rib:rid = lobe:load = cub:cud = ... = pip:pit = hip:hit = limp:lint = cup:cut = ... = reave:wreathe, etc. or leave:lees, etc. ... = dim:din = shim:shin = damn:Dan = ram:ran = hum:Hun = ... = roof:Ruth, etc. or miff:miss, etc. ... = labial:apical (for the time being). (5) bet:jet = bug:jug = bake:Jake = back:jack = ... = pit:chit = pat:chat = pink:chink = ... = fun:shun = fin:shin = ... etc., etc., = labial:palatal. But this is very likely to be considered a two-step analogy, consisting of the labial:apical series of (4) and an apical:palatal or non-affricate:affricate or quiet:noisy ratio – debt:jet = dug:jug = ... = tat:chat = ... thin:shin (or sin:shin), etc. ... (6) bet:bait = red:raid = men:main = ... = but:boat = hum:home = bud:bode = ... = bit:beet = hit:heat = rim:ream = flit:fleet = ... = should:shooed = could:cooed = ... etc. = something like checked:free or lax:tense or short:long or simple:complex. (7) Let us adopt the hypothesis suggested above that opposes *bet* directly only to *bit, bat* and *but* (and only via them to the others). Then we have bet:bit = let:lit = set:sit = net:knit = ... = pen:pin = ... = beg:big = ... = peddle:piddle = ... etc. = bait:beet = laid:lead = same:seem = nape:neap = ... = pain:peen = ... = bake:beak = ... Huck:hook = luck:look = buck:book = ... boat:boot = coat:coot = shoat:shoot = ... This might be named mid:high, or half-open:close (other names will be discussed later). (8) bet:bat = met:mat = set:sat = net:gnat = ... = pen:pan = ... = beg:bag = ... = peddle:paddle = ... etc. = bait:bite, etc. (or perhaps = came:calm) = Huck:hock = luck:lock = buck:bock = ... boat:bought = coat:caught = loan:lawn = ... This we could call mid:low or half-open:open. (9) bet:but = met:mutt = jet:jut = ... = pen:pun = ... = beg:bug = ... peddle:puddle = ... etc. ... = bait:boat = laid:load = tame:tome = ... = kick:cook = lick:look = whiff:woof (for some speakers) = fit:foot = ... = sheet:shoot = beet:boot = reel:rule = ... etc. This is 'front:back' in old-fashioned terms. (10) bet:beck = sit:sick = mat:Mack = coat:coke = ... = bad:bag = sad:sag = rid:rig = ... (initials) debt: get = dab:gab = dame:game = dole:goal = ... = tape:cape = tough: cuff = top:cop = till:kill = ... etc. = apical:velar. (11) bet:*bep = pet:pep = yet:yep = cat:cap = sat:sap, etc., the same analogy as (4), apical:labial. (12) bet:*betch = hut:hutch = mat:match = coat: coach = peat:peach = ... = lead:ledge = rid:ridge = head:hedge =

... = stop:affricate or perhaps alveolar:palatal. (cf. under (5), above). (13) bet:Beth = root:Ruth = pit:pith = mat:math = ... = laid: lathe = load:loathe = breed:breathe = reed:wreathe = ... = stop: fricative or perhaps alveolar:dental. (14) bet:Bess = sit:sis = mat: mass = cut:cuss = mutt:muss = kit:kiss = ... = hid:his = quid: quiz = said:says = had:has = bud:buzz = bead:bees = freed:frieze = teed:tease = tweed:tweeze ... = stop:sibilant. (15) bet:bed, etc. is the same as pet:bet, the analogy of (1), voiceless:voiced or tense:lax.

So much for the boring examples. Sets of analogies like those given above may easily be summed up by such descriptions (voiced:voiceless) as those appended in each case here. If no term may be neatly inserted in the middle of such pairs, they are thought of as 'minimal contrasts' and christened 'distinctive features' or 'phonological components'; and we shall discuss them at greater length in another chapter. The point here is that it is in terms of such features (or, more basically, the analogies which they represent) that we can give an answer to the question "Is this the same word as that or a different one" (excluding here the question of syntactic and semantic analogies which might lead one to say that 'know' is a different word from 'no'). "This is an instance of *bet*, not of *pet* or *vet* or *debt* or *get* or *bat* or *bit* or *bot* or *bed* or *beck* or *Beth* or *Bess*." There are only a small number of such binary decisions which have to be made; no fine decisions or subtle graduations, no intermediate qualities are relevant for the listener. Speakers may, of course, produce an infinitely graduated range of some of the sound qualities implicit in these analogies, but neither they nor their hearers need pay attention to that range. So here is an essential function of analogy. But this is not the only kind of phonological analogy – indeed few people ever notice that it is an analogy. There is another kind which is more often viewed in this way.

Consider the proportion ma:a or ŋa:a or na:a = nta:ta = mpa:pa = ŋka:ka .... (Here I am abbreviating by using a for all vowels, t for all apical stops, p for labial stops, etc.) This is equivalent to a rule stating that either (1) nasals assimilate to a following stop, or (2) the contrast among nasals is suspended before a following stop. Or pha: ap − # = tʰa:at − # = kʰa:ak − # = ma:am# = ra:ar# = ba: ab# ... This is equivalent to an allophone rule: voiceless stops are aspirated initially (or prevocalically) but unreleased finally. Or try ma: mama = na:nana = pa:papa = da:dada = la:lara = ra:rala .... This is a dissimilation rule: "If two consecutive syllables would begin

with the same liquid, the second must be dissimilated." Many phonological rules rest upon such proportions (or rather on the fuller proportions built up of the actual forms here schematically represented), but
not quite all. Rules of non-occurrence, for instance, cannot be derived
from any set of occurrent forms. If it is true (in English, for instance)
that the velar nasal is prohibited in initial position, an analogy like
ar:al: am: an: aŋ = ra: la: ma: na is only a tentative expression of this,
though if we allow a dummy element meaning 'prohibited', say $,
then we can have am:ma = an:na = aŋ:$. And if we are willing to say
that an initial ŋ would be replaced by n, then we can write am:ma =
aŋ:na = an:na. Suppose we have a language where no word is longer
than five syllables: S/word:SS/word = SS/word:SSS/word = SSS/
word:SSSS/word = SSSS/word:SSSSS/word = SSSSS/word:$ or
(if we believe that we can predict deletion of, say, the first syllable when
a sixth is added) = $S_1 S_2 S_3 S_4 S_5$/word:$S_2 S_3 S_4 S_5 S_6$/word. Proportions such as these seem counterintuitive, however. How about rules of
the type of this one: 'If an English word begins with three consonants,
the first one must be s, the second a voiceless stop (p, t, k) and the third
a liquid or semivowel (r, l, w, y)'? Can they be regarded as basically
analogies? Here again only partial formulations seem possible (e.g. o:
so = no:snow = mall:small = fear:sphere = law:slaw = tie/die/
thigh/thy:sty = peer/beer: spear = kale/gale: scale = pray/bray/fray:
spray = true/drew/through:strew = cram/gram:scram = chin/gin:$
= hat:$ = quirt:squirt = rub:shrub = vat:$ =... for the first
series). And the reason is clear. Analogies reflect decision procedures,
and the basic form of an item in the lexicon involves no decision; it is
given. It is true that language-learners may have to revise their inter-
nalized lexicon at some point to conform to analogies of this type, but
these decisions are made once for all.

But rules of pronunciation, i.e. rules leading from orthography to
phonology, are clearly proportional. So *hotter*:/hɔtr/ = *foxy*:/fɔksy/ =
Boston:/bɔstn/ = *foster*:/fɔstr/ = *lodge*:/lɔj/ =... states the general
rule (which can, of course, be incorporated in an even larger analogy, a
more general rule about vowel letters – a, e, i, o, u, y, æ, œ – before
consonants) that the letter *o* before a double consonant (i.e. *x* or two
consonant letters – *h* is not such a letter – which may be alike or
different) is pronounced /ɔ/.[1] But this is subject to certain prior analogies,

---

[1] The symbol /ɔ/ represents whatever sound you normally use in these words, phonetically most often [a], or perhaps[ɑ].

such as this: *colt*: /ko·lt/ = *fold*: /fo·ld/ = *poll*: /po·l/ = *soldier*: /so·ljr/
= *roller*: /ro·lr/ = *holster*: /ho·lstr/ ... etc., equivalent to a rule that if
the first consonant is an *l*, then *o* is pronounced /o·/, instead. (This can
also be incorporated in a larger rule involving *a* and *u*.) But as time goes
on, the bigger analogy tends to swallow up the smaller; even now we may
note *doll*: /dɔl/ = *moll*: /mɔl/ = *Poll*: /pɔl/ etc., not to mention *dollar*:
/dɔlr/ = *hollow*: /hɔlw/ = *follow*: /fɔlw/ = etc., which could have been
excluded by a different formulation of the rule above. And people who
do not encounter cotton bolls as children very often attach *boll* to the
larger analogy (along with *doll*, etc.) instead of the smaller one. (So in at
least three different recorded versions of the semi-popular (1966–7) song
In Them Old Cotton Fields Back Home.) In the case of another small
analogy, monk: /moŋk/ = compass: /kom'ps/ = front: /front/ = Monday: /mondy) ... etc. (/o/ here roughly = [ʌ]), where the rule probably
reads or once read "If the first consonant letter after it is a nasal (not
followed by an apostrophe) and the second a stop or fricative, *o* is
pronounced /o/", pressure to swing these words back to the majority has
been strong and has been going on for a long time, so that most words
(e.g. all those in final -*omp* and -*omb* – though /bom/ for *bomb* was
normal in my early childhood – -*ond*, *bronc*, *conch* and *honk*, all words
in -*ong*) have long since joined the larger analogy, leaving only *front*,
sponge, *month*, *once*, *monk* and *tongue* among monosyllables, and a mere
handful of longer words like *compass*, *monkey* (*donkey* also only or
mainly in New York City), *comfort*, *condom* (but the word is rapidly
becoming obsolete now) and a few more, and even these are feeling the
pressure. It is this kind of 'analogical change' which is generally
referred to as 'spelling pronunciation', and it has probably been the
greatest single cause of phonological change in modern English, both
British and American.

It is a remarkable characteristic of several Indo-European languages,
most familiarly Latin, that there are sets of affixes superficially different
in form from other sets, but filling exactly the same function – the so-
called declensions or declension-types. These are pure analogies, often
of many terms: singular:plural = anima:animae = animae:animārum
= animae:animīs = animam:animās = animā:animīs = homo:
hominēs = hominis:hominum = hominī:hominibus = hominem:
hominēs = homine:hominibus = gladius:gladiī = gladiī:gladiōrum =
gladiō:gladiīs = gladium:gladiōs = etc., etc., where the correspondence
is between singular cases and plural cases. (The case specification is

assumed to be in each instance a part of the omitted environment in the above proportions – i.e. anima/nominative:animae/nominative = animae/genitive:animarum/genitive, and so on.) And, condensing for the moment all first declension nouns into one, all second declension nouns in one, etc., poēta:gladius:homo:cīvis:senātus:diēs (:nominative singular) = poētae:gladiī:hominis:cīvis:senātūs:diēī (:genitive singular) = poētae:gladiō:hominī:cīvī:senātuī:diēī (:dative singular) = ... etc., which can as easily be formulated as poēta/nom. s.:poētae/gen. s.:poētae /dat. s.:poētam/acc. s.:poētā/ abl. s., etc. = gladius/n.s.:gladiī/g.s.: gladiō/d.s.:gladium/acc. s.:gladiō/ab. s., etc. = homo:hominis:hominī: hominem:homine, etc. = cīvis:cīvis:cīvī:cīvem:cīve, etc. =... and so on through all the declensions. In short, a conventional paradigm is merely a handy representation of one of these long proportions. Paradigms which extend in two or more dimensions (e.g. 'number' and 'case' in these Latin examples) are equivalent to intersecting chain analogies. Such paradigms are nowadays often referred to as matrices by followers of the linguist Kenneth Pike. Native speakers, perhaps, do not normally have paradigms stored in their brains in matrix form; they do have instant access, however, to dozens of analogical chains. The native speaker does not ask "Is *blātus second declension or fourth?", for example, but he often does ask – or at least wonder – "Do you say *blātī like gladiī or *blātūs like senātūs?" So we may say "Is *fit* like *hit* or like *pit*?" when wondering about a past or a participial form. Such multi-dimensional continued proportions as those of Latin, Greek or Sanskrit are not frequent in languages of the world; many of them do have verb systems of 500 or more distinct forms, but as a rule all verbs will make these in the same way, with simple and obvious morphophonemic adjustments (i.e. d after other sounds but t after s, k, p, etc., but not like IE, where suppletion of affixes may show -ī after nominal o-stems, -ius after pronominal stems, or -m after nominal o-stems, -d after pronominal, or -e after consonant-stems, -d after vowels, -bi- after ā or ē, but -ē- after consonants or ĭ).

The name suppletion is most often reserved for stems, however. In English there are few good examples: two are *go:eat:walk:row* ... = *went:ate:walked:rowed* ... where *go* and *went* have virtually no phonological similarity, and *am:be:are:is:was:were:been* = *go:go:go:goes: went:went:gone* = *eat:eat:eat:eats:ate:ate:eaten* = *walk:walk:walk: walks:walked:walked:walked* ... etc. Not only are most of the forms of *be* (except *was – were* and *be – been*) quite dissimilar phonologically, but they mark at least three, often four more distinctions than are made in any other verb. Latin, like English, has only a few examples, *fero*:*tulī* = *amō*:*amāvī* = *cupiō*:*cupīvī* = *moneō*:*monuī* ... somewhat like *go – went*, and *sum*:*esse*:*fuī*: etc. = *amo*:*amāre*:*amāvī* :etc. exactly equivalent to *am – are – be –* etc. But Greek and Sanskrit have many examples. Greek suppletive verbs with three stems include *horɔ̂*:*ópsomai*:*eîdon* ('see') = *phérɔ*:*oísɔ*:*énenka* ('bear') = *érkhomai*:*eîmi*:*ɛ̂lthon* ('go, come') = *légɔ* (-*agoreúɔ* in compounds):*erɔ̂*:*eîpon* ('say') = *esthíɔ*:*édomai*:*éphagon* ('eat' – here the first two stems are distantly related) = *pɔl^*:*pɔlésɔ*: *apedómɛn* ('sell'; only two stems up to here, but a third appears in other forms, the perfect *pépraka*, for instance). Most of these verbs also have numerous compounds made with prepositional prefixes, e.g. *diaphérɔ*: *dioísɔ*:*diénenka* ('differ', 'surpass', etc.) = *apagoreúɔ*:*aperɔ̂*:*apeîpon* ('become tired' etc.) = *parorɔ̂*:*parópsomai*:*pareîdon* ('concede', 'neglect', etc.). Compare English forego – forewent – foregone.

Two stems are also exhibited by some verbs, with the second stem entering at various spots in the paradigm. *Hairɔ̂*:*hairésɔ*:*heîlon*, 'take' (a third stem is associated with this as a passive, *halískomai*); *erɔtɔ̂*: *erɔtésɔ*:*erómɛn* (the stems are obviously related, but not in a regular way) 'ask'; *ékhɔ*:*héksɔ* or *skhésɔ*:*éskhon* (again the stems are historically related) 'have'; *zɔ̂*:*biɔ́somai*:*ebíɔn* (historically related in the remote past) 'live'; *trékhɔ*:*dramoûmai*:*édramon* 'run'. There are a few other cases like *hairɔ̂*:*halískomai* of verbs with a partially suppletive active-passive relation, e.g. *diɔ́kɔ* ('pursue', 'prosecute') often has *pheúgɔ* ('flee', 'be prosecuted') as its passive, and *apéthanon* ('died', 'was killed') may function as the passive of *apékteina* ('killed'). Similarly, *keîmai* ('lie', 'be put') frequently functions as the perfect passive of *títhɛmi* ('put'), especially in compounds, and compounds of *eimí* ('be'), frequently act as perfect forms for compounds of *gígnomai* ('become'). The nearest thing to this in English is the use of 'have been' as a kind of experiential perfect for 'go' or 'come' (in 'He's been to the movies, to Spain, to Europe, to graduate school, here, etc.'). Suppletion in nouns is also possible, though rare: so *person* in part may function as a singular of *people*. In Greek the word for 'lamb' is usually *amnós* in the nominative singular, but *arn*- (ós, -í, etc.) in the remaining cases (historically unrelated); *Zeus* has the stem *Di*- in all other cases (historically related). A striking example is the Indo-European first singular pronoun, *I, me*, etc. in English, *ego, mē*, etc. in Latin, *egɔ, me*, etc. in Greek, *aham, mām*, etc. in Sanskrit; English also has *we – us* and *she – her*, while Sanskrit shows *yayam – asmān – nas*, etc. (we – us) and *yūyam – vas*, etc. (ye – you); oddly enough, Bilin, a Cushitic language of Ethiopia, shows a similar phenomenon.[1]

Many dictionaries and some grammars are inclined to weasel about these proportions; it's as if it were incestuous for forms of the *same* lexeme (word, lexical unit) to be phonologically unrelated. They suggest sometimes that *went* is not the past of *go* but a defective synonym which happens to occur only in the past, while forms of *go* are defective in that they just happen never to be past. Now and then usage gives them a little help, when alternate forms from two stems which are otherwise suppletive compete with each other. So in Greek, although the aorist *éleksa* (from *légɔ* 'say') is quite rare and *eîpon* is very common, some writers (e.g. Thucydides) do use both of them. Curiously enough, it can even be shown that there are certain contexts in which they are not free variants, hence differ slightly in meaning.[2] Therefore (they would argue) *éleksa*, not *eîpon* is the true aorist of *légɔ*, and *eîpon* is defective, without any true imperfective stem. But the fact remains that we can find dozens of passages where the speakers are clearly applying an aspect-shifting transformation rule to an expression containing *légo* and come out with one containing *eîpon*. When we ask someone "Where *did* you *go*?" and he answers "I *went* to X" with high consistency, it becomes almost paradox for its own sake to deny the existence of suppletion. This kind of suppletion in verbs is quite typical of some (not all) Indo-European languages; it is also well attested in a number of American Indian languages and some New Guinea languages.

But there is a type of synonymy which is suppletive in a somewhat different way. Consider such sets as the following: Chemistry Building: this building = Ballantine Hall:that building = Schermerhorn:that other building, etc. Buildings on a college campus are all buildings (except perhaps for gyms, auditoriums and field houses), but their names, under certain conditions, contain the word *Building*, under others *Hall* (both of which are normally freely deletable), and in still other cases (at least in normal college speech) nothing. In some sense *Hall* is either a synonym or a suppletive alternant of *Building*, while zero seems to be a third.

But, you may say, these are proper names, not ordinary English

---

[1] F. R. Palmer in *Lingua* 17:207–8 (1966).

[2] Similar specializations occur in English, e.g. (as noted by D. L. Bolinger, *Aspects of Language*, Harcourt, Brace and World, 1968, p. 127), speeded = drove over the limit, sped = went fast.

expressions. Very well, try these. *Cases*: in five ... the verb was passive = *instances*: in five ... the nouns were in different cases. It is a rule of English style that, unless you are intentionally making a joke (hence the common use of "No pun intended"), you cannot use homonyms or "the same word in two different senses" (zeugma) in the same phrase or sentence. And on nearly every occasion when we apply this stylistic rule, there is an acceptable synonym available. Not quite always; occasionally we have to back up and start over. But nearly always. Is this not clearly also a kind of suppletion? The evidence is very similar. Just as a child who says "We goed to the store" is often absent-mindedly corrected, "Went, Johnny, went", so a man who absent-mindedly writes "Smith's thesis in his Ph.D. thesis is that X", absent-mindedly (or amusedly or in annoyance) goes back and revises – perhaps changing the first 'thesis' to 'main point' or 'claim' but more easily the second one to 'dissertation'. This sort of linguistic behavior is by no means unusual. And yet many linguists (and others) not only refuse to consider these events as involving cases of suppletion, they are not even willing to treat them as synonymy. One reason for this last has been pointed out by John Lyons.[1] A feeling has somehow arisen that "X is synonymous with Y" ought to mean "X can be replaced by Y in all possible contexts without change of meaning" where change of meaning is to be determined by differences, however subtle, in the hearer's attitudes and behavior. But it takes no great depth of penetration to see that if this definition is correct there can never be synonyms. Even if one throws out the cases of hypostasis (or mention or citation: e.g. " 'Hall' can be replaced by 'Building' ") and cases of assonance, pun and rhyme ("I like Ike" is obviously different from "I admire General Eisenhower" in influence on the listener, as is "Rub-a-dub-dub, three men in a tub" from "Rub-a-dub-dub, three men in a vat"), there will still remain contexts where some sort of secondary associations are different and relevant. There may be an element of arbitrariness in distinguishing potential synonyms from apparent variants (maybe in most cases dialect variants) of the same word. "Cherry-pip" and "cherry-pit" seem to be in a different relation than either of them has with "cherry-stone" or "cherry-seed". Is "a bumbling idiot" synonymous with "a bungling idiot", or merely a variant? How much or what kind of phonological resemblance is sufficient to tip the scale toward the

---

[1] J. Lyons, *Structural Semantics*, Oxford, Basil Blackwell, 1963. (Publications of the Philological Society, xx), pp. 74–5.

'variant' hypothesis and away from 'synonym' candidacy? If a given definition of 'synonym' leads to the conclusion that the word 'synonym' is useless (except in negative contexts), why not accept, with Lyons, the easily definable and frequently useful notion of 'synonym in a context'?

This brings us back to the question, are some cases of synonym-in-context actually better considered as suppletion, i.e. not another way of saying the same thing, but the same word in a different guise, somehow? The main difficulty with the suppletion hypothesis seems to be that the requisite complementary distribution is never quite perfect; there are nearly always *some* environments in which both X and Y occur, though often with very different frequency (e.g. X 99 per cent of the time vs. Y 1 per cent) and with no discernible difference in purport or response. Whereas, among adult 1960–70 speakers of American English, "*I goed to the store" and "*I'm wending to the store" are absolutely non-occurrent in ordinary non-jocular speech, although "I went to the store" and "I'm going to the store", and the like, occur frequently and would be regarded as normal and correct expressions by most speakers, similar unity of feeling is not to be found about the instance of "case" and the case of "instance" or such other similar pairs as "the fact that" and "the idea that", or (linguistic) "corpus", "texts" and "data", or "exceptionless" and "invariable", or "paper" and "article", to mention only a few. By and large, then, we must conclude that the general refusal to consider these things instances of suppletion is well founded, though there may be a handful of pairs in English where this is not true.

In any case, it would be difficult to find pairs or sets which could be put upon the same analogical basis as Latin declensions; proportional contexts for several complementary pairs would be a minimum requirement, and it seems doubtful if even two pairs can show this kind of proportion. If we shift to the realm of pairs differing by a single feature, however, we find them easily: cow:bull = ewe:ram = mare:stallion = sow:boar = female:male = lioness:lion = etc., or, in the same portion of the lexicon, cow:calf = horse:colt = sheep:lamb = hog:shoat/pig = x:x cub (where x may be bear, wolf, lion, etc.) = cat:kitten = adult: young ... etc. These are the most commonly cited examples, but others are available – blue:pale blue = green:pale green = red:pink ... where – in my dialect at least – *pale red is impossible ('light red' is possible, but just barely).

In derivation just as in lexicon there are many cases of synonymy as well as suppletion. So, corresponding to *certain* we have both *certainty* and *certitude*, to *move* both *motion* and *movement*, to *beauty* both *beauteous* and *beautiful*, and so for all kinds of nominalizations and adjectivalizations – verbalizations, too, as in *equal* (adj.) corresponding to *equal* (vb.) and *equate* (here, as often, there is a tendency to use one verb as transitive and the other as intransitive) or *black* (adj.) to *black* (vb.) and *blacken*, or *long* to *lengthen* and *elongate*. In all such cases the well-known tendency to specialization which Bréal[1] was so fond of is generally at work, so that the synonyms differ, to some extent at least, in various ways – in stylistic flavor if nothing else. In setting up proportions this can be noted by subscripts: $black_1 : black = black_2 : blacken = long_1 : lengthen = equal_1 :$ equate, etc. The equivalents to these proportions in a generative grammar would lie in two places: a feature [+Verb] or [+Adjective] (or, possibly, [−Verb] or [−Adjective]) etc. added to the lexical entry at some point, and a later look-up procedure or lexical rule which says that *black* with the feature [+Verb] ([−Adjective]) is to be written *blacken*, at least under certain specified conditions. *Pink* could be handled the same way – i.e. a semantic feature [+pale] attached to color terms could be brought on the line ('segmentalized') as the word *pale* except when the item is *red*, in which case it must be changed to *pink* and *pale* optionally deleted – or else it could be treated as a fairly late 'spelling' rule which operates on the sequence *pale red* replacing it by *pink*. *Cow*, *ewe* and the rest could also be handled in either of these ways. The brain, I suppose, does neither, but recognizes the proportion.

If we turn now to the realm where decisions have to be made most often, we get a notion of the vast network of analogies which is sparking in our brain every time we speak. Let us take a simple sentence like "John is writing a book" and look at some of the analogical chains that it fits into. (1) John:John is writing a book = my uncle:my uncle works for Macy's = the rug:the rug is on the floor = ... for millions of examples which can be summarized as Subject:Sentence. (2) is writing a book: John is writing a book = works for Macy's:my uncle works for Macy's = is on the floor:the rug is on the floor = ... for millions (the same millions, sliced differently) that add up to Predicate:Sentence. The two chains together are equivalent (or partly equivalent) to a rule S→NP + VP, or Subject+Predicate. Separate justification for some of these names (e.g. NP) depends on other, intersecting analogical chains.[2]

---

[1] See M. Bréal, *Semantics*, New York, Henry Holt, 1900 (New York, Dover Publications, 1964).

[2] It is perhaps worth while to specify more clearly here exactly what goes into a syntactical analogy. When we say, for instance, x : xyz = q : qpr etc., we are saying two

Many proportion-chains can be shown to lie behind various syntactic categories (or categorizational features); indeed there is very little else to these categories or to most rules that contain them except shorthand expression of long chain proportions. The man reads:the man speaks: the man thinks:the man decides:the man intends to ... = the woman reads:the woman speaks:the woman thinks:the woman decides:the woman intends to ... = the professor ... = the lady ... = the intelligent being from outer space ... = ... etc., etc., with the terms vastly extended in both directions, provides two categories: 'human' noun phrases (and, in the simplest case, animate nouns), and verbs (or rather predicates) which take 'human' subjects – or, conversely, 'rational action predicates' and nouns which take rational predicates. If one of these is prior to the other, the ground for choosing has not yet appeared.[1] Predicates like these, in general, *must* have subjects like these, while 'human' or 'rational' subjects, in the main, are also 'animate' and belong to sets like – the man drinks water:the donkey drinks water:the spider drinks water:the rattlesnake drinks water ... = the man is asleep:the donkey is asleep:the spider is asleep:the rattlesnake is asleep

things, equivalent to assertions (a) that x is a specific constituent of xyz and q the same sort of constituent of qpr, and (b) that the relation of x to xyz is the same as that of q to qpr, i.e. that a certain meaning is associated with it. There may also be purely constituent analogies, as for instance: The man came : I saw the man : he's with the man:who is the man : etc. = fourteen tall boys came : I saw fourteen tall boys : he's with fourteen tall boys : who are fourteen tall boys : etc. = ...which is equivalent to specifying an entity like 'animate noun phrase' or 'human noun phrase', depending on how the proportion is continued.

Furthermore it cannot be doubted that the analogical chains in our brain include *inequalities* as well as equalities, i.e. information that certain things are *not* analogical to certain others, the result, one supposes, of tentative attempts at extending a chain which are in some way rebuffed.

And, though we can economically summarize the value of many, many chain proportions by minimal ordered rules, there is no reason to suppose that analogies have to be minimal. In fact, those which we can observe in operation as speakers try to extend the frontiers of their language are often complex, to be represented not by a single rule, but by half a dozen rules, or even more. George Lakoff's comments in 'Empiricism without facts', *Foundations of Language* 5:125–6 (1969) are irrelevant for this reason, as well as for assuming that preknowledge is the only possible explanation. Just as I could never learn what a chair is if I didn't have an innate idea of a chair at birth, so I could never form correct analogies involving NP's if I didn't have an innate idea of an NP. Many people believe that this is self-evident.

Incorrect analogies can, of course, be formed, and often are; some of them eventually become correct analogies (language change), but most meet with some discouraging reactions and are dropped. An incorrect analogy is equivalent to a false rule (or sometimes several false rules), and subject to the same controls as all false beliefs which must be put to the test. (Those which cannot be properly tested, which include many superstitions and political beliefs, may last throughout life.)

[1] In spite of (e.g.) Chomsky's argument in *Aspects*, pp. 114–15.

... = etc., etc., and 'solid material objects', which appear in analogies like I hit the man: I hit the donkey: I hit the table: I hit the stone ... = the man fell down: the donkey fell down: the table fell down: the stone fell down ... = etc., etc. But the statement may again be turned upside down: predicates like *fell down* may be called 'material event predicates' and it may be said that 'rational predicates' are a subclass of 'vital predicates' which are, in turn, a subclass of 'material event predicates'.

Rules of the sort that used to be called transformational (still so for Zellig Harris[1] and many Pikeans[2]) appear in analogies like these: someone ate the meat: the meat was eaten = someone broke the glass: the glass was broken = someone is swimming the channel: the channel is being swum = someone can see you: you can be seen = ... etc. This corresponds to a simple rule converting active transitive sentences with indefinite ('someone') subjects into equivalent passive sentences without an agent expression. (A more general passive rule would require somewhat more elaboration and variety in the proportion.) He told me "Come!": he told me to come = we bade them "Go away from here!": we bade them (to) go away from here = I'm ordering you, "Do it!": I'm ordering you to do it = ... This is a rule converting direct to indirect commands (some linguists would prefer it to go the other way, which is possible; a proportion works either way). We can also observe Come!: He told me "Come!" = Go!: He told me "Go!" = Do it!: He told me "Do it!" = ... etc., and Come!: I told you to come = Go!: I told you to go = Do it!: I told you to do it = ... Similar but slightly different analogies exist for many other verbs, e.g. "I want you to come", etc., "asked you to go", etc., all of which form another analogical dimension. Related to this set are proportions like the following – he's coming: they said he was coming = he'll be there: they said he'd be there = he can do it: they said he could do it = he's been robbed: they said he'd been robbed = he was robbed: they said he'd been robbed = ... – and similar sets with 'thought', 'heard', 'believed', 'claimed', 'alleged', and many more, as well as Is he coming?: I don't know if he's coming = did you see him?: I don't know if you saw him = where is he?: I don't know where he is = who called?: I don't know who called = why did he say that?: I don't know why he said that = ... and dozens

---

[1] See 'Co-occurrence and transformation in Linguistic Structure', *Language* 33:283–340 (1957).
[2] See, e.g., R. E. Longacre, *Grammar Discovery Procedures*, The Hague, Mouton, 1964.

more with 'wonder', 'ask', 'learn', 'inquire', 'discover', 'find out', 'tell', etc., etc.

One more example. Dick knows/John knows: Dick and John know: they know = Bill sees/Henry sees: Bill and Henry see: they see = You're here/I'm here: You and I are here: We're here = He's here/I'm here: He and I are here: We're here = You're here/he's here: you and he are here: you're (both) here = . . ., and, at a slight angle to that one, I came with Dick/I came with John: I came with Dick and John: I came with them = I saw Bill/I saw Henry: I saw Bill and Henry: I saw them = He'll find you/he'll find me: he'll find you and me: he'll find us = You know him/you know me: You know him and me: you know us = I know you /I know him: I know you and him: I know you (both) = . . . and so on for many more. Here are parts of several rules, including conjunction of noun phrases with 'and', agreement of pronouns with antecedents, agreement of present tense verbs with subjects, generation of plural personal pronouns, and probably one or two more.

We've come a long way from the undefined notion of similarity with which we started. But we seem to have added nothing more; all the most complicated chain analogies are built up using only this. The most important (if vague) principle involved here is what may be called the principle of hasty generalization (by which we live and assuredly talk):

Things which are similar in one way are probably similar also in another (different, dissimilar) way.

The kind of linguistic change known as analogical change is not a change from non-analogy to analogy or one *caused by analogy*, as is sometimes mistakenly supposed, but a change *from one analogy to another*, a transfer of a pattern or item from one proportional set (usually a short one, even unique in one dimension) to another (usually a long one with two-dimensional similarity throughout). So when nouns pass from the Old English situation of many different plural patterns to the modern one with the basic pattern (-s) and a minute set of 'irregular' patterns, short chains (man: men = foot: feet = goose: geese = mouse: mice = . . . ox: oxen [entirely isolated and now almost purely literary and archaic] . . . = child: children [almost suppletive] . . . etc.), it is not necessary to suppose that all formations except -s were unique ('irregular') along the way. Even now, it is difficult to see how anyone examining the Old English or Middle English situation could predict the eventual triumph of -s, except on grounds of phonological simplicity and convenience. As it happens -s is, within the English phonotactic system, about the most convenient and shortest possible suffix, which undoubtedly explains its parallel success in several other functions, particularly the third-person singular present where its exact starting point (conceivably *is*) is hotly debated. Here the original chain had only zero or -(e)th, and the shift to -s must have been for some time a transfer from a longer to a shorter analogy. The expression of analogical changes in terms of features or rules lies often in the elimination of special categories (and marks of membership in these categories) so that the scope of a rule (the Structural Description, as it is called) becomes gradually wider and less restricted. Sometimes it involves the deletion of special rules, reordering of rules, or simple changes in the phonological specification of morphemes.

Analogical change in syntax is quite similar, though not often as sweeping. A word lexically marked for one structure the same as another semantically similar word, but differently in the case of another structure becomes like it in both. For instance, an analogy which in the more old-fashioned form of modern English might be given as *persuade him of it: convince him of it = persuade him that it is so: convince him that it is so = persuade him that he should go: convince him that he should go = persuade him to go: convince him that he should go* is altered to make the last term the currently popular (*) *convince him to go.* In this case there is probably also an accompanying change in the relative frequency of the two verbs, and eventually an alteration of the semantic features which distinguish them.

Much or most borrowing by one language from another is by way of bilingual proportions – so all cases of calque or loan translation, e.g. Fr. *ça va* and *sans dire:ça va sans dire* = English *that goes* and *without saying:that goes without saying* (semantics or context is again omitted from the proportion).

Enough has been said to show the great role of analogy in forming the structure in a man's brain which is his language. We have also noted the convenience and economy, in talking about such proportions, of using conventionalized summarizing devices like rules, features, paradigms, and matrices. From now on we shall use these devices most of the time; but we should not forget that each of them rests on one or more proportions or sets of proportions. And if, in one sense, rules and features are merely arbitrary fictions (while only the utterances and proportions are real), there is also another, paradoxical, manner of speaking in which only they are real while actual utterances are merely conventional abbreviations for the rules and features. Many linguists prefer this paradoxical sense of 'real'.

6 *Mood, modality and illocution*

Communication is not all the same. It is natural and perhaps proper to assume that assertions or statements are the basic class of messages, and to derive other kinds from them, but that does not relieve us of the responsibility of asking how many kinds there are and what they are. We may then compare the various possible kinds with the varieties of expression available in different languages and notice points where the correlation is imperfect. Or we could start with the various forms of expression and look for the nature of the messages which they convey. Or, finally, we can[1] consider the words we normally use to distinguish these various kinds of messages – *tell, ask, order, question, claim, believe, hope*, etc. – and go from there to both the meaning and the form. In this chapter we will follow the first method, starting with aprioristic message types and using the structural and lexical correlates of these to support our classification.

There are two traditional starting-points, both of which seem to be relevant: truth-value and speaker's attitude. To certain sentences we can say, "No, that's not so" or, "Yes, that's true", while to many others we cannot. By this test, for instance, we can divide the following sentences quickly into groups A (with truth-value) and B (without) (I exclude here such verbless types as 'Goodbye', 'Thank you', 'Hello', etc.):

A: (6-1) This book is (not) red.
 (6-2) Johnson is (not) president.
 (6-3) I'm (not) sitting in the lounge.
 (6-4) Coal is (not) white.
 (6-5) Books are (never) printed on paper.
 (6-6) It is (not) 11.45 a.m.
 (6-7) We went (didn't go) to Woolworth's yesterday.
 (6-8) I can (not) read French very well.
 (6-9) We're (not) going to be late.

[1] In this chapter I am indebted in various ways to J. L. Austin, *How To Do Things With Words*, New York, Oxford University Press (1965) [GB 132].

B: (6-11) It may (not) rain (tomorrow).
  (6-12) (Don't) Read your book (now).
  (6-13) I wish you would(n't) do that (now).
  (6-14) Who's Johnson?
  (6-15) (Don't) sit in that chair (ever).
  (6-16) I would(n't) have been president (then).
  (6-17) I hope it does(n't) rain (tomorrow).
  (6-18) I'll (I won't) read it (tomorrow).
  (6-19) You can (can't) come in (now).
  (6-20) Are(n't) you ready (yet)?
  (6-21) Shall I answer the phone (now)?
  (6-22) He ought to have (shouldn't have) said that (yesterday).
  (6-23) I wonder if he's (not) coming.
  (6-24) I advise you to mind your own business.
  (6-25) He may (not) be there now.

Several things are immediately obvious in this rather heterogeneous looking collection. In A, all the sentences are explicitly or implicitly either present or past ((9) clearly implies an inference from known present distances and speeds, i.e. "we've got 100 miles to go on foot and only five minutes to do it in" or the like) and all but (4) and (5) must be placed in a specific context with specific individuals saying them. In B, sentences (11), (17), (18), and (19) are quite clearly future, and (12), (13), and (15) are likely to be future, though they may also be, in some sense, present, while only (16) and (22) are past. And indeed we may have some qualms about the truth-value test as applied to (16) and possibly even to (22), (11) or (25): somebody *could* answer "No, that's not so" or "I don't believe it", so perhaps, at least sometimes, they belong in A. All questions and commands are in B; but about questions there is a further point: the possible answers to some (e.g. 14 and 20) will have truth-value and belong in A, whereas for others (e.g. 21) this is not the case. We may then ask whether questions should not be treated much like negatives (notice that all sentences except B (14) may either be positive or negative); all the sentences in A have matching questions (remember to interchange *I/we* and *you* in converting) and so do all the non-questions in B except (11) and (23) (and perhaps 13, 17, 25). Sentence (11) seems to represent one position on a scale of possible answers (It might, it will, it could, it ought to, it should, etc.) to one single question "Will it rain tomorrow?" or "Do you think it will rain tomorrow?"; and (25), similarly (He is, he must be, he might be, he could be, he should be, he has to be), to the single question "Is he there now?" Most of these may also be negatived. For sentences (13), (17), and (23) there are *grammatically* matching questions (Do you wish I would(n't) do this? and Do you hope it doesn't rain? and Do you wonder if he's coming?), but the emphasis has shifted to the *wish, hope* and *wonder* in a way that can be matched in a non-question only by stressing these words or negating them (I don't wish ... I don't hope ...), in which case they immediately acquire truth-value and belong in A. And the archaic equivalents "Would that you were not doing that/didn't do that!" "May it not rain!" like the recent colloquial "Hopefully it won't rain tomorrow" and perhaps "Ideally you wouldn't do that", cannot very well be interrogativated at all.

Let us then extract interrogativization as a process like negation[1] that can be applied to any (non-interrogative) sentence with truth-value, and to many (but not all) of those without. This leaves us with the following sentences in B: 11–13, 15–19, 22–24. Of these, (12) and (15) are formally imperative, and the others seem to be somewhat varied, mostly lacking any generally accepted name, though (13) is sometimes called an ideal wish, and the very similar

(6-13a) I wish (= would that) you hadn't done that (yesterday)
(6-13b) I wish (= would that) it were tomorrow (already)

are called unreal wishes or unfulfilled wishes, while (17) is a real or fulfillable or attainable wish.

Let us return to the question of B (16); is it or is it not appropriate to call such sentences true or false? Some cases seem clearer than others. Consider, for example, 16(a): If Dewey had received 10,000,000 (or 10,000) more votes (*ceteris paribus*, of course), he would have been president. We might reply (to the 10,000,000 proposal), "That's true, he would have", or (to the 10,000) "I don't think so; surely it would have taken more than that."

On the other hand, consider 16(b): If I were a fairy tale prince, I would shower you with millions of precious stones. Here a response of true or false, or even "I believe you" or "I don't believe you" seems

---

[1] Austin envisaged questioning as an illocution like any other, implying that only constatives (i.e. statements) could be questioned. He did not consider negation at all in this connection, though he does put some negative verbs (e.g. *deny*) in his Expositive class (statements, etc.) and would probably have put others (e.g. *forbid, prohibit*) in his Exercitive class (commands, etc.) if he had thought of them.

D

quite out of place. In other words, the same grammatical form may be used both for relatively realistic assertions about the logical consequences of particular false suppositions, and also for quite fantastic sentences intended only to convey some sentiment or prejudice in an indirect manner. Incidentally, it is worth remembering that the conclusion corresponds to a false statement when the condition is a simple 'if' or 'only if' but to a true one when it is an 'even if': 16(c) Truman would have been elected even if Dewey had not been overconfident. This suggests that *even* is equivalent to two negatives, one negating the whole sentence, the other the conclusion alone: 16(d) It is *not* so that Truman would *not* have been elected if Dewey had not been overconfident. Finally, a quite non-fanciful use exists which, nevertheless, seems to lack truth-value: 16(e) I would(n't) sit down if I were you. This seems to be rather a weak imperative in force.

The truth-value test, then, seems to make a dichotomy of sentences which is at least partially related to grammatical form. But it is not always unambiguous, and it certainly doesn't go far enough for a grammarian. How about the other proposed criterion, the speaker's attitude? Is it any better? or any good at all? And how can we describe or determine it?

First, let us make clear that the speaker's emotional state is beside the point: We do not care if he is angry or hurt, irritated, tired, or bored. What we are concerned with can be put like this. Conceive, first, of the pure, unmodalized heart of the sentence, a subject and predicate which are, somehow, merely juxtaposed.[1] Then the speaker ('I') must somehow convey to the listener ('you') how he wants him to apprehend the juxtaposition: is he (1) to know it, (2) to verify it, (3) to bring it to pass, or what? This is what we mean by the speaker's attitude as conveyed to the listener. These three would correspond rather well to assertions, questions and commands, respectively. Very similar but more complex attitudes may include as one component the speaker's belief or assumption that the hearer is unable or unwilling to do any of these things; in this case he is merely (4) guessing (or supposing, or opining – or quoting – "They say he's a secret drinker!"), (5) wondering ("I wonder what time it is" differs from "What time is it?" in not explicitly expecting an answer) or (6) wishing or hoping. In many cases, of course,

---

[1] This is called the 'phrastic' by R. M. Hare in *The Language of Morals*, New York, Oxford University Press (1964) [GB 111]. The signal of illocutionary force he calls the 'neustic'.

the speaker is merely pretending, and really expects some action from the listener. There is also one situation (7) where the speaker himself can make the prediction come true and is reassuring the listener of his intention, i.e. promising ('I will do it' or 'He will'; 'You will' obviously has to be different).

The only questions so far accounted for from this point of view (2) are what might be called information questions, which can be looked upon as a compound of (3) and (1) – The listener is to bring it to pass that the speaker knows. What about (8) advice ('deliberative') questions, in which the speaker wants the hearer to tell him to do (or not to do) something? This could be considered a reflexive application of (3), though both here and in the information question case the first response is only verbal, while the second can be anything. If I say "Shall we go?" the response may be "O.K., let's go" or "No, let's wait a while", but only elliptically (and I think we must recognize the existence of total ellipsis) will it be for the listener to arise and start for the exit. "Do you want me to go?" or "What do you say I go?" or "How about me going?" or "Shall I go?" or "Should I go?" – depending somewhat on speaker and dialect – are in the same case, but it is also possible (9) to say "Shall I ask you what I'm wondering about?" or "Shall I tell you what to do?", where both responses will be verbal unless the first one is negative.

As (7), (8) and (9) show, all these criteria are closely bound up with person; and yet, curiously, in most natural languages every mood has a complete battery of personal forms, with the exception of the imperative, which frequently (but by no means always) lacks a first person singular ('I') form, sometimes lacks third person ('he' and 'they') forms, and occasionally lacks a first person plural ('we') form. In all cases, of course, equivalents for the missing forms are supplied by periphrasis (as English 'let's' for the we-form, non-interrogative) or from other paradigms. Some periphrastic patterns in English, e.g. *Why don't/doesn't —?* or *Suppose —*, both of which yield slightly weakened imperatives, may function with any personal pronoun at all (or any noun phrase subject).

On the other hand, perhaps it is worth while to digress here for a moment on the relation between subject-person and illocutionary force (to use Austin's term for this phenomenon – assertion, will, question, wish, doubt, wonder, guess, accusation, etc.). Consider a simple past statement in the third person: "He was here at 5.30." Clearly this is most likely an assertion, with speaker's guarantee either based on direct observation or on fully reliable hearsay. Shift it now to first: "I was here at 5.30." Now the claim for reliability is much stronger, and hearsay is obviously ruled out. But put it in the second person and see what happens: "You were here at 5.30." Several interpretations are possible, but the two most plausible are (1) that this is an accusation, the speaker is daring the hearer to deny it, and implying that retribution is nigh, and (2) that this is a disguised question, perhaps elliptical for "Do you say that you were here at 5.30?" or "Is it true, as I hear, that you were here at 5.30?" It obviously cannot often have the force that first and third person sentences can of teaching the listener something he didn't know before (except in cases where the listener has just awakened from a trance or coma or is suffering from amnesia).

The present tense immediately raises the question of the shared knowledge of speaker and hearer (if face-to-face; in telephone conversations the present is much like the past); many statements in the third person would be very odd in first or second, if the present is an immediate, moment-of-speaking, temporary present (as opposed to more or less durative presents like "I'm living at the Y.M.C.A.", which also behave much like pasts). "He's standing on the grass" is quite likely purely informative, "I'm standing on the grass" is most likely a corrective statement, calling the hearer's attention to a fact he must have known, but forgot to take into consideration; "You're standing on the grass" might also be corrective, but is more likely to be a polite invitation to get off (as "You're stepping on my toe" would invariably be), calling the hearer's attention to something he should have noticed himself.

What about 'will', 'may', 'must' and 'can', however?[1] "I'll be there" is normally a promise, equivalent to "I intend to be there" or "I promise to be there", and unlike "I'm going to be there" which is a more neutral statement of expectation, not commitment. "He'll be there" is also very often a promise or guarantee, "I personally vouch for his attendance" or the like, but may be slightly weaker, a reassurance given to someone who has expressed skepticism "Don't worry, this time I think we can count on him", or something of that sort. But it can never be an assertion, a communication of factual information as third-person pasts and presents may be. "You'll be there" may be a polite command, "I'm telling you to be there", or, quite like the second-person pasts, an implied quotation of the hearer or an unexpressed question

---

[1] For a more detailed consideration of some of these expressions, see Angus McIntosh, 'Predictive Statements', *In Memory of J. R. Firth*, ed. C. E. Bazell *et al.*, London, Longmans (1966), pp. 303–20.

("Won't you?"), perhaps with the added tone "I hope". Try 'must'. "I must go" is normally an apology, "I have to go now" in more colloquial style; "He must go" is likely to be an edict – "Either he goes or heads will roll" or whatever other sanction may be appropriate (and again "He's got to go" may be the equivalent) though it may instead be an implicit quotation "He says 'I've got to go' "; "You must go" may be another sort of polite command, or a reminder "Don't forget that you told me 'I must go' ", and again "You have to go" (not, in my dialect, "You've got to go", which is stronger) is a close colloquial equivalent, or it may be said with a questioning air, "I know you said 'I must go', but won't you please reconsider?" There is also a homograph 'must', always with full grade vowel, which marks an inference – hence rarely occurs in the present with 'I' or 'you' except in expressions like "I/you must be out of my/your mind", and in general is almost confined to progressive or perfective contexts except with 'be' and 'have', as in "He must be in New York by now" or "He must have read the book already". In literature 'will' occurs in a similar function.

'May' is also a pair of homonyms, the more colloquial of which is equivalent to "It is possible that", and otherwise is parallel to 'will' in its distribution with the persons: "I may be there tomorrow" a weak promise; "You may be there tomorrow" a quotation or half-question; "He may be there tomorrow" a weak prediction implying some inside information. Command interpretations are unlikely. The other use of "may" is permissive. "I may go" is a half-question or quotation, "You are giving me permission to go (?)"; "You may go" is a permission which in some contexts is equivalent to a firm command; "He may go" is an indirect permission: "Tell him, 'You may go' " or "Don't stop him if he starts to go".

All this has gradually led us off into modals and the question of modality; but we haven't really finished talking about mood or illocutionary force yet. Let us try to average the results of our bidirectional assault on moods, statuses, illocutions or sentence-types. There seem to be only two basic types, each with matching negations, questions and perhaps negative questions: *will* and *assertion*.[1] I say 'will' as a more general (and traditional) term than 'command'; because the latter would

[1] If negation and question are absorbed here, we'll get illocutions: positive will, interrogative will, negative will, negative interrogative will, positive assertion, interrogatived assertion, negatived assertion, negative interrogatived assertion. But for our purposes it is simpler to narrow the application of 'illocution' than to coin a new name for the will vs. assertion category.

tend to suggest imperatives only, while *will* can cover also optatives and hortatives as well as unreal wishes and conditions. *Assertion* is not so vague a term as we might wish, especially since 'interrogative assertion' seems self-contradictory, but essentially it will cover indicatives, including (in general) the modals which we are about to discuss. Austin's 'constative' sounds O.K., but 'constation' does not. 'Subjective' for 'will' and 'objective' for 'assertion' might be better except for the unfortunate fact that both terms have other uses in grammar.

Is there no neutral mood, no form of predication without illocutionary force? Not in independent sentences, except perhaps for the explicit performatives, such as 'I want —', 'I bid —', 'I wonder —', etc., which are overt expressions of illocutionary force. But in certain types of subordinate clauses there does seem to be such a possibility, though some embedded predications are marked, in one way or another, as either will or assertion. "I sent him downtown to buy groceries" clearly incorporates a 'will' expression, "buy groceries!", and this is the case even with first-person contexts, as "I went downtown to buy groceries". Many languages, in fact, use their independent imperative forms in such expressions of purpose. And "I was all tired out from buying Christmas presents yesterday" clearly incorporates the assertion "I bought Christmas presents". Even "Flying planes can be dangerous", in either of its ordinary interpretations, implies an assertion: "Planes (sometimes) fly" or "(Some people sometimes) fly planes". And in "I didn't wait for John to cross the road" there is an implicit *negative* assertion "John didn't cross the road (on this particular occasion)", just as there is in "If I hadn't arrived just then, John would have crossed the road". (Though we have the corresponding *affirmative* implication in the superficially similar sentence "Even if I hadn't tried to stop him, John would have crossed the road.") But in such sentences as "Selling beer on Sunday is illegal", we have neither an affirmation that anyone actually does sell beer on Sunday, nor a denial, and the same is true in the related sentence "If anyone sells beer on Sunday he may get in trouble with the law." Nor is there any implication of a will to sell beer; there is indeed a kind of hint that someone's will is opposed to selling beer, but that comes from the other parts of the sentences, "illegal" and "get in trouble", not from the portion ending with the word "Sunday". About all that such forms can be said to imply (a third would be "It would be risky for anyone to sell beer on Sunday") is that it is possible to *imagine* the predication embedded as true. So we can say "Talking to centaurs is said to be risky" or "If anyone has the Midas touch, he'll starve to death" or "It might be fun to ask the Sphinx a riddle."

There are two possible ways we might derive such moodless or 'subjunctive-infinitive' forms: one by first giving the clauses to be embedded a specific illocutionary mood (say *assertion*) and then deleting this at the moment of embedding, the other by making mood optional to begin with, but requiring moodless sentences to be embedded in some appropriate frame and not left running around by themselves. Although certain forms of speech come close to being moodless: "The (very) idea of John sitting in a Rolls Royce!" or "To think of John etc.", such sentences generally imply that another speaker has either reported seeing John in the Rolls or hearing John talk about riding in a Rolls, or has proposed a practical joke involving putting John in a Rolls, or something of the sort. But none of this is either clearly will or clearly assertion.

Now are these really all the basic moods, or are there perhaps others which have simply not occurred to us because of the limited sample of languages we are basing our guesses upon? What about irony, for instance? If this belongs on our list, it must be somehow in the same class as Question, since both statements ("A fat lot you know about it!") and commands ("All right, be a wise guy!") may be ironical, but questions apparently cannot, though one or two fixed ironical expressions have interrogative form. Here we run into conflict with the use of rhetorical questions as emotionally colored rejections of the corresponding statements. Possibly a sentence like "Boy, are you stupid!" might be regarded as a double reversal, rhetorical question yielding "You are not stupid", irony then altering that to "You are stupid". But more likely this is to be regarded as an exclamatory sentence, derived directly from an assertion "You are stupid" by a rule which happens to produce the same word order as the question transformation. However, this coincidence of form occurs in many languages, so possibly it *is* more than coincidence. We may return to exclamations later; irony in English is marked by a variety of devices. (1) Special intonation or voice qualifiers nearly always; (2) special vocabulary – "fat" in the first sentence cited above occurs as a qualifier of "a lot" only or chiefly in ironical sentences; (3) word order: "A lot you know" is invariably ironical, while "you know a lot" is only very rarely so; (4) special adverbs and parenthetical expressions: these are relatively less common in English than in some other languages, "yet" being confined mostly to Jewish dialect anecdotes

and "forsooth" being long since obsolete, but in general strong pro-
testations of truth tend to be reliable markers, though by no means
infallible – "really and truly", "ask anyone!", "believe it or not",
"I give you my solemn word", and many more. Other languages have
particles which are said to be consistent, even obligatory marks of irony.
But part of the charm of irony is often to leave the hearer a little up in the
air as to whether or not the speaker is ironical, so that an obligatory
marker seems self-defeating. Excessive and elaborate praise is nearly
always ironical in English, but in many languages is normal social coin,
which can lead to cross-cultural misunderstanding on occasion. It may
well be that some languages never make use of irony, though it has been
reported from many quarters of the globe. So what about it? Is it a
grammatical phenomenon, on a par with Question, for example, or is it
purely stylistic? The answer for any language in which formal devices
occur (as in English "A lot you know about it") must certainly be that it
is, to that extent, grammatical. But in cases where its recognition depends
on the wit of the hearer, perhaps it should be considered as stylistic;
certainly the elaborate irony of literary items like Swift's *Modest Proposal*
must be considered stylistic. It is interesting that many speakers in
many countries avoid it entirely in their own speech and are baffled or
made uncomfortable by it in the speech of others. It is not a necessity of
language; question, negation, and the two primary illocutions are.

We noted above that there are certain grammatically distinct forms of
exclamation in English, which resemble questions in form. Unlike irony,
but like questions and commands, distinct 'explicit performatives' can
be added: "(I am amazed, astounded) how stupid you are!" So it
would be perfectly possible to suppose that all exclamations without
explicit performatives are derived by deletion. It is impossible to treat
them as special 'uses' of questions, since some of them are distinct in
form, e.g. "What a fine day it is!" and all sentences beginning with *what
a*, to mention only one type. But, just as in the case of questions, assertions and commands, deletion of explicit performatives seems to be the
backwards way of doing things; intuitively (that is, by my intuition; yours
may be different) "What fun!", does not seem to be *derived from* "I
am delighted at discovering what fun this is!", but rather to be *embedded
in* it. So it looks as if we might add a third illocutionary force Exclamative
or the like, commutable with (i.e. not co-occurring with) Assertive
and "Hortative" or whatever we choose to call the others. But perhaps
it is rather commutable with Question; the matter needs investigation.

Are we done now? How about such emotional colorings as *rage, disgust, delight, tenderness,* and the like? Are they relevant here? Well, do they have systematic grammatical correlations? So far as I can discover, the only effect of any of these is on such phonological features as pitch, amplitude, rate of speaking, and precision of articulation, not structure or vocabulary. On the other hand there are categories like *hope, wish, suggestion, proposal, opinion* and the like which are, in some cases, grammatically marked.[1] Though not universal, these must surely be dealt with in appropriate ways in writing the grammars of individual languages. In Classical Greek, for instance, the basic illocution of Will has got to yield, in the end, not only the imperative forms but also the subjunctive and much of the optative (the rest of the optative must come either, like the indicative, from the Assertive base, or, in some cases, from the moodless base). And secondary illocutions applied to the Assertive are going to give us, in all languages, the modalities. So let us look at them for a minute.

As discussed in logic, the notion is due to Aristotle (*De Interpretatione,* 12–13, 21a–23a, and *Prior Analytics I,* esp. 25a–b), who argues for two basic modalities only, 'possibility' and 'necessity' (approximately *may* and *must*), various others being reducible to these two in one way or another. One thing that reveals itself strikingly as one reads Aristotle's discussion is that the modalities are essentially quantifiers of the predication,[2] so that 'possibility' (*may*) is analogous to *some* with noun phrases, and 'necessity' (*must*) is analogous to *all* (or *no(ne) ... not*) – while its opposite, 'impossibility', clearly corresponds to *no(ne)*. We might add that plain statements of a *particular* fact correspond to singular nominal expressions ('terms') like *Socrates*. "This boy may be a murderer" is analogous to (not synonymous with) "Some such boys are murderers",

---

[1] Austin's treatment implies at least as many illocutions as there are explicit performative verbs, but he does group them into five classes, of which his Verdictives and Expositives (except for *question* and *ask,* in part) seem to be clearly assertive, differing sociologically rather than linguistically. His Exercitives and Commissives include nearly all performatives of Will (though he never places *hope* and *wish* on any list), differing in that the former are second-person expressions ("My will is that *you* do something") while the latter are first ("My will is that *I* do something"). His class 4, Behabitives, includes a subclass 4 'attitudes' which belong to Kiparsky's Factive class (i.e. presuppose the truth of their objects), but are not moods in our sense (and the embedded clauses are surely assertive), and subclass 7 'challenges' which may be a kind of Will-verbs. The others don't seem really illocutionary at all (*thank, apologize, condole, curse,* etc.).

[2] Modern logicians have not overlooked this point either; see A. N. Prior, *Time and Modality* (Oxford University Press), p. 6, and the passage he refers to there in G. H. von Wright, *An Essay in Modal Logic* (Amsterdam, 1951).

and "This boy must be a murderer" to "Every such boy is a murderer". ('Synonymy' can be achieved by quantifying a noun like *chance*, or *probability*: "There is some chance that this boy is a murderer", "There is no chance that this boy is not a murderer", etc.) And just as, in ordinary speech, *some* can be varied in all kinds of ways – to *few, many, several, two, five, thirty-seven*, etc. – so *may* has a considerable variety of slightly different substitutes.

Aristotle was concerned with other implications, however; he developed a theory of the logical relations of sentences containing such modals, a topic which has been treated since, but does not concern us. We are concerned rather with two questions: What are modalities? and are there only two? and perhaps also, If there are just two, why is that the case?

First, what are modalities? The name 'modal' is often applied to the class of auxiliaries in English consisting of *can, could, will, would, may, might, must, shall, should,* and sometimes *need (not)* and *dare (not)*. A few linguists call attention also to *ought to, have (got) to, be to, be able to, had better, be supposed to* (in spoken use only), *had/would rather* and possibly *can't help* and one or two more, in spite of certain formal differences. Is there anything semantic that all these have in common? In particular, can they all be regarded as various shading of Aristotle's two basic modalities? If not, can we name a third? I think we can quickly see one that, in many cases at least, is not obviously potential, and is certainly seldom necessary, *will*, and one other that was not a strong candidate for admission in the first place, *I'd rather*. Both of these seem, in fact, to be somewhat similar to one of our basic moods (Will) rather than to either of the modalities. Nevertheless, there are some occasions where *will* implies necessity, and others where it is plainly only probability (a variety of possibility) that is suggested. If we were to add a third modality for *will*, we could easily explain Aristotle's omission as due to the structure of the Greek language, in which the verb has an inflected future form. And Aristotle does note in the *De Interpretatione*, 9, 18a–19b, that propositions in the future tense are different and special in certain ways. On the other hand, it is not correct to say that *will* in English is restricted to future contexts; it has a limited use in present and past contexts, where it does indeed convey the notion of probability. So I think we must agree that *will* is modal (in our present sense) only in so far as it conveys ideas of possibility or necessity, and Aristotle's two basic modalities (along with the third, zero modality, simple assertion of something –

present or past – as a fact, without colorings of possibility or necessity) are indeed all that are needed, as a base. But each of them may be richly varied in many ways. Possibility may range along a scale from 'barely imaginable' to 'almost inevitable'; both possibility and necessity may be attributed to various causes – possibility, for instance to the physical or mental qualifications of a human subject, to the known fulfillment of necessary (but not sufficient) conditions, to the laws of inference; necessity to physical non-human force, to human use of power, violence or authority, to logical consequence, to moral obligation or duty (of various kinds). Note that many of these causes are not truly necessary causes in the narrow logical sense, but languages tend to treat them indistinguishably from those which *are* strictly necessary. So, if we say we have to do something, or we'd better do something, or we ought to do something, or we must do something (as opposed to "we can't help doing this"), it is not often really inevitable that we do this – indeed with *ought* in ordinary use (as opposed to philosophical use, in which it is *the* auxiliary of duty) as with *be supposed to* it is the rule that we *don't* do it, and in present or past contexts *ought* in fact *always* presupposes the falsity of its prediction – "He ought to have been there yesterday" means that he certainly wasn't, as "He ought to be here right now" means that he isn't, though in the case of "I ought to go see him, I suppose" it occasionally happens that I go.

Can the modalities be combined? To some extent this seems perfectly O.K. – we can say "It is a fact that it may turn out that I'll have to go" or "It is true that it must be the case that he can do it" and many more things of the same sort. In English the modals of the first list are mutually exclusive, and indeed so are those of the second list with each other and with members of the first list, except for *have to, be able to,* and *be supposed to,* which can be preceded by most of the others. Combinations that sound implausible to me are **must have to, *dare (not) have to, *be able to have to, *dare (not) be supposed to, *have (got) to be supposed to, *be able to be supposed to, *had better be supposed to,* but probably a few of these could be made credible in the right context; repetitions are also excluded – **have to have to, *be able to be able to,* and **be supposed to be supposed to* – and some of the other unlikely combinations are with such near synonyms that it is almost a case of recursion; beyond that, *dare (not)* and *be able to* seem to be most restricted as first members. Some combinations, like "He may have to go" are quite normal and frequent in ordinary use, and the restrictions on *be able to* as a second member are so scanty that its claims to be considered a modal must be viewed with some 'skepticism. And combinations like *may have to* can be interpreted as referring to different times, as equivalent to "It is *now* possible that he will *in the future* have to". But this is not always so, and "It must be that he can do it" seems to show both modalities. But here it may be argued that *must* refers to our knowledge of the facts, not to the facts themselves, i.e. this sentence means "It must be that when we learn the truth we'll find out that he can do it". And this seems to take care of all combinations which cannot be dealt with by the time-difference hypothesis. So we conclude that, in strict use, modalities cannot be combined.

And they cannot combine with Will (here again *be able to* is O.K. and hence seems not to be modal); *dare* in the imperative is not alleged to be modal. But they can be negated and questioned without trouble, at least most of the time. So we might consider incorporating them in our provisional basic rules somewhat as follows:

1. U→S +Ill (+Q)

   I.e., an utterance may be questioned or not, but must be given an illocutionary mark. Possible *Excl* belongs here as an alternative to Ill (+Q).
2. S→S′ (+Mod)

   The predicational heart of an utterance may have some modality.
3. S′→Snu (+Neg)   The sentence nucleus may be negative.
4. Ill→Assn, Will
5. Mod→Poss, Nec

Variations on the values of Will, Poss, and Nec will be established differently in different languages by later rules. The complete U will be embedded then as the complement with performative verbs like *ask, tell, learn, hear, request, demand* and the like; S will be used, for instance, in many conditions and result clauses; S′ for purely abstract infinitival and gerundial complements; Snu in a few such sentences where negation is excluded. In particular, we may note that if Will (without Q) is chosen in rule 4, then the U will select verbs like *ask, tell* and *request* with an infinitive transformation (I asked/told/requested him to leave), and verbs like *ask, request, demand,* and *suggest* with a that-plus-subjunctive transformation (in American use: British use prefers indicative or a modal; "I suggested that he go" American = "I suggested that he went/should go" British). If *Assn* (without Q) is chosen, then governing verbs like *say, tell, hear, report* and the like are required, most generally with a sequence-of-tense rule; "I am going" is embedded as "He said he was going". If Q is taken, then *ask, tell, learn, hear, determine* and similar verbs may be used with either Will (infinitival) or Assn (indicative) complements; "I asked him what to do, where to go, whether to join, how to write", etc. for Will, "I asked him what he was doing, where he was going, whether he was joining", etc. for Assn. With Will modal expressions may also be used: "I asked him what I should do, where I should go, whether I should join", etc., where the immediate source can be thought of as already in question form: "What shall I do, where shall I go, shall I join", etc., whereas the infinitival complements are embedded before Will +Q has been converted to "Shall I". This looks simpler than the equally possible alternative that they are derived by deleting "Am I" from direct questions of the form "What am I to do, Where am I to go, Am I to join, How am I to write", which seem to have specific semantic suggestions quite different from those of the indirect sentences.

There is a lot that remains to be learned about both mood or illocutionary force and modality, but this is at least the heart of what is interesting about these matters for one linguist. One final note. Rules 1–5 above are written in a style in which the various symbols on the right are treated as all of a kind. A more honest style would probably recognize two types of symbol, symbols for segments or stretches of speech and symbols for features or characteristics. In this style Ill (and its values), Q, Mod (and its values) and Neg should probably all be features, even though their ultimate representation in English or in some other languages may be by distinct words or affixes which are arranged sequentially. Adopting the convention that segment-symbols are enclosed in brackets and that feature symbols are attached after a right-hand parenthesis with hooks (^), the first three rules would appear like this:

1. U→[S] ^ Ill(^ Q)
2. S→[S](^ Mod)
3. S'→[Snu] (^ Neg)

This could be telescoped into one rule by eliminating S and S'.

1. U→[[[Snu] (^ Neg)] (^ Mod)] ^ Ill (^ Q)

But, as we mentioned above, S and S' are very useful for making complex sentences.

These features may be represented in actual speech ('surface structure') in various ways. Q will appear mainly as intonation, order-change, etc., since "I ask you ..." is not a genuine performative in English, but if Q is combined with a feature which might be called 'You-neutrality', with which the speaker professes indifference or scepticism about the responses of the listener, it appears as "I wonder ..." When this feature combines with Will, the result is a wish, "I hope ..." or, in some combinations, "I wish ..." And the rich variety of explicit illocutionary performatives (in Austin's sense) must similarly derive from the combination of various optional features of this sort (politeness, forcefulness, hesitancy, and so on) with Ill ^ Q, Ill, Mod ^ Ill, etc.

We have arranged things so that recursion is possible only by combining two U's – i.e. no term occurs twice. But this is perhaps wrong for the Neg feature or segment, and if it can appear twice we will need only one value for Mod, namely Poss, since "It is not possible that S did not happen" is precisely equivalent to "It is necessary that S did happen". But to do this our U must consist of at least two segments, unless we are to allow significant ordering of features. Perhaps the answer is that in the ultimate underlying structure we will have a logically ordered string of segments, each of which consists of exactly one feature. But much remains to be done.[1]

---

[1] Similarities of the above with various other proposals, such as Fillmore's (in 'Case for Case' published in Bach and Harms' *Universals of Language*) or Seuren's (in *Operators and Nucleus*, Cambridge University Press, 1969), or Jackendoff's ('Speculations on Presentences and Determiners', 1968 (unpublished)) are independent, but not (of course) entirely coincidental since the evidence is the same for all of us. The scheme offered by J. R. Searle in *Speech Acts* (Cambridge University Press, 1969), especially on pp. 31–2 and 66–7, allows negation of other illocutions but not questioning of them. The view that all these things are "really" performative verbs, whether real ones (according to Langendoen, for instance) or abstract ones (Ross, Lakoff, McCawley, Robin Lakoff) if other than notationally different, is hard to defend, in my opinion. Leech's stimulating book (G. N. Leech. *Towards a Semantic Description of English*, Indiana U.P. 1970) reached me too late for consideration here or on p. 91, n. 2, or in ch. 15.

7 On rules of grammar, ordered and unordered

A grammar of a language, in the sense of a book describing or specifying this language, can be seen to consist (in general) of rules, examples, and lists. The purpose of examples is almost always to aid the reader in understanding a rule (or, sometimes, to convince the reader that the rule is correct); so, if the rules were all perfectly couched and misunderstanding was impossible, examples could be dispensed with. If this is done, the grammar consists exclusively of rules and lists (which may, indeed, be regarded as a special kind of rule or as a special part of many rules). As we have said above, the 'grammars' in our brains are, no doubt, strange and wonderful things, containing many examples almost certainly – examples linked by a complex network of analogical chains; and if they contain rules (as they must in some way), most of them are in the form of open analogical chains with general instructions to extend.[1] But this is a space-wasting and messy business to represent on paper, so an ideally economical 'model' of it (in the sense of a device which would give the same output under specifiable conditions) would consist of rules and lists. About this much linguists are agreed; what they quarrel about is the specific rules and the conventions for writing these rules. In this chapter we will examine a number of types of rule, and a number of ways in which such rules are combined into grammars.

First let us get rid of one naive feeling about rules found (at least subconsciously) in many of us. This is the feeling that rules are needed only for those parts of grammar in which we frequently go wrong, and that where we rarely or never make a mistake, there we need no rule. The cause of this feeling is the experience we may have had with English lessons in school. In my childhood we were taught not to say *ain't* (so effectively that many people nowadays consider the word an artificial literary dialect item, said – if ever – only as an affectation), i.e. not to substitute *ain't* for *am not*, *are not*, *is not*, *have not*, or *has not* (and it is

---

[1] Many linguists, including Noam Chomsky, believe that the brain contains something much more precisely like rules than this, but it is not clear what form they would have.

quite dispensable for four of these, since *aren't, isn't, haven't* and *hasn't* are available; for *am not*, however, there is no acceptable substitute, since *am I not* is literary and both *amn't I* and *aren't I* sound insufferably cute and little-girlish to many of us). This rule actually is a kind of non-rule, or second-order rule. It instructs us to *eschew* a rule of substitution or contraction, not to apply this rule. Not all our school-rules were of this kind, though; such rules of agreement as "two singular subjects linked by *either – or* or by *neither – nor* require a singular verb" are real rules. This one is designed to prevent you from saying "Neither John nor Bill are here" and persuade you to say instead "Neither John nor Bill is here". You are advised to apply this rule rather than another which would read the same except for the next-to-last word; which would be *plural* instead of *singular*. The reason why you might have interiorized such a rule is that it can be combined with others to yield a more general rule: "Any compound subject (two or more nominal expressions linked by any conjunctions at all) requires a plural verb."

Very often your school grammar would give nice, logical arguments to show why their rule was right, and the rule they were implicitly attacking wrong. Since, in most cases, your childish instinct tended toward the rejected rule, which was never dignified by being formulated or called a rule (even a bad rule), it is natural that you might develop the notion that rules exist only to correct you and that where you don't need correcting there are no rules. But this is a narrow and prejudiced view. There are good rules and bad rules (i.e. rules which are good or bad for some specific purpose), but everything we say can be brought under one or fifty rules of some kind or other.

A few of us derived our notions of grammatical rules from the school grammars of Latin which were once sold to high school students in their third or fourth year of study, such grammars as those of Allen and Greenough, Hale and Buck, Gildersleeve and Lodge, Lane, Bennett, and others, varying slightly in length and scope, hardly at all in approach and method of presentation. Such grammars generally had a few brief remarks on *Phonology* (or *Sounds* or *Pronunciation*), including usually a bit on Indo-European origins and some of the major historical developments from Italic or Old Latin to Classical (or sometimes to Late or Vulgar) Latin, some remarks on *Word Formation* (occasionally placed after the next section) with a few examples, a long section on *Accidence* or *Inflection*, first *Declension* of nouns, adjectives and pronouns, then *Conjugation* of verbs, another long section on *Syntax* (or on *Sentences*, as in Lane), treating first (after some preliminary remarks on concord, government, co-ordination and the like) the various uses of the cases, then those of verb-forms, most especially the subjunctive and the infinitive (usually organized in part by function of the subordinate verb or clause), and finally (sometimes) short sections on metrics and figures of speech (and occasionally miscellaneous topics like *The Calendar, Oratorical Terms, Roman Government*, etc.). In all sections one could find expressions which would count as rules, but the most typical rules for most students were those of the syntax section. I will quote a few examples here from G. M. Lane's *Latin Grammar* (New York, American Book Co., 1903, etc.), an excellent one of this class. Here are six picked at random (from paragraphs 1023–2299) by consulting a telephone directory.[1] 1033 says "The third person plural often refers to people in general..." This appears to be a semantic note, or possibly a deletion rule, equivalent to "*homines (omnes)* as sole and complete subject is regularly deleted". 1066 is a rule of concord, which must be combined with 1064–5 and 1067 to make a complete rule. This portion reads "Often, however, with two or more singular subjects, the verb is put in the singular." These sections 1064–7 are equivalent to a set of rules for adding a feature of number to a complete noun phrase formed by compounding smaller noun phrases, plus a later rule for duplicating this feature on the verb or shifting it to the verb. 1303 reads "This ablative is used (*a*) with such verbs as mean *abstain*, abstineō, dēsistō, supersedeō; *am devoid of*, careō, vacō; *need*, egeō; and in addition to the accusative of the object, (*b*) with verbs used transitively, such as mean *keep off*, arceō, exclūdō and interclūdō, prohibeō; *drive away, remove*, pellō, moveō, and their compounds; *free*, expediō, līberō, levō, solvō and exsolvō; *deprive*, orbō, prīvō, spoliō, nūdō, fraudō." This purports to be (a) a complete list of verbs taking the "ablative of the thing from which separation takes place" as Lane calls it in 1302, and (b) a semantic specification of these verbs and any others which might have been overlooked but which would belong to the same list. So it is equivalent to a statement of the presence of certain syntactic features on these verbs, conditioned by certain semantic features.

1541 (1) reads: "The present and perfect [sc. of the subjunctive of

---

[1] For people unfamiliar with how to use a phone book as a table of random numbers, here is the procedure: open the directory to any page; copy the last four digits of the seventh (or eighteenth, if you like) number; turn to another page; repeat; continue until you have enough. If certain digits never occur in last place (or first) allow for that.

wish] represent a wish as practicable; although a hopeless wish, may, of course, if the speaker chooses, be represented as practicable: as [then 10 lines of examples]." This is a rule of interpretation, saying that 'practicable' wishes (i.e. hopes) must be expressed with a primary tense of the subjunctive. Few models are available yet for expressing such a rule, but it could be done by having a rule which takes Will (see above, ch. 6) and makes it Command, Wish, Request ... etc., and then one which marks Wish as Hopeless or Hopeful, then converts Hopeful into Primary on the verb.

2173 is an explicit rule: "The subject of an infinitive is put in the accusative." This can hardly be said much differently, and it is also quite easy to formulate as a feature-attachment rule.

2337 reads "The reflexive sometimes refers to a word not the subject, when that word is specially emphasized or easily made out from the context. This holds chiefly for *suus*, which is used with great freedom ..." and examples are given. The conditions here are not clearly enough stated to permit reformulation, but the rule would obviously be part of a larger rule or set of rules for replacing some noun phrases of identical reference by pronouns.

There are the six random examples. What do they show? One thing is quite different from our grade-school English rules: *they* nearly always envisaged a pseudo-moral situation, a dilemma for the speaker, where one alternative was wrong and the other right; these rules are not concerned with right and wrong, but only with specifying the practice of the Romans as accurately as possible, and giving hints for interpreting what they wrote. A familiar expression of this difference is the saying that our English school grammars are 'prescriptive' and grammars like Lane's 'descriptive'. None the less, both consist of rules, and rules of much the same general sort; the difference is that Lane's rules seldom indicate variation (2337, 1066, and part of 1541 are slightly exceptional) whereas the prescriptive rules *always* imply a variation; and when such variation *is* mentioned by Lane, no qualitative judgement is ordinarily made (even in 1066, where the equivalent English statement is quite strong: "John and Bill is" is wrong, "John and Bill are" is right). The variation can generally be expressed as a pair of alternative rules or as the addition or deletion of a rule, and prescriptive grammars very often say nothing at all about English structure *except* where this competition exists. If native speakers do not sometimes use the 'wrong' rule, there is no point in mentioning it. But Lane must try to give *all* rules, whether or not such competition exists, and when it does exist he must report it, sometimes adding his judgment as to the significance (early vs. late, prose vs. verse, colloquial vs. literary, Hellenizing vs. native Latin – but very rarely [if ever] correct vs. incorrect). In other words, Lane is trying to recover and report *all* the rules implicit in our texts of classical Latin, i.e. all the rules unconsciously used by extant authors, or better, all the rules which can serve to characterize as simply as possible the Latin sentences preserved from antiquity.

Both of these kinds of rules are generally expressed in words, though here and there one may run into rudimentary types of abbreviation or geometric schemes (such as sentence-diagrams in English or inflectional paradigms in Latin). But of course, the same rules may be expressed in other ways, often much more economically. In recent years such devices have become extremely common; the two commonest are probably the tagmemic[1] formula and the generative rule. I will say nothing here about the former, though it has one or two advantages. The latter has more advantages, and is much more widely used in textbooks of all kinds (even English school grammars in which the prescriptive element is reduced). Such success, even if undeserved, would be a sufficient reason for using this notation here and now.

How would the English and some of the Latin rules mentioned above look in this system? In the case of *ain't*, the rejected or incorrect rule might read:

$$(7\text{-}E4) \qquad \left.\begin{array}{l} \text{amn't} \\ \text{aren't} \\ \text{isn't} \\ \text{haven't} \\ \text{hasn't} \end{array}\right\} \rightarrow \text{ain't,}$$

in which case it would perhaps follow a rule (E3) $X\#\text{n't} = X\text{n't}$, to delete phonological 'disjuncture' or separateness before *n't*, and this in turn would follow some rule or rules introducing *n't* in certain positions under certain conditions. E4 would be a rule which could be applied only fairly late, after many other rules. The preferred or correct grammar would not have rule E4 at all, but perhaps

$(7\text{-}E5)$ amn't $\Rightarrow$ *am not, aren't* (under specified conditions; obligatory perhaps for some, optional for others).

---

[1] See below (7-1.6, 7-2.4), etc.

This has the odd effect of making the 'correct' grammar seem simpler than the 'incorrect', even though we (or, at least, I) intuitively feel that it's much simpler to say *ain't* for all five values than to keep them distinct. This intuition seems difficult to represent, except by ordering the rule attaching *n't* earlier than the replacement of [BE] by *am, are, is* and of [HAVE] by *have, has.*

The incorrect rule for the compound subject reads something like this:

$$(7\text{-}E11) \quad NP[(C')\ NP_1\ (+X)+C+NP_2]\ \widehat{}\ number$$
$$\Rightarrow NP[(C')\ NP_1\ (+X)+C+NP_2]\ \widehat{}\ pl$$

or, in shorter form:

$$\widehat{}\ number \rightarrow \widehat{}\ pl/NP[(C')\ NP_1\ (+X)+C+NP_2]\_\_\_\_.$$

Here a symbol like NP placed directly before brackets (other people sometimes place it after, or both before and after, but lowered) means that the whole expression within the brackets *is* or *functions as* an NP. This is called a labeled bracketing. The inclusion of an item within parentheses means that it does not matter whether this item is present or not (but if present on the left it must remain on the right). C means any member of the set *and, or, nor*, and C' means correspondingly *both, either, neither*. The item represented by X includes additional pairs of C (or 'comma') followed by NP, if present, in any number. Symbols attached by hooks, like *^number* and *^pl(ural)* are called features. A more common notation, but more awkward to write and print, is to place them below the line, inside square brackets. Here the best place would be under the labeling NP at the beginning:[1]

$$NP \ldots \rightarrow NP \ldots$$
$$[\text{number}] \quad [\,+\text{plural}].$$

Alternatively, the left-hand side can be depicted as lacking any feature or as being labeled [r plural], where r means 'relevant'.

The correct pair of rules would include an E11 just like this except that C includes only *and* and C' only *both*, and an E12 just like it but with C *or, nor* C' *either, neither* and the value *^sing(ular)* on the right, provided that NP₁ and NP₂ are both marked *^sing* already, otherwise with the value *^pl*.

---

[1] Andreas Koutsoudas has recently denied (*Linguistics* 46:11–20, December 1968) that conjoined NP's constitute an NP. If this view prevails, then this rule becomes a little awkward to write.

Lane's 1033 might (under one interpretation) correspond to a rule (perhaps obligatory) X + Subject [homines] + Y ⇒ X + Y. It might also be interpreted on the assumption that one possible expansion of the subject NP would be to label it with a feature ^*indeterminate* and then have a rule which reads:

Subject [NP] ^indeterminate → Subject [NP] ^indeterminate ^pl,

and later have a rule (after the verb agreement rule) which deletes this item entirely, so that no surface form is dominated by this NP node. Lexicalization is here assumed to follow at least some transformations.

1066 is similar to the English rule already discussed, but would have to specify random choice of ^*sing* or ^*pl* ([− plural] or [+ plural]) under certain conditions.

1541 would take a pair of semantic features and add a mood feature:
    1541A ^wish ⇒ ^subjunctive,
    1541B ^hopeful ⇒ ^primary,
    1541C ^hopeless ⇒ ^secondary (or sometimes ^primary).
The converse is a rule of interpretation:
    ^subjunctive ^secondary = hopeless,
    ^subjunctive ^primary = hopeful (or sometimes hopeless).

The arrows are an unsuitable notation here; there is as yet (1971) no established convention.

2173 could perhaps be handled as follows: various embedding rules would delete all but voice and aspect marks from verbs, and add ^*infinitive* ^*Acc*. A later rule would go:

Subj [NP] + VP ^infin ^Acc ⇒ Subj [NP] ^Acc + VP ^infin.

Or the ^Acc could be added outright in this rule; and other devices are possible.

The rule of 2337 might be something of this sort. Assume that a semantic identification tag is put on every noun phrase in a discourse.[1] Let's think of it as a feature ^*identity K*, with K taking any integral value you like, so that every NP marked ^*identity* 3 (for instance) would specify the same individual or class, but different from all NP's not so marked, those labeled ^*identity* 4 would all indicate a different same individual or class, and so on. All occurrences of each such tag after the first would also bear a feature ^*anaphoric*.

(It is here assumed that cases where the pronoun precedes its antece-

---

[1] As suggested by (among others) Noam Chomsky in *Aspects*, p. 145.

dent, which happens more often in Latin than in English, are due to later reordering.) Then a set of rules would go:

NP ^identity K ^anaphoric ⇒ Pronoun A ^identity K

where Pronoun A would repeat certain features of the NP (for Latin, this would include number and gender only). Then another rule would say:

Pronoun A ^identity K ⇒ Reflexive ^identity K/
Subj [NP] ^identity K + X ____

where X does not include any sentence boundaries. Actually several more conditions must be specified (for instance verbs must be ranked as to dominance, and the only Subject NP's which can condition the application of this rule must belong either to the same verb, or to one of higher rank than the pronoun) and for *suus* (and some other words) a device converting genitive case into number-gender agreement would also be required. But there is nothing in the least outlandish about such rules; though conventions are not yet agreed upon, they can be devised by the dozen.

So much for a sample of grammatical rules as they are and as they might be written. How are they to be put together in a grammar? How can one test a grammar for completeness? Here the notion of the grammar as algorithm which we owe to Noam Chomsky has been extremely fruitful; indeed it is impossible to imagine a truly useful grammar which cannot be expressed as an algorithm.

But what is an algorithm? An algorithm may be loosely described as a complete and explicit set of instructions for specifying (or 'describing' or 'generating') all the entities (mathematical or symbolic) of a certain desired class, *or* for converting any entity (or set) of one type into a corresponding entity (or set) of another type. An algorithm of the first sort might be given for the class of entities called 'natural numbers'.

(A) 1 is a natural number.

(B) Any natural number increased by one is a natural number.

This algorithm presupposes the ability to *add one* as known in advance, and all algorithms presuppose some small set of undefined or given operations, and most of them also presuppose some given entities as well.

Algorithms of the second kind are the procedures for adding, multiplying,. dividing, extracting square roots, etc. which we learned in school. The algorithm for adding a pair (ultimately any number) of n-digit numbers requires several prior abilities: (1) knowledge of the sums of all pairs of numbers less than ten; (2) identification of the 'last' or 'units' digit and of 'the next digit to the left'. Then we may have rules:

(A) Set the two numbers one above the other, so that the units digits are in column, the next digits to the left in column, and so on.

(B) Add the last digits which have not yet been added; if the result is 9 or less, write it down below these digits in a 'sum row'. If it is 10, write a zero in that position and add one to the next-digit-to-the-left in the upper number (if there is one; otherwise the lower, if there is one; otherwise write a 1 down to the left of the first digit in the sum row); if it is any two-digit number other than 10 (necessarily less than 19), write its last digit down below the given digits and add one to the next-digit-to-the-left in the upper number (if there is one, etc., as above).

(C) Add the next-digit-to-the-left, using the same instructions, which now apply one column to the left. Continue until the instructions can no longer be applied.

That's clumsy, and can be improved, but it will give you the idea. Instructions must be complete and explicit.

The invention of the modern digital computer gave a big boost to algorithms, because this is essentially all a computer can do, execute algorithms. And if they are not complete or explicit, the algorithm (=computer program) will fail. Computers also encourage algorithm writers to break operations down into a multitude of tiny steps such that each one is minimal, involving only one indivisible change. It is often helpful to do the same thing in writing grammars, though most linguists lack the requisite patience and most readers would be bored stiff by a truly minimal-step algorithm. The examples given here have rather long and complicated steps, not too complex for us to follow, but quite beyond the average computer until they have been broken down. Programmers often use the device called 'flow chart' to represent the various steps (not usually minimal; some steps may stand for complete flow-charts known to exist elsewhere), and this is easily used for some kinds of simple algorithm. I will not put in a flow-chart here, but I will try to arrange the equivalent for a simple algorithm which will test any

single-digit number for evenness, divisibility by two. The only operations are registering the number, subtracting one, and reporting the
register empty (or that it reads 'zero').

	Operation	*Question*	*If yes*	*If no*
1.	—	Is reg. empty?	Enter number	Go to 2
2.	Subtract one	Is reg. empty?	Number is not even. END	Go to 3
3.	Subtract one	Is reg. empty?	Number is even. END	Go to 2

In principle a grammar could equally well be a set of rules which would
take some string of symbols as input and give as a final output the decision whether or not this string is a sentence of the language, like the
above elementary algorithm for detecting even numbers. This is (in a
rough way, at least) a third type of algorithm, distinct from both the
enumerative or generative devices and the operational or transformational
devices (like the rules for addition mentioned above). In fact, however,
such a device for discriminating well-formed strings has so far proved
too difficult to write, in spite of some interest in the possibility on the
part of mathematicians and logicians. So all recent attempts have been
directed toward grammars which are enumerative devices, such that a
properly programmed computer using this grammar as the essential
basis of the program (if instructed to make all free choices in a random,
unprejudiced way), would ultimately print out the vast majority of all
possible sentences of the language.[1] If sentences were assumed to have
an upper bound in length (on the ground of finiteness of human life, or
of the brain, or dysgenic consequences of linguistic infiniteness for the
species), so that the total number of possible sentences was finite, and
if this upper bound were added to the program, then it could be expected
to crank out every single possible sentence – and no non-sentences or
sentences belonging to other languages. This goal, too, is hard to reach;
but progress toward it has been fast.

What kinds of rules should we have, and in what order (if any)
should they apply? Such questions are answered, of course, by a list of
super-rules (a 'theory of grammar'), which are somewhat like a publisher's style-sheet or the rules of a game, except that they should not
be wholly arbitrary. At the present moment no such conventions are
accepted by all grammarians, and the dispute about which rules
should be accepted seems to require a set of super-super-rules (a 'theory
of theories' or 'metatheory of grammar') to help us decide which

---

[1] This use of 'grammar' and 'language' corresponds to the mathematician's use;
linguists often use 'language' where mathematicians say 'grammar'.

conventions to prefer. Perhaps it is arbitrary, in which case a roll of dice or a consultation of astrologers should be suitable methods. But many linguists and philosophers believe that, even if some individual choices are arbitrary, some of the important and fundamental decisions are not. If this is so, we should choose the natural (or 'correct') conventions rather than unnatural ones. This question is still in the air, but for the time being we shall pretend that many, at least, of these conventions are arbitrary and cannot be either right or wrong.

First, then, what kinds of rules have been proposed? (1) Context-free phrase-structure (PS) rules, of which most tagmemic formulas and some immediate-constituent (IC) rules may be considered variants, are of the basic form:

(7-1.1) $A \rightarrow B + C$ or   B C, or
(7-1.2) $A \rightarrow B + C + D$ B C D, or
(7-1.3) $A \rightarrow B + C + D + E$ B C D E, or
(7-1.4) $A \rightarrow B + C + D + E + F$ B C D E F, etc.

They must have (1) a single symbol on the left of the arrow; (2) one or more symbols linked by a concatenation symbol (plus or space) on the right; (3) until special theoretical provision was made for it, the symbol which appears to the left of the arrow was not supposed to be repeated on the right, i.e. $*A \rightarrow A + B$ was not a legitimate rule (though Chomsky allowed one such rule in his 1957 and 1960 sketches of English). In 1965 Chomsky allowed S to appear on both sides, and more recent grammars grant this recursive possibility also to NP and sometimes other symbols. (4) Nothing is said about what precedes or follows the left-hand symbol ('context-free rules'), nor about its source in earlier rules ('mother-symbol', '[immediately] dominating node', etc.). (5) Occasional suggestions have been made to limit the form to $A \rightarrow B + C$, where exactly two symbols appear on the right. Obviously any rule of the form $A \rightarrow B + C + D$, $A \rightarrow B + C + D + E$, etc. can be converted to two (or more) rules like $A \rightarrow B + C$ applied consecutively, e.g. $A \rightarrow B + Q$, $Q \rightarrow C + D$ and $A \rightarrow P + Q$, $P \rightarrow B + C$, $Q \rightarrow D + E$, etc. The trouble with this restriction as applied to natural languages is that it seems sometimes (at least) to be *ad hoc*; occasionally a construction containing three words does not seem to be built up of two dichotomies. Is 'red, white and blue' to be analyzed as 'red' plus 'white and blue' or as 'red, white' plus '(and) blue'? Why? On the other hand, many complex constructions do seem to be built up of successive binary ones.

This same class of rules in IC form might be represented (there are many notations) as:

(7-1.5)   (B + C) = A, or

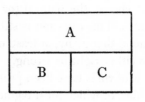

or in tree form

a form used also by transformational grammarians. Tagmemicists add a slight complication: each element on the right must consist of two symbols, one marking function (or 'slot') the other form ('filler'). Hence:

(7-1.6)   A = +B:b +C:c

The plus here is not a concatenation symbol, but an indicator of obligatory occurrence.

Rules of the given form are pure single rules; for reasons of simple economy of space, nearly all grammatical notations involve devices for conflating several rules into one (usually if and only if the left-hand symbol is the same). (a) A pair of rules:

(7-2.1)   A→B +C and
(7-2.2)   A→B +C +D can be conflated as
(7-2.3)   A→B +C (+D),

where the parentheses indicate optionality. The tagmemic equivalent is '±' ('plus or minus'):

(7-2.4)   A = +B:b +C:c±D:d

(b) A pair of rules of the form:

(7-3.1)   A→B +C and A→B +D are conflated as

$$(7\text{-}3.2) \qquad A \rightarrow B + \left\{ \begin{array}{c} C \\ D \end{array} \right\} \text{ or} \rightarrow B + C, D.$$

The alternatives are either placed one above the other inside braces or one after the other separated by commas. A conflation of this type is generally understood to convert two *mays* into one *must*: i.e. The first pair of rules read "A *may* be a $B+C$ or it *may* be a $B+D$"; the conflation goes "A *must* be either $B+C$ or $B+D$". In tagmemics alternation applies only to fillers, not slots, and the usual convention is the solidus;

$$(7\text{-}3.3) \qquad\qquad A = B{:}b + C{:}c/d.$$

(c) Occasionally one sees conflation of rules like:

$$(7\text{-}4.1) \qquad\qquad A \rightarrow B + C + D + E \text{ and}$$
$$(7\text{-}4.2) \qquad\qquad A \rightarrow P + C + D + Q \text{ into}$$

$$(7\text{-}4.3) \qquad\qquad A \rightarrow \begin{bmatrix} B \\ P \end{bmatrix} + C + D + \begin{bmatrix} E \\ Q \end{bmatrix},$$

here the square bracket convention requires that corresponding lines must be chosen, i.e. $*A \rightarrow B + C + D + Q$ is not a possible reading. This also is a *must* alternation.

(2) Most of the remaining conventions concern context-sensitive rules only. They may be written in two styles:

$$(7\text{-}5.1) \qquad X + A + Y \rightarrow X + B + C + Y, \text{ or } A \rightarrow B + C/X\_\_\_Y.$$

Either form is read "A is (necessarily or optionally) represented by $B+C$ when it occurs with an X before and a Y after it". Nearly always there is at least one other rule, whether or not it has been conflated with this one, to indicate what an A is when it is *not* surrounded by X___Y. And on this point there are conflicting conventions and hence misunderstandings possible. There are two possible cases: either the other rule or rules are context-free, hence should apply also in the X___Y case, or they are context-sensitive, and apply only in the elsewhere-case (all environments except X___Y; we might use the logical negation symbol and write $\overline{X\_\_\_Y}$, i.e. $/\overline{X}\_\_\_, \_\_\_\overline{Y}$, *either* preceded by non-X *or* followed by non-Y and *not* $\overline{X}\_\_\_\overline{Y}$, which means *both* preceded by non-X, *and* followed by non-Y. The first case may be written:

$$(7\text{-}5.2) \qquad\qquad A \rightarrow \left\{ \begin{array}{l} Q + C \\ B + C/X\_\_\_Y, \end{array} \right.$$

with the understanding that every A *must* be dealt with by this rule, and that only if the environment is X___Y *may* the second line be chosen.

This can be represented less ambiguously as follows:

$$(7\text{-}5.3) \qquad A \rightarrow \left\{ \begin{array}{l} \left\{ \begin{array}{l} Q \\ B \end{array} \right\} + C/X\_\_\_Y, \\ Q + C \end{array} \right.$$

where the second line can only be understood as meaning 'elsewhere', but the symbol Q is required one extra time. The multi-line rule where all lines are context-sensitive and mutually exclusive can be arranged in any order,

$$(7\text{-}5.4) \qquad A \rightarrow \left\{ \begin{array}{l} B + C/X\_\_\_Y \\ Q + C \; (/\overline{X}\_\_\_, \; \_\_\_\overline{Y}, \text{ i.e. elsewhere}) \end{array} \right.$$

or

$$(7\text{-}5.5) \qquad A \rightarrow \left\{ \begin{array}{l} Q + C \; /\overline{X}\_\_\_, \_\_\_\overline{Y} \\ B + C \; (\text{elsewhere, i.e. } X\_\_\_Y) \end{array} \right.$$

and the convention is often followed of omitting the 'elsewhere', taking it as understood that the last line of such a rule is always context-sensitive even though it looks context-free. Notice that both lines in such a rule are *must* rules, whereas in (7-5.2) line 2 is optional, while line 1 is obligatory only if the context is $\overline{X\_\_\_Y}$, (i.e. "not preceded-by-X-or-followed-by-Y").

The only remaining conventions of critical importance are the convention of executing the rules in a fixed order[1] and the conventions of

---

[1] A note on the various and possibly confusing ways in which the terms *order* and *ordered* are used by linguists (especially) is perhaps in order here.

(a) Rules may, by convention, be printed in the order in which they must be executed; this means that the last occurrence of a symbol as part of the right-hand (expansion) side of any rules must precede its occurrence on the left (to be expanded). If a convention is adopted of never executing an earlier rule after a later one, it sometimes becomes necessary to repeat rules (which is generally regarded as a defect). However, *this does not necessarily make the rules ordered rules* in the technical sense here discussed, unless another criterion is fulfilled.

(b) If two or more rules are so related that they can actually be executed in either or any one of several orders so as to yield different outputs, then they are called *ordered* in the strict sense. This is *extrinsic* order as defined by Chomsky in *Aspects*, p. 223, n. 6. This happens mainly when a symbol appears on the right of some rule after it has already occurred either on the left (itself rewritten) or as part of the contextual restriction of an earlier rule.

(c) The order of elements as they are spoken or written is here called sequence, or sequential order. In this sense the compound term *word-order* is familiar.

(d) Logicians and mathematicians, and people who use their language speak of ordered sets, ordered n-tuples (couples, triples, quadruples, quintuples, etc.) or ordered n-ads (dyads, triads, tetrads, pentads, etc.). This means that the members of the set are different in kind or function or relation; e.g. in the ordered couple (John, features or cross-classification. The best examples of the utility of the fixed-order convention that I have been able to find come from rules which have to do with phonological shape (including order of constituents or elements in the string, which is also, at this end, purely phonological, the difference between *gob* and *bog* or between the shapes of *come in* and *income*, of *gum-chewing* and *chewing gum*.).[1] One example may help to make this clear.

Suppose we wished to handle the English forms *wolf, wolves, safe, safes, dove, doves, lunch, lunches,* in such a way as to have (a) only one plural suffix, /z/, (b) one basic stem form for each noun, and (c) no special morphophonemic symbols unusable elsewhere. Without ordered rules this may be impossible; with them it may be done as follows (as well as other ways, no doubt).

    o. Earlier rules have produced N and N +Pl.

(7-01) N→wulv, se:f, dovǝ, so:fa, lonč

(7-02) Pl→z

(7-03) v# →f# (i.e. absolute final v is devoiced. A complete grammar would also cover the cases of ð→θ and perhaps *house, houses*).

At this point *wolf* and *wolves* are already O.K.

(7-04) Xǝ→X/—(z) # (i.e. stem-final ǝ drops before final z or finally; other contexts would be specified in a complete grammar).

Now *dove* and *doves* are O.K.

(7-05) z→ǝz/S— (S represents any sibilant or the sibilant feature, i.e. s, z, š, ž, č, ǰ).

Bill) which is present in the sentence "John shot Bill", the first term marks the subject agent or shooter (in this case), whereas the second is the object or victim. Interchanging the two changes the meaning.

[1] Since 1965 *all* transformations are phonological in this sense, at least in most familiar variants of the theory. They *also* generate derived phrase-markers. Even so, *most* of the orderings which have been proposed for them by Fillmore, Klima, Ross, Lakoff, Rosenbaum, or Jackendoff, etc. are *intrinsic* only: The Structural Description by itself excludes misapplication. The most plausible examples yet offered involve the rules of pronominalization or NP-deletion and rules of passivization or extraposition, and I strongly suspect that a more general constraint needs to be formulated to cover not only these cases where ordering *can* be used to prevent ungrammatical output, but also various other cases for which (e.g.) Ross formulated a number of specific constraints in his 1967 thesis. One intuitively plausible constraint might be this: "Constituent structure must be recoverable."

    In phonological rules labeled bracketing can do the same work as linear extrinsic ordering so that, e.g., an [f] which is derived from an underlying [v] (perhaps v[f]) would be distinct from one which is not. This would even handle cases where no single unique order is possible – i.e. where rule A must be before B and B before C, but C must be before A – if any such can be found.

Now *lunch* and *lunches* are all right.

(7-06) a→ə/—(z) # Environment mainly lack of stress, but here we need only that of rule (7-04).

Now *sofa* and *sofas* are fixed.

(7-07) z→s/K— (K represents any voiceless phoneme or the feature of voicelessness, p, t, k, f, θ here; by rule (7-05) s, š, č won't occur in this position).

Now *safe* and *safes* are ready.

After the operation of rule (7-02) we have *wulv, wulvz, se:f, se:fz, dovə, dovəz, so:fa, so:faz, lonč, lončz*. After (7-03), as noted above, *wulv* becomes *wulf*; after (7-04), *dovə* and *dovəz* become *dov* and *dovz*, after (7-05) *lončz* becomes *lončəz*, after (7-06) *so:fa* and *so:faz* become *so:fə* and *so:fəz*, while rule (7-07) changes *se:fz* to *se:fs*. These rules are ordered in such a way that (7-03 to 7-07) pretty well have to follow (7-02); if 7-03 came before, then *wulv* would become *wulf* everywhere and rule (7-07) would change *wulfz to *wulfs. Rule (7-04) has to follow (7-03), or else *dov* would be changed to *dof*; (7-05) must precede (7-07), but otherwise could come anywhere after (7-02), while (7-06) must follow (7-04), or else *so:fə* and *so:fəz* would become **so:f* and **so:fz* (which, by (7:07), would then turn to **so:fs*). Rule (7-07) has to follow (7-05), or else *lončz* would become *lončs.

In general if the output of a rule k would be eligible as input to a rule j which must not apply, then simply placing k after j will produce the desired result; if rule j *must* apply, then placing k before j will do. If the output of j does not satisfy the specifications of input to k, nor the output of k those for input to j, then the relative order of the two rules is indifferent.

The principal alternative to ordered rules for handling problems like this is the labeling or indexing procedure (violating restriction (c) above, about special morphophonemic symbols), which marks differently a /v/ which may become /f/ from one which may not, or an /f/ derived from a /v/ from one not so derived. In such a system of inherently unordered rules, the same part of the grammar might look like this.

(7-701) N→wulv$_1$, se:f, dov, so:fə, lonč

(7-702) Pl→z

(7-703) z→əz/S—

(7-704) v$_1$→f/—#

The metagrammar includes a convention to delete all subscripts after the last rule has applied.

(7-705) $z \rightarrow s/K$— (here K means non-sibilant voiceless, ptkfθ only).

In this particular case the unordered grammar seems to the layman a trifle more economical; this is not always so, and even when it is so the ordered rule procedure often marks out regularities which the index procedure would leave unnoticed.

Let us also look at a case involving sequence: consider only the rules which invert subject in questions and which contract *not* to *n't*. We want to allow *I will not go, I won't go, Will I not go, Won't I go*, but *not *Will not I go* or *Will In't go*.

Using M to represent *will, can*, etc., *am, is, are*, etc., and Pron for *I, you, he, we*, etc., we might have the following rules:

(7-11) X +not $=$ Xn't (where X can only be a member of M, because of earlier rules. This is an optional rule. We can make it obligatory by adding a trigger element Ctr [for 'Contract'] on the left).

(7-12) NP[Pron] +M(n't) $\rightarrow$ M(n't) +Pron/—Q (where Q means some marker in the string which indicates 'question').

If the order of these two rules is reversed, both will have to be revised and made more complex, something like this:

(7-21) Pron +M +Not $\Rightarrow \begin{Bmatrix} \text{M +Pron +not} \\ \text{M +not +Pron} \end{Bmatrix} /$—Q.

(7-22) M +not $\Rightarrow$ Mn't obligatory in env.____Pron, optionally elsewhere.

But, as it happens, (7-11) and (7-12) cannot be applied wrongly anyway, hence do not need the kind of strict ordering convention needed for rules (7-04) and (7-03).

The order involved here is the order of application as determined by the 'Structural Description' to use a familiar name for the left-hand side of a transformation. But are there pairs of rules involving order conventions like those for (7-03) and (7-04)? In general no, at least not as rules of sequence are ordinarily formulated. Ordered rules are useful, we must remember, when a given left-hand side might be derived from two different right-hand sources, and yet we wish to restrict the rule to the case derived from one of those sources, and do so by placing it after that source rule but before the other. Rules involving sequence generally arise in a part of the grammar where it has been customary in the past to require indexing (as the metarule is often expressed, "transformations operate on P-markers, not on strings"), so that any pair of symbols derived from different sources would *be* different symbols (at least in indexes or labels). Hence order conventions are unnecessary. But we can give an example of a situation where they have been favored by many linguists. Suppose we start with an active structure:

(7-31) *John$_1$ saw John's$_1$ wife.

If we next apply a pronominalization rule which specifies that in such sentences the second co-referential NP must be pronominalized, we'd get:

(7-32) John$_1$ saw his$_1$ wife.

If we then passivize, we'd have:

(7-33) *His$_1$ wife was seen by John$_1$.

(Throughout here co-referentiality is marked by subscript identity.) But if we first passivize (7-31) to

(7-34) *John's$_1$ wife was seen by John$_1$.

and *then* pronominalize, we get:

(7-35) John's wife was seen by him.

Unfortunately, however, (7-33) is not really impossible, especially if it is lengthened a bit:

(7-33A) His$_1$ wife was seen by John$_1$ slipping jewels into her pocket at Cartier's.

But, at any rate, this illustrates how the principle might work.

Another kind of ordering is the cyclic principle, according to which transformational rules are first applied to the most deeply embedded S, then to the next, and so on. A simple but cogent example of this is hard to find, but the earliest use, to specify relative degrees of ideal stress in English, is reasonably clear. The notorious *air-raid warden post stairway* of the 1940s consists basically of five monosyllabic words (including *stair* and *way*) and one dissyllabic word with stress only on the first syllable. It could be bracketed as follows:

(7-34) N[N[N[N[air-ráid] warden] post] N[stair way]].

Suppose we label stress as '5' to begin with, and then subtract one every time a stress is lowered. Then we'll start with [[[[5-4]5]5][5-4]]. Remove the innermost brackets and subtract: [[[5-3-4]5]4-3]. Then the next pair: [[5-2-3-4]4-3]. And finally: [5-1-2-3 4-3]. This is the ideal, but most people like me have only two or three degrees here: [5-3 5-3 5-3] or even [4-3 4-3 5-3].

A good illustration from syntax is hard to find, but the example used by Jacobs and Rosenbaum in their recent textbook is instructive. Start with an underlying structure like this, with two steps of embedding:

(7-35) NP[it S[that NP[it S[for Icarus to fly] VP[is unnatural] VP[is obvious]

From this we wish to derive:

1. That for Icarus to fly is unnatural is obvious.
2. That it is unnatural for Icarus to fly is obvious.
3. It is obvious that for Icarus to fly is unnatural.
4. It is obvious that it is unnatural for Icarus to fly.
   But not:
5. *That it is unnatural is obvious for Icarus to fly.

Jacobs and Rosenbaum postulate two rules, 'Extraposition' and 'It-deletion' to apply in this order and cyclically for this purpose. Stated in words (Jacobs and Rosenbaum avoid formalization in this text), Extraposition says, roughly speaking, "An S embedded in an NP may optionally be moved out to the end of its matrix S, after its VP", and It-deletion says "An *it* which is left in front of its S inside an NP must now be deleted". The above four sentences are derived as follows:

1. (a) delete *it* before innermost S; (b) delete *it* before higher S.
2. (a) extrapose inner S; (b) delete *it* before higher S,
3. (a) delete *it* before inner S; (b) extrapose higher S,
4. (a) extrapose inner S; (b) extrapose higher S.

Unfortunately this does not seem to be the only way of achieving precisely this result; another way which uses neither cycle nor ordering is this:

Assume that the two rules, since they can never *both* apply at the same point, but one *must* apply, are really a single obligatory disjunctive rule, more or less like this:

$$(7\text{-}36) \quad \begin{matrix} \text{X} & \text{S[NP[\textit{it} S] VP]} & \text{Y} \\ 1 & 2 \quad 3 \quad 4 & 5 \end{matrix} \Rightarrow \begin{cases} 1\ 2\ 4\ 3\ 5 \\ 1\ \emptyset\ 3\ 4\ 5. \end{cases}$$

In words, "Any embedded S preceded by *it* must either be extraposed

E

after the next higher VP, or else must have the *it* deleted." Here there is neither ordering nor cyclic application – i.e. whether you work up from the bottom, down from the top, or both ways from the middle, results will be the same.

A different sort of ordering occurs in connection with direct and indirect questions.

Given a sentence "Where did he go?", we may consider that this is derived from "He went somewhere." and itself is embedded to yield "I wonder where he went." This order of derivation supposes a double reversal of order: first "he went" to "did he go", then "did he go" back to "he went". Such double changes seem uneconomical, so Chalao Chaiyaratana in her English grammar adopted instead the hypothesis that the correct order is "he went", "I wonder where he went", "where did he go?" deriving all direct questions from indirect, instead of *vice versa*.[1] And this is a reasonable hypothesis, in view of what Austin has pointed out about illocutionary performative verbs. But even if we reject that hypothesis and want to have a rule of this sort:

(7-37) $Q + he + \text{Past} \, ^\frown go = \text{Past} + he + go?$

we can still do it by making this the second option in a two-line obligatory rule whose first option is:

(7-38) $Q \rightarrow I$ *wonder, I ask, I inquire,* ...

Then only if the lexical expansion of Q is rejected does the metathesis rule go into effect. And actually, this seems more elegant than many devices I have seen used for this purpose. Still another way which also involves order (but not the strict ordering convention) is to have all embedding rules operate on unlexicalized strings, i.e. strings of class-symbols and formatives (NP, Plural, Verb Phrase, etc., or clusters of syntactic features). Then the 'did he' rule would necessarily be in a later portion of the grammar, and the absence of embedding could be a condition for its applicability.

I think this discussion may at least suggest that a strict ordering convention may well be unnecessary and certainly forces the linguist into counter-intuitive analyses.[2]

Occasionally, in the early (1957–64) literature on transformations, one found discussions of the possibility of applying two transformations in

[1] Rules 56, 138, 145 in her 1959 Indiana University Ph.D. thesis.
[2] For more on this point, see section 1.3 in F. W. Householder *et al.*, *Linguistic Analysis of English*, Final Report to the National Science Foundation under Grant GS-108 (1964), available from CFSTI as PB 167 950.

different orders with either different results or with ambiguity. Even this seems to be due to a misunderstanding. Of course, if one embeds "He is going" into "He says X" to yield "He says he is going" and then converts to a question "Does he say he is going?" the result is different from what happens if we convert "He is going" into "Is he going?" and then embed to yield "He wonders if he's going". But here we are not merely applying the two rules in different order, we are applying them to different input. On the other hand, a sequence "John killed him" → "He was killed by John" → "Was he killed by John?", presumably is not distinct from "John killed him" → "Did John kill him?" → "Was he killed by John?", and more recent styles of grammar which introduce both Passive and Interrogative as formatives in the base do not allow such pseudo-ambiguities.

In the last few examples several of the rules have been of the kind called transformational rules (T-rules). These are of several general types (though the number of types can be reduced in various ways by compounding, i.e. breaking a rule down into two or more steps):

(I) transposition rules, of the form $A + B + C + D \Rightarrow A + C + B + D$ or $A + B + C + D \Rightarrow D + B + C + A$. Note that while the first rule might be written $B + C \Rightarrow C + B/A\rule{1em}{0.4pt}D$, there are still two symbols on the left. Another notation is

$$\text{SD} \quad A \quad B \quad C \quad D \quad \text{SC} \ 1 \ 3 \ 2 \ 4 \quad \text{or} \quad 4 \ 3 \ 2 \ 1$$
$$\phantom{\text{SD}} \quad 1 \ \ 2 \ \ 3 \ \ 4$$

(II) Insertion rules, of the form

$$A\,B$$
$$A + B \Rightarrow A + C + B, \quad \text{or} \quad \text{SD} \quad 1 \ 2 \quad \text{SC} \ 1 \ C \ 2.$$

Here a similar *string* would result from either of two P-rules: $B \rightarrow C + B/A\rule{1em}{0.4pt}$ or $A \rightarrow A + C/\rule{1em}{0.4pt}B$, but the structures in the three cases are or may be quite different. In the first case, assuming $A + B$ was a Q, the result will be $Q[A + C + B]$; in the second it will be: $Q[A + B[C + B]]$, and in the third $Q[A[A + C] + B]$.

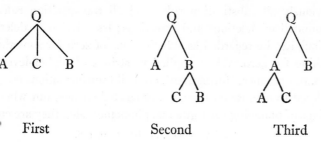

First   Second   Third

Special variants (sister-adjunction, Chomsky-adjunction, etc.) create different types of structure, including additional nodes sometimes. SD A B   SC $1 + $ C 2, 1 C $+2$ yield trees

    1 2

(III) Deletion rules, of the form

$$A + B + C \Rightarrow A + C, \text{ or SD ABC   SC } 1 \varnothing 3.$$

                    $1\,2\,3$

A somewhat similar P-rule would have the form $B \rightarrow \varnothing / A$___C, but this is generally allowed only in the case of contrastively significant zeros. Furthermore, the T-rule actually erases the B without a trace, while the P-rule leaves the structure $A + B[\varnothing] + C$.

(IV) Substitution rules are not commonly used, perhaps because they look so much like P-rules.

$A + B + C \Rightarrow A + Q + C$ erases the B and puts a Q in its place; the corresponding P-rule $B \rightarrow Q / A$___C merely brackets the Q as a B, leaving $A + B[Q] + C$.

(V) Portmanteau rules, of the form $X + A + B + C + Y = X + Q + Y$. Rules of this type are generally allowed only in phonology or morphophonemics, as

(7-41) PAST $+$ COME $\rightarrow$ CAME,

but it is easy to look upon lexical selection rules based upon syntactic and semantic features as essentially the same[1], the features corresponding to $A + B + C$ (although in principle unordered and without structure) and the lexical item itself to Q. From a phonological point of view the Q is then expanded to another sequence (of phonological segments, each of which may be regarded as a structureless set of phonological features).

Obviously all substitution rules and all transposition rules can be compounded of deletions and insertions; less obviously deletions and insertions can be regarded as substitutions of zero for something or of something for zero. When applied to strings of higher-level symbols (words, morphemes, 'formatives', etc.) all transformations are generally considered to operate on *trees*, i.e. bracketed strings, but when applied to strings of phonological segments, phonemes, etc., they are considered

---

[1] Cf. Chomsky, in *Aspects*, p. 108.

not to have (except in the case of the phonological cycle) or produce any structure. But all this is mechanical detail, easy to adjust in whatever way you prefer and not very revealing about the real structure of any real language. So for our purposes here we will generally confine ourselves to the five types of transformation exemplified above.

The big excitement of 1963 was about a new form of rule, the complex symbol (C.S. – not to be confused with context-sensitive) rule which finally appeared in Chomsky's *Aspects* in 1964. This type of rule is concerned with what has sometimes been called the cross-classification problem, which arises from the necessity of writing rules in which one part of a sentence determines some feature or vocabulary item in another part of it, rules of 'collocation' or 'co-occurrence restriction', of which our old friends agreement (or concord) and government (or rection; "X *takes* the dative") are special cases. So let us start with a quick look at the nature of the problem and the various attempts to solve it.

There are several noteworthy syntactical differences between what are called 'countable' or 'count' nouns, which occur with *a* or *an* as indefinite article, may be pluralized, and in the indefinite singular are referred to as *one* ("I've got one", "Give me one"), *another (one)* ("I want another (one)"), etc., and 'uncountable' or 'mass' nouns, which occur naked (or, in certain cases, with *some* /sm/) as indefinites, cannot be pluralized (without change of meaning), are referred to as *some* /som/ ("I want some", "Give me some"), *some more* ("I want some more"), etc. Suppose we decided to symbolize these as N_{co} and N_{un}. Now the distinction between animate and inanimate nouns is also important, and they can be regarded as subclasses of N_{co} without much difficulty (though conceivably 'virus' or 'plankton' might be regarded as animate mass nouns for a very few contexts). So we have a rule:

(7-51) $$N_{co} \rightarrow N_{an}, N_{in}.$$

Fine. But suppose we next come to a classification (important in many languages) of nouns into relative (or obligatorily possessed) and absolute (unpossessed or optionally possessed) nouns. Among the relative nouns are, say, *brother, cousin, heart, spirit, fingernail, pet, footprint, blood, shadow* and *wedding*; among the non-relative are *man, girl, cane, nail-file, cat, water, shade,* and *ceremony*. Some of both are animate, some inanimate; indeed there are mass nouns, too, in both classes. If we proceed to subdivide N_{an} into N_{anrel} and N_{anabs}, N_{in} into N_{inrel} and N_{inabs}, and

N_{un} into N_{unrel} and N_{unabs}, we still cannot write rules about N_{abs} or N_{rel}, since these categories do not exist (although I am always allowed for convenience to say "In this rule N_{rel} is to be taken as an *ad hoc* abbreviation for the logical sum of N_{anrel}, N_{inrel} and N_{unrel}"). On the other hand, if I go back before my split of N's into N_{co} and N_{un} and there introduce a rule $N \rightarrow N_{rel}$, N_{abs}, I will be even worse off. For now I have to divide N_{rel} into N_{relco} and N_{relun}, N_{abs} into N_{absco} and N_{absun}, then N_{relco} into $N_{relcoan}$ and $N_{relcoin}$ and N_{absco} into $N_{abscoan}$ and $N_{abscoin}$, etc., and I have no way of talking about N_{co} and N_{un}, which don't exist unless I arbitrarily introduce them as cover symbols.

This kind of notation, in which the subclasses were represented by subscripts, suggested the obvious solution to the problem: treat the subscripts as entities of the grammar. And this is exactly what almost everyone was doing within two or three years after *Syntactic Structures*. By the conventions that then grew up, N meant the disjunction of all classes marked by subscripts of N, N_{an} or N^an then meant all animate nouns, whatever other classes they belonged to, N_{rel} or N^rel all relative nouns, $N_{an; rel}$ or N^an^rel all nouns which were simultaneously *animate* and *relative* (the logical product of the classes), and so on. A third notation was introduced at M.I.T. on the analogy of the system used for writing phonological features:

$$N$$
$$\begin{bmatrix} +an \\ +rel \\ +co \end{bmatrix},$$

i.e. the subscripts are all treated as binary features and arranged in column inside square brackets. This is a suggestive notation in many ways, though awkward to manage. In any of these notations, it is a logical next step to regard N itself as being merely one of the linked features; this can be shown best in the second style by reducing the capital letter to yield n^an^rel, and in the third style by adding another + and lengthening the brackets:

$$\begin{bmatrix} +N \\ +an \\ +rel \\ +co \end{bmatrix}.$$

The first notation, which singles out the N by making it both uppercase and on the line while the features are lowercase and subscript, has less flexibility in this regard. Presumably in all notations the 'N' or 'n' would still be first in line (at left or top), which gives it some sort of special status. But two oddities arise here: (1) there are a bunch of binary features [±N], [±V], [±Adj.], etc. which are, in general, mutually exclusive: i.e. it looks like rather a single four-or-five-valued feature 'Word-class' than four or five binary features, though it is inevitable that such binary features should inspire interpretations for, e.g. [+N, +V], [+V, −Adj.], etc.; (2) anything which is *animate* or *relative* or *countable* is automatically bound to be a noun, i.e. N as a feature may be redundant. So perhaps it is best regarded as a shorthand notation for the union of all classes in which such features as [±countable], [±animate], etc. appear. This is not to say that there may not be languages in which one or more of these features apply to verbs – e.g. a language in which "he took a walk" or "he walked once" or "he walked several times" might be expressed as single verb forms to which the feature *countable* was relevant, whereas in "he walked" or its equivalent this was not the case. But the *complete list* of all features which are relevant for nouns must be somehow distinct from the complete list of all features relevant for verbs. If it were not, *then* indeed the feature *N* (or *V*, if it is not merely [−N]) would be nonredundant. It is conceivable (though it does not now seem likely) that this state of affairs could be achieved by a more careful treatment of nouns and verbs than has yet been managed.

Now most of the subclasses of verbs which are discussed in grammars are based upon the subjects, objects, prepositional phrases, dependent infinitives (participles, gerunds, etc.) or subordinate clauses which occur with them or are prohibited from occurring with them. So, for example, in Lane we have lists of verbs with the genitive (1271–94), with the accusative gerund/gerundive (2250–2), with the ablative (2254–7), with the accusative (Transitive, 1133, etc., defined but not listed), with two accusatives (1138), with accusative and dative (1192–9), without accusative objects (Intransitive, not listed, 1479), with dative (1181–91), without subjects (Impersonal), with infinitives 2208–10, with genitive 1283, classified 815–16, etc.), with complementary infinitive (2168–71), with infinitive of indirect discourse (2175–84), with other types of infinitive (2185, 2186, 2187–8, 2189–92, 2194, 2195, 2196, 2197, 2198–2202, 2203, 2204–6, 2207–15), with complementary final (i.e. purposive) clauses (1949–56, 1957–9, 1960), with complementary consecutive (i.e.

result) clauses (1965–9), etc., etc.[1] Consequently Chomsky (in *Aspects*) hit upon the Complex Symbol convention. Roughly it goes like this: let your rules produce a sufficiently detailed classification of everything that precedes and follows a verb: then (and in this way C.S. rules are necessarily ordered) by means of a rule.

(7-61)   V→C.S.

require that whatever pieces of environment have been selected in the generative process up to that point must now be reduplicated as subscript features of the verb, e.g. if we come up to this rule with a string

(7-62)   NP   +V +NP   +Prep. +NP
           [+animate]   [−animate]

then the V will become:

(7-63)   V
           [+ [+an.]___[−an.], Prep., NP]

and when we come to select specific verbs from our lexicon, we will look for one with that rather cumbersome-looking feature attached to it. There are several details that we need not go into here (why both subject and object environment must be considered at once, for instance), but it is clear that this will yield many classes which are quite similar to those set up for Latin by Lane (though he does not say much about verbs restricted as to animateness of subject or object, since these features are in general, for him, logical consequences of the semantic features – *thinking*, for instance – which he considers basic, and would also, from his point of view, coincide almost perfectly with the same features as applied to the English equivalents of these Latin verbs). Curiously enough, Chomsky's earlier rules are so designed that the class of Impersonals could not be naturally established in this way (as verbs not accompanied by any subject), but the rules could easily be altered to achieve this result for Latin if one so desired. Actually Chomsky has

---

1 We should not forget that there is *also* a great deal of syntactic classification by semantic features, e.g. Verbs of Perceiving, Knowing, Thinking, Saying (2175–84), or Accusing (2185), of Hoping, Promising and Threatening (2186), of Emotion (2187–8), of Desire (2189–95), of Accomplishing (2196), of Teaching and Training (2197), of Bidding and Forbidding and of Allowing (2198–203), of Will (1950), of Aim (1951), of Resolving (1953), of Fear, Anxiety or Danger (1957–9), of Avoiding, Hindering and Resisting (1960), of Happening (1965–6), etc., etc. In fact, in most cases, the correct semantic specification allows correct specification of the construction. But this is not relevant to Chomsky's convention.

two separate C.S. rules, one before (strict subcategorization) and one after (contextual) the attachment of features like [+animate] to nouns,[1] but this does not alter the essential operation of the rule. Note that since ' + ' on the line means something quite different (concatenation) from ' + ' inside feature brackets, it must be replaced by something else (space, juxtaposition, or comma) when brought down.

This completes the roster of the main types of rules; one other type which is no longer in use might just be mentioned, the double-base (or 'generalized') transformation. This differs from the ordinary (single-base, singulary) transformation in having *two* strings on the left (S D, structural description) but only one on the right. A simple example with actual words might be the indirect statement embedding:

(7-71) (a) I said ⟨that⟩ D
      (b) He will be here   ⟩ ⇒ *I said* ⟨that⟩ *he would be here.*

Here we should note that this rule is obligatory for strings like (a), since otherwise the D-symbol would be left unexpanded and result in a non-sentence. (Alternatively one could have a pronominal object in the frame-sentence e.g. *something* or *this*, omitting the conjunction from the left-hand side.) I will not explore the notational variants on this pattern, since it has been almost universally abandoned and the same results are achieved by using S (instead of D, here) and sending the user thus back to rule 1 of the grammar. The double-base pattern has one strong advantage over the S-recursion device, which may lead to some modification of the latter, and that is that it allows restrictions to be placed on the form of the sentence to be embedded (e.g. (b), above) as well as on the matrix sentence ((a), above). In the case of verbs of saying, this makes little difference, but in other cases (e.g. relative clauses) it does. Suppose one has a string NP(The man +S) + VP(came in the house), and then goes back to expand the S designed to modify 'man' here. There is nothing at all to prevent this S being expanded as 'Procrastination is the thief of time' or 'The girl is my daughter' or 'Go to school, Johnny', or in a host of other ways, when what is required is some sentence containing "A man___" (or perhaps, as some prefer, "The man___"), e.g. "A man was whistling" to yield either "The man who was whistling came in the house" or "The whistling man came in the house". However nicely the new procedure may work as a model of a speaker's

---

[1] For an argument that neither rule is needed, see McCawley 'Concerning the base component of a transformational grammar', *Foundations of Language* 4:243 (1968).

competence (i.e. something which can duplicate his output), it seems highly implausible as a model of his performance (i.e. a map of the way a speaker produces a sentence). One difficulty has already been suggested on p. 122, n. 1. It is possible, in many cases, to predict all the syntactic features of a verb from a knowledge of one or a few semantic features. But if the C.S. rules attach only *contextual* features to V's for the purpose of lexical search, it is difficult to make economical use of this predictability. It pretty well has to be reversed; i.e. we have to have rules that will take a set ('matrix') of syntactic subscripts or features and automatically substitute certain semantic features (taken quite often from a disjunctive list), i.e. something like this:

$$(7\text{-}72) \qquad \begin{bmatrix} +V \\ \\ +\underline{\quad}NP+to+NP \end{bmatrix} \Rightarrow \begin{bmatrix} +V \\ +\underline{\quad}NP \\ +motion \end{bmatrix},$$

or some equivalent. In some cases part of the contextual feature may remain, in other cases it may be entirely replaced by semantic features.

The possibility of a converse type of C.S. rule, in which the verbs are first categorized and then their syntactical surroundings are specified by such a rule, is rejected by Chomsky, but seems actually somewhat closer to the speaker's performance. In this case, for instance, after the feature [+motion] has been optionally attached to the Verb, a C.S. rule would immediately add the feature [+ [+motion]___] to the complement, and this would in turn be rewritten as

$$\rightarrow \text{Prep. Phrase}$$
$$[+\text{motion}]$$

and that as

$$\text{Prep.} \qquad +NP,$$
$$[+\text{motion}]$$

and finally motion prepositions such as 'to', 'from', etc. would be extracted from the lexicon. In the same way a verbal feature [r intentional] (where r means *relevant*, i.e. it is relevant to ask whether the verb signifies an intended or unintended event) would rapidly condition on the subject a feature [+___[r Intentional]], i.e. [+Animate], or possibly [+Human]. The question whether *all* co-occurrence restrictions are more properly handled in this way or in the reverse way is hard to answer without first writing complete grammars in both styles and then testing them. It is certain, for instance, that in many languages (probably all) a feature *intentional* or the like is going to be needed for verbs in any case – for instance it is deviant to have a purpose clause accompanying a verb which is marked non-intentional, e.g. *It snowed last night in order to whiten the ground. Such sentences, of course, occur, but are regularly understood as figurative, humorous or the like, as is the case with other types of semantically deviant sentence.

This pretty well completes our projected examination of rules and of the advantages of ordering, i.e. allowing several rules with the same *input* (and others with the same *output*) so arranged that if taken in another order a different (and incorrect) result will occur. We decided that the evidence so far available shows few or no cases where ordering in this sense is advantageous, except for the special C.S. rule and rules concerned primarily with the 'surface' of language, that is, the phonological shape (including the sequential order of words and other elements in the final string). Even here we have seen reason to be mildly skeptical about extrinsic ordering in the transformational component. In the base component, then, and probably also in the transformational component, the input specification for each rule should be unique, so that the correct order of application can never be in doubt; if an obligatory rule *can* be applied, it *must* be applied.

8 Subgrammars, planes, levels and components

Old-fashioned grammars were divided into sections, as we mentioned above: 'Phonology', 'Sounds', 'Spelling and Pronunciation', 'Rules of Sandhi' or 'Euphony' (i.e. morphophonemics, the adjustment of sounds to adjacent sounds) and the like usually forming the first section; then, for languages like Latin, 'Inflection' (or 'Accidence'), 'Derivation' and 'Compounding' the second section, sometimes called 'Morphology', or 'Morphology and Word Formation', while the third and last main section dealt with 'Sentence-structure' and 'Syntax'. The rationale is ultimately derived from the way in which school teachers in ancient Greece taught their pupils to read. You can't read texts until you can read words, and you can't read words until you know the alphabet (at least that's what *they* thought). And later grammarians believed they could see a justification for this organization in a certain independence which they felt to belong to each of these sections. The principles by which words (considered *merely* as pronounceable entities) are built of syllables and syllables in turn of vowels and consonants (meaningless units, in essence) seemed to be quite different from and largely uninfluenced by the way in which meaningful words were derived and meaningful categories indicated by inflection, and this is turn different in kind (though perhaps not as completely) from the way in which words were combined into sentences to convey effective messages of one kind or another.

Since the nineteenth century there has been a certain amount of scholarly bickering about the exact number of such divisions of grammar and the exact degree and kind of independence which they possess. In various modern systems of grammatical nomenclature we hear talk of two or three, or four or five (or more) *strata* or *levels* or *ranks* or *planes* or, most recently, *components* of a grammar. The 'levels' of the tagmemicist and the 'ranks' of a Firthian[1] are closely similar: word, piece, phrase or

---

[1] We learned a little about Kenneth Pike and tagemics in the last chapter, and will hear more later. J. R. Firth of the School of Oriental and African Studies of the University of London trained many British linguists, among whom M. A. K. Halliday has

word-group, clause, sentence, paragraph or dialogue, discourse are the entities of successively increasing length.[1] But the boundary between phonology and morphology (or anything assumed to be higher) is obviously more than a matter of increasing length, and so, perhaps, is that between syntactic structure and interpretation of meaning. Hence another principle of division appears, crossing the one based on length. Glossematists[2] recognized two dichotomies: one into content and expression, the other into form and substance. *Expression substance* is essentially phonemes (or letters of the alphabet; writing also belongs to language in this view), *expression form* rules of phonological structure; *content substance* is meaning, *content form* rules of syntax. But the theory has never been carried much beyond this promising point. Stratificational grammar, a theory still being actively modified by its proprietor, Sydney Lamb, sets up strata descending from a topmost 'sememic' stratum (similar to, but not quite the same as Hjelmslev's content substance) through lexemic, morphemic and phonemic strata. Above the sememic stratum there may be some kind of non-linguistic meaning layer, just as below the phonemic there is a phonetic layer. Between adjacent strata are transitional layers: semolexemic, lexomorphemic, morphophonemic. We may return to these later, but all we wish to do now is note the general arrangement of the grammar, through which Lamb envisages the speaker as descending from top to bottom and the hearer rising in symmetry.

Now the models proposed by Chomsky (and most of the variations suggested by other transformationalists) differ from nearly all of these notions in not implying a single, straight-line motion through the levels – at least this is true of all except perhaps the earliest version. In *Syntactic Structures* Chomsky does seem to imagine a linear sequence through two partly distinct components, the first a phrase-structure grammar which turns out simple kernel strings (i.e. it contains the lexical rules, but not all, at any rate, of the morphophonemic rules), the second a transformational component which takes kernel strings and performs various

offered the most explicit proposals, e.g. in *Word* 17:241–92, 'Categories of the Theory of Grammar'.

[1] Tagmemicists and Firthians also have another organizing principle, which divides language into phonology, grammar and lexis (Halliday) or phonemics, morphemics and tagmemics (Pike).

[2] See especially Lamb's appreciation of Louis Hjelmslev, the chief founder of glossematics, 'Epilegomena to a Theory of Language' in *Romance Philology* 19:531–73 (1966). For glossematics see also E. Fischer-Jørgensen, 'Form and Substance in Glossematics', *Acta Linguistica Holmiensia* 10:1–33 (1966).

optional and obligatory operations on them, some of which are partly syntactic in nature, the others purely morphophonemic. Still, we do not seem justified in splitting this into a syntactic transformational component and a morphophonemic one. But since those days a whole semantic component has grown vastly in dignity, the lexicon has become a distinct component for some, and the purely syntactic portions of the syntactic

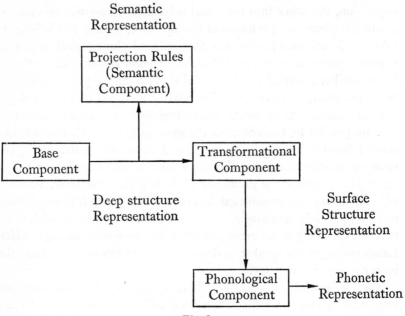

Fig. 8.1

transformations have largely been incorporated in the kernel grammar, now called the base. The result (*c.* 1966) may perhaps be best understood with the aid of a diagram (see figure 8.1).

Chomsky himself (in 1964, at least) supposed that the base might include some language-specific features, but many other linguists are inclined to aim at or postulate a wholly universal base, identical for all the languages of the world. It would then contain or account for all or most of the non-phonological universals of language.[1] The really odd

---

[1] Many linguists who believe this assume as the combined semantic and base component a set of universal semantic features and a handful of logical operators. There have been attempts to establish the existence also of transformational universals, but most of them are of uncertain validity, and may follow from some simpler underlying principle of communication.

feature of this model is the direction of the arrow *from* Base *to* Semantic Interpretation, emphasizing a somewhat artificial-seeming parallel with the Phonetic component: "Just as the phonetic component provides a phonetic interpretation of surface structure (output of the transformation box), so the semantic component gives a semantic interpretation of the deep structure (output of base)." It is hard to see much more here than a bit of play on the word 'interpretation'. The parallel of semantics with phonetics is, of course, real and has often been commented on by glossematists, among others: these are the two links between language and the real world, phonetics via real articulated sounds and semantics through referential relations to things meant in the world. The kind of rules offered by Katz and Fodor[1] in their initial assault on this problem also made a similar odd assumption, that the principal function of semantic rules was to eliminate ambiguity caused by lexical homonymy (or polysemy; it seems doubtful whether they would make such a distinction). This in turn is related to the manner in which a 'lexical entry' is identified. Fodor and Katz (and Chomsky also, at one time; perhaps following Zellig Harris) considered that identity of morphophonemic shape means lexical identity, or at least initial identity of a lexical entry. What is the lexicon where the items are entered? Presumably it is a better-than-real model of the language storehouse in every speaker's brain. Is it necessarily the case that my brain has only one entry for 'flat' meaning an apartment and 'flat' meaning slightly lower in pitch? And does it then necessarily have two entries for 'go' and 'went'? The lexica that we use as reference books, our monolingual and bilingual dictionaries certainly have only one entry for 'go', including 'went', perhaps with a cross-reference under 'went' (e.g. 'see *go*' or 'past tense of *go*'). How many entries they have for 'flat' and similar cases usually depends on a fact which we (including Chomsky as well as Katz and Fodor) should be inclined to consider irrelevant (though sometimes, perhaps, suggestive) since it is not normally known to native speakers: historical identity. If both uses of 'flat' can be traced back to figurative uses (let us say) of the adjective 'flat' meaning 'smooth and level, two-dimensional', then they will be entered in the same place, but if one of them is an old inherited Middle English word and the other is a nineteenth-century borrowing from Hindustani or the like, then the dictionary provides two entries. There is a reason for this which is

---

[1] 'The Structure of a Semantic Theory' in *Language* 39:170–210 (1963). Several times reprinted.

perfectly sensible for dictionary makers: if they are going to give etymological information for each entry, it would be wasteful to have two entries with the same etymology. Distinct form-class membership – what part of speech it is, noun, verb, etc. – is sometimes allowed to guarantee distinct entries in spite of identity of etymology, but not always in all dictionaries. And it probably shouldn't in a good model of a speaker. And of course there is another reason; the procedure for searching, for retrieving an item from a printed dictionary is based on alphabetical order. Even when the dictionary is one like Roget's thesaurus in which meanings are of primary importance, the alphabetical arrangement is still generally used for at least some part of the search. But no one supposes that any close analog of alphabetical order exists in our brains.

Let us quickly recapitulate. We see that most traditional grammars are (as they have been since antiquity, in some measure) organized into a phonological section, a morphological section, and a syntactical section, usually without any clear explanation of the rationale. And we see linguists paying attention to two or three different organizing principles in this traditional arrangement, evaluating them in many different ways. The first one we mentioned above is the principle of increasing length, often combined with a second notion of composition: phonemes are put together to make morphemes, morphemes are put together to make words, words are put together to make (phrases, phrases to make clauses, clauses to make) sentences. Immediately our third criterion, degree and kind of freedom, originality, or productivity, leads us to examine "are put together". By whom? How freely? How often? As soon as these questions are asked we see a considerable difference between the first steps and the later ones. By and large *no* speaker ever puts together phonemes to make new 'morphs' or 'morphemes'; at most he may indulge in some sort of linguistic play involving nonsense-words or nonsense-syllables, but these cannot immediately join the language nor can they be assigned meanings (and some meaning must be attached if they are ever to be used by other speakers) in a wholly arbitrary way. (Cases like *Kodak* are exceptional.) The principal ways in which rules of permissible sound combination affect the individual speaker are in contributing redundancy to overcome noise and in judgements of 'acceptability' or 'normality' of the new words (including names) which he hears. In the combining of 'morphemes' into words there are two quite different degrees of freedom, corresponding to the traditional division between inflection and word-formation (including derivation and compounding in most traditional European grammars). How freely does one make new combinations of stem and inflectional ending? In one sense, not at all; suppose a speaker is using a Latin noun in a prepositional phrase which requires the accusative case, can he be said to have exercised freedom in attaching an accusative ending? On the contrary, he seems to have no freedom to *avoid* attaching that ending, whether it is for the first time in history or something which has been said a million times. And just in case it *is* for the first time in history, will he know it? This seems most unlikely. When a young child is acquiring control of his language it may be possible to record the first occasion on which we hear him utter a particular combination of stem and inflectional affix, but even then can we be sure he is 'newly creating' the form rather than repeating something he has heard already made?

In the case of compounding and derivation, it is almost a rule of linguistic structure that a speaker is never compelled to create a new form. The resources of the language always provide other ways of 'saying the same thing'. But many word-formation patterns (e.g. suffixation of -ness in English) are so common that the speaker may be unable to say whether he is creating a new form or merely recalling a word he has heard. At this level a little freedom is certainly possible, even though we may not always know when we are exercising it. In an earlier chapter I suggested that there may be differences in the inventiveness of individual speakers; some of them may never in their whole lives utter a word which they have not heard from other speakers, while a few may coin two or three new derivatives or compounds every day – though that is probably high; a careful inspection of many recorded conversations leads me to believe that we are prone to overestimate our own inventiveness.

But once you come to sentences and longer stretches the situation changes sharply; now it is taken for granted that almost every sentence uttered by any speaker at any time is a brand new one, and even if by chance it is not, neither speaker nor hearer is ever aware of this lack of originality except when quotation (or plagiarism) is involved. (Quotation depends for its effect on being quickly identified as quotation – hence obvious stylistic marks are desired; on plagiarism see ch. 14.) As I suggested earlier, it is quite possible (though evidence is almost wholly lacking) that there is a good deal more repetition of whole sentences and largish chunks than we are conscious of. But there is obviously a striking difference between words and sentences; unless we have evidence to the contrary, we assume that any *word* we hear is an old one (against which we may sometimes make the claim "There's no such word" or "That's not in the dictionary"), but any *sentence* we hear is a new one (it is impossible to claim "There's no such sentence", but only that a sentence is nonsensical, or ungrammatical, or deviant in some other way). Words are (in our folk taxonomy of language) normally supposed to pre-exist, sentences to be made up.

The criterion of originality, then, suggests something like two principal 'levels' or 'components' with a third in between: a phonological component virtually devoid of originality which specifies acceptable shapes for (rarely occurring) new morphs, which surprisingly often are identical with old ones (this component also includes – or perhaps refers to the general theory for – rules to make loan-words native), a syntactic component with almost complete originality to specify acceptable structures for sentences, and a word-forming or compounding-derivational component with much more freedom than the phonological specifier but much less than the sentence specifier. A few patterns are perhaps so productive that they may be shifted (as many linguists do with all word-forming) into the sentence specifier, but in general the gap is considerable.

If the distinction between the phonological and word-forming components is reduced, one could have the former specify *phonological* morphs or words (i.e. shapes only) and the latter *morphological* words (i.e. morphemic trees or IC patterns without shape). This would help to dispel the notion that the sole difference is one of length. On the contrary, the difference of length, where present, is more or less irrelevant. A phonological word is specified as being like other words in varying ways and degrees solely from the point of view of sound (a phoneme can naturally – from one logical viewpoint – be thought of as a set of words similar to each other in one way, just as a phonological feature is a class of phonemes similar in one way and just as the number two is defined by Russell as the class of all pairs), whereas a morphological word is at least partly specified as being like other words from the point of view of syntax (form-class, part of speech, grammatical-category, etc.) and of meaning (semantic features of the parts and any features which may be contributed by the rules joining the parts).

It has never been clear (to me, at least) precisely how Chomsky would handle these two specifiers; certainly they are not (as described here)

components of his grammar, but they are somewhat sliced up and re-
distributed so that some of the phonological specifier is merely embedded
in the lexicon, most of it somehow incorporated into the sequence of
phonological rules, while part of the morphological specifier (perhaps a
very small part) is in the lexicon, part of it in various rules adjusting
embedded S's to their surroundings.

And it is clear from any point of view that inflectional elements (meaning those which mark syntactic relationships and relationships among
utterance, speaker, hearer, and place and time of speaking, in so far as
they are parts of words rather than free forms) certainly do belong well
down in the grammar, definitely later than lexical selection and application of transformational rules, though necessarily before most of the
morphophonemic rules which (among other things) adjust the shapes of
inflections. Their occurrence and use (like that of any free particles with
similar functions) must be conditioned by features attached to the
sentence, to the verb (or verb phrase) or to some noun phrase; the
older view that they are 'morphemes' quite parallel to verb stems or
noun-stems is also popular now. All this rather resembles the Saus-
surean distinction between 'semantemes' (i.e. independently meaningful
units like noun-stems, etc.) and 'morphemes' elements like affixes and
sentence particles). But the division rests on criteria of another sort.

There is no doubt that one can write grammars corresponding to each
of these types of structure: a pure phonological grammar to generate
purely phonological words (i.e. all – or nearly all, excluding a very
few marginal items – existing words and all potential shapes which could
be assumed by loan-words and proper names not marked as foreign);
or, by prefixing one or two rules to add intonations and related phenomena (much more would be needed for the phonological side of real
sentences; here we are concerned *only with pure sound*), phonological
sentences; a morphological word-grammar (or, in some cases, fixed-
phrase grammar or idiom-grammar[1]) to generate secondary words
(i.e. derivatives and compounds); and, finally, the usual sentence-grammar or syntactic grammar. Note that each of the last two must have a
'phonological' or morphophonemic part or component, and that the
sentence-grammars will also have morphological rules of a kind. There
can also be no doubt that these three grammars correspond to quite
different performance abilities: *everyone* above the age of two, more or

---

[1] 'Idiom' is Hockett's term for a lexical meaningful unit, whether it is an affix or a
phrase.

less, is constantly (over 100 times a day) exercising a function which is modeled by the sentence-grammar, and can scarcely avoid doing so; *some* individuals freely and frequently (i.e. several times a week or year) perform the operations of the morphological grammar to construct new lexical entries, whereas others seldom or never do so; and *most* individuals for a short time in childhood and again perhaps as parents of young children exercise a function represented by the phonological grammar, but very rarely (once or twice per decade) during the rest of their lives, mainly perhaps to try out the sound of a strange word. In spite of this difference Chomsky and Halle have vehemently and violently argued[1] for incorporating the phonological grammar into the morphophonemic rules of the sentence-grammar (an easy thing to do, for the most part), on the ground that our non-exercise of these rules is only superficial; deep down we are constantly applying them to control the shape of every word we say. If this is so, it is obviously done in some inaccessible operation of the brain and there is no chance of our being able to devise a means of finding out about it, at least not with the psychological technology which is at present available.

My distinction between the phonological grammar and the sentence grammar (ignoring for the time being the word-forming grammar) is very much the same as Hjelmslev's between expression and content (that between form and substance, on the other hand, comes closer to the difference between structural rules and lexical rules or lists), and is also what Hockett (as cited in ch. 3, above) refers to as duality of patterning. In each grammar or on each plane there are a number of basic entities (which may themselves be complex in some way, but which are primitives within this system) and a number of regularities of co-occurrence or combination, and, by and large, the regularities on one plane have no link with regularities on the other. It is probably some tagmemicists who have pushed this the farthest,[2] but all talk of phonotactics, of canonical form or of syllable-types is a step in the direction of phonological grammar.

Is this really just *duality* of patterning, as Hockett would have it, or it is rather triplicity or something higher? There is certainly no doubt that the rules of phonological structuring are different from and independent of the rules of syntactic structuring, and furthermore, that

[1] In *Journal of Linguistics* 1:2, 97–138 (1965). Cf. now G. Sampson *Lg.* 46: 586–626 (1970).
[2] But see B. Sigurd, *Phonotactic Structures in Swedish* (Lund, Uniskol, 1965), or M. Yasui, *Consonant Patterning in English* (Tokyo, 1963), for other elaborate treatments.

meaning must be irrelevant in the first case and relevant in the second. If there is a third kind of patterning, what is it? Something related to our morphological grammar, perhaps? But the structure of complex words is in some way related to syntax and to meaning, and, on the other side, to phonology. Nevertheless there are striking differences between languages precisely at this point: some languages have mostly one-morpheme words, others have long polymorphemic ones as well; some languages use nothing but prefixes, others have suffixes, still others have infixes (so most of the Indonesian languages, where, e.g. Sundanese cïrik means [*he*] *cries*, carïrik means [*they*] *cry*); some allow extensive compounding (however one chooses to define this elusive word), others use mainly fixed phrasal constructions (English (a) milk-bottle, French (une) bouteille à lait, Modern Greek (mia) botilia tu ghalaktos, Turkish (bir) süt şişesi; contrast English (a) bottle of milk, French (une) bouteille de lait, Greek (mia) botilia ghála, Turkish (bir) şişe süt) which function much like compounds and have the same sort of status intermediate between independent free forms and freely invented phrases; some make almost no phonological adjustments in such complex or compound words, others have elaborate rules for internal morphophonemic changes (internal sandhi). So one must say that in some sense such an intermediate third kind of structuring exists, even though it is only partially independent of the other two.

Is there a semantic structure which is quite independent of the syntactic? Lamb suggests that there is, but does not give a wholly convincing account of what it is like. The splitting favored by many linguists (including Chomsky, of course) of syntactic structure into two parts, deep structure and surface structure, is amenable to the interpretation – not favored by Chomsky himself – that the deep structure *is* solely semantic structure (and hence should have in it no anticipations of peculiarities of individual language surface structure), while the surface structure is most of what we have long been regarding as syntactic. But obviously the two are not totally independent; (syntactic) surface structure must somehow provide representations of most of the deep (semantic) structure, and the rules linking the two seem to be the most genuinely linguistic part of the grammar. In spite of the labors of many linguists, philosophers and psychologists, furthermore, we do not have as clear and sharp a notion of pure semantic structure as we might wish for. But maybe it is real.

What about phonetic structure? Is there such a thing? Here again we may be in the realm of universal grammar, with rules telling us what restrictions on phonetic sequences are necessarily present in all languages, such as (perhaps) that all languages must have some sounds which are pronounced with voicing (though some seem to lack any sounds whose voicelessness is distinctive); or that all languages must have sounds pronounced with outbreathed air, though some may have others, like clicks, which use no breathed air at all; and other things of this kind. But this does not seem to be enough for a purely phonetic structure; perhaps the picture given by a sound spectrogram represents pure phonetic structure. If so, it is very highly dependent on the phonemic (or phonological) structure, much more so than is the case with the deep and surface structures of syntax.

A few years ago (at least *sub specie aeternitatis*) we were often warned not to mix levels. What was this all about? The levels in this case were again much the same as the two basic ones we have been discussing, phonological and morphological-syntactical. But the context was that of discovery, about which we will say more in a later chapter. It was the belief of Trager, Smith and many other American linguists that there were two distinct stages in the analysis of a language: first one determined the phonological structure, the inventory of phonemes and the essential nature of their contrasts without reference to any other aspect of language except the notion of sameness or difference – "Are these two the same in sound, or different?" was the first legitimate question. If they were said to be different in sound, one could then ask, "Does this difference in sound ever make a difference in meaning?" If the answer to this question was "No", then the difference was probably not a relevant one phonologically, but if the answer was "Yes", careful attention had to be paid to the other occurrences of the same difference, whether or not (in any given instance) it did make a difference in the meaning. Two separate onslaughts were made upon this principle: one by Pike in *Word*,[1] and the other by Chomsky, Halle and Lukoff in an article which may now be recognized as epoch-making.[2] Pike's article attempted to show that a more intelligent attack upon the problem of phonological distinctiveness could be achieved if the linguist made conscious use of his knowledge of morphological structure; Chomsky, Halle and Lukoff argued simply that the boundaries which were most relevant

---

[1] 3:155–72 (1947), 'Grammatical Prerequisites to Phonemic Analysis'.
[2] 'On Accent and Juncture in English' in *For Roman Jakobson* (The Hague, Mouton, 1956), pp. 65–80.

phonologically could only be determined from an examination of the syntactical surface structure, and this, in turn, was to be considered an intuitionally given fact, not subject to determination by any mechanical procedures. In essence they argued, as Chomsky has argued many times since then, that the method of discovery employed by a linguist is not relevant or subject to legislation, that the only legitimate questions which can be asked are about the correctness of the description which he finally produces, regardless of how he arrived at it. At the time this constituted a real declaration of independence, a sudden and abrupt shift of direction in linguistics, where previously the correctness of discovery procedures had been assumed to be the sole imaginable guarantee of the correctness of the results. Can we now, after this brief lapse of time, make a sound judgment about this? Perhaps not, but it is surely worth the effort. Why was such emphasis placed upon discovery and the use of rigorous principles of discovery? Beyond doubt it depended on the basic notion of replicability. If one scientist cannot duplicate the work of another with the same results, doubt may be legitimately cast upon those results. In order for the work to be replicable, it must be described in very explicit terms, and the rules to be followed must be agreed upon. All this is clearly based upon the rules for experiments in the natural sciences. Is the analysis of a language, then, analogous to an experiment or series of experiments in physics or chemistry? Or is it rather, as Chomsky seems to maintain, analogous to the formation of a hypothesis? I think we must now agree, at this distance, that Chomsky was right. A linguistic description is a hypothesis, and like hypotheses in other sciences it is of no direct relevance to its truth how it has been arrived at. Once given, it can be tested, and either accepted or rejected on the basis of suitable tests. It is these tests which are analogous to experimentation in the physical sciences, not the procedures used in forming the hypothesis originally.

But there is a good and valid model for the kind of discovery algorithm favored by the linguists of the period from 1930 to 1956, and it was undoubtedly one which had some influence on Bloomfield, at least, and probably on most of these linguists: the operational definition. Charles Sanders Peirce gave several good examples of this, most often defining minerals or simple inorganic substances. Suppose an operational definition of *water* were wanted (no doubt by a creature from outer space who had never encountered the substance); you could instruct him, if you had him in your home, let us suppose: "Go into the kitchen; locate a white depression (called 'sink') about a foot deep and two feet wide with a round hole in the bottom partly covered by some kind of shiny metal piece; note a pipe-like projection above it ('faucet') with a pair of levers near its base; turn one of them in a horizontal plane in whichever direction it will turn (clockwise or counterclockwise); note if a clear liquid then rushes out of the faucet; if not, try again; when it does, that liquid is the desired substance, water." Now just in case there might be some malevolent race who were feeding some other liquid into the water mains at that moment, further instructions might be given: "Take a sample of presumed 'water' and test for the following properties: it will dissolve sugar, salt, . . . etc.; it will extinguish a match with a hissing noise; it will freeze if cooled down below 32° F (0° C); when frozen its volume will be greater, so pieces of it placed in liquid 'water' will float; etc., etc." In case the tests all fail, then instructions must be given on where to go for another sample – perhaps to the rain-spout on a very rainy day – and then the tests must be applied again; eventually, in principle, the Martian is bound to come up with an indubitable sample of water and be certain that it is water.

What would a linguistic analogy be? Perhaps something like this, for enabling the Martian to identify a sample of the English phone or phoneme /p/: "First observe an English-speaker talking (while simultaneously recording his speech and his actions on television tape and the functioning of vocal cords, movement of air from nostrils or mouth, and other movements as well with some sort of recording apparatus for instant replay); watch until he closes his lips completely for a brief moment (2 to 5 centiseconds, generally); replay this bit and check that no air is coming from nostrils and the vocal cords are not vibrating during most or all of this closed-mouth period; if both tests are met, and if the vocal cords are vibrating immediately before or immediately after this mouth-closure, so that the sound appears to be either cut off or abruptly begun by it, then you have located a specimen of /p/." This is, of course, greatly simplified, and the instructions would have to be made considerably more explicit to work properly, but something of this sort could be done. But note that the man who is making up the instructions for the Martian himself knows perfectly well (we hope) what a /p/ is and can identify one instantly when he hears it, just as he knows in advance what water is and can identify a specimen of it, in the ordinary run of things, almost instantly.

Can we devise a mineralogical or chemical equivalent of a discovery algorithm for the phonemes of a language? Not very easily; perhaps something like this would do: given a large pile of mixed sand containing a considerable but unknown variety of simple and compound inorganic substances, write a procedure which would enable (let us say) an ancient Greek or Roman to *discover for himself* all the relevant facts of inorganic chemistry and identify and measure the quantity of every chemical element present in the pile, without giving away to him any chemical information, or not more than some very general statement such as "There are less than a hundred irreducible elementary substances present in this pile or any other such pile". Is such an algorithm utterly outside the realm of possibility? I think not, once a certain looseness and vagueness of specification is cleared up in the right way. But certainly it would be difficult, essentially to lead a naive but intelligent man to recapitulate in a brief space of time the entire development of chemical science over several centuries.

All this is based on the supposition that a phoneme discovery algorithm starting from scratch is what people had in mind. Suppose, instead, that we seek a somewhat more modest algorithm, one which takes as given a fully segmented sample of speech (as large as you please) and will take any pair of segments and answer the question "Are these two segments phonemically different?" Perhaps the program requires two stages: (1) "Are these two segments instances of the same sound?" and (2) "Are these two sounds phonemically different?" Certainly some of the classical proposals for phonemic analysis were designed on some such model as this. Is this also related to operational definition? Tests very like this one often form a part of the second stage of any operational definition; indeed one can easily convert this procedure into an operational definition by saying, "Given a segmented corpus, classify all segments by successive applications of the 'phonemically different' test; the result will be a number of classes such that the members of each class are not phonemically different from each other, but are distinct from the members of all other classes. Then each such class is a phoneme. (e.g. /x/) and each member of it an instance or token of the phoneme /x/." A close analog of such a procedure is not too hard to construct in Peirce's favorite realm, though botany might be better if we assume clear-cut species only: "Given a large collection of plants, compare them pair-wise to detect specific differences; each class of plants no member of which differs specifically from any other member of the same class, but each of which does so differ from all other plants constitutes a species." The difficulty here is the same as in the case of the phoneme; how does one determine which differences are specific (phonemic) and which sub-specific (sub-phonemic)? We will return to this question in a later chapter; but now it is time to abandon this line of discussion and get back to the injunction against level-mixing which started us off.

It was the notion of Trager and Smith that once a corpus had been segmented and classified phonemically in this manner it could be represented as a sequence of phonemes, and that a similar procedure could then be applied to recurrent phoneme sequences by which they could be classified into morphs and later into morphemes by different but analogous procedures answering the question "Is this pair of morphs morphemically different?" The injunction against mixing levels, then, states that it is never necessary to know the outcome of the morpheme-classification algorithm before making decisions in the phoneme-classifying tests; if it were, we should be caught in a vicious circle, because we must have the strings of phonemes before we can group them into morphs to be classified into morphemes. No one seems to have ever proposed that the circularity be evaded by inserting the morph-and-morpheme routines in between the phone-classification routine (our stage 1) and the phoneme routine (stage 2). And yet there seems to be no obvious reason why such an ordering of algorithms could not work as well (or as badly) as the one favored by Trager and other contemporary linguists. And if this ordering is adopted, then morphemic evidence could easily be used in the phonemic tests. We shall return to this matter in a later chapter; here we must note that there does seem to be a partial similarity between this use of the term 'level' and the ones we have spoken of earlier. The level of morphemic analysis, though approached from the opposite direction, seems to correspond in some way to Chomsky's lexicon along with some of the phonological (morphophonemic) rules, and very closely to Lamb's morphemic stratum; even in systems like Halliday's or Pike's where nothing corresponds precisely, the *difference* between this level and the 'level of phonemic analysis' finds its match.

It has often been pointed out that certain sets of grammatical facts or rules form such neat and self-contained little sub-routines that they may very easily be detached from the rest of the grammar and considered in isolation. The most familiar of these, perhaps, is the set of rules and lists designed to specify all the case forms of nouns in Latin or Greek or Sanskrit. In such a sub-grammar one may use rules which could not occur at all in a complete grammar, e.g.:

(8-2)   1. Noun→Nst^No^Ca
            2. No→Sg, Pl
            3. Ca→Nom, Gen, Dat, Abl, Acc, Voc.

Here the first rule is mildly unlikely to occur in a full grammar, though some linguists might include such a rule solely in order to establish a node for 'case', and the third rule simply could not occur, since it implies that there is a free choice of case, whereas in a sentence-grammar case is always predetermined by the context or the operation of a syntactic rule. Is there any utility to such sub-grammars? Of course exercises based upon them are no doubt of some value in second language instruction, but do they correspond to any feature of linguistic competence? Here it will not do to investigate cultures where public education is well established, since in most such countries school children are given formal instruction in exactly such exercises (a practice established by the ancient Greeks and continued by the Romans). Once again what little evidence we have is anecdotal. Many linguists report that when they were eliciting paradigms (verb-systems more often than declensions, of course) their more intelligent informants quickly grasped what was wanted and proceeded to reel off complete paradigmatic sets in some sort of systematic order. The evidence in this form is probably unreliable, but if some sort of experimental procedure could be established and communicated quickly to field linguists in places like New Guinea where unschooled natives still speak elaborately inflected languages, it might be possible to collect some better testimony. If true, what would it show? Presumably the existence of well-worn associational (analogical) paths linking the various related forms together, and providing one of the search and retrieval techniques which must be under extremely rapid control by every fluent speaker. These paths are the native speaker's equivalent of the dull student's search in dictionary (for morphophonemic classification "what declension is it?") and grammar (to run down the paradigm and determine the correct form).

Besides declensions and conjugations there is one other such subgrammar that is often discussed,[1] that which will produce all the expressions for cardinal or natural numbers up to a certain point (no natural language, curiously enough, seems to have a built-in device – e.g. a

---

[1] See, e.g., in the first issue of *Foundations of Language* (1965), articles by A. Van Katwijk (51–8) and H. Brandt Corstius (59–62).

suffix meaning 'exponent' – to generate numbers without limit, though the limit is often very high). If the largest possible number in a given language is 10 or less, then no sub-grammar is likely to exist, but where millions are discussable, there one can spell out an algorithm.

A similar sub-grammar generates arithmetical sentences:

(8-3)

$$X + \left\{ \begin{array}{c} \text{times, minus} \\ \text{over} \\ \text{divided by} \\ \text{and, plus} \\ \text{from, to the} \end{array} \right\} + Y + (\text{Neg}) + \left\{ \begin{array}{c} \text{makes} \\ \text{gives} \\ \text{equals} \\ \text{is} \end{array} \right\} + Z(+Q).$$

Only a few modifications of the basic pattern are possible:

(8-4)

$$\text{If you} + \left[\begin{array}{c} \left\{ \begin{array}{c} \text{multiply} \\ \text{divide} \end{array} \right\} \\ \text{add} \\ \text{subtract} \\ \text{raise} \end{array} \right] + X + \left[\begin{array}{c} \text{by} \\ \text{to} \\ \text{from} \\ \text{to the} \end{array} \right] + Y,$$

$$+ \left[\begin{array}{c} \text{the} \left\{ \begin{array}{c} \text{answer} \\ \text{result} \end{array} \right\} \text{is} \\ \text{you get} \end{array} \right] + Z \ (+Q),$$

for instance, or

(8-5)

$$\text{The} + \left[\begin{array}{c} \text{quotient} \\ \text{sum} \\ \text{product} \\ \text{difference} \end{array} \right] + \left[\begin{array}{c} \text{of} \\ \text{of} \\ \text{of} \\ \text{between} \end{array} \right] + X + \left[\begin{array}{c} \text{divided by, over} \\ \text{and} \\ \text{and, times} \\ \text{and} \end{array} \right] + Y + \text{is}$$

$$(+ \text{ not}) \ Z \ (+ \ Q).$$

Sentences produced by this sub-grammar can enter into the general grammar by way of certain embeddings and shifts: e.g. they can be quoted, linked to each other by conditions or causal or concessive clauses, and so on in a limited way, but nothing much in the way of complements or modifiers can be inserted in them, nor can they, except for the verbs of 8-4 (*multiply, divide,* etc.) be made into direct commands (even if you can imagine giving orders to a number: *"Five! be three plus three!"), although they may be made into suppositions ("Let A + B be C" or "Suppose that A minus B equals C").

Such sub-grammars as these may be incorporated whole, as they stand, into the main sentence grammar, but they have little or no need of its base rules – indeed not much above morphophonemics

$$\text{(e.g. five} \rightarrow \text{fif-/}\_\_\_ \left\{ \begin{array}{l} \text{-ty} \\ \text{-teen or } one + teen \rightarrow eleven, \text{ etc.)} \\ \text{-th} \end{array} \right.$$

in short they are semi-independent.

Some years ago[1] I suggested that several modes of word-formation might well be regarded as little sub-grammars of a similar sort. So a large number of phonaesthetic words (to use Firth's name), words involving sound symbolism, ideophones (in part), can be generated by the following rules.

1. $W \rightarrow C_1 + V + C_2 \ (+l,r)$.
2. $V \rightarrow a, e, i, o, \mathfrak{o}$
   (i.e. the short vowels of pat, pet, pit, putt, and pot – but not put).
3. $C_1 \rightarrow C, (s) + (K) + L, s \left\{ \begin{array}{l} m \\ n \end{array} \right\}$
   (where C is any English consonant except z, ŋ, ð, K is ptkbdgfθ and L is lrw. Co-occurrence restrictions are as in English words generally.)
4. $C_2 \rightarrow f, š, (N) + \left\{ \begin{array}{l} ptkč \\ bdgǰ \end{array} \right\}$
   (N is the homorganic nasal).
5. $W \Rightarrow W + W$
   (once only. Any W may be repeated. This is a transformation.)
6. $X_1V_1Y_1 + X_1V_1Y_1 \Rightarrow X_1iY_1 + X_1AY_1$
   (A = a, o, ɔ. This is an optional transformation to yield sets like zig zag, ding dong, etc.)
7. $X \begin{bmatrix} l \\ r \end{bmatrix} V X \begin{bmatrix} l \\ r \end{bmatrix} \Rightarrow X \begin{bmatrix} l \\ r \end{bmatrix} V X \begin{bmatrix} r \\ l \end{bmatrix}$
   (i.e. two l's or r's dissimilate.)

These rules are, of course, incomplete, probably contain some errors, and need additional restrictions, to exclude (e.g.) forms ending in -nĵl or -nrĵ and maybe even -nĵ. And there are undoubtedly a few good phonaesthetic words which don't fit this pattern. But the general structure is clear, and if anyone coined an expression /kronk/ or /blagr/

---

[1] In 'On Linguistic Primes', *Word* 15:231–9 (1959). For a similar portion of Azerbaijani, see *American Studies in Altaic Linguistics* (Bloomington, 1962), pp. 115–22.

and used it in the right type of context,[1] none of his listeners would be particularly surprised – as they might be if, instead, he used a word like /spe·jn/ in the same context. Such a sub-grammar would correspond to two abilities exercised by native speakers: (1) the ability to coin such expressive words on rare occasions; (2) the ability to classify words heard from others for the first time as being potentially expressive. Hundreds of perfectly ordinary non-expressive words also fit these patterns. A third ability has not been taken care of in these rules, but could be: the assignment of potential meaning, partly by choice of C_1, partly by choice of V and partly by choice of C_2. Certain combinations may perhaps be semantically incompatible, i.e. necessarily non-expressive.

In the same article I noted the ease with which a small sub-grammar could generate Latinate vocabulary (i.e. words like *produce, induce, refer, defer, desist, persist*, etc.); in general a large part of the devices available in any language for the formation of compounds and derivatives can be taken aside, and made into a number of small, self-contained grammarlets. But such grammarlets cannot be independent in the sense in which phonology is independent of syntax; each one must include its own set of morphophonemic-phonological rules, and (if meanings are to be assigned) its own set of semantic rules. In the case of the phonaesthetic grammaticule, these semantic rules are undoubtedly special and vaguer than semantic rules in the sentence-grammar. For compounds Lees[2] did not specify semantic rules, but the line of generation which he followed was designed to provide a distinct source for every possible interpretation of each compound; that is, he attributed all uncertainty here to genuine *ambiguity* (with a definite listable set of interpretations) rather than to *vagueness* (where the discreteness of interpretations is not presumed). Of course, it is possible that we have both vagueness and ambiguity, i.e. a small number of distinct sources, each of which is inherently vague in certain respects. The same would seem to be often true of derivational properties. Instead of a series of special verbal features ([+remove], [+attach], [+seek as food], [+transport], etc.) being distinct (ambiguous) zero verbalizers attached to English nouns, perhaps there is only one such (vague) feature [+relevant action]. The relevant action involving *skin* and *deer* is removal, for *shingle* and *house* it is attachment,

---

[1] A detailed specification of appropriate contexts for such words is beyond our scope here, but in a general way they would be colloquial, affective, imprecise, concerned especially with noises, movements, speaking, insults, etc., such that the communicative burden of the word itself is minimal.

[2] R. B. Lees, *The Grammar of English Nominalizations* (Bloomington, Indiana, 1960).

for *fish* or *berry* it is hunting and gathering, for *truck* or *cart* with *logs* or *stones* it is transportation. In a very few cases there may be more than one relevant action: "He stoned them" might mean "pelted the men with stones" or "lined the wells with stones", and "We shelled them" could be "We removed their shells" or "We fired shells at them", and "String them" may mean "Remove the strings from these beans" or "Insert strings in these rackets, bows or violins". Rarely the same objects may be involved in two different ways, as "He spotted the coat" may refer to a child accidentally putting spots on, or to a cleaner taking spots off (to say nothing of the detective spying the stolen stole).

Besides looking at levels and components from the point of view of a speaker or in the ideal purity of linguistic theory, it is also possible to appreciate the matter from the vantage of a hearer, for whom there are three typical situations. (1) When you are told the wholly unmotivated local dialect word for such-and-such a piece of harness (say it is */floč/, *flutch) or an equally arbitrary family name (perhaps */grɔist/ *Groist), you hear it solely in terms of phonology. (2) When you learn a partly new word or a new combination of old morphic elements (not necessarily morphemes, or meaning-preserving), say */θwaklbery/ *thwackleberry (which is, let us say, the name of a berry), or */hwipstod/ *whipstud (which is, perhaps, the name of a wildflower and has no connection with whips or studs) then you hear in terms of morphs, the larger chunks of pure phonological material about which you know only that they must mean something, though you may make partially correct guesses about what they mean. Much the same thing is true of family names like */giːzlsn/ *Geezleson, or place names like */teːbltn/ *Tableton, except that there is no meaning to guess. *Each language seems to have a definite (if large) store of morphs, phonological shapes to which various functions or meanings may be attached, and this store changes only slowly.* (3) But when you hear an ordinary sentence built entirely of familiar lexical items in familiar patterns, then you are hearing in terms of morphemes, words, phrases and the like – so much so that you may not even notice quite scandalous distortion, which would render a type 1 situation (wholly new) hopeless and often lead to error in type 2 (partly new). The 'redundancy', as they say, is very high in most cases, so that a *phonological* misunderstanding is relatively rare ("Did you say you bought the baby a bassinet or a Bathinette"), though lexical or structural ambiguity is not so unlikely. In such rare cases, the hearer is abruptly shifted into a type 2 or type 1 mode of operation momentarily.

Let us try to sum up. There are in all languages rules of structure and distribution to which the *meaning and use* of the forms are *irrelevant* and other rules which are *closely related* to the meaning and use of forms. This corresponds well to the general distinction between phonology and the rest of grammar (sometimes called 'grammar' *par excellence* and opposed to phonology). Is there also a distinction between rules for which the *surface structure* is irrelevant, and those for which both meaning and form are relevant? We suggested above that this was so, that the purely semantic-syntactic or deep structure rules illustrated the former class, while the so-called transformational, lexical and morphophonemic rules represented the latter. The question still remains open whether pure deep structure is linguistic (i.e. varies from language to language) or non-linguistic (i.e. logically rather than accidentally universal). These are the distinct structural levels, and grammatical components producing or linking them are essential. The possible sub-grammars which we mentioned are not levels in any sense, nor components in the same sentence-grammar, though they do often show clearly some of the effects of levels. In Austin's terminology[1] the phonological component is relevant to the *phonetic* act, the morphological (and in part the syntactic) to the *phatic* act, and the semantic-syntactic to the *rhetic* act, all of which together make a *locutionary* (as opposed to *illocutionary* and *perlocutionary*) act.

[1] *How To Do Things With Words*, p. 95.

9 Phonemes and distinctive features: I

Whether or not you believe that phonological structure[1] is in some way independent of semantic-syntactic-morphological structure, you cannot doubt that it exists, for any normal spoken language; and if beings on another planet communicate by manipulating radio waves or smells, they will have some counterpart of phonological structure in their special sensory domain. Motivations for the study of phonology are various, but for centuries the principal reason has been to arrive at a permanent visual representation which is relatively unambiguous and can be linked to the phonological data by relatively simple rules. In another chapter we will say more about writing, but here let us concentrate on one type of representation, that which aims at (1) bi-uniqueness of segmental representation – i.e. "one sound, one symbol" – allowing anyone who knows the system to *write* down whatever he hears (whether or not he understands it) and *read* it back with minimal distortion, so that any competent speaker of the language who could understand the original utterance would also understand this rendition; and (2) stability of morphic (as opposed to morphemic) shape, permitting accuracy of representation of the sound to be sacrificed, on occasion, to consistency of spelling. This is a kind of morphic bi-uniqueness, so that (e.g.) *says* is written like *say* plus *s*, even though it rhymes not with *haze* but with *fez*. Obviously these two principles clash, and all practical systems of writing have adopted various kinds of *ad hoc* compromises, now favoring segmental accuracy, now morphic consistency. Nowadays linguists make a strong effort to keep both principles by having two systems of representation linked by a series of rules. But in this chapter it is mostly the segmental system – not the morphic one – that will concern us.

---

[1] Please remember that this chapter (like the rest of the book) was originally written without access to three books which are now all available: P. Lieberman, *Intonation, Perception and Language* (Research Monograph No. 38) Cambridge, Mass., M.I.T. Press, 1967; Paul Postal, *Aspects of Phonological Theory*, New York, Harper and Row, 1968; and N. Chomsky and M. Halle, *Sound Pattern of English*, New York, Harper and Row, 1968, referred to as *SPE*. See also W. L. Chafe, 'The Ordering of Phonological Rules', and W. S-Y. Wang, 'Competing Changes as a Cause of Residue', *POLA Reports* 2nd series, No. 2, October 1967.

F

The principle of bi-uniqueness forces the inventor of writing to practice a kind of economy of symbols, so that if he can't *hear* a distinction between some class of utterance-pairs, he can't *write* one, and if he *does* consistently hear a distinction, he must write it or fail the read-back test. All or nearly all systems tolerate some ambiguity for the sake of economy, an ambiguity which is seldom important because of the redundancy of language. Bi-uniqueness, in other words, is most usually violated in the direction of representing distinct utterances as if they were the same, spelling different sounds the same way. But several early Mediterranean alphabets have examples of the opposite defect (if you so regard it), writing (e.g.) Q before O and U, K before all other letters (only and always). This does not mean that Q and K did not perhaps correspond to sounds which could be distinguished by a competent speaker of the language if it were desired, but only that no speaker ever needed to be able to discriminate them. And what we don't *have* to do, we generally don't do, and often *can't* do without special effort of some kind.

Thus the earliest and perhaps still the primary function of phonemic analysis (to use a name from the 1940s) is to provide the base for an efficient writing system, one that is easy for native speakers to learn, easy to write and easy to read. In some nineteenth century instances, missionaries devised writing systems which were easy for them to use, but hard for the natives because they attended to distinctions which are significant in English (say) but irrelevant in the other language. If such a system ever catches on and is put to regular use by the natives on their own, then the irrelevant distinction is either dropped or handled by a predictable spelling rule (of the 'i before e except after c' variety) so that the two representations are, as it were, allographs of one grapheme, combinatory variants.

Now since an efficient writing system should represent units which are somehow natural in the language, linguists readily took the next step of asking for the nature of the 'psychological reality of the phoneme', speculating on the entity in speakers' brains which corresponds to the single phonemic representation. The first answer, of course, is that phonetic similarity provides the required unity; this seems to have been the ancient Indian view, the Greek view, and the medieval view as well, so that it was quite natural for it to become the prevailing view among nineteenth century linguists and phoneticians (and, in part the justification for the existence of phoneticians). The implied assumption is something like this: human speech organs can produce a large number of sounds, but these are assignable to a relatively small (200 at most) number of distinct types; in every language the distinguishable and significant types are all identifiable with types from this basic list, or sometimes with small sets (couples or triples) of these types; an ideal international alphabet will provide one symbol for each of these types, so that two people knowing the alphabet can correctly write and read (aloud) utterances in any language. For practical orthographies, types never distinguished by the native speaker need not be distinguished in writing, but a scientific transcription will always distinguish all types. This attractive assumption is the basis of the high development of phonetics, particularly in Europe, where its influence and prestige are still quite high. But, as more languages were studied, more types had to be distinguished, so that the small basic alphabet had to grow and grow. Given a type A and a type B, it happened again and again that both had to be split into A_1, A_2, B_1 and B_2, because, besides the languages for which A (i.e. A_1 plus A_2) and B (i.e. B_1 plus B_2) were valid types, there were others where 1 (i.e. A_1 plus B_1) and 2 (A_2 plus B_2) were the identifiable types. In the case of the consonants this process was not so important as the mere discovery of new types (made by articulations which the earlier phoneticians had never even thought of), but the two processes together ran the number up into the thousands, which made the procedure seem difficult if not infeasible.

From the earliest times, again, it had been recognized (a) that the types were not all totally dissimilar and unrelated, but fell easily into *classes* marked by perceptible qualities or *features*, and (b) that there were (in many languages) some such qualities which, though relevant, could easily be ignored for economy's sake.

First (a). The Greeks classified their consonants very much as we do: they gave names to the stops, and separately to the voiced stops, the plain voiceless stops and the aspirated (voiceless) stops, to liquids, nasals and to sibilant(s). The classification of voiced stops and of nasals appears to have been made already by the Semitic speakers from whom the Greeks got their alphabet: the second, third and fourth letters are B, G, D, and two consecutive letters along in the middle are M, N. Classes and features are, of course, two nearly equivalent expressions: from one point of view a class of stops is the same as a stop feature, and so on down the line. Only in the case of aspiration did they actually make use of this way of talking, because of the fact that when a vowel is elided before /h/, a preceding plain voiceless stop combines with the h to become an aspirate.

The Indians had an even more regular and symmetrical classification of consonants than the Greeks (partly because they had more consonants and more classes, partly because the earliest phonologists hated to see an empty hole in the grid), with specific words for many classes, and an alphabetical order wholly based on this classification. Features are used in several rules, particularly voicing, aspiration, retroflexion and palatalization.

Now (b). Perhaps the most frequently ignored features (though even these are sometimes redundantly written) are those of tone or accent, and length, so that for some linguists these are the prosodic features par excellence. Length of vowels was rarely indicated in Latin (whether by diacritics or by doubling), and only coincidentally in Greek (two long vowels happened to be qualitatively quite distinct in Attic-Ionic). Linear B, like the Cypriote syllabary, has no convention for indicating length, nor do many of the systems derived from the Semitic. Exceptionally the Indian scripts (Devanagari, etc.) do mark long vowels – but not vowel length as a separable feature. No alphabetic or syllabic script of Europe or India marked tone as a regular thing; systems were devised for Greek and for Sanskrit (mainly Vedic), but otherwise only a few modern systems indicate accent. On a smaller scale nasalization of vowels fairly often goes unmarked, as well as (more rarely) contrasts like laxity and front vs. back (e.g. in Arabic writing of Turkic languages).

Aspiration and voicing are probably the most frequently omitted features of the 'non-prosodic' set. Neither is indicated in younger runes, in Cypriote or in Linear B except for /d/ as opposed to /t/, /th/, an opposition of frequent relevance or functional yield. Early Greek alphabets often ignored aspiration, and several alphabets of Italy ignore voicing in some cases – *perhaps* because Etruscan had no voicing opposition. Hieroglyphic Hittite ignores voicing. This feature was marked by a diacritic in some Southeast Asian scripts, a diacritic which (like others elsewhere) was often omitted. A similar development has been noted in some syllabaries devised for native American languages. Finally, the kinship of liquids (the various kinds of l's and r's) is often noted by a failure to distinguish in writing, e.g. in Linear B where the same series of five signs serves for ra, re, ri, ro, ru and la, le, li, lo, lu. Do not forget that in all the cases mentioned here the distinction that was not noted is one which was an essential (phonemic) distinction in the languages in question. So, in English, the contrast of voicing is never marked for /θ/ as opposed to /ð/, except in a limited way (e.g. initial *th* must be /θ/ unless the word is pronominal; in Greek loans *th* is regularly /θ/; otherwise intervocalic *th* will be /ð/, even if the second vowel is a 'silent e'), and is sometimes indeterminate for /s/ opposed to /z/ (e.g. *loose* is /luːs/ but *choose* is /čuːz/).

Note that what is recognized here is *similarity of the differences* between sounds which contrast. When, for instance, p, b and pʰ are all represented by the same sign or set of signs (as in Linear B), this is a recognition that they are all *labial* stops (as opposed, e.g., to velar or dental stops), as well as a kind of deliberate ignoring of the ways in which they differ (voicing and aspiration). Interestingly enough, there seems to be no case where the difference between p and t or t and k or b and g is deliberately disregarded, though there are a few cases of partial non-representation of contrast between velar and palatal k's (e.g. in the romanization of Azerbaijani used before 1940 in the Soviet Union). Nor is it easy to find a clear case of suppression of a stop-fricative contrast (e.g. between p and f or k and x), though the similarity of Devanagari signs for *b* and *v* suggests that India might be a place to look.

The phonemic features which are most often ignored by conventional writing-systems then, are the following: for consonants, *voicing, aspiration, palatalization, gemination* (or *length*), *lateral* vs. *trill* (or whatever the essential base of the l-r opposition may be); for vowels, *length, nasality, diphthongization* (e.g. a vs. ai, as in Linear B), and *tone* or *accent*. Some cases exist of ignoring the contrast syllabic vs. non-syllabic (e.g. i vs. y), but usually it can be argued that the difference is predictable, hence non-phonemic. However, in Latin, *volvit* 'he rolls' and *voluit* 'he wished', though differing as dissyllabic vs. trisyllabic, were both normally written VOLVIT by the Romans.

Oppositions which seem to have been seldom or never ignored are those of stop or fricative apical vs. labial vs. dorsal articulation (i.e. t, p, k), stop vs. fricative,[1] stop vs. nasal (i.e. b vs. m), stop vs. liquid (d vs. l or r), stop vs. glide (b vs. w), nasal vs. glide (m vs. w; though there are languages like Hidatsa in which these are not phonemically distinct), nasal vs. liquid (n vs. r; Egyptian may be an exception,

---

[1] Except in the younger futhark. See the excellent article by Jørgen Rischel, *Phoneme, Grapheme, and the 'Importance' of Distinctions*, published as Interim Report No. 1 of the Research Group for Quantitative Linguistics (KVAL PM 260), no date (but probably about 1967), for an account of the nature of the oppositions ignored in this writing system.

though some scholars believe that at least one dialect – like Hidatsa again – did not distinguish the two), sibilant vs. non-sibilant (s vs. θ), and several more; among vowels, low vs. high (a vs. i or ɯ), except in scripts which ignore vowels entirely, like the basic Semitic script from which all alphabets are derived.

We should not overlook the fact that when Linear B, for instance, uses the same five symbols for long or short pa = ba = pha, pe = be = phe, pi = bi = phi, po = bo = pho, pu = bu = phu (not to mention pa = pai = bai = phai, pe = pei = bei = phei, po = poi = boi = phoi and pa = spa, pe = spe, pi = spi, po = spo, pu = spu) it is using one type of economy, one which has seemed universally a more obvious type than the Semitic device of using the same three symbols for (let us suppose) p = pa = pi = pu, b = ba = bi = bu, ph = pha = phi = phu, even though it was only the Semitic economy which led to the device of using two (or more) letters per syllable, of which one represents a consonant and the other a vowel. The most natural form of segmentation seems to be everywhere syllabic[1] (i.e. include a following vowel, if there is one, with each consonant) rather than segmental (consonant-vowel), and it is more natural to abstract features from the vowel and consonant portions of the syllable (for economy's sake) than it is to separate the two segments.

The degree of classification or feature specification represented by the efforts of ancient grammarians and reflected in writing practices is essentially what was used by linguists down through the nineteenth century and into the twentieth. The phoneticians of the late nineteenth and early twentieth century indeed introduced refinements, but mainly in the way of phonetic detail. The study of new languages, especially in Africa and America, added to the list of ignorable features (e.g. glottalization) and absolute types (e.g. clicks; a click is not *minimally* different from *any* non-click), but the essential framework was not affected. Then Trubetzkoy attempted a codification of this basic phonological framework, inspired in part by the various attempts (in Prague and elsewhere) to refine the relatively new term 'phoneme', basing many decisions on broader evidence than had previously been used. We may have to say something more about Trubetzkoy's *phoneme*

---

[1] A syllabic script is not one which has only as many symbols as there are vowels in a word, but more nearly one which has as many symbols as there are consonants. A word like English *strength* for instance, would not be written with one symbol but with at least *three*: one for the *t*, one for the *reng*, and one for the *-th*, and might use five: s-t-re-ng-th.

(essentially also the phoneme of standard average American linguistics for several decades), but let us now turn to the strange case of Roman Jakobson. Jakobson made three basic assumptions and shook the faith of many men. These assumptions were: (1) all phonological oppositions are privative (where for Trubetzkoy only some were); (2) since speech is transmitted acoustically, the oppositions are basically acoustic and should be renamed accordingly; (3) since some oppositions (as previously named) apply only to vowels, and some only to consonants, perhaps if we switch from articulation to acoustics we can determine them to be the same.[1] Let us discuss these assumptions and their consequences a little more fully.

(1) All oppositions are privative.[2] This meant not only that they are all binary, but that one term (and always the same one) of the opposition is 'marked', the other 'unmarked'. And 'unmarked' implies *not* the absence of the feature in question, but its complete indeterminacy – it may or may not be absent. The notation used in *Preliminaries* and now very widespread has + for the marked member and − for the unmarked member.[3] This distinction implies a procedure for discovering which term, in any given case, is marked. The first and principal test was neutralization; whichever member stands for both in positions of neutralization is the unmarked (−) member. Furthermore, the unmarked member should allow a wider range of free variation (in the general direction of the marked member). So non-nasal vowels may have a considerable amount of irrelevant nasalization, but a phonemically nasalized vowel cannot drop below a rather high minimum of nasality.

---

[1] For the first point see especially the opening paragraph of *Zur Struktur des russischen Verbums*, reprinted in Vachek's *Prague School Reader in Linguistics* (Indiana, 1964), p. 347, as well as in *Readings in Linguistics* II (Chicago, 1966), p. 22. For the others, read the earlier pieces in Jakobson's *Collected Works*, vol. I.

[2] Jakobson seems to have altered his view on this point later, allowing both privative and polar oppositions, and even that the minus member of an opposition necessarily lacks the feature.

[3] For a different (and now orthodox) use of the notion of markedness, see *SPE*, 402–35. In the Chomsky–Halle theory the values ('coefficients', 'specifications') + and − of any feature are unordered – i.e. it seems to be entirely arbitrary which is called by which name. Thus [+Voiced] and [−Voiceless] are equally good names. But the values m and u (for *marked* and *unmarked*) are not used in exactly the same way as Prague + and −, since m may end up as either a + *or* a −, and so may u. This is a distinct advantage for handling the difference between intervocalic position and utterance–final position, for instance, with regard to voicing. A theory which allowed m to become either + or −, but u to become − only would again imply a distinction between the terms such as we assume here. See also B. Mohr and W. S-Y. Wang, 'Perceptual distance and the specification of phonological features' (perceptual tests for markedness), *POLA Reports* 2nd series, No. 1, September 1967.

The marked member should be further from a neutral acoustic quality and a neutral position of the articulators. Finally, in any language where the opposition in question is firmly established (not just coming in or dying out), the unmarked member should be statistically more frequent in random samples of running speech. By inverting Zipf's law we should be able to infer from its frequency rank order the approximate number of oppositions for which a phoneme is marked.

(2–3) The oppositions are basically acoustic. The great virtue of this principle was to allow the identification of features articulated in quite different ways as being really the same. The most celebrated example of this is the identification of dorsal articulation of consonants (i.e. velar or palatal stops and fricatives) with maximally open articulation of vowels (i.e. [a] [æ], [ɑ], etc.) under the label *compact* (since 1951; before that called *chromatic, farbig,* or *saturated*). The subconscious motivation for this no doubt goes somewhat as follows: "the minimal stops are p t k, the minimal vowels are u i a; we can see a labial similarity between p and u, and the tongue-tip is up for i and t and down for a and k." Now the odd thing about this is that it is very easy to progress from k to a vowel (though not so easy from p or t), via g, ɣ, and finally ɯ, and it is also easy to go from i and u to stops, via fricative y, front g' and k' in the first case, ɣ^w, g^w and k^w (a labialized velar stop) in the second case, but /a/ fits nowhere in these schemes. Clearly *all* dorsal consonants are closely related to high vowels – and high vowels were regarded by Jakobson as *diffuse* (*diluted*) or *non-compact* (i.e. unmarked for compactness) and later by Halle as *diffuse* (marked for diffuseness). So Jakobson's brilliant stroke led to an identification of opposites in the case of a and k. This makes no difference for rule-writing, since dissimilation is exactly as economical to write as assimilation; e.g. [anything] → [α feature]/____[α feature] is an assimilating rule, but →[– α feature] is a dissimilating rule.

The other effect of this principle was to introduce a series of novel terms for old oppositions: 'grave' and 'acute' (earlier 'dark' vs. 'bright') for back vs. front (vowels) and non-apical vs. apical (consonants), 'flat' versus 'plain' for rounded vs. unrounded (later 'pharyngealized' was also added to the domain of 'flat') – especially confusing since in a vague associational way 'flat' seems the opposite of 'round' – 'sharp' for palatalized, and 'strident' vs. 'mellow' for (a) sibilant vs. non-sibilant, (b) loud friction vs. weak friction (an unfortunately indeterminate criterion), and (c) affricate vs. plain stop. Most of the other features retained older names which were specifically articulatory: consonantal–vocalic (later split into consonantal–non-consonantal, vocalic–non-vocalic), voiced–voiceless, continuant–intercepted (or interrupted), nasal–oral, tense-lax.[1]

(3) The cases of identification of vocalic with consonantal features included, besides the *compactness* example just discussed, also *gravity*, which, for vowels, means back articulation or a low second formant (below 1,200 Hz or so), while for consonants it means non-apical (also non-laminal, i.e. not articulated with the front part of the tongue), with a relatively low burst (if any) and low extrapolated F_2 (a bit vague, since some k's overlap with some t's in this regard). It is unfortunate that, for consonants, only F_2 is available to specify both *compactness* and *gravity*, except for some small relevance of F_3. *Flatness* was generally applied only to vowels, but was also available for labialized consonants. However, in the paper (written jointly with John Lotz) called 'Notes on the French Phonemic Pattern',[2] Jakobson did not use the feature *flat* to identify the front rounded vowels; instead they were marked as $\pm$ (called 'complex') for gravity, as if they were central vowels, neither front nor back but halfway between. This notation was also used for two other purposes; /r/ and /l/ were so marked for the feature *vocality* (i.e halfway between consonant and vowel) and the mid vowels /e/, /ê/, /E/ (a neutralization vowel or 'archiphoneme'), /o/ and /ô/, as well as the nasalized /E/ and /O/, are treated as $\pm$ for saturation (compactness), i.e. as halfway between open and closed or high and low. In terms of F_1 position, this is certainly correct: a high vowel (e.g. /i/) has an F_1 generally under 400 Hz, a low vowel like /a/ has an F_1 over 700 Hz as a rule (for men), while the mid vowels have F_1 values somewhere in between. Later treatments by Jakobson and Halle got rid of this fourth value (the other three are plus, minus and zero[3]) by the device of splitting features. Instead of Vocalic vs. Consonantal, we had Vocalic vs. Non-vocalic and Consonantal vs. Non-consonantal; in this scheme liquids could be plus for both and /h/ and /ʔ/ (called *glides* by Jakobson

---

[1] But see the article by Chin-W. Kim, 'On the Autonomy of the Tensity Feature in Stop Classification', *Word* 21:339–59 (1965).

[2] In *Word* 5:151–8 (1949).

[3] Note that there are two kinds of zeros, as Robert D. Wilson remarks in 'A criticism of Distinctive Features', *Journal of Linguistics* 2:196 (1966): *specific* (i.e. neutral or irrelevant) zeros and *universal* zeros, where other values would be either impossible or contradictory. A four-valued system is equivalent to making '+' and '−' into independent binary variables, yielding the combinations 'plus but not minus', 'plus and minus both', 'minus but not plus' and 'neither plus nor minus'.

and Chomsky and Halle, though quite unlike what most phoneticians call by that name) could be minus for both features. And by splitting Compact–Diffuse in the same way, we can make e, o, etc. – for both (+ for both would seem to be more in line with the notion of markedness discussed above, but by this time the criteria for telling which term is plus have become lost to view). Since French did not really have front, central and back rounded (or unrounded) vowels – and indeed there seems to be no language which does have three vowels at the same level which are all alike in degree of rounding – it was not necessary to split grave–acute.

Since 1964 a number of changes have been proposed which have the effect of virtually abandoning Jakobson. Of the old features, Grave, Diffuse, Sharp, Continuant, Compact and Flat are dropped entirely or renamed.[1]

Let us examine all these old and new features in some detail, to see if we can get a clear idea of whether they are privative and, if so, which term should be regarded as marked by the criteria mentioned above.

For each feature we will give a clue to its scope by listing typical phones alleged to be marked (+) for it, then the relative frequency evidence for correctness of marking ("yes" means minus items are in general more frequent, "no" means the opposite), next the neutralization evidence for correctness of marking ("yes" means the presumable neutralized case is represented by the minus member, "no" by the plus member; a blank means insufficient or contradictory evidence), then the evidence of historical change or merger if any ("yes" means the change usually goes from + to −, "no" the opposite), and finally various comments including some on utility in rules. The frequency counts most used were of English, Modern Greek, Azerbaijani, and Ancient Greek; some others are cited from an article in *IJAL* 29:93 (1957), which tabulates a number of American Indian languages, and one by Bengt Sigurd in *Phonetica* 18:1–15 (1968). (See table commencing on p. 158.)

Considering the proposed reforms (features marked *SPE*, '1967' or 'new') as a whole, it seems clear that Jakobson's original premises have been abandoned. (1) There is little concern for distinctiveness or phonemicity at all, but much for possible utility in generative rules or articulatory descriptions. The goal seems to be something vaguely akin

---

[1] For the official Chomsky–Halle discussions of features and markedness, see *SPE*, 298–329 and 402–5.

to Daniel Jones' broad phonetic transcription. (2) The notion of attaining economy by avoiding articulatory terms and using acoustic ones has been dropped. All the new terms are articulatory. (3) The notion of oppositions has almost vanished (replaced by a kind of 'additive component' theory in many cases), and with it the axiom that all oppositions are privative. (4) Although several new features seem designed mainly to provide a reversal of sign from the old ones, there is not always a clear rationale for the reversal – or for failure to reverse.

What are some of the questions which have been raised in connection with binary oppositions? (1) Are all minimal oppositions alike (whether or not they are all privative)? From Trubetzkoy to the present, many linguists have maintained that they are *not* all alike, and that they differ from one another in more than one way. We noted earlier in the chapter that certain oppositions are very commonly – almost universally in some cases – ignored in writing systems. One of these is the opposition between long and short vowels, which is in fact put into a special class by Jakobson. But in addition to this, we noted also the frequency with which the voicing opposition is ignored, and we showed earlier (in chapter 4) that voicing or the vibration of the vocal cords is one of the two fundamental carriers on which all other variations (including unvoicing) are imposed as modulations. Plainly this is a genuine privative opposition; the only caution is to distinguish those cases in which the voiced term must be considered marked from those in which the unvoiced term is marked. These features belong to the class called SGC (series-generating components) by C. F. Voegelin,[1] along with *aspiration* (also sometimes ignored in orthographies), *glottalization, prenasalization* (fairly common in several parts of the globe: sounds which are transcribed *mb, nd, ng* or the like), *implosion* (resolvable into *voicing* plus *glottalization* perhaps) and simple *nasality* (i.e. m, n, ŋ, etc.; quite important in Australia where the other SGC's are rare) and perhaps one or two more. The literature refers to these categories collectively as "manner of articulation". Affrication is often classed as a manner of articulation, but it is uncertain whether it should be treated as a clear-cut privative opposition (SGC). Very often a language has only one affricate, and its point of articulation is not the same as that of any plain stop, so that it might be considered another stop whose point of articulation necessarily (i.e. redundantly) induces affrication. There are also lan-

---

[1] Earlier called additive components, e.g. in *Word* 12:429–43 (1956). The term SGC appears in *Anthropological Linguistics* 1 (1959), No. 6.

	Relative frequency	Neutralization and range	Historical shift	Comments
1. Consonantal (originally) + all consonants and r, l − all vowels and r, l (early vocalic is simply the reverse of this)	Yes	The case is rare maybe yes in Gudschinsky's Maxakali[1]		No rules known which reverse the value of this feature; doesn't seem naturally privative.
1a. Consonantal (later) + consonants and r, l − vowels and h, ʔ, w, y	Yes	Yes		Only rarely do h and glottal stop behave like vowels.
1c. Sonorant (*SPE*) + vowels, liquids, nasals, semivowels, h and ʔ − obstruents	No	No	No	Signs seem wrong; rules changing the value of this feature from − to + are not uncommon (d→r, γ→y, etc.).
2. Vocalic (goes with 1a) + vowels, and r, l − consonants and h, ʔ, w, y	No			Neither feature 1 nor 2 will isolate the syllabic central vocoids, nearly always a necessary class.
2b. Syllabic (new)	No (i vs. y, u vs. w)			Generally redundant rather than distinctive.
3. Grave (old and new) + a, o, u, p, k, q − (Acute) æ, e, i, t, č	Yes; but in Kaiwa labial stops are the most frequent	Yes, but see comments	Yes, except Hawaiian, Samoan etc. where t→k	A single permitted final nasal is [ŋ], e.g. in some Spanish dialects, in Quechua, etc. In Bengali k is more frequent than t.
3a. Back (*SPE*) + k, q, pharyngeals, w, uvular R, back vowels − apicals, labials, y, front vowels	Yes (in general)	No	No	Sign-changing rules seem to be rare. Anterior (*SPE*) is not quite the reverse of this, being + only for labials, dentals and alveolars.

Feature				Comments
3b. Coronal (*SPE*) + t, d, n, č, ś, ţ, ţ, r, retroflex vowels − labials, dorsals, normal vowels	No (consonants). Yes (vowels)	No	No	Sign-changing rules seem to be rare.
4. Compact (old) + a, æ, α, k, č, g, š − i, u, uu, p, t, b, f, s, etc.	Yes	Yes	No (with exceptions)	Rules which apply to this feature are generally limited either to vowels only or consonants only. Final [ŋ] again, like Hawaiian k, is odd.
4a. Compact (newer) + a, æ, α − e, ε, o	No, though in Bengali e, o outnumber a	No	No	Evidently the signs are wrong.
4b. Compact (1966) + a, α, − most open vowels only − all consonants, all other vowels	No	No	No	Same comment. The class of all phonemes except /a/ is seldom useful.
4c. Low (*SPE*) + open vowels, pharyngeals, h and ʔ	No	No	No	Perhaps a little more useful than 'Compact'.
5. Diffuse (newer) + i, uu, u, ü − all other vowels (i all consonants)	No; but in Bengali e, o, are more frequent than i, u	No (usually)	No (usually)	Possibly the fully relaxed position of the mouth favors a mid vowel, rather than open or closed.

¹ S. C. Gudschinsky, Harold Popovich and Frances Popovich, 'Native reaction and phonetic similarity in Maxakali phonology', *Language* 46:77–88 (1970).

	Relative frequency	Neutralization and range	Historical shift	Comments
5a. Buccal (1967) + e, o, ö, labial and apical consonants − i, u, ü, w, y, velar and palatal consonants	No (except rarely /i/)	No	No (except Hawaiian k again)	Better reversed as [HIGH], as in *SPE*
5b. High (*SPE*) Exact reverse of 5a	Yes	No	Yes (but not common)	
6. Strident + f, s, c, v, ĵ, ř − φ, θ, t, β, d, r	No, except for stops as opposed to affricates	No, (again excepting stops)	Usually the reverse (e.g. θ→f, β→v, etc.)	For languages in which only one or two consonants are [+ strident], the feature has some utility. Probably this should be split so that affricates are [+], but not f, s, v, etc.
6a. Secondary (1967) + f, s, š, c, t, q, ř, v − φ, θ, t, k, r, s, β	No	No	Usually no	Almost the same mixture as the old [strident]. Notice that here, too, /f/ and /θ/ must differ by at least two features, though maximally similar to the ear.
6b. Distributed (*SPE*) + š, č, t′, ž, p, φ − s, c, t, z, f	Yes	Yes (often)	Examples are few	Defined as having a longer area of contact.
7. Voiced (as usually understood)	Intervocalically, No; Initially, or finally, Yes	Intervocalically, No; Initially, or finally, Yes	Intervocalically, No; Initially, or finally, Yes	If the positions are lumped together, markedness is inconsistent.

8.	Continuous (or Continuant) + f, θ, s, š, x, l, y, w, vowels − p, pf, t, tθ, c, č, k, r, nasals In SPE 318 r often +, l sometimes −	No (with some exceptions)	Goes both ways	No (generally)	The grouping of /r/ and nasals with stops, and fricatives with vowels is seldom useful. There are some cases where [continuous] might be the marked term, e.g. for fricatives like f and θ, but generally the evidence is against it.
8a.	Abrupt onset (new) is simply a sign-reversal of 8; therefore an improvement				
8b.	Instantaneous release (*SPE*) or abrupt offset + t, p, k, b, d, g − ts, ph, kx, s, f, x, v, ð, γ (fricatives and affricates) (also with reversed signs as Delayed release *SPE*)	No (affricates are always less frequent; fricatives may do better on occasion)	Ambiguous	Yes (but the reverse also occurs)	Takes over some of the work of Strident, but reverses the signs. Again, affricates probably should be +, but not fricatives. Delayed release (*SPE*) is probably a better feature.
8c.	Released (new) + all pre-vocalic consonants and some others − many pre-consonantal and some final consonants	No (indeed some languages have only pre-vocalic consonants)	Indeterminate	Indeterminate	This is usually a superficial phonetic fact without significance; occasionally languages oppose 'loose' to 'tight' consonant clusters but most analyses handle these by inserting a vocalic segment (e.g. English *blow* vs. *below*). Used to differentiate the two parts of a geminate.[1]

[1] For an argument claiming the necessity of this feature (especially for Korean) see J. McCawley in *Language* 8:120–3 (December 1967).

	Relative frequency	Neutralization and range	Historical shift	Comments
9. Nasal + nasal consonants (m, n, η) and nasalized vowels – perhaps also prenasalized stops – all others	No (for consonants), Yes (for vowels)	Yes for vowels, at least	No (e.g. in assimilation)	One of the clearest of privative features. Apparently nasalized vowels are marked, but nasal consonants unmarked. Yet a relaxed velum is lowered.
10. Tense + generally voiceless or aspirated stops, long vowels, peripheral vowels – voiced, unaspirated, or unreleased stops, short vowels, neutral or central vowels	Yes (where this is not so of consonants, the opposition is regarded as [VOICED] instead)	Yes	Difficult to know	There are few rules which can apply to *both* vowels and consonants. Many attempts have been made to establish this as a distinct feature, independent of length, of which Kim's (p. 155, n. 1) is the best.
11. Lateral (new) + liquid l-sounds, lateral fricatives, laterally released affricates – all others	Yes (r generally ahead of l; Navaho c and λ are about equally rare). See comments	Yes	Little evidence; the feature is very stable as a rule, but probably Yes	Jakobsonian analyses regard l as a continuant which is both vocalic and consonantal. Lateral stops and fricatives are sometimes made [+strident]. In Samoan the most frequent consonant is l.
12. Flat (old) + u, o, ü, ö and other rounded vowels; labialized consonants; later Arabic emphatics (pharyngalized) are included – unrounded vowels, unpharyngalized and unlabialized consonants	Yes, for consonants and front vowels. No, for back vowels	Yes (generally)	Yes (Kurylowicz's theory of the origin of Western IE labiovelars is contrary to this)	Non-labialized consonants are not often a useful class.

12a. Labialized or Rounded (same as older Flat)				In *SPE* some African labiovelars (double stops) are counted here.
12b. Pharyngalized (new) Combined in Low in SPE	Yes	Yes	Yes	This may be a prosody or harmony-style feature.
13. Sharp (later sometimes called Palatalized) + Palatalized consonants − others. Not used for vowels	Yes	Yes	Yes	This could be applied to vowels in several ways.[1] *SPE* uses High and/or Distributed for palatalized consonants.
14. Long + long vowels − short vowels	Yes, (except in some S. Asian languages)	Yes (generally)	Yes (generally)	Long treated as a separable feature for vowels (less often for consonants, where gemination is the favoured notation). Jakobson put it in a separate class of prosodic features.

[1] The possibility of using this feature for vowels seems not to have been considered by Jakobson, though there are three easy ways in which it could be done: (1) treat ü as a sharpened u rather than a rounded i. If this were done for Azerbaijani, the frequencies would be right for regarding the sharp term as marked. In Turkish it might be justified in the occasional influence of palatal consonants on following vowels. But, in the main, rounding appears to be the relevant feature in Turkic languages. (2) Treat English [yu:] as in *beauty*, *music*, etc. as a sharpened form of /u:/. The change from [yu:] to [u:] in words like *rule*, *lute* and often (in U.S.) *tune*, *due*, *news*, would be reversal of this feature rather than loss of a segment. (3) Treat front-rising diphthongs as sharpened correlates of their first members, i.e. English [ay] in *like*, *tie*, etc. would be the sharpened form of [aː] in *palm* or of [æ] in *lack*, *tap*, etc. – though in the latter case there is also a tense–lax difference. Any one, or all three, of these possibilities seems worth exploring; all offer some economies. A count of my own speech shows [yu:] less frequent than [u:] and [ay] as less frequent than [æ] but more so (by far) than [aː].

	Relative frequency	Neutralization and range	Historical shift	Comments
15. Obstruent + stops and fricatives − vowels, semivowels, liquids, nasals (the reverse of sonorant)	Yes (minimal pairs are rare, but most obstruents are below 9th in rank, non-obstruents above 10th)	Neutralization appears unlikely	Dubious, there are many instances of a change w→v	Very similar to consonantal or non-vocalic. Here, too, rules changing the sign are not common.
16. Checked + glottalized consonants, including implosive − non-glottalized	Yes			The languages containing these consonants (in many parts of the world) have little historical data available. Glottalized vowels might also be specified in this manner, as well as unreleased final stops.
*16a. Implosion (Glottal Suction) (*SPE*) + implosives only − all others	Yes			
17. − ? On other features, such as [Click] (or Velaric Suction), [Labiovelar], [Covered], [Glottal constriction], [Ejective], [Heightened Subglottal Pressure] etc., it is difficult to get enough information; superficially, however, all of these seem to be rare articulations whose presence is surely marked (+).				

guages in which it looks as if *prestopping* is an SGC which may be added to continuants of various kinds, and when a fricative is so modified, an affricate results. Other prestopped sounds may be noted *dl, dn, bm,* for instance.

Oppositions of this class are often treated as separate segments, especially as some of them are so easily split phonetically. Aspirated stops are given as ph, th, etc., glottalized as pʔ, tʔ, kʔ, etc., affricates as ts, tš, pf, tl, etc. To write the nasals as tN, pN, kN, etc. (for n, m, n) is much less common, as is notation with two letters for voiced stops (e.g. tD, pD, kD for d, b, g), though a proposal has been made to write unvoiced stops in English as clusters with h (dh, bh, gh or hd, hb, hg for t, p, k). What about fricativeness? Is this also a privative opposition? Though non-writing of this opposition is rare, there may be a few genuine cases, and indeed the use of h as a feature-marking device is familiar to us in English (ph, th). Once again though, as in the case of the affricates, the point of articulation is seldom the same; English f is labiodental,[1] while p is bilabial; θ is apicodental but t is alveolar, while s, though perhaps alveolar, seems to be usually lamino-alveolar, not apico-alveolar, i.e. it is generally made with the tongue tip down by the lower front teeth, while t has it against the alveolar ridge; š (in *shush*) may correspond with č (in *church*), though sometimes they show the same sort of difference as s and t. It is easy and undoubtedly correct to say that this has the effect of optimizing or maximizing the opposition – a fricative articulated against the teeth (like f and θ) or sibilated, pronounced with eddy noise (like s and š) is louder and more clearly distinct from a related stop than it would be if it were articulated in the same position and with the tongue in the same attitude as for that stop. But, at the same time, this detracts from its privative nature; only š, ž and č, ǰ seem clearly privative in English, and this may be a prestopping ('abrupt onset') opposition rather than a simple fricative one.

The opposition of p to t, or t to k is intuitively felt by most of us to be of a different order. Jakobson thought we were being misled by articulation, but recent experiments incline us to believe that we hear in terms of our own imaginary articulations, not in terms of pure acoustic quality.

[1] We use here the system recommended by Hockett and others, in which the first Latin stem indicates the articulator, the second marks the point of articulation: labio-dental is (lower) lip against (upper) teeth, apico-alveolar is tongue-tip against ridge between gums and hard palate, etc. Note that the term labio-velar does not belong to this system in either of its possible senses: (1) Indo-European labialized dorso-velar, or (2) African double-stopped bi-labial dorso-velar. Bilabial is equivalent to labio-labial, lip against lip.

When an experimenter feeds us a sound that seems now like a k, now like a t, this experience has the baffling character of fluctuation between discrete qualities, as if we saw a colour which seemed at one moment to be red and at the next green. It is quite unlike the uncertainty whether something is medium dark green or very dark green, or even, in listening to vowels, whether what we hear is a slightly higher or slightly lower variety of e. In the case of vowels, however, we sometimes have (conditioned by our native language) a similar set of arbitrary boundaries between (e.g.) [ɪ] and [e˙]., i.e. there are shifts that seem almost as abrupt as that from t to k. Languages do occasionally exhibit change across these boundaries, and it always upsets linguists if they are not clearly assimilative, as when Umbrian makes -ns into -f.

So I think our answer to question 1 is, "No, oppositions are not all alike". In particular, while many are clearly privative in character, others require some effort of thought to be seen in such a light.

(2) Question number 2 is this: Are all oppositions *inherently* binary? This question is usually raised in connection with vowel systems, but it may also arise in relation to a consonant series (e.g. p, t, k). Many languages have three front vowels, something like i, e, æ (or ɛ, in IPA symbols). Jakobson handled this in terms of his compact–diffuse contrast by making i diffuse, æ compact and e simultaneously both (or perhaps neither: ±). This is equivalent to admitting a third value, neither marked nor unmarked but half-marked ('complex'). In some later work Halle solved this by splitting the features in two: i was [+diffuse] and [−compact], æ was [+compact] and [−diffuse], while e was [−diffuse] and [−compact]. As we noted earlier, this is an unfortunate choice, since it implies that e is unmarked for both features, although in general it is less frequent. In English, for instance, /i/ ranks first or second, /æ/ about ninth, and /e/ tenth or eleventh. In Azerbaijani the situation is worse: /æ/ ranks second, i is third, while e is twelfth with about a third as many occurrences as either i or æ, and in the back vowels a is first, ɯ is seventh (high-back-unrounded) while o is tenth and u (high-back-rounded) is eleventh. There is no unrounded partner for o. If we made e (and o) [+diffuse] and [+compact], it would obviously be better both from this Zipfian viewpoint, and – as far as the evidence goes – for historical change (o→u, o→a, e→i, e→æ all seem more frequent than the reverse changes). But there are languages which are said to have *four* front vowels: i, e, ɛ, and æ. In this case ± cannot be made to work, nor is it easy to see how a simple diffuse-nondiffuse and compact–non-

compact set will work either. Hence many people have favored a three-
or four-valued feature of tongue-height (i.e. value of Formant 1).[1]

In the case of point-of-articulation or point-and-articulator, it is also
often argued that binarization is arbitrary, that p, t and k are in some
sense three absolute values, not reducible to binary oppositions, or to
scalar values either. Various other types, c or t^y or k^y or k^w or a back
velar q or a retroflex ṭ, can be linked in binary (even privative) ways with
one or more of the basic three, but it is in nature impossible (if this is
not pure transcriptional prejudice) to modify p into t or k by imperceptible steps; and though one might proceed gradually from k to t or t to k,
nevertheless at some point the listener feels an abrupt shift in quality.
And unconditioned mergers are rare. Against this it may be pointed out
that some of the modified types (like c, k^w, etc.) may provide links: so
k^w is a good link between p and k, k' or c between k and t. But it is still
hard to link p with t.

Nothing that has been said here is an argument against using a wholly
binary analysis if some provision can be made for distinguishing the
natural privative oppositions from the more arbitrary ones.

(3) Are there some unshared features? If some phoneme has a unique
feature, participates in a unique opposition, then obviously the feature
is essentially identical with the phoneme. In most European languages
such a status has been claimed for l, though Jakobson tried to make the
lateral articulation a purely phonetic, predictable development from
other more general features. Similarly, in languages where [s] is the
only strident, this feature may become a non-distinctive, redundant,
predictable or merely phonetic one. Systems which use features that are
phonetic and non-distinctive anyway do not mind a language in which
[a] is the only compact phone, but in the older system where features
had to be distinctive or phonemic, this tended to cause distress.

In practice it is certainly easy enough to dispense with unique
features in any given language, but is it perhaps arbitrary to do so?

(4) Finally, is it proper to regard oppositions as the same which are
quite obviously different in respect to articulation; in particular, is it
right to use several features in one sense for vowels and in a different
sense for consonants? In Jakobson's system this was the case for grave–
acute, compact–diffuse, and perhaps for tense–lax. The feature HIGH

---

[1] See, e.g. H. Contréras in *Language* 45:1–8 (1969), and Frank W. Heny, 'Non-
binary phonological features' and 'Toward the separation of classificatory and phonetic
features' in *Working Papers in Phonetics* 7, November 1967, U.C.L.A.

(SPE) for 'diffuseness' is quite satisfactory: "[+HIGH] sounds are articulated with the tongue near to or touching the hard or soft palate, and have relatively low first formants." The gravity feature seems reasonable in an *acoustic* definition (e.g. "[+GRAVE] sounds have relatively low second formants"), but it is difficult to pin down the way in which the *articulation* of [p] resembles that of [a] (for instance).

Still, it is such an obvious economy to be able to use the same features for vowels and consonants that we should perhaps not mind some measure of artificiality. And the 'high' consonants and vowels, at least, are linked by phonological rules in various languages: in Azerbaijani, the palatal stop g′ under certain conditions varies freely with y; under other conditions a y raises preceding vowels to i. In some Southeast Asian languages where clusters (phonetically dissyllabic) of ia, ua, ɯa are a common type of syllabic nucleus, each of these tends to develop a transitional glide – [iya], [uwa], and [ɯɣa], the latter with good back velar friction.

But if you are willing to go this far, where should you draw the line? In the old system four features were contrastive only in the case of consonants: *obstruence, stridency, voicing* (cases like Keresan where phonemic voiceless vowels are postulated by some linguist can always be handled in other ways) and *continuity*; *checked* was probably also intended as a purely consonantal feature. In newer systems *obstruence* retains its old character, while *compact* becomes relevant only for vowels, and *lateral, implosion, velaric suction, ejection, instantaneous release,* etc., are only for consonants. Certain features show even narrower limitations: [+syllabic] cannot co-occur with [±delrel] for instance in the new system, nor [+compact] with [+diffuse] in the earlier. An effort must be made, of course, to find a phonetic basis for uniting a vowel feature with a consonantal one; mere complementary distribution is not enough. We have seen what that might yield in the case of *checked* or *interrupted* applied to vowels; *secondary* (defined as 'with tongue horizontally shifted from basic position') could specify centralized vowels (or even lax vowels).

Various older systems supposed that some features were basically segmental while others extended over longer domains; Firthians treated the first kind under phonematic units, the second as prosodies. Jakobson himself originally set length, stress and tone aside as prosodic. The newer theory makes no difference in the features, but only in the rules. If, for instance, it is the case that in some Turkic language the vowels in a single word must be either all front or all back, then Firthian phonematic-prosodic linguistics (cf. also Lightner's proposal in *Word* 21:244–50 ([1965]) assigns a feature of *backness* (= Jakobson's *gravity*) to the whole word, without locating it in any segment; Halle-style rules (so far) assign the feature to some one segment in the lexicon, then replicate it in others. Are all features equally likely to behave in this way? By no means. In the system of *Preliminaries*, there is no such likelihood, so far as we know, for Consonantality, Vocality, Obstruence, Stridency, Continuity, and Checkedness, which are always purely segmental, or at most subject to infrequent assimilation by directly adjacent segments; the same is true in later systems of Syllabicity, Consonantality, Obstruence, Compactness, Secondariness, Abruptness of Onset, Delayed Release, Coronality, Anteriority, Distribution, Continuance, Suction, Pressure, Laterality and Checkedness. Laterality is, of course, often liable to distant dissimilation within the word, but this is not the same. This leaves, in system No. 1, Gravity, Diffuseness, Compactness, Voicing (perhaps only in adjacency; Whisper must be something else), Nasality, Tenseness, Flatness, and Sharpness. The first three and the last three are involved in various sorts of Vowel Harmony; *consonantal* Gravity and Compactness are never prosodic, Flatness and Sharpness only to the extent of adjacent phonemes. Turkish harmonizes on Gravity and Flatness, though Sharpness might be involved in some consonantal harmony effects. Nasality, in some languages, may be a matter affecting both vowels and consonants within a certain domain; Tenseness also. In later schemes the potentially prosodic features are *high, low, back, nasal, tense, labialized, covered, pharyngalized,* and *sharp. Pharyngalization* appears to affect both consonants and vowels within its domain in certain Semitic languages.

What more do we need to consider? The importance of starting with *oppositions*, not with phonetic qualities, should not be forgotten, since it is reasonable to believe in a small number of kinds of opposition for all languages, but against all evidence to believe in a small number of phonetic qualities. We should also strive to choose features in such a way that at least some rules in some languages will involve each feature singly, and few rules in any language will involve complexes of four or more features. This is not to say that some economy cannot be achieved by using arbitrary binary features which in themselves mean nothing, but certain pairs and triplets of which have useful phonological values. Here is a crude example[1] of such a system, based on a phonemic analysis of English which treats one feature (/:/ 'tenseness plus diphthongiza-

---

[1] Presented by me at an Indiana University Linguistic Seminar in 1961.

tion' or something of the sort) as a segment, so that the phonemes of the system are these: h p t k b d g f θ s š č ǰ v ð z ž m n r l w y u i e o a ɔ /:/. The scheme uses seven unnamed 'features', which accomplish seven distinct dichotomies of the inventory, and they are distinguished by position. The whole of any segment (or class of segments) is represented by a seven-digit binary number (e.g. h = 1010110 and voiceless stops – ptk- = 1XXooXo), with a third symbol X indicating irrelevance of the feature in question. Roughly speaking, the features are as follows:

1st digit – 1 = approximately obstruent, including h.
2nd digit – 1 = consonants except some apicals (tdθs) and h.
3rd digit – 1 = h, velars and palatals (š č ǰ ž), semivowels and l.
4th digit – 1 = voiceless fricatives, z, ž, nasals, non-high vowels.
5th digit - 1 = h, θ, s, č, ǰ, v, ð, z, ŋ, w, y, non-low vowels.
6th digit – 1 = h, p, b, f, š, č, ǰ, v, ž, m, w, back vowels.
7th digit – 1 = voiced consonants (including liquids, nasals, semi-vowels) and the tenseness segment /:/.

No one value of zero or 1 by itself is particularly meaningful phonetically, but most desirable features may be easily specified:

stops (p t k b d g) = 1XXooXX
m n r l = o1XXoX1
p b f v m = X1oXX1X
t d θ s = XooXXoX
f θ s š = XXX1XXo
nasals = o1X1XX1
w y = o11o1X1
vowels = oooXXXo
front vowels = oooXXoo
low vowels = ooo1oXo.

The number of unmarked features (o's) in the specification of any phoneme correlates roughly with its frequency (i.e. many zeros, high frequency) in running text[1]: so t, y, æ and tenseness each have a single 1; d, s, r, u, e, and ɔ have two, and so on.

The specifications were arrived at purely empirically (and it is frustrating to discover the incompatibility of the two aims; you cannot appreciate this fully until you try it for yourself), by trial and revision

[1] Ten of the leaders in English text frequency, as given by various sources, are: ə, i, n, t, r, e, s, l, d, æ. See A. H. Roberts, *A Statistical Analysis of American English*, The Hague, Mouton, 1965.

and compromise. Though 31 phonemes could be specified (in principle) in binary notation with five digits, this leaves so little freedom that no other requirements can be satisfied. When Jakobson and Lotz specified French phonemes with six features in 1949[1] it must not be forgotten that they were allowing three contrasting values for three of their features, which meant that they could, in principle, have specified 216 distinct phonemes, where purely binary features would allow only 64. By using only one more digit for English, the features could be given very reasonable definitions one by one. Clearly the amount of freedom needed is about seven or eight times – i.e. to specify 30 phonemes you should use a scheme capable of specifying between 210 and 240.[2]

[1] 'Notes on the French Phonemic Pattern', *Word* 5:151–8 (1949).
[2] Throughout this chapter I have made little use of the criterion of economy in rule-writing. For more on this, see R. T. Harms, 'The measurement of phonological economy', *Language* 42:612–11 (1966). For other criticisms see Peter Ladefoged, *Linguistic Phonetics* (Working Papers in Phonetics 6, U.C.L.A., 1967), and Geoffrey Sampson, 'On the need for a phonological base', *Language* 46:586–626 (1970).

IO   *Phonemes and distinctive features: II*

Let us now consider the central question: Is there some small number of truly *distinctive*[1] (not merely 'phonetic') features which correspond to all the phonological distinctions attended to by speakers of any human language? What are they? If they are not all alike, how many kinds are there, and what are they?

1. There does not appear to be any good reason yet to doubt that some small number of universal features can do the job, possibly less than 18. A larger number is required if you shift from *distinctive* to pure articulatory *phonetic* features.

2. There seem to be three kinds: substantive segmental features, assimilable (privative) features, and prosodic features (which we will not discuss in this chapter). We are here talking about the features of lexical items alone; if the domain is shifted to the phrase or sentence, then a fourth type must be added, intonational features.

(a) Substantive features for consonants correspond loosely to Firth's phonematic units, and to the positional (point-of-articulation) classes or features of most non-Jakobsonian American linguists and of André Martinet (for instance). All labials in English, say (p b f v m), are identical in one substantive feature (if these are made binary, two or more may be used simultaneously). The first problem is this: are there seven or eight totally distinct *positions*, or are there three or four types which may then be modified (perhaps by something analogous to McCawley's [+secondary], a point-of-articulation shifter)? Suppose a language has p t< t ṭ ƛ k' k q, i.e., from front to back, labial, dental, alveolar, retroflex, lateral, prepalatal, prevelar, and velar (or uvular) stops, is the difference between all pairs the same, or are some pairs (in the psychology of the native speakers) more alike than others? Our own first feeling is that t< and ṭ are modifications of alveolar t, but that may be solely because (i) we use the same Roman letter, t, in all three cases, and because

---

[1] A truly distinctive feature is one term of an opposition; i.e. there must be utterances in which a change in the value of the feature immediately changes the sense or makes it nonsense (without, e.g., giving it a foreign accent or making it sound as if the speaker has a speech defect).

(ii) English has alveolar but not retroflex or dental stops. Many languages of India have dentals and retroflexes while Australian languages often have all three. Some linguists from India have (apparently spontaneously) chosen to regard retraction or retroflexion as a modification of dental articulation. Interestingly enough, Indians normally render English alveolars as retroflexes. I do not have any evidence about the reaction of Australian aborigines to these contrasts, though some of their languages exhibit assimilation or dissimilation among the apical articulations. In the case of the front and back velars I have noted a little free or individual variation in Persian loans in Azerbaijani, but there are other factors involved in those cases; however, in much of the vocabulary, these palatals and velars are in complementary distribution before (or after) front and back vowels, respectively. In some American Indian languages, like Chinook, for instance, there are also morphophonemic relations between the velars and the postvelars. Between labials and apicals there seems to be no evidence of relationship (except for the fairly common $\theta \rightarrow f$ shift); between apicals and dorsals or apicals and laterals there is a little. If apicals are palatalized, so that not just the tip but a half-inch or more of the tongue comes in contact with the front of the palate (the *SPE* feature [+distributed]), there is a gradual transition possible to palatalized dorsals, where not just the hump of the tongue but a half-inch or more of the surface in front of it touches the palate. Phoneticians are often in disagreement whether to write k̇ or ṫ in a particular language (e.g. in Tabriz Azerbaijani), and either of them may gradually shade into an affricate č. Possibly, then, we might settle on four basic substantive articulatory features (or sets): labial, apical, dorsal, and lateral. Each of these (though rarely the lateral or labial, except nondistinctively for the sake of optimizing a fricative) may have two or three modifying features imposed upon it. The apical may be (a) neutrally postdental; (b) positively interdental; (c) alveolar, or (d) retroflex (i.e. palatal, except that this term is now by custom reserved for blade contact, not tip contact). The lateral may be either (a) 'velar', with dorsum lowered, or (b) 'palatal' with dorsum raised. The dorsal may be either neutrally velar, prevelar, postvelar (uvular), or possibly even pharyngeal. There is no evidence that any language has more than three apicals or three dorsals (indeed two dorsals is probably the maximum; a number of languages have two without and two with labialization – k^w, q^w – but this is another kind of modification). Retraction (i.e. retroflexion of apicals, uvularization or pharyngalization of dorsals) produces a similar acoustic modification in both cases (a lowering of F_2 and F_3), and fronting (dental articulation for apicals, palatal for dorsals) also yields the same result in both cases (a raising of F_2 and perhaps also F_3). So two mutually exclusive privative features capable of applying to the basic segmental type are adequate to the job, or alternatively, a single three-valued feature (fronted, neutral, backed). But these are not assimilable features; i.e. fronting of a k does not induce fronting of an adjacent t.

And let it be remembered that economy is against specifying p t k with three mutually exclusive binary features ($\pm$ labial, $\pm$ apical, $\pm$ dorsal, where only three or conceivably four of the eight possible combinations would be legal). A single four-valued feature (to include laterals) is simpler. Let us represent these *values* (arbitrarily) by P, T, K, and L, rather than [P point], [T point], [K point], [L point].

Are there also segmental vowel features, or is there just one, 'Vowel'? When Jakobson (influenced by C. Stumpf) first hit upon the identity of a and k (in *Les Lois Phoniques du Langage Enfantin*, for example, of 1939), he seemed to be supposing a primitive or basic triangular vowel system (a, u, i) parallel to the triangular consonant system (k, p, t). But it seems a good deal more obvious that u and i have something in common (high tongue, low F_1) than that p and t do, so that we might cut to *two* basic vowels, A and I. But if a neutral vowel segmental symbol (E) is needed anyway, then surely a, i, and all the rest should be handled by ordinary binary features (unless, perhaps, we feel the need of a four-valued feature of Height or Openness). Are any other segmental features needed? What about liquids, undifferentiated (i.e. assimilated) nasals, semivowels, h and glottal stop? The liquids (in most languages) could be represented by one such feature (call it R), whereas for the assimilated nasal, the h and the glottal stop we can use the feature O (equivalent to [+segment] merely), unspecified for point-and-articulator, which can then be binarily specified for nasality, stopping or aspiration. The semivowels might also be treated with O as segmental feature, binary features being the same as for i and u (for example). Occasionally a language has more semivowels (glides in this sense, not in the Jakobsonian sense) than high vowels. Some languages of Australia, besides y and w (corresponding to i and u) have a peculiar retracted palatal glide – often transcribed R – which sounds a bit like y and a bit like American r; in any case there is no corresponding vowel. Maybe IE laryngeals (whatever they were) or Salishan pharyngeals require another feature; it is not clear.

Sibilants cannot always be treated as merely apical fricatives which are non-distinctively sibilated. On the whole it seems best to have one further segmental feature (S), all of whose other features are predictable if there is only one sibilant (as in Ancient Greek, for instance), and all but one or two in languages with more, like English (s š z ž) and Sanskrit (s ś ṣ).

Before we move on to the list of reasonably certain privative features, we might take a few moments to discuss a question which was a burning issue of the thirties and forties, but has been strangely ignored in recent discussions: how to tell a feature from a segment. The problem was often couched in terms like 'biphonemic' or 'monophonemic' interpretation,[1] and has been raised primarily in connection with affricates, diphthongs, long vowels (long consonants are in practice almost invariably treated as two segments, usually geminated, sometimes consonant plus a special symbol – /q/ or /:/), glottalized phonemes (especially stops), aspirated stops, trilled r, and naturally enough such oddities as labiovelars (African style), and prenasalized or pre-aspirated stops. Two lines of argument have been followed: (1) one school argues that such stretches as these are 'clearly' two *phonetic* segments, and the question therefore is how to decide when two phonetic segments may be phonemically one. (2) The other school argues that many or most of these, though composed of two phonetic *phases* (in articulatory or acoustic terms) are produced by a single stroke or motion of the articulator(s), the two phases being an automatic and inescapable consequence of the position and direction of the stroke, or, if there are two articulators, that their action is simultaneous. If the first line is taken, criteria of the type known as 'pattern congruity' are called upon to solve the problem: is the distribution, the phonotactics, of the stretch of sound being tested more like that of indubitable unit phonemes, or more like that of undoubted clusters? This test will not always work. In English, for instance, č and j may occur initially, medially and finally, quite like such clusters as /st/ (though recently some Indo-Europeanists have advocated regarding these s-clusters as 'pre-sibilated' unit phonemes), though unlike /ts/ or /dz/ (which do not occur initially except in words agreed by most speakers to be foreign-sounding); on the other hand, they do not form any initial clusters at all, quite unlike p t k b d g which all may occur with

---

[1] See, for instance, E. Vasiliu 'The Phonemic Status of Rumanian Affricates', *Proceedings of the 9th International Congress of Linguists* (ed. H. Lunt), Mouton, 1964, pp. 589–92.

following r l or w. One other distributional criterion is that of frequency: no cluster may be more frequent in any position than one of its members. This gives a clear unit decision for ǰ, since ž (if truly a phoneme) is a much rarer segment, in all positions, than ǰ, and in some of them carries the notion 'foreign' with it. As a matter of consistency, if ǰ is a unit, č must be. A good argument from morphophonemic rules assumes that it is better not to change the number of segments. Since the final of *speech* is related to the final of *speak*, which is clearly one segment, č should be one segment, too. Some of the English diphthongs (e.g. /ay/ or /ai/ as in *wild*, *find*, etc.), have as much distributional freedom as the tense pure vowels; /ay/ occurs before clusters like ld, rd, nd, for instance, and even nt, though not before a long list of other types. Since they also occur finally (where lax vowels do not occur), it has been common to analyze all tense vowels and diphthongs as sequences of (lax) vowels followed by other segments (w, y, u, i, h, /:/, etc.). Only a few linguists, like Jakobson, favored treating long vowels as single segments (with the prosodic feature of length), but diphthongs as sequences. The treatment of Halle and Chomsky starts with single long vowels in the base lexical form, which are then converted to sequences by a series of rules.

If the second line is taken, that the sounds are single units in the articulatory sense, then the burden of the argument is shifted to those who prefer a diphonemic interpretation. They may simply deny the unitary claim, but this is often difficult to argue. Take the case of English /ay/ once again. X-ray studies generally show that the tongue is in smooth continuous motion during its articulation, and sound spectrograms show a smooth gradual rise of F_2 and dropping of F_1. Nowhere is there a natural boundary between two parts or 'segments'. The case of /ɔy/, as in 'boil', 'coin', etc., is different. Here there are three phases usually detectable in X-ray pictures and sound spectrograms: an opening /ɔ/ phase, a brief transition, and a final /y/ or /i/ phase. Affricates show a smooth articulatory movement, in general, but a sharply segmented spectrogram. The same thing is true of aspirated stops and glottalized stops (ejectives). Most often, therefore, linguists who start with the second line of argument reinforce this with material drawn from the first line. And this is not unreasonable.

A third line of argument, very difficult to manage, is sometimes taken from the intuitions of the native speaker, or his reactions to being taught one or another system of writing his own language. This is hard to manage and treacherous for several reasons. One is that it may carry you farther than you wish to go, when the native is happiest with a system which treats a *syllable* (e.g. *ba*) as the minimum and unanalyzable unit. Another is that native speakers, even if not themselves linguists, are fully as suggestible as linguists are. Nor do they always agree among themselves. But, in spite of all these dangers, it is likely that we ought to try to collect this evidence, because in some cases it will be clear-cut and consistent. And who should have a better feeling for the segments of a language (if there are any) than the man who speaks it?

(b) The point of all this digression has been to prepare the way for one kind of uncertainty in the listing of privative features: can this feature be treated as (or, is it not in reality) a segment? I do not know a universal answer to this question, and have a feeling that what is a segment in language A may be a feature in language B at the same level in the system. (Of course all hands admit that a deep-structure or morphophonemic or systematic phonemic representation may have a different number of segments from the corresponding surface structure, phonemic, systematic phonetic representation.)

1. Voicing. It appears to be clear that many languages have several pairs of phonemes which differ solely in that one term is voiced and the other voiceless. This should be accompanied by a caution that there is almost certainly at least one other privative opposition which *in some cases* entails a voicing difference. As we have seen, however, since optimal (non-nasal) obstruents are voiceless, but other optimal phone-types are voiced, the marked term should be Voiced for obstruents and Voiceless for everything else.[1] This could be handled by a feature called 'non-optimal voice'. (See under 3 below for an alternative notation.) In general non-obstruents would be simply unmarked for the feature, but if there are genuine cases of distinctively voiceless vowels or liquids, they will be marked (i.e. + in Jakobson–Halle notation) for this feature, as will all the distinctively *voiced* stops and fricatives. Non-distinctive phonetic voicing or unvoicing is a matter for general phonetic theory, except when it belongs to the tabulation of idiosyncrasies which mark speakers of a particular dialect.

---

[1] A rule for assimilation of voicing of obstruent would have the segment start as unmarked (−, i.e. voiced) and then become marked (+, i.e. voiceless) just in case the adjacent segment is both obstruent and [+voiceless]. Languages in which, e.g., an underlying voiceless stop is voiced by the adjacency of anything except another voiceless obstruent would require an intermediate unconditioned unmarking of the underlying stop. But one might question whether the underlying stop really is voiceless.

2. Nasality. This is quite clearly something distinct and distinguishable, both in articulation and in sound. Even though it is admitted that nasalized vowels may be so in varying degrees, it is everywhere the case that functionally either nasality is entirely irrelevant or is regarded as being definitely there or definitely not there. As in the case of voicing, however, there seems to be a difference in direction of markedness between nasalized vowels and nasal consonants. Nearly everywhere m's are more frequent than b's (or v's or w's) and n's more frequent than d's (or ð's or z's; with r's the race is closer); so the optimal basic non-syllabic segment would appear to be nasal, whereas the optimal vowel is non-nasal. Again we need a feature non-optimal nasality to meet the needs of the situation.

3. Labialization or rounding. Jakobson argued for including pharyngealization as an articulatory variant of the same feature on the grounds that no language contrasts labialized with pharyngealized phonemes, and that the acoustic qualities are similar. There are a number of problems here, one that mainly Semitic languages seem to have pharyngealization, at least on such a scale, and that in them it behaves very definitely like a prosody, something whose domain extends over several segments.[1] This is not often the case with labialization. But the fact mentioned already, that our feedback appears to be in the main kinesthetic, i.e. based on articulation, would seem to be a clincher against Jakobson.

Optimal back vowels are regularly rounded; hence rounding is the feature for all other phonemes, but unrounding is marked for back vowels. From now on we will take the descriptive adjective *non-optimal* for granted as applying to every feature. Many linguists like to use a value *marked* for such non-optimal cases, converting then by rule (e.g.) [m rounded] to [−rounded] on back vowels, to [+ rounded] on front vowels. This makes m and u upper level feature values, + and − low level or intermediate phonetic values.

Rounding of consonants is one of the features which is easily viewed as a separate segment. It is especially common on back velar consonants, which resemble high back vowels in this respect, though we cannot say that optimal back velars are rounded – at least I have no arguments to prove this. But wherever labialization is applied to a consonant, we may debate whether to write tw or t^w, sw or s^w, and so on. From this point

---

[1] A category of such features, which is closely related to distinctive tone in some languages, is sometimes postulated as 'phonation-type' or 'register'. Vowel glottalization ('creaky voice') or fricativization ('breathy voice') are examples. See E. J. A. Henderson in *Lingua* 15:400–34 (1965).

of view w might be specified as a zero consonant (or non-syllabic, or whatever we choose as basic) marked solely as rounded.

4. Palatalization falls in the same class. Many hot debates have been concerned with the question whether to write ty or t^y (or t', another common notation), ny or ɲ, ly or λ, and so on. Like labialization, palatalization is particularly common for dorsals (to which l is closely related). Jakobson used to argue strongly for distinguishing languages with palatalization, a feature combinable with many different consonants, from languages with palatal consonants, i.e. dorsals articulated on the hard palate. But the only plausible way of doing this would be to assign palatalization to two different categories, making it a segmental feature in the 'palatal' languages and a kind of semiprosodic feature in the palatalizing languages. In any case, y could be considered as marked only for palatalization.

The possibility of palatalized vowels was mentioned above, where three interpretations were suggested, (1) diphthongs with front-falling on-glides or (2) front-rising off-glides and (3) fronted opponents for back vowels (so that [ü], for instance, might be a palatalized u in one language and a labialized i in another). The last interpretation seems best, and in this sense, then, all optimal front vowels are palatalized. From this point of view i or ɯ might be a depalatalized i instead of an unrounded u.

5–6. Some feature or features are agreed to be required for specifying stops and fricatives. The older scheme makes stops [+obstruent] and [−continuant]; more recently we find [+obstruent] and [+abrupt onset]. (*SPE* has them [−sonorant] and [−continuous].) All specifications include affricates. We also find 'instantaneous release', which applies to nasals, flaps and trills as well as to stops, and 'released' which (as we have seen) is rarely a *distinctive* feature.

Since the optimum non-nasal consonants are (in general) the voiceless stops, we surely do not want to require two marked features to specify them, or even one, if we can avoid it. Fricatives, however, are somewhat less than optimal, and do need a + feature. The simplest solution is to view non-nasal P, T, K (our segmental feature-values) as automatically voiceless stops unless otherwise marked, and to make use of a feature of 'fricativeness' or 'frication' to specify the corresponding fricatives f, θ, x; but not s, which is optimal in another way – optimally 'strident', in Jakobsonian terms. Affricates, on the other hand, would be made from fricatives and sibilants by adding a feature of 'prestopping', obligatorily in cases like Spanish where the corresponding sibilant is lacking.

So in the end we want two privative features here, one of 'frication' and one of 'prestopping', but their domains are smaller than those of similar features in other schemes.

7. Glottalized consonants are of three kinds: ejectives, or glottalized voiceless stops, which are made by raising the larynx to compress the air behind the oral closure (with glottis tightly closed), then releasing the two closures, oral first; implosives, or preglottalized, or glottalized voiced (occasionally voiceless) stops made by lowering the larynx to rarefy the air behind the oral closure (with glottis leaking enough to vibrate, or, less often, tightly closed), then releasing the oral closure (or both closures simultaneously); glottalized continuants, which are simply continuants interrupted in the middle or near the end (less often near the beginning) by one or more glottal constrictions. Vowels may also be glottalized in this way. The proposed feature 'checked' does not appear properly named to cover all of this, and might also cover the case of final voiced consonants which are cut off and devoiced by a glottal constriction (as happens most of the time with unreleased stops). There seems to be no strong objection to classing all these phenomena together (though most of them are sometimes analyzed as sequences of the basic segment and a glottal stop) under the same feature, even though the mechanism and acoustic effects for ejective and implosive consonants is something quite special and different from the others, and what is in language A a glottalized long vowel /a: ʔ/ may be *phonetically* identical with a three-segment sequence of vowel, glottal stop, vowel in language B /aʔa/. So we have a privative feature *Glottalization* which may be applied to nearly any type of segment, which is always marked (so far as we can tell), and which, like palatalization, labialization, and aspiration, is frequently treated as if it were a separate segment. The scarcity of this feature in languages of Europe and Asia is no doubt one reason for its low-rating by many linguists.

8. Clicks and (African) labiovelars are similar in many ways to glottalized (ejective and implosive) stops, but are not quite the same. And some languages apparently have implosive labiovelars, which would seem to require both features. Let us at least add a feature *Click*, as has often been proposed.

9. Some feature similar to McCawley's *Secondary* is needed to specify different apicals and different dorsals; it doesn't seem to be naturally

privative, however. In fact, we ought to have at least three values 'Fronter', 'Backer' and 'Unmarked'. This treats alveolar t's as neutral, in contrast to dental and retroflex, and midvelar k's, as opposed to palatovelars and postvelars (uvular).

10. Do we need both a feature of *Tenseness* and a feature of *Aspiration*? or neither? or only one? Most writers[1] agree on only one, *Tenseness*. Where do we need it? For consonants it seems to be wanted in cases (like Azerbaijani) where members of one class of phoneme are, in varying situations, voiceless lenis stops (finally unreleased), voiced stops, voiced fricatives, voiced frictionless glides (e.g. p, b, β, w), while the opposed class includes voiceless aspirated stops (released if final) or voiceless fricatives or sometimes long (geminate) voiceless stops (p^h, ϕ, pp). In spite of the superficial phonetic diversity, native speakers hear all these variants as essentially the same. When, as here, the lax, lenis, sometimes voiced phoneme is the more common term of the opposition, then the other term should be marked. In some languages this other term may be always an aspirated stop, but to allow for cases where this is not so, *Tense* would seem to be a reasonable name. Aspiration, then, is in such cases just *one* sort of tenseness, and Korean, for instance, would need another similar feature. But is this true in Indic languages which have both voiced and voiceless aspirates (the voiced ones often more readily identified in the following vowel)?[2]

Once more, aspiration is frequently treated as a segment; often, but not always, correctly. This is a modulation of a modulation.

11. The ancients recognized a special kinship of r and l (as 'liquids'), which is not directly realized in the systems we have been examining. In the old scheme (and the first *SPE* system) they can be specified with two features as [+consonantal] and [+vocalic]; some late schemes need three [+consonantal], [−obstruent] and [−nasal]: the second *SPE* (p. 354) scheme uses [+consonantal], [+sonorant] and [−nasal]. Most systems can specify the l, m, n, r or liquid-and-nasal class with two features [+consonantal, −obstruent], but none seems able to handle the sonorant class of r, l, m, n, w, y, without a fully predictable feature [+sonorant] or [+resonant], which is sometimes used, though [−obstruent, −syllabic] does pretty well for the non-syllabic variants of these in one recent scheme. Recent systems can single out the l with one feature [+lateral], however.

[1] Except Kim, cited above (p. 155, n. 1).
[2] See *SPE*, 326, for the feature of Heightened Subglottal Pressure proposed to deal with Korean and Indic.

All this seems a mite uneconomical, not to say inconvenient. And I think we can see a good reason: there are more mutually unrelated natural phonetic classes than can be economically used as features. That is, although features 1–5 or features 3–7 may equally well be used to specify all the phonemes of language X, features 1–2 and features 6–7 are both valuable and necessary for some rules. In this specific case, for instance, we wish to link m with p and b, n with t and d, etc., and furthermore link w with u (and back-rounded vowels) and y with i (and front-unrounded vowels), and still group r, l, w, y for certain rules and r, l, m, n for others, but never m, n, w, y (let us say). This would seem to demand *seven* binary features to specify six phonemes, and perhaps four of these features would not apply anywhere else in the system. And this is not all. We should also be able to relate y directly to the palatalization feature and w to the labialization feature, and somehow show the relationship of these two features to each other.

Can we have features of features? Something like 'modification-by-glide', perhaps? Why not? Are there other pairs or sets of features which share a super-feature? Many analyses of American Indian languages treat aspiration and glottalization as such a pair, sharing perhaps 'modification-of-release'; we have not chosen to consider aspiration a basic feature, but have treated it as one variant realization of tenseness, a more general feature. And, in at least some cases, tenseness is not marked solely in the release (though this is usually the case). Is there any alternative other than superfeatures? One could, of course, have an automatic feature such that whenever [+labialized] or [+palatalized] appeared, [+glide-modified] would also be added, but this is obviously an *ad hoc* or 'conventional abbreviation' device to save us breath when we would otherwise have to say 'labialized and/or palatalized'.

One difficulty with r's and l's seems to be a lack of harmony with the articulatory-position features. It is common in the older literature to list both l's and apical r's under the apical column (along with n, t, d, etc.), though occasionally it is noted that the anchoring of the tongue-tip for an l does not prevent the dorsum from doing some articulating on its own (hence 'velar' and 'palatal' l's, which people are seldom bold enough to put in the velar or palatal columns). And the articulation of r's may vary greatly even in closely related dialects of the same language. Still, it might be possible to combine semivowels with liquids and attach a joint liquid feature (R) to the positional feature-values proposed above, so that P^R would be a /w/, T^R some type of apical

/r/, S^R some other type, L^R an /l/, palatalized K^R a /y/ and velar K^R a glided /γ/ or uvular /r/. But this makes it very difficult to separate w and y or r and l into distinct classes, or to link w and y with u and i, or with the features of labialization and palatalization. If we set up a *segmental* feature-value R, and use (perhaps) some of the vocalic features with it to distinguish r from l, we lose the link with y, w and nasals. If we redefine R to include y and w, then we can perhaps assign them features similar to those for i and u, but may have to make some unhappy choices for r and l.

I think it is likely that our proposed ideals are incompatible. We cannot maximize all our virtues in one system. I will leave the machinery available for both solutions, considering that possibly one way will be more appropriate in some languages, the other in others. We leave unmarked (for the moment, at least) the similarity among palatalization, y and frontness ([−grave]), or labialization, w and backness ([+grave]). And, under either solution, we can easily specify r l w y, less easily r l or w y, and only disjunctively (or by a redundant feature) r l w y m n.

Incidentally the question what makes an /r/ what it is, whether it is a trill, a flap or a glide, an apical or dorsal, I am here leaving out of account. Certainly one could assume that all r's in all languages are basically some one of these things (say an apico-alveolar glide, just to be perverse), and then derive all the other shapes by rules. But this seems unsatisfying.

12. Of the vocalic features, we have already mentioned backness ('gravity' in Jakobsonian), the feature specified by the position of F_2 or the size of the cavity in front of the tongue. Is this a genuine privative feature? Both in articulation and in spectrum this dimension is objectively a continuum; can it be always contrastively binary? There are languages (like Vietnamese) with many qualitatively distinct vowels; isn't a third degree of gravity ever required? Apparently not. In every case where several F_2 classes are needed, the others can be handled by the feature of non-optimal rounding discussed above, i.e. they are either the front rounded or back unrounded vowels. Talk in the literature about 'central' vowels is either low-level fine phonetics or a simple error for 'back unrounded' or sometimes for 'lax'.

Some scholars have expressed doubts about the psychological reality of an association between u and i or o and e. It is perfectly true that naive speakers are not as likely to find *boot* similar to *beet* as they are to find it like *boat* (for instance). But in the set of English lax vowels, this difficulty disappears. *Fit* and *foot*, *bed* and *bud*, *hat* and *hot* are all acceptably close (indeed sometimes confused). In part this is because the lax back vowels are not rounded like the tense ones,[1] and in part because both front and back vowels are more centralized, closer to the neutral position, and hence closer to each other. But I think there is little to be gained by clinging to the Jakobsonian term 'grave'; everybody else has spoken of *back* vowels (and *front* ones) for years, and the terms are clear and unlikely to cause misunderstanding.

Even if we decide in the end to economize on features by slicing up our four-valued articulator-position feature into three (or more) binary features, *Backness* would still be as good a name as Gravity (even if /p/ as Back sounds odd). *SPE* uses anteriority (for p and t), and coronality (t), making High and Back values redundant except for complex articulations.

13. In the vertical dimension three levels of vowels are quite a common event, four not unheard of. We discussed above the Jakobson (three-valued) method of dealing with this and the Halle (2-feature) method,[2] objecting to the latter that it ends up by making e and o doubly minus when their relative infrequency suggests that they ought rather to be doubly plus. McCawley's *buccal* and *compact* features make them singly plus ([+buccal]) and make i and u doubly minus (which is not bad for i in languages like English where it is one of the most frequent of all phonemes), but *buccal* seems against nature for the consonants. I suppose one could argue for a feature of *non-optimal buccality* or *dorsality* or *height* which would mean 'open' for vowels but 'palatal or velar' for consonants. But if one wishes to cling to the long-favored dimensions of High and Low, a definition which makes [i, ɨ, ɯ, ü, ʉ, u] [−Low] and all other vowels [+Low], but [æ, a, α, ɒ, ɔ] [−High], while all the rest are [+High] yields pretty appropriate values all the way for a three-level language. For four levels it is necessary to consider Low as equivalent to Open in the old-fashioned sense, so that i is High and non-Open, e is High, Open, ɛ is non-High, non-Open, and æ is non-High Open. This makes ɛ doubly minus, i and æ singly plus, and e doubly plus. I don't have available a frequency count for such a language, but I suspect that a more appropriate feature might be the 'Mid'

---

[1] This is true of most American dialects. The vowel of *foot* is not, for most of us, distinctively different from the Trager-Smith /ɨ/, nor is there any 'New England short /o/' for most of us. When *foot* is pronounced with lip-rounding, the speaker is usually pegged as a foreigner.

[2] First suggested in print, as far as I know, in my own article on 'Unreleased p t k' in the volume *For Roman Jakobson*, Mouton, 1957, pp. 235–44.

feature I once proposed. Using it, /i/ would be [+High, −Mid], /e/ [+High, +Mid], /ɛ/ [−High, +Mid], and /æ/ [−High, −Mid]. If /i/ turns out to be more frequent than /æ/, then *Low* and *Mid* should be the two features. A four-valued feature (say i = [4 High], e = [3 High], ɛ = [2 High] and æ = [1 High]) makes a general lowering or raising rule easier to write. At any rate, whatever the precise choice, only two features ever seem to be required in this dimension.

What if these features are used to help chop up our P, T, L, K values of the consonant segmental feature? Then, as we have seen, there are strong reasons for assigning K and probably L values like [+High]; neither Low, Open, nor Mid could be justified for consonants – at least not without some pretty tricky arguments.

14. These three features (i.e. [+Back], [+High] and [+Mid] or [Low], or [Open]), when combined with the feature of [+R-U] – non-optimal rounding or unrounding – will yield a 16-vowel system. It's a very rare language which cannot be made to fit this framework, though very often we may also need *Length, Nasality, Glottalization,* and various values of a tonal feature or features. Certainly there seem to be languages where length must be handled as a privative feature – though in some others (e.g. Greek, Latin, Sanskrit, most Polynesian languages) it seems better to treat it as a segment, as is sometimes the case for Nasality and Glottalization though rarely for Tone. In Latin, for instance, this segment permits a more economical statement of the base form of such endings as accusative plural (-:s). Such a segment may be viewed as simply a vowel in the lexicon, which becomes a copy of its predecessor by late rules.

Finally we come to the question whether we need features like Consonantal, Vocalic and Syllabic, and if so, how many. If we are to keep our features truly distinctive, i.e. use them only where not redundant, all of these are hard to justify, even though we keenly want classes like 'Consonants', 'Syllabics', 'Vowels', etc., for our rules in many languages. In some Jakobson–Halle analyses /k/ may differ from /ʔ/ only in the feature 'Consonantal'; but in Polynesian languages (and many more) it makes no sense to treat glottal stop as [−Consonantal]. And furthermore, it does not always seem to be more closely related to /k/ than to /t/. Similarly, in some Jakobson–Halle analyses a lax /i/ differs from a light /l/ solely in the feature *consonantal,* and from a /y/ solely in the feature *vocalic.* Such a linking of i and y (as also of u and w) seems natural and desirable, but this is not as true of i and l. The substitution of

Syllabic for *Vocalic* does not substantially alter the /i/ – /y/ relationship, and does make /ʔ/ as much like /p/ or /t/ as it is like /k/, but the feature of laterality separates /l/ from all other phones. A syllabic glided /r/, i.e. one in which no contact is made (hence no instantaneous release), however, could still be minimally distinct from lax /i/ by virtue of the Consonantal feature; if nonsyllabic, it should naturally differ also in the syllabicity feature.

None of this offers very strong arguments for the Vocalic feature; it appears to remain a needed grouping for various rules, but not a truly distinctive feature. Syllabicity is scarcely better; most of the languages which (like English) have syllabic liquids and nasals, have them predictably. E.g., in English, r, l, m, n will be syllabic between two consonants (and even if we abandon a consonantal feature, we will have unambiguous extensive definitions of consonants) or between consonant and juncture (word-boundary or affix-boundary), as in *redden* /redn/, *reddened* /rednd/, reddening /rednŋ/ where we may need to specify a morph juncture /redn'ŋ/. Furthermore, if (like Jakobson) we are going to treat /y/ as a non-syllabic /i/, it seems poor strategy to turn around and treat /i/ as a syllabic /y/, which is precisely what is needed for Indo-European, where r, l, m, n, w, y must go through an identical set of positional changes.

So, tentatively at least, we will exclude both vocalic and syllabic from our set of privative distinctive features. Can we keep Consonantal? We've already seen that w and y cause a real difficulty, no matter what we do: if we make them differ only as Consonantal from u and i, we cannot easily *identify* them with the features *labialized* and *palatalized*, as we would like to (though we can, of course, make every i and y redundantly palatalized as every u and w are labialized). And for most consonants we cannot even imagine what a [– Consonantal] match would be, just as for vowels other than the highest ones we cannot imagine a [+Consonantal] partner. So, on the whole, it would appear that Consonantal is not a *distinctive* feature, either, though it certainly refers to a natural class.

We have now a system with two successive segmental feature cuts, one of which says *Segment* must take one of two values E or O. O takes the second cut, being a four-valued feature with *values* G, S, R and null (i.e. none of the three). G is the point-and-articulator feature, S the sibilant (which might perhaps be treated as a value of G), R the liquid-and-semivowel. G is in turn a four-valued *feature* with the values P T L K (labial-apical-lateral-dorsal). Each of these is now subject to modulation by one or more of 12 privative (binary) features, as follows:

E may be modified by one or more of the set 10, 11, 12 – Back, High, Mid and also by 2 Nasal, 3 Labial, possibly 4 Palatal, 7 Glottal, 9 Tense. Of these all combinations seem to be possible. Unmodified E is some sort of schwa.

The values of G are, if unmodified (i.e. unmarked for all other features), nasals – roughly /m n ŋ/ – except that unmodified L is the ordinary liquid /l/. If modified it may take one of the set 1–10, but not 11–13. L with [+Liquidity] might mean non-optimal liquidity, i.e. the lateral affricate (which is also [+Nasality], and [+Prestopped]). Otherwise, taking T for an example, [+Voice] yields /d/ (and co-occurs with [+Non-optimal Nasality], i.e. stop value or [+fricative] or [+ Glottal] and possibly with [+Tense]); [Non-optimal Nasality] makes /t/, and also co-occurs with all the rest; labialization gives t^w, d^w, n^w etc. depending on the other values; palatalization yields t', d', ɲ, etc.; fricativization makes θ, ð (with voice), and may also combine with labialization, palatalization, prestopping and glottalization; prestopping if added alone gives d^n, the prestopped n, but if added after fricativization with or without voice yields $t^θ$, $d^ð$, and if added with Liquidity gives d^r, a prestopped gliding r; glottalization without voice gives $t^ʔ$, with it ɗ (implosive); glottalized $n^ʔ$ requires also nasality, but other combinations seem to be impossible. [Click] alone here yields the 'ts' type; with tenseness added the popping Xhosa click, and no other combinations are possible (except for voice and nasality). Tenseness requires at least non-optimal nasality, and may have labialization, palatalization, frication, or prestopping as well; liquidity rarely co-occurs with nasalization (which is, here, non-optimal) or devoicing or tenseness or click or fricativization, and may, therefore, rather be a third *value* for one of those (most likely fricativization), not a separate binary feature; combined with T it yields a gliding /r/ (similar to the American type, but not as retracted). Is it likely that any of the ten besides liquidity are values rather than features? Possibly click and glottalization are two values of the same feature. And, along with liquid and fricative, non-optimal nasal seems to be another value of a feature /Manner/. But a final solution of these questions is not going to come immediately; let us just note here that they are questions. Certainly it is wrong to have R in here both as a value of O and as a binary feature combinable with G. All we can do is test out the two routes to see how they work. Suppose we try combining

R; it cannot take voice or nasality, but it might seem that we could use labialization to make /w/ and palatalization for /y/, except that then everything else would be redundant, and we want to use High Non-back for /y/ and High Back for /w/, since those are the values needed for /i/ and /u/. Fricative r's must be regarded as purely phonetic in most languages, and fricative l's must come from the positional feature-value L; but prestopping is allowable, as well as glottalization and tenseness.

If we now try the unlimited O for binary modifications, we can see that with (unmarked) nasality we may get the positionally unspecified nasal which we often need, with *tenseness* (or possibly *frication*) we get /h/, with *non-nasality* and perhaps *glottalization* we get /ʔ/. Indeed we could also get /w/ and /y/ again by adding labialization and palatalization, or even with various combinations of features 11–13. Clearly R is unnecessary, except for the advantage of being able to specify simply the class of liquids or liquids-and-semivowels.

Finally, S may combine with voice (not nasality), labialization, palatalization, non-optimal frication or prestopping (to make affricates), glottalization, click, tenseness and perhaps liquidity (to make one type of apical /r/), but not with features 11–13.

Before we conclude the chapter, we should re-evaluate the effort to specify P T L K in terms of the binary vowel-features 12–14. This, after all, was Jakobson's most revolutionary proposal, and it does achieve economy. We have seen that the highest vowels (i, ɯ, u, etc.) shade naturally into palatal or velar fricatives of one kind or another; what more natural, then, than to cut K off from the rest as [+High]? But the next step, marking P K as [+Back], is somewhat harder; possibly it can be done on the basis of the inherent quality of the voiced fricatives (the /β/ and /γ/ being back-vowel in character, while /ð/ is fronter), or of the neutral release vowels after stops. And even though this is plausible as *classification*, it is not so as *privative features*. We can envisage a gradual fronting of /u/ toward /ü/ or a backing of /i/ to /ɯ/ or an opening of /i/ to /ɛ/, but we cannot as naturally front a /k/ into a /t/. So if we choose to substitute *these* binary features for the articulator-position values, we do so mainly on grounds of economy, and must assign a different reality to them here than when used to specify vowels. And specifying L in these terms would be unnatural.

Now we must see what the important questions are that our attempt at solution has brought to light.

(1) The goals of truly *distinctive*, *phonemic* features on the one hand

and *useful, natural* morphophonemic classes, on the other, are not identical. In any morphophonemic rules or specifications of historical change, there are two ways in which features or classes may appear: (a) a feature value may be changed, or (b) it may specify the environment (simultaneous or adjacent) in which the change occurs. It is only the genuine distinctive (privative) features or purely phonetic (redundant) features which are capable of changing; classes like *Consonants* are useful to mark an environment (either the given change takes place – or cannot take place – adjacent to a consonant, or it takes place – or fails to – in a segment which is a consonant), but it would stun anyone if he found a rule [α Consonantal]→[−α Consonantal].[1] We saw above that any attempt to arrange for a natural class m n r l w y (the IE sonorants) except by making it a wholly redundant feature would lead to loss of economy or 'observational adequacy' elsewhere in the system. This class is affected (*inter alia*) by a phonetic change from non-syllabic to syllabic in certain environments – specifiable in terms of classes like *Consonant*. The Greek, Oscan, or p-Celtic change from /qʷ/ to /p/ involves a shift from a binary feature (*labialized*) to a segmental feature value (*labial*) with loss of the original segmental value (*velar*). But all features and values involved are distinctive, even though a neat way to write the rule does not spring instantly to mind.

(2) Now the question what are features and what are values of the same feature is not easy to answer, even if one adopts the metarule that all features are two-valued. In many systems, 'labial' is represented by a simultaneous pair of feature values [+grave, − compact] or [+anterior, − coronal], while labialization is a value of a single feature [+flat] or [+labialized], and the system is incapable of showing any similarity or relationship except by arbitrary rules. If we have a four-valued feature Articulator with one *value* labial, as well as a binary feature *labialized*, we have a similarity of name, but no reason to asign any significance to this similarity. I can see the possibility of building in a device to handle this by having in the system a distinction between primary and secondary features, with 'labial' or [+labial] somehow possible in both, so that one special type of rule might have the function of shifting a value from the primary to the secondary matrix or vice versa. In the case of vowels we could easily take the line that tongue height is a single four-valued feature; the metarule here would state that in any feature with more than two values, changes must proceed in linear fashion, from value 1 to 2,

---

[1] On some incredibilities of alpha-rules, see below, ch. 14.

2 to 3, 3 to 4 or 4 to 3, 3 to 2, 2 to 1, but never directly 1 to 4 or 3 to 1. In any case where two or more binary features are mutually exclusive – e.g. Compact and Diffuse in the early system, or Liquid and Fricative in the scheme suggested above, i.e. where only three out of the possible four combinations can be interpreted (or, in the case of three such features, three out of eight), it seems likely that each 'feature' must really be a *value* of some more general feature. As we noted above, given three mutually exclusive and exhaustive qualities or categories A, B and C, we can (uneconomically) set up three binary features [±A], [±B], and [±C], or a single three-valued feature [D^A], [D^B], [D^C], or two binaries E and F, such that [+E, −F] = A, [−E, −F] = B, and [−E, +F] = C.

(3) As the number of such categories grows, the economic advantages of the last solution increase. Two features allow only four values, three allow eight, four sixteen, and so on (2^n). In cases where all combinations are allowed, this is rightly the preferred procedure. Our three features for specifying vowels are of this kind: such an exhaustive vowel-system may be diagrammed as the eight vertices of a cube where the top four are +HIGH], the right four are [+BACK] and the front four are [+MID].

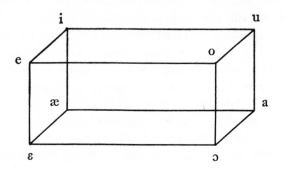

Another fully utilized feature would require a fourth dimension to represent in the same way, as the sixteen vertices of a hypercube. But in many cases attempts to produce this kind of analysis have not encountered universal acclaim. One difficulty is this: suppose you have nine vowels to account for. This requires four binary features (since three will yield only eight), seven combinations of which will go unused. But there are very many ways in which four features may be used to make nine phonemes, something like 1,430 altogether, and to be sure which one of those 1,430 is the best way is not easy. On the other hand, a pure hierarchical taxonomy[1] which subdivides each successive branching according to new and independent criteria, has the disadvantage that all the upper nodes seem to be redundant, mere *ad hoc* cover-symbols. Suppose we had one like, for instance, that shown in figure 10.1.

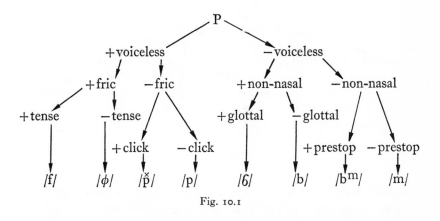

Fig. 10.1

Probably no language has exactly that set of eight labial consonants, but many will have five or six of the eight. No feature appears twice anywhere on this tree And if, for instance, the apical and dorsal trees look like figure 10.2, then only these two features are cross-classificatory, the

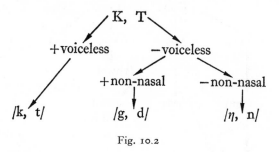

Fig. 10.2

other 5 purely subclassifying. And this sort of thing is not rare, as we noted above for 'Consonant'.

[1] See H. Conklin in *Problems in Lexicography* (ed. Householder and Saporta; Bloomington, 1962), pp. 132–6. A feature-value which at the next step becomes a feature with various values is the sort of thing which in strict binary analyses is handled by a hierarchically arranged set of features, with rules like [+such]→[±thus] [−such]→ [±so-or-so]. The notion of a feature of a feature (like the 'labiality' or 'rising glide' suggestions above) corresponds to a redundant feature: [±thus, −such]→ [+so-or-so].

More complex is the case where two different branching routes may lead to the same final list, yet there is no way of incorporating the two routes into a single system. Consider the case of the IE sonorants,

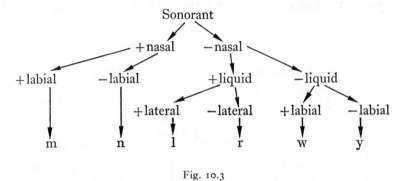

Fig. 10.3

idealized in figure 10.3. This tree does suggest also a kinship between m and w, which might be useful in some languages (though not in IE).

Re-arranging the hierarchical order in the last tree (figure 10.4) will not help much; if we put Voc above Cons, we will have nasals and semivowels

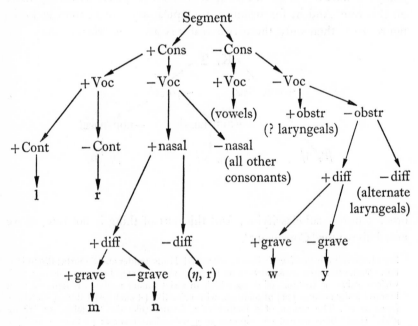

Fig. 10.4

in the same branch, but that is all. The only real help would be to decide that both r and l were [+diff] and then put diff above Voc. This might also bring i and u a little closer to y and w, but would separate the non-high vowels very far from the high ones, as well as putting palatals, velars and labialized velars farther away from dentals and labials. But there is no way of inserting a feature 'Sonorant' into the last diagram, unless we arbitrarily move both Voc and Cons way down to the bottom of the tree.

The conclusion seems to be that not all binary (or non-binary) natural divisions of phonemes which are used in rules need be built into a *distinctive* feature system.

II *Discovery and testing*

I *Phonology*

In an earlier chapter we remarked that the chief domain of scientification for linguists of the thirties and forties (and for many linguists, such
as the missionaries of The Summer Institute of Linguistics, even today)
was in procedures for discovering the structure (phonological and
morphological, at first; later also syntactic) of new languages. By
scientification here I mean reduction to rules and principles such that
(after due perfection) any two properly trained linguists independently
approaching a hitherto undescribed language, if they spent sufficient
time in applying them to the data of the language, would come up with
the same description, in the same form, order and notation. It was
usually taken for granted that this would also be in some way or other
the best description, though few linguists had as yet attempted to explain what made it the best until the doctrine of total accountability
(sometimes attributed to Pike) came along in the early fifties. This de-
clared that *one* feature of the best description would be that it accounted
for everything in the data and in any further extension of the data. This is
approximately what was later narrowed down a bit and christened observational adequacy, though in intent it was much closer – since its
proponents were sensible men – to descriptive adequacy. The term
'account for' is perhaps vague, but was usually understood to mean that
for any feature of any sample of the data one could find in the description
a relevant rule or classification. Obviously this could easily be pushed
toward Chomsky's descriptive adequacy; all that is needed is the notion
of an explanatory universal theory. And in phonology such a theory was
well on the way to being formulated.

We mentioned earlier that it is denied that the methods developed in
the period 1930–57 are either of the slightest theoretical interest or have
any applications as practical heuristic procedures. Some linguists
grant that it may be possible to devise heuristic procedures, but doubt
if they will have any similarity to the methods known as phonemic

analysis (including distinctive feature analysis), morphemic analysis and immediate constituent analysis. Nevertheless, it seems worth our while to examine these various methods, and any others we can come up with, so that, if in the end we decide to reject them all, we may at least know what it is that we are rejecting.

In this chapter, first, phonemic analysis. Here the theoretical foundations are given by Bloch's 'Postulates', Trubetzkoy's *Grundzüge* and Hockett's article on 'Descriptive Phonology';[1] Twaddell's 'On Defining the Phoneme'[2] and Y. R. Chao's 'On the Nonuniqueness of Phonemic Solutions of Phonetic Systems',[3] though reverently referred to by many, had little effect on actual practice. Pike's *Phonemics* (University of Michigan Press) became the standard practical guide upon its first appearance in 1947. The basic message of all these writers (and it struck its own era as just as much of an apocalyptic glory as Chomsky's *Syntactic Structures* in more recent times) can be summed up as follows: (1) Linguists analyzing other languages tend to hear and note well only the distinctions which are significant in their own language and to ignore or to treat as difficult distinctions peculiar to the strange language. The most notorious case of this is probably to be found in the accounts and dictionaries of African tone languages which entirely ignore the tone (except perhaps to say that you must try to imitate a native informant). Therefore the linguist must take special pains to discover exactly the set of distinctions the native speaker attends to (ignoring non-distinctions which may resemble distinctions in some other language). (2) These distinctions must then be represented by means of a minimal alphabet. This economy is achieved by considering the position in which the longest list of distinctions is maintained, and using for all other positions letters selected from this list only, provided there is sufficient phonetic similarity. (This last provision occasioned many debates about what is similar enough.)[4] This is the principle of complementary

---

[1] B. Bloch, 'A Set of Postulates for Phonemic Analysis', *Language* 24:3–46 (1948); slightly revamped in 'Studies in Colloquial Japanese IV', *Language* 26:86–125 (1950). N. Trubetzkoy, *Grundzüge der Phonologie* (*TCLP* 7) Prague, 1939; reissued by Vandenhoek and Ruprecht (Göttingen) in 1958; issued in a French version (tr. J. Cantineau) by Klincksieck (Paris) in 1949; English, tr. by C. A. M. Baltaxe, by University of California Press in 1969; C. F. Hockett, 'A System of Descriptive Phonology', *Language* 18:3–21 (1942); reprinted in Joos' *Readings*.

[2] Language Monograph No. 16, 1935, reprinted in Joos' *Readings*.

[3] *Bulletin of the Institute of History and Philology* (Academia Sinica) 4:363–97 (1933); reprinted in Joos' *Readings*.

[4] For a recent answer (two phones are similar enough if a change from one to the other is historically attested somewhere) see Shirô Hattori, 'The Principle of Assimilation in Phonemics' in *Word* 23:257–64 (1967).

distribution. As can be seen, the two together cover all cases of non-distinctiveness; two phone-types which the linguist suspects of being different may turn out to be non-distinctively different (not in contrast, not opposed) either (1) because they (a) are different only from a fine phonetic point of view or (b) may be unpredictably (or predictably) substituted for each other at any time, or (2) because they never occur in the same environment. The first case is ignored if it is believed to be a matter of fine phonetics, classed as *free variation* otherwise. The line is somewhat arbitrary, but most linguists tend to use the term free variation if and only if the two phone-types are known to contrast in some language. This is the international phonetic purpose for which Chomsky first favored distinctive features. But by no means Jakobson, who loved to cite the case of Danish stops, where a voiced stop initially contrasts with a voiceless one, but medially with a voiced fricative, so that the medial voiced fricative may be the same phoneme as the initial voiced stop, distinguished by the same feature (say Laxness) from the medial voiced stop as the initial voiced stop is distinguished from the initial voiceless stop. This sounds confusing, but is easy to represent as a proportion d:ð/medial = t:d/ initial; i.e. initial [t] = medial [d] = /t/, initial [d] = medial [ð] = /d/. This says that identical phones in different positions may be distinct phonemes. American linguists generally rejected this (called phonemic overlap), and required at least three phonemes (/t/, /d/, /ð/) for the Danish case. Here the [t] and the [ð] never occur in the same environment, but are not enough alike, and (more important) do not differ from [d] in ways which are alike. Jakobson says they differ from [d] in ways which are precise contraries, i.e. that the [t]:[d] contrast is identical to the [d]:[ð] contrast. So it is not *phones* which are in complementary distribution, but *contrasts*. Some American linguists more or less implicitly followed this principle, but their explicit doctrine was generally about the phonetic similarity of phones.

In languages like English it often happens that different inflections and derivatives containing the same morph exhibit the same segment of it now in initial, now in medial, now in final position. Though all three are rare, two are common: final and medial—grea*t*-grea*t*er, bea*d*-bea*d*ed, le*g*-le*gg*ing, etc.; initial (pretonic) and medial (posttonic)—geo*m*étric-geó*m*eter, *n*ot-can*n*ot, *t*one-ìnto*n*átion, *n*ote-dè*n*otátion; e*d*ítion-é*d*it, *m*e-gí*mm*e, *p*ose-dè*p*osítion, a*pp*éar-à*pp*arítion, and many more, almost all of Latin origin; final and pretonic (initial)—u*p*-u*p*ón, India*n*-Indiá*n*a-Indiá*n*ápolis-*N*aptown (which includes all three positions), ad*d*–ad*d*ítion, complemen*t*–complemen*t*árity (and many more of this general type), for*m*–for*m*álity, a*t*–a*t* áll, with–withál, look–look óut (meaning "Danger!"), ge*t*–ge*t* úp (flapped variety), etc. For such languages it is possible, in some measure, to escape the arbitrariness that has bothered many people (Chao, Twaddell, Harris quite as much as Chomsky). But suppose we have a hyper-Sinitic type of language in which all words are single morphs, all morphs are single syllables, and all syllables are made of one of ten initials – [ptk bdg shwy], three vowels – [aiu], and five finals – [mnzrʔ]. There will never be any etymological link between one of the initials and one of the finals (forgetting about the vowels). Obviously one here has two choices: either say that *order* of segments is non-distinctive (in which case [pin] may be indifferently represented as /pin, pni, inp, ipn, nip/ or /npi/) and all the phones are phonemic, or say that order is distinctive and (using Jakobson's approach) say that the contrast between m and n is the same as that between b and d (or p and t, – but here most people let the irrelevant voicing influence them) and that the difference between n and r is the same as that between d and s (this requires a little more faith), and finally, perhaps, that the contrast between [ʔ] and the other finals is the same as that between [h] and the other initials (this takes even more). But we cannot stop at [pid], since that leaves the position of i still predictable. The obvious next step is to say that i differs from u as y from w (and who would deny it?), while [a] does not contrast with zero. So, if order is made significant, we can now write [pin], [tan], [buz], [sam], [hir], [yuʔ] [haʔ] as /pyd/, /td/, /bwg/, /sb/, /hys/, /ywh/, [hh]. And, as a matter of fact, that makes a readable orthography. But is it some sort of truth? This is much harder to say. Note that one could also regard *either* the initial [h] or the final glottal as zero, but not both, (if the [h] is zeroed out, then [ʔ] may be represented as /ʔ/ in spite of defective distribution [final only] – unless /a/ is kept). If h is treated as zero, then the third-from-last word above would be written /ys/, the next-to-last /ywʔ/, and the last /ʔ/; if the glottal is zeroed, the three words will be /hys/, /yw/, /h/; if both are zeroed, then /tad/ and /sab/ have to be written for the second and fourth words, and the last three will be /ys/, /yw/ and /a/. It is quite normal for h's and ʔ's (when fully predictable) to be regarded as phonemic zeros – and usually corresponds well with the native speakers' intuition (as far as we can tell); it is a little less usual for /a/ or /ə/ to be so regarded, but still by no means unexampled (languages like Moroccan Arabic and Upper Chehalis spring to mind).

And the native speaker's reaction was considered a legitimate test by many linguists, in particular the missionaries of the Summer Institute of Linguistics. The principle could be formulated in two parts, one for free variation and one for complementary distribution. If the linguist teaches a native to read and write in his proposed phonemic orthography, but (1) the native keeps confusing two 'phonemes' which occur in the same position, then perhaps they are free variants and do not contrast, whereas if he has trouble reading the linguist's transcriptions of a single 'phoneme', asking "which way do you mean this one?" or the like, probably the linguist has missed a contrast. (2) If the native has trouble with the spelling of the same 'phoneme' in different positions, or flatly says "No, this isn't the same as that" then a wrong use of complementarity has perhaps been made. So if an untutored Dane had said to Jakobson (as numerous somewhat tutored ones in fact did), "No, no; medial [d] is the same as initial [d]!" this would have to be considered relevant.

These two basic principles, (1) native-speakers' distinctions only and (2) economy as long as it is not rejected by the native speaker, and the two positional types of economy (1) free variation and (2) complementary distribution, provided the basis for all the practical procedures recommended by Pike (and some pseudo-practical ones discussed somewhat later by Harris),[1] but a third check on the freedom of the linguist has received a high degree of notoriety through its being regarded as the single important test by some linguists and rejected as worthless and irrelevant by others. I mean *bi-uniqueness*. As generally stated this is a test of an orthography or transcription, rather than of an analysis: "For a transcription system to be correct, speakers must be able to write isolated words – even nonsense syllables – of their language so that other literate speakers can read them back without error." Now any good phonetic transcription automatically satisfies this requirement, but phonetic transcriptions are not economical. As just now stated, however, we really have only half of the bi-uniqueness requirement. The other half goes like this "Two writers transcribing (correctly) the same utterance in this system must always give the same transcription." Without this restriction, there might again be a loss of economy. There could be two or three letters unambiguously representing each 'phoneme' or phone, and the first test could be passed with flying colors. But the second one could not be passed on brand new nonsense syllables unless the subjects were using two systems, one for known words (which could

[1] *Methods in Structural Linguistics*, University of Chicago Press, 1951, ch. 3 and 4.

be learned perfectly by both) and a different, unambiguous one for nonsense syllables. This implies a third test, which is not often explicitly mentioned: "All familiar words must be spelled exactly as if they were nonsense syllables." Stated otherwise this means "A non-speaker of the language can learn the system well enough to transcribe every word perfectly even though he does not understand a single one." It might in theory be possible to fudge this test; a non-speaker might be taught a large vocabulary of words, none of which he understands, but which he can nevertheless learn to spell correctly in an ambiguous system. But it is generally supposed that such an elaborate cheat would not be worth-while.

Now how is the bi-uniqueness requirement usually stated? Chomsky's statement is perhaps the best known:[1] "Each sequence of phones is represented by a unique sequence of phonemes, and each sequence of phonemes represents a unique sequence of phones"; a footnote modifies the second half into "each sequence of phonemes represents a sequence of phones that is unique up to free variation". This phrasing would not be acceptable to either Praguian or Bloch–Tragerian or Pikean phone-micists because of the word 'represent', chosen by Chomsky, perhaps, out of his belief that phones are real while phonemes are hocus-pocus. Furthermore, this wording doesn't take us away from the orthographic or notational interpretation of the phoneme, according to which phonemes are notational devices to symbolize or 'represent' phones. The contrary view was more usual in the forties and fifties: phones somehow repre-sent or 'realize' phonemes; they are the actual sound-types which speakers employ to signify the more abstract entities which are called phonemes. However, if we substitute some more neutral verb for 'represent' we can arrive at a statement of the principle which will fairly well fit the usage of all Classical Phonologists (as Sydney Lamb calls them) except sometimes Jakobson: "Any given portion of an utterance in any language can be set in systematic correspondence with one and only one sequence of phonemes; furthermore, given any se-quence of phones there will be a single sequence of phonemes corres-ponding, and given any sequence of phonemes there will be a single sequence of phones (except for possible free variation)." The second half is not quite a necessary consequence of the first half because the first half does not exclude the possibility that another given utterance-

[1] In *Proceedings of the 9th International Congress of Linguists* (ed. H. G. Lunt), The Hague (Mouton, 1964), p. 954.

sample might have the same corresponding phone-sequence (or phoneme-sequence) as the first one, but a different corresponding phoneme-sequence (bzw. phone-sequence). In some versions of Jakobson's theory, however, it looks as if phones are eliminated from the picture. This makes it a good deal harder to state the principle, since everyone admits that no two utterance-tokens are the same. However, if we substitute "class of utterance-tokens" for "sequence of phones", it would perhaps come out like this: "Every sequence of phonemes is realized by a unique class of utterance-tokens, and the class of utterance-tokens which realizes a given sequence of phonemes cannot also realize any other sequence of phonemes." I think this would be acceptable, and has free variation built in. The point here is that, while most American (and some British) linguists regarded a phoneme as a class of distinct phones, each of which could be specified in absolute terms without reference to the possible existence of other phones, Jakobson regarded a phoneme as one term (simultaneously) in a small number of distinctive oppositions. So, in the Danish case mentioned above, we would have a number of utterance-tokens each of which contained (at some fairly definitely specifiable location) an end term ("unmarked for tenseness" or perhaps "marked for laxness") which is simultaneously an end term in a number of other oppositions. The only meaning of 'phones' in this scheme is "closely resembling distinctive segments in some known language". So, in terms of Danish alone, there is no [d], but only the lax phoneme /d/ and the tense phoneme /t/. But it does happen that some instances of /d/ and some of /t/ closely resemble the French (or German, perhaps) phoneme /d/, while other instances of /d/ resemble the English phoneme /ð/ and others of /t/ resemble the French /t/.

A phone notation [d] then means merely "Like a phoneme /d/ in some language X," in the sense that a speaker of language X who was ignorant of the language (L) under discussion might use his phoneme /d/ to imitate a speaker of the Language L. This is by no means unreasonable, and recognizes the fact which first initiated phonemic theory, that our hearing is always (even after much phonetic training) conditioned by the phonological system of our native language. Under this view "phonemic overlapping" cannot occur, because within the native speaker's system the two entities alleged to be the same phone are not the same at all.

Firthian linguistics dodges the complementary distribution problem by specifying (more or less in Twaddell's manner) that the system of commutable entities at position 1 is necessarily independent of that at position 2, and any identification is purely conventional for the purposes of practical orthography. Danish initial [t] and [d] are part of the Danish initial system, while medial [d] and [ð] are part of the medial system, and these two are separate and independent; the need for economy which leads to attempts to match the members of one set with members of the other is relevant only for a practical (i.e. theoretically irrelevant) orthography.

So what do we decide about bi-uniqueness? (a) For practical orthographies a considerable measure of it is desirable, though some relaxation in the direction "several symbols – one sound" may be O.K. In particular, if it is convenient in language L to spell[1] initial /s/ with *s* when it begins a noun, and with *x* when it begins a verb, or to distinguish pairs of homonyms by such variant spellings, why not? – provided the learning burden placed on the school-child is not too great. And it would hardly be greater than the spelling burden of English-speaking children. (b) For linguistic truth, the answer is more difficult, since this presumably depends largely on the intuitions of intelligent but unschooled native speakers, and these may not always be consistent. But if we take the phone-bypassing approach given above, and add a restriction to a single dialect, a single style and limited time (since we must allow change), it would seem impossible to reject bi-uniqueness. Let us restate it: "Every grammatical sequence of phonemes corresponds (for a given speaker) to a unique set of utterance tokens, no member of which may correspond (for that speaker) to any other sequence of phonemes." This amounts to a flat denial of intermediate or indeterminate tokens, tokens which may serve equally well (say) to represent 'gum' as 'come', or 'thin' as 'sin' or 'ran' as 'rang', etc. Now it is a matter of common experience that such uncertainties do occur, but this is irrelevant unless it can be shown that native speakers have and use such an intermediate category, so that, to a given stimulus, some will respond "He said 'sin'", some "He said 'thin'", and others– in some cases a majority – "He said the word intermediate between 'thin' and 'sin'". I think it is clear enough that no such category exists, that no matter how indeterminate or blurry a given utterance may be, each native speaker must either assign it to a specific phoneme sequence (or the equivalent) or give up, saying "What's that again?" or "I'm sorry,

---

[1] The notation between asterisks here means orthography, written representation, letters of the alphabet, as opposed to solidi which indicate phonology, phonemes, abstract classes of speech-sounds. Others use angle brackets ⟨ ⟩ for orthography.

I can't understand you." So, if we are willing to have phonemes or phones of any kind, they must surely have this kind of bi-uniqueness. Even the relation between phones and phonemes, or phonemes and letters must certainly be characterized in considerable measure by bi-uniqueness, though in the latter case it is a practical concern.

What about the other principles mentioned by Chomsky – linearity and local determinacy for instance? As he himself admits, not all Classical Phonemicists maintained these 100%, though as rough empirical propositions they will serve: in general, phonemes are consecutive and two distinct consecutive phonemes do not correspond to a single uniform stretch of sound. But, as we remarked in an earlier chapter, it is quite usual for some linguists to assume that occasionally two consecutive phonemes match a single articulation and a single acoustic segment, though it is hard to suppose this of discontinuous phonemes.

But, for this chapter, we want to note merely the heuristic methods which have been devised as consequences of (a) the doctrine that natives hear nonsense syllables or new names in their own language in a different manner from non-natives, and (b) the desire to minimize the inventory, without (c) loss of bi-uniqueness or introduction of ambiguity.

Let us consider these methods first for those who proceed from phones to phonemes. The linguist asks the native speaker to utter for him a series of short words (monosyllables, if there are any, otherwise the shortest available) one at a time, and writes them down as best he can. This first transcription will necessarily be largely in terms of the linguist's own phonemic system; if he happens to be a native speaker of two or more languages, he will be able in some cases to shift his hearing base from one to another, and if he has been well trained in producing (and, of course, discriminating) the sounds of many different languages, he may possibly miss none of the significant distinctions on the first go. But he will also (unless he is very unskilled or the phonological system is very close to his own) transcribe differences that the informant does not care about. As he keeps up this process of transcribing lists over a longer period of time, he will gradually become aware of differences he missed at first and of unnecessary distinctions, and will revise his transcription accordingly, without special procedures. The most serious problem here lies in the vowel system; if the linguist speaks a language which cuts up vocalic space[1] into twelve distinct types and is listening to

1 In this space the horizontal dimension represents frontness vs. backness (with front to the left) or Formant 2 (with high values approaching 3,000 Hz to the left), while the

a language which divides the same space into only five, he may persist in writing irrelevant distinctions for quite a while; and even if both languages have (say) four vowels, but these four are differently placed and have different areas, he may both overdiscriminate and underdiscriminate for a while. Consider vowel systems A and B, here:

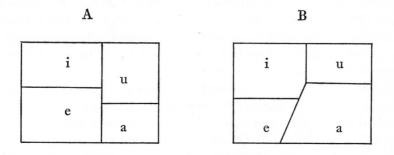

Suppose A is the linguist's system and B the informant's. Then some instances of B's i and a will be noted as e, some of B's a will be noted as u, though all of u and e will be consistently noted as u and e. Two things may then happen: he may say that in language B, under some conditions, there is free variation or complementary distribution between i and e, e and a, a and u, or (if he becomes somewhat fluent in the language himself) he may cease to hear in his own frame and hear instead the way the B-speaker does. In this case, as he looks back at his first transcriptions he may wonder a bit at the odd fluctuations he indulged in.

Eventually the linguist becomes pretty consistent and complacent about his transcriptions, and the testing begins (although much of this in most cases has been done as he went along). The usual first test is the search for minimal pairs of words or utterances. The phone-oriented linguist means by minimal "differing at only one point", whereas the feature-oriented one whom we will discuss later means "differing (at one point) in such a way that no third term can be inserted between the members of the pair". For instance, a pair like English brig:brim is minimal for the phone-starter, but not for the feature seeker, since a term *bring* may be inserted, which is more like each of the pair than they are like each other. In fact, however, it is mainly this 'feature' kind of minimal pair which provides a useful test, even for the phone-linguist, because it is mainly in cases of *close* resemblance in sound that the

vertical dimension represents openness or height (with high vowels at top) or Formant 1 (with high values around 1,000 Hz at the bottom). See ch. 4.

investigator has doubts. It is quite unlikely that there is any language in the world in which (say) [big] and [bim] represent two variant pronunciations of the same word, indistinguishable to the native speaker.

Let us take a specific instance. In the Azerbaijani of my first informant I early noted that a palatal fricative [ç] occurred finally and before a few consonants, always preceded by a front vowel (i, e, æ, ü, ö), never a back one. (Azerbaijani has both front–back and rounded–unrounded vowel harmony in suffix syllables.) In many cases the final syllable was a suffix or part of a suffix (infinitive, first-person plural, future, diminutive, etc.). And the back-vowel form of this suffix ended in [x]. The question, then, is this: are [x] and [ç] capable of contrasting or not? If not, then we can consider them both forms of /x/, say. After some searching it turned out that they *could* contrast, that there were several minimal pairs with the vowel [æ] before final [x] and [ç]. Of course this does not end the testing. As it happens, when a suffix beginning with a vowel is added after [x] or [ç], these two are voiced into [ɣ] and [y], respectively. So, can [x] contrast with [ɣ]? Can [ç] contrast with [y]? Once again the answer is yes, and minimal pairs can be found, although final [ɣ] and [y] are nearly confined to monosyllables. Neither [ɣ] nor [ç] can occur initially, though [x] and [y] do. But back velar lenis [q] and front lenis palatal [g′] as well as aspirated palatal [k′] – but rarely (never for some speakers) an aspirated velar [k] – do occur initially. Can [q] and [ɣ] ever contrast? Not initially and finally, as we have seen, but medially, yes. [g′] and [y] both occur initially, so the remaining question is, what about [k′] and [ç]? The first answer is that they cannot contrast, and may therefore be regarded as one phoneme. It is true that eventually it appeared that [k′] could occur (very rarely) in final position in Persian–Arabic loans of a certain stylistic level, hence making contrast with [ç] theoretically possible (though no minimal pairs could be found). So in a very rigorous phonemic analysis (e.g. of the Trager or Harris varieties) all seven of these phones, though linked many different ways by morphophonemic rules and free (i.e. stylistic) variation, would be distinct phonemes. This is clearly on the ground that the distribution shows native speakers able and eager to distinguish them all. And the one case ([ç] vs. [k′]) where they have some trouble distinguishing is just the one for which phonemic unity could be argued, up to a point.

The minimal-pair-testing procedure applies, as we have seen, only to phones in comparable positions (both final, both intervocalic, both initial, etc.), and is to distinguish free variation and over-fine phonetic discrimination from contrast. It may also, on occasion, call attention to over-coarse phonetic discrimination. To make this test the linguist collects instances of homonyms (the shorter the better, of course), and somehow persuades the informant to record each of the pair in exactly the same frame, amplitude, tone, rate of speed, etc., noting carefully on the tape which member of the pair is being elicited. The next step is easy to perform when you have access to a lab, but tough in the field. Duplicate both utterances half-a-dozen times, and dub them off on another tape in random order (without the identification). Then play them to the same informant and to other informants, and see if they can discriminate. Often they cannot (even when they think they can), but sometimes they can. And then the linguist's job is to find out how. This is not always easy; it is surprising what a slight difference may be significant. There must be a threshold value here, of course, but it is remarkably low. The opposite, how great a difference may count for nothing, is not usually so surprising, though some people are surprised to learn that in Niihau [t] and [k] are not distinguished, or [m] and [w] in Hidatsa. But very great differences may often be taken as indications merely of physical defect or foreign origin. The cleft-palate speaker cannot produce true aspirated voiceless stops or non-nasal vowels (among other things), and yet such speakers get along in the community without attention, even though their substitute articulations may be quite elaborately different from those of the normal speaker. And Greeks or others who substitute [x] for initial /h/ in English get along quite well, and the normal native reaction lumps this in with a bunch of other deviation as a "guttural accent" or maybe just a "thick accent". If I substitute initial voiced implosives for ordinary voiced stops, most people won't notice, although that is a rather big difference, and important in some languages.

I have described these tests so far as if they were always clean-cut, unambiguous and two-valued in their results: x and y *are* distinguished in position P, or x and y are *not* distinguished in position P. And this is sometimes the case. But not always; very often an informant will discriminate "correctly" 60% of the time, or 75%. Or one informant will discriminate 95% correctly, but another only 45%. This last case is not too bad; one merely assumes that the two speakers' dialects have different systems at this point, which is not unusual even in speakers who have grown up next door to each other and speak indistinguishable dialects in all other respects. A few points in American English where this has been recorded are the following: (1) distinction between *latter* and *ladder* and similar words (in spite of Webster III's assumption that no American makes it); (2) between *war* and *wore*, *horse* and *hoarse*, and similar pairs; (3) in parts of the South the distinction between *pen* and *pin*. Furthermore, most people can hear more distinctions than they use in their own speech (though this is not often the case with the three I have just cited); so-called r-less dialect speakers who never pronounce *law* differently from *lore*, or *caught* from *court*, or *canna* from *canner* can nevertheless distinguish these words perfectly when someone else pronounces them. In many areas certain mergers or discriminations are considered in the local folklore to be characteristic of people from certain other areas, shibboleths. Very often the belief is correct; sometimes it was formerly correct but is not any longer, and sometimes it has never been correct but is just close enough so that it is never refuted.[1]

But whatever the situation is in any of these respects, it is always capable of description in yes–no terms, with supplementary information about style levels, dialect differences and social prestige factors. One's feelings for economy are often upset by a situation in which a certain discrimination is very rarely used. In Iranian Azerbaijani, for instance, the back velar stop is normally lenis only, unopposed by any fortis aspirated [k], although occasionally a speaker may accidentally (as it were) give a fortis pronunciation to a word normally pronounced with the lenis [q]. But there are a few loan-words, mostly from European languages (Russian, French or English), in which the fortis, aspirated k is pronounced consistently by some speakers. (A similar situation is said to exist in Moroccan Arabic.) Since all the other stops occur in pairs (p–b, t–d, k–g, c–j), it seems natural that the velar stop should too. And yet it is uneconomical to have this fortis k for most of the normal vocabulary. But anyway, the facts are easily taken care of, in spite of the awkwardness, though the principle adhered to by some Classical Phonemicists (called "once-a-phoneme-always-a-phoneme"), which requires careful reporting of all the ordinary free-variation words to indicate which variant has been chosen, would make for loss of economy. Here the Prague archiphoneme notion (avoided with revulsion by many Americans in the forties) comes in handy. The ordinary vocabulary contains words which have neither the aspirated tense /k/ nor the lenis lax /q/ but a velar stop unspecified as to tenseness. (The value 'un-

---

[1] W. Labov has recently reminded us that speakers may use distinctions without being aware of it.

specified' for features must be added to the values 'marked' (' +') and 'unmarked' (' −').) In terms of phonological rules, this archiphoneme could either go to phonetic specification direct in rather low-level rules, or first go to 'plus tense' or 'minus tense' by some probabilistic rule (i.e. 'plus tense 16·3% of the time', 'minus tense 83.7% of the time'), after which these 'plus tense' items join the others (which have been so specified all along) in their progress toward phonetic shape. In old-fashioned language one would say that the archiphoneme /Q/ is realized by lax [q] 83.7% of the time, by tense aspirated [kʰ] the rest of the time (assuming there is no third variant, or gradient values of tenseness). A few loan-words, on the other hand, would contain either the fully specified tense velar or (rarely) a fully specified lax or lenis velar stop.

But whatever solution linguists of the Lost Generation adopted for problems like this, their abiding compass-rose was to match the native-speaker's ear as closely as possible. This was the case also with problems of monophonematic and diphonematic interpretation, which have to do with the number of phonetic segments in comparison with the number of phonemes in the corresponding string. In English the most frequent discussions of monophonematic interpretation had to do with the alleged diphthongs in *bait* and *boat* and with the prevocalic portions of *chew* and *Jew*. Were there sequences /ey/ and /ow/ or the like in the first case or unitary tense vowels /e/ and /o/? Were there simple affricates /č/ and /ǰ/ in the second case or clusters /tš/ and /dž/? Arguments were based on economy, phonetic realism, and various other things, but 'pattern congruity' – which was a vaguely formulated device for guessing at the native speaker's subconscious analysis – was generally regarded as able to override both the others. In the case of *chew* and *Jew* it would go like this: if one analyzes the initial in Jew as /dž/, then this cluster will be more common and occur freely in more positions than one of its components, /ž/; such a situation is incongruous, and hence /ǰ/ must be a single phoneme. But if /ǰ/ is, then /č/ must be also, for it would be incongruous to have the voiceless term of an opposition structured differently from the voiced term. An argument similar to the /dž/ – /ž/ one would apply to /ow/ if the Smith–Trager line were taken that pure /o/ is a sporadic dialect feature occurring in a few items like 'gonna' in New York, or 'road' in Maine. But if the Bloomfield line that /o/ is the stressed vowel in *bud, hut, rug*, etc. is adopted (as in this book), then this argument won't work. And at the Fall of Phonemics in the early sixties, though the one-phoneme analysis of /č/ and /ǰ/ was almost universally accepted, the two-phoneme version /ey/ and /ow/ – or /ei/ and /ou/ for some – though favored by a majority, did not have the same settled status. One curious thing about this problem is that a pure feature approach does not get rid of it. Two examples of a diphonemic interpretation concern the post-vocalic portion of *hang* and the vocalic portion of *can't* or *think*. Final [ŋ] (and intervocalic [ŋ] as well as [ŋ] before suffixal [z] [d] and probably [θ]) could be treated as two segments /ng/ without much difficulty, by adopting a rule:

(a) /ng/→[ŋ]/____#, suffix,
(b) /ng/→[ŋg] (elsewhere)

except for the odd fact that although [ŋ] stays the same before most vowel-initial suffixes, the words *long*, *strong* and *young* have instead [ŋg] before comparative *-er*, superlative *-est*, and (optionally, at least, in some dialects) before the particle *enough*. And, of course, all the monomorphemic words like *anger*, *bungle*, *dingus*, *thingummy* (but *thing-a-ma-jig* and *thing-a-ma-bob* must be polymorphemic, with [ŋ]) have [ŋg]. And other monosyllabic adjectives (e.g. *wrong*, and nonce-adjectives like *wing*, *zing*, etc.) keep [ŋ] even before *-er*, *-est*. This makes the rule rather awkward to write. But it can be done with a notation of morph-boundary (e.g. ' + ') by saying:

(a) /ng/→[ŋg] in *long*, *strong*, *young* except when followed by #,
(b) /ng/→[ŋ]/____ #, +
(c) /ng/→[ŋg].

(Accounting for *length*, *strength*, and *youth* will need some other rules.) Another solution has also been proposed, which consists in spelling *long*, *strong*, and *young* with an extra /g/ in the lexicon: /longg/, /strongg/ and /yongg/. Then after rules (b) and (c) are applied ((a), of course, is not needed) a general rule dropping final [g] after [ŋ] would be applied. This solution, however, is no more economical and introduces rather counterintuitive geminates. As for the nasalized vowels in *can't*, *lamp*, *hank*, etc., diphonematic interpretation is universal, so far as I know, partly because for most speakers there is completely free variation between [kæ̃t] and [kæ̃nt], [læ̃p] and [læ̃mp], [hæ̃k] and [hæ̃ŋk], and indeed most people would have a hard time deciding (without instrumental aid) which pronunciation they were themselves using, let alone which another speaker was using at any given moment.

A most delicate question (first raised, I think, by Jakobson in a vague way, and used, in a more precise form, by Chomsky to demolish the entire edifice of phonemic procedure) concerns the case of contrast of sequences reversed or of sequences with their members. A permissive rule which I formulated (a wee bit sloppily, as was amicably pointed out) in *Journal of Linguistics*[1] for handling this situation, one used more or less subconsciously by most Classical Phonemicists, runs something like this: "If a tentative phonemicization includes distinct phonemes A and B, then this phonemicization should not be rejected for lack of contrast even if A is never directly opposed to B, provided that AB is opposed to BA or that AB (or BA) is opposed to B or to A." If the doubly-negative formulation is not satisfying, we might try this: "Two distinct phones A and B may be said to contrast even if A and B do not occur in the same environment, provided that AB contrasts with BA, or AB or BA contrasts with B or A." One obvious case is that of vowels which seldom contrast directly with consonants (a thing which was frequently taken for granted). But it is also useful for some other types of sequence of restricted distribution, and can even be used to support some diphonematic interpretations of diphthongs and affricates.

One proposal for discovering vowel systems recently made by Scholes[2] is of some interest. As it now stands it will only take care of two-dimensional ($F_1 \times F_2$) systems, without regard to nasality, quantity, glottalization, creaky voice, or any such modifications. A set of synthetic vowels is prepared covering the entire practicable area (F_1 250–850 Hz, F_2 800–2,600) for a male speaker, by steps such that 70 distinct vowels (7 values of F_1, 10 values of F_2) are synthesized. Various randomized sequences of these vowels are played to native speakers of the language being investigated, who are asked, if a vowel sounds possible in their language, to write down a short word containing the vowel, but if not, nothing. When the results are plotted, there is generally a pretty correct picture of the number of distinct vowels in the language and their approximate ranges in F_1–F_2 space. Numerous refinements can easily be devised.

A perusal of Pike's *Phonemics* and some of the vast literature (not yet completely finished) on procedures of phonemic analysis will show many more proposed tests, tests in general use, theoretical principles, rules of sequential operation and even rules for theoretically automatic

[1] I (1965) p. 130; cf. p. 27. Chomsky and Halle's kindly reply appeared in the next issue.
[2] Unpublished final report under an Indiana Language Program Grant, entitled *Categorial Responses to Synthetic Vocalic Stimuli by Native Speakers of Various Foreign Languages*, by Robert J. Scholes.

algorithms (which all too often require information derivable only from an enormous corpus, and one which must be perfectly homogeneous in style and dialect), but none of them rest upon any other principles than the two I have mentioned: basically native speaker's phonological performance, secondarily (provided there is no conflict) economy. The literature on phonemics also includes a goodly portion of scattered items dealing with ideal orthographies, writing schemes for hitherto unwritten or badly written languages. We shall say a little more about this in a later chapter, but here we should point out that a third principle is often brought into these accounts, what might be called morphemic bi-uniqueness, which implies two consequences: (1) the same morpheme is always spelled the same unless this results in horrendous misrepresentation; (2) homophones (if not truly polysemous single morphemes) must have distinct spellings unless their distribution guarantees freedom from ambiguity.[1] Part (1) has always been much more popular than part (2), and underlies the dodges often resorted to to achieve a convenient pseudophonological representation for the base form of each morpheme. Part two is sometimes rejected on the ground that a single lexical entry should correspond to a unique base form.

But what about the direct discovery of distinctive features? Jakobson has a number of scattered remarks, and other writers occasionally say something relevant, but I know of nothing that could be called a manual of procedure. And yet, in general, it is clear that many of the same operations must take place, and (in particular) that minimal pairs in the narrow sense of that term must enjoy a dominant role. Although it is probably true that precise segmentation (into phones) is unnecessary as a preliminary step to forming oppositive pairs (of words or perhaps morphs, if citable), since some sort of generic localization ("at the end", "at the beginning", "between the beginning and the vowel", "after the vowel", etc.) is sufficient to establish a class of utterances A which contrast with another class B at such and such localities, it is hard to avoid the feeling that such a class-forming operation is logically equivalent to establishing a pair (or a number of pairs) of phones. The vaguest part of Jakobson's theory was always the rule for recognizing that x and y were both instances of the same opposition. In practice it was normally done (by Jakobsonians of my acquaintance) in terms of lists of phone-types. The investigator learns, for instance, that the s:θ opposition in

---

[1] So, in English, *bank* might be used of a shore, *banc* of a shelf or row of things, *banque* of a financial institution.

any language is a case of strident–mellow, as is the c:t (affricate–plain stop) opposition, and a whole list of other pairs. But he never learns how to hear for himself the special quality of this opposition, so that he could identify hitherto unexampled specimens of it in languages being studied for the first time. Jakobson was believed to have a special gift which resisted simple explanation. He could hear that the k:t contrast was identical in quality with the a:i contrast, or that Arabic laryngealization was the same as labialization. The famous *Preliminaries*[1] was a valiant but not wholly successful attempt to provide some sort of objective criteria. It also began the slow shift from specification of *oppositions* to specification of articulations and spectra of particular sounds. That is, we now get a description of /a/ and of /k/ in the absolute, not an account of the *difference* between /a/ and /i/ or /k/ and /t/. But even in 1962 Jakobson himself was adamant about the essential nature of *distinctiveness* as opposed to phonetic (acoustic or articulatory) description, whether fine or coarse.

In practice, then, most people simply followed the same procedures (more or less) as those codified by Pike, and then converted this into a distinctive feature analysis by consulting a table of equivalences. Still it seems in principle possible to imagine a procedure something like this (involving features more like those suggested above in chapter 9):

(1) Listen to words for clear indications of labial-apical-dorsal opposition or some part of it.

(2) Within apical or dorsal, listen for front vs. back contrasts or palatal vs. plain.

(3) Listen for stop–nasal contrasts;

(4) For voiced–voiceless or tense–lax contrasts;

(5) And so on through other contrasts, noting them down on some sort of musical score, in which each test word is allotted a simple staff and each part of the word a corresponding part of the staff (without rigorous segmentation). Eventually one might have a complete feature scoring without ever having once written a single alphabetic symbol. For us with our ingrained alphabetic habits this would be impossible to test fairly, but perhaps a Chinese linguist who had not been much exposed to alphabetic language material might be able to do it. In principle, if the oppositions are explicitly described, the whole process

---

[1] *Preliminaries to Speech Analysis* by R. Jakobson, C. G. M. Fant and M. Halle, M.I.T., 1952. Minor variations of the theory appear in the items on pp. 442–658 of Roman Jakobson, *Selected Writings I* (Mouton, 1962).

H

might be performed by a computer (though I shudder at the complexity of the program).

If we turn now to an alternate view of features, that their function is to provide useful classes of phonemes for specifying phonotactics and morphophonemics (distribution and sandhi) and historical changes, then another set of heuristic procedures becomes available. Once again the investigator completes a Classical Phonemic analysis (possibly stopping short of unifying major positional variants), and prepares a large corpus, transcribed in the corresponding notation. He then conducts exhaustive distributional searches of the corpus: what phonemes or phones may begin an utterance? end one? never do either? How many phonemes may precede the first vowel (the identification of vowels and consonants is usually assumed to have been independently made)? What are they? If there are C_1C_2 clusters in initial position, which phonemes may occur as C_1? as C_2? as C_1 before particular members of C_2? as C_2 after particular members of C_1? and so on and on. The classes that result from such an examination have been studied in great detail (e.g. by Bengt Sigurd[1] for Swedish), and we shall see later how features may be derived from such lists. Now to this add information about morphophonemics: what phonemes change in what ways when affixes are added to stems? when words are combined in sequence? when words are compounded? In English, for instance, f and θ are related to v and ð by certain rules about singular and plural (and sometimes noun and verb). s, z, and iz are variant forms of the plural noun suffix, the third-singular-nonpast verb suffix, and various other suffixes; in words of Latin origin there are complicated interrelations of vowel quality with position and stress – and so on.

Suppose we consider here an attempt at an algorithm for classifying English phonemes, which we will rephrase as a set of distributional classes, and see what features suggest themselves to account for these classes.[2] The phonemicization with which I start has the following peculiarities: the vowels of *bat, but, hot, beat, bait, yacht, boot, boat, brought,* and *Hoyt* will be represented respectively as /a, o, ɔ, iː, eː, aː, uː, oː, ɔː, ɔy/, the stressed nuclei of *mirror* (=*beer*) *berry, barrow* (=*care*),

[1] *Phonotactic Structures in Swedish*, Lund, 1965. Note also the excellent bibliography on pp. 210–17.
[2] 'The Distributional Determination of English Phonemes' in *Lingua* XI (1962), 186–91. See also the literature there cited, to which might be added the passage in Edward Sapir's *Sound Patterns in Language* (reprinted in Joos' *Reading in Linguistics* I; 24, col. 1) where he lists seven distributional and morphophonemic criteria for specifying ptk as a class in English.

jury (=*poor*), *hurry* (=*word*), *story* (=*fort*), *sorry* (=*short*), and *starry* (=*part*) will be /ir, er, ar, uːr, or, oːr, ɔːr, aːr/ respectively. The consonant phonemes are pretty well the standard list.

(11-1) The first class is "phonemes which may occur initially, but not finally", and consists of h and the six simple vowels. There is apparently no single distributional rule for which we need only the class of simple vowels, except perhaps something like this "single phonemes occurring between initial s and final t" – but my algorithm is assumed to start without any knowledge of s's or t's. However, let us for convenience sake make our first cut between *vowels* and *non-vowels*. This requires a second cut as follows: "If the first *two* phonemes of any words are both members of class one, then the first is h; all other members of class one are vowels."

(11-2) My second class is "phonemes which occur finally but never initially" and includes /ŋ/, /ž/ and /ː/. Those who object to /ː/ as a phoneme and who treat /ŋ/ as /ng/ would have only /ž/ in this class. None of these groupings looks very charming for real phonetic features.

(11-3) My fourth and fifth cuts yield the semivowels /w,y/ as the only non-vowels occurring after initial /h/. If /yuː/ is treated as vocalic throughout, /üː/ or the like, or as a falling diphthong /iw/, this won't work. Postvocalic w and y are harder to single out, though groups like r, y, w or ː, r, y, w, or maybe ː, l, r, y, w are not impossible.

(11-4) My first subclass of vowels consists of i, a, ɔ, o, the four vowels which occur before final (or prefinal) /ŋ/. (If we use instead final /sk/, we exclude only /u/, not /u/ and /e/. Call it class 4*a*.)

(11-5) My second (independent of the first) yielded the two open vowels "which can occur before final y or w". People who phonemicize /iy/, /ey/, /uw/ and /ow/ couldn't use this criterion.

(11-6) My next (large) class contains all phonemes except y, w, ž, ŋ, ː, h, and vowels; I call them consonants. No new criteria are needed; this class is made up of all phonemes not in classes 1–5.

(11-7) Initial three-consonant clusters establish three more classes, one consisting of s alone, one of p, t, k – the simple voiceless stops – and one of r, l (w and y have been excluded, but otherwise r, l, w, y could be derived here). These are useful for the algorithm but /s/ can be otherwise specified.

(11:8) The class of non-vowels which may follow initial s is next: ptk, mn, l, f, w. (If [šr], as in *shrill*, etc., is treated as phonemically /sr/, then /r/ may be added. Speakers of the old-fashioned type of English in which *sphere* was /spir/ would exclude /f/ from this class. It's a pity we don't still talk that way. Initial /sθ/ is no problem, since my algorithm uses only monosyllables.

(11-9) Another subclass of vowels is picked out as occurring before final r: i, a, o. Since there are almost as many ways of handling these vowels as there are analysts, and since dialects differ widely here, this is obviously only one possibility.

(11-10) Vowels followed by /:rk/ include (in my dialect) o, ɔ, a, as in *pork, fork, park.*

(11-11) An important subclass of consonants is "those which occur initially only before a vowel or y, w: čj, mn, vðz – affricates, nasals and voiced fricatives". There may be a few expressive items in vr- or zl- for some people, but they are (as has often been remarked) expressive in part because they break this rule.

(11-12) Initial phonemes (h or consonant) which may be followed directly by /yu:/ include, for me, only the labials, velars, and h: p b f v m, k g, h.

(11-13) Those which may be followed directly by /w/ include some apicals, the velars and h: t d θ s š k g h (note that ðzn are not included). If you cannot say /šwa:/ in your dialect, š is excluded.

Joint membership in these last two classes yields kgh. The residue from 12 is then labials only – p b f v m; the residue from 13 is t d θ s š, the most generally useable apicals.

(11-14) Our next criterion is "initial followed by l or r". This gives ptk, bdg, fθ, sš. If [šr] is treated as /sr/ and the expressive words in /šl/ are excluded, š will fall out of the class.

(11-15) The final C of any final CCC must be θ, s, z, t, d – and is nearly always a suffix if we wish to consider morphological classes.

(11-16) Consonants which occur before final /s/ are ptk, fθ, mn, lr. If you put a p in *glimpse* or a t in *fence* and *else*, mn and l may be deleted from the list.

(11-17) Non-vowels which occur before final /t/ are pčk, fθsš, mn, lr, yw, :. If you put a p in *dreamt* or *prompt* m can be removed. If you exclude cases where there is a morph boundary before the t (i.e. where -t is a suffix), the list will lose č, θ, š.

(11-18) Consonants before final /z/ are bdg, vð, mn, lr. Again, if you put a /d/ in *lens*, n will come off the list. Note that mnlr is the intersection of 16 and 18.

(11-19) Non-vowels before final /d/ include bgǰ, vðzž, mnŋ, lr, yw, :. The intersection of 17 and 19 gives /mnlryw:/.

(11-20) Always preceded immediately by a vowel: ŋ, :.

Let us now lay out these twenty natural (phonotactic) classes (really 21, since rule 7 marks two classes) in a matrix, omitting minuses after column 6. (See Table 11.1.) Note that 7a is needed to separate p from f, 7b to distinguish l from n, 20 to get ŋ away from ž (the class defined

Table 11.1

	1	2	3	4	5	6	7	8	9	10	11	12	13	14	15	16	17	18	19	20
i	+	−	−	+	−	−			+											
e	+	−	−	a	−	−														
a	+	−	−	+	+	−			+	+										
u	+	−	−	−	−	−														
o	+	−	−	+	−	−			+	+										
ɔ	+	−	−	+	+	−			+											
h	+	−	−	−	−	−					+	+								
p	−	−	−	−	−	+	a	+			+		+		+	+				
t	−	−	−	−	−	+	a	+			+	+	+	+						
k	−	−	−	−	−	+	a	+			+	+	+		+	+				
č	−	−	−	−	−	+				+					+					
b	−	−	−	−	−	+					+		+			+	+			
d	−	−	−	−	−	+						+	+	+		+				
g	−	−	−	−	−	+						+	+	+		+	+			
ǰ	−	−	−	−	−	+				+						+				
f	−	−	−	−	−	+		+			+		+		+	+				
θ	−	−	−	−	−	+						+	+	+	+	+				
s	−	−	−	−	−	+						+	+	+		+				
š	−	−	−	−	−	+						+	+			+				
v	−	−	−	−	−	+					+	+				+	+			
ð	−	−	−	−	−	+					+					+	+			
z	−	−	−	−	−	+					+			+		+				
ž	−	+	−	−	−	−											+			
m	−	−	−	−	−	+		+			+	+			+	+	+	+		
n	−	−	−	−	−	+		+			+				+	+	+	+		
ŋ	−	+	−	−	−	−													+	+
l	−	−	−	−	−	+	b	+			+				+	+	+	+		
r	−	−	−	−	−	+	b				+				+	+	+	+		
w	−	−	+	−	−	−		+							+		+			
y	−	−	+	−	−	−									+		+			
:	−	+	−	−	−	−									+		+	+		

under 31*b* in my article is incorrect, since ž is not a member of C),
4*a* for u (from e) and 10 for o (from i). The only phonetically plausible
vowel class is 5.

Could we do better with the vowels (in the sense of approximating
phonetic 'nature') by using classes derived from morphophonemics?
Scarcely at all. The high vowels could be picked out as related somehow for the umlauting plurals of *tooth* and *goose*, but the strong verbs
are of little help; a small class of verbs like *wake* and *break* provide a link
for /e:/ and /o:/, a few verbs link two of the tense rounded vowels (as
in *grow–grew*), one verb alone (*eat*) links the corresponding front vowels
(for American speakers). The most frequent patterns are i – a – o (as in
sink) or two of the three (and they are three of the four in class 4),
/i:/–/e/ (as in *read*), ay – o: – i (as in *write*, etc.) or two of the three,
/i:/–/o:/ (as in *steal*), and /e:/–/u/ (as in *take*). These could, of course, be
used but would not yield any more phonetically 'correct' classes than
we already have. This leaves the alternation in words of Latin origin,
i.e. the variant (stressed) pronunciations of written a, e, i, o, u (etc.; ae
and oe should be identical with e, y with i, and eu always /yu:/). But this
system is, if anything, less helpful:

Letter	− CV/ − ‡	− C‡/ − CC	− rC	− riV/ − reV	− rV (non-final)
i	/ay	i	o	i	i/
e	/i:	e	o	i	e/
a	/e:	a	a:	e:	a/
o	/o:	ɔ	ɔ:	o:	ɔ/
u	/yu:	o	o	yu:	yu:/

Of course, it is easy enough to make this system the result of applying
a long series of rules to something quite phonetic and symmetrical. But
that does not help our problem, to derive good natural classes from the
surface facts of phonology.

The twenty classification principles given above do not have to be
regarded as twenty binary features; as we noted in the preceding chapter, it is quite possible to arbitrarily represent these twenty classes (and
many more) with a much smaller number of binary features. The coding
given there made use of seven features, and eight would make the job
easier. But even with those seven, most of our classes can be nicely
specified. The vowel coding given in chapter 9 is fine for phonetic
classes; a somewhat different vowel coding gives classes more like our
distributional and ablaut groups.

i = 0001011   u = 0011001

e = 0010001   o = 0000011

a = 0000111   ɔ = 0010111

The vowels of *sing–sang–sung* (which is also class 9) are now specified as oooXX1X. To add ɔ to this class (as in *song*), ignore the third digit and consider only the sixth digit–1. The vowels of *steal-stole* end in –011; those of *take–took* in –001, etc. Slight modifications will make it even better for these purposes, though it will lose its phonetic plausibility very soon (perhaps it already has).

Let it be said at once that English is a remarkably skew language in respect to phonotactic and morphophonemic classes; many other languages would yield classes phonetically much more 'natural' – and without the intervention of elaborate sets of ordered rules. Let it also be recognized that for many languages *nothing* of this sort would be possible: all syllables end in vowels and begin with consonants, there are no clusters, and co-occurrence restrictions are minimal (perhaps the same C cannot occur at the beginning of four successive syllables) or non-existent. No sandhi changes occur either within words or between words, and there are no irregularities of inflection or derivation. The most one can establish in such a language is the C–V dichotomy (unless, perhaps, one uses frequency data). Even in English, if we operated with a pure twelve-vowel analysis it would be virtually impossible to classify the vowels. However, where it *can* be applied, the method often yields interesting results.

12   Discovery and testing

II   *Morphology, syntax, semantics*

The practical manual for morphological discovery that for years stood side by side with Pike's *Phonemics* is Nida's *Morphology*.[1] Whereas problems of segmentation are relatively unimportant in phonemics (not that there hasn't been enough hassling about them), a morphemic analysis seems to depend very strongly on how the raw data is chopped up. The same paradigmatic set of forms may often be sliced in three different ways, one which makes the stem invariant and the affixes variable, one which makes the affixes firm and the stems variable, and a third which inserts a variable zero-element or process in between two non-varying morphemes. Take three Latin verbs, for instance:

	I	II	III
(a)	port-ō	mon-eō	reg-ō
	port-ās	mon-ēs	reg-is
	port-at	mon-et	reg-it
(b)	port-ō	mone-ō	reg-ō
	portā-s	monē-s	regi-s
	portat-t	mone-t	regi-t
(c)	port- -ō	mon-e-ō	reg- -ō
	port-ā-s	mon-ē-s	reg-i-s
	port-a-t	mon-e-t	reg-i-t

These are all simple cuts: by adding morphophonemic processes (phonological rules), either style (b) or style (c) can be made more regular. Even style (a) could be made more regular, although most of the linguists who favor this variety of analysis are (or were) implacable foes of morphophonemic rules (often described by them as illicit injection of historical linguistics into the esthetic limpidity of description). With only

[1] E. A. Nida, *Morphology, The Descriptive Analysis of Words* (Ann Arbor, University of Michigan Press, 1946, etc.). On the general topic of this chapter (and the preceding), see also R. Quirk and J. Svartvik, *Investigating Linguistic Acceptability*, The Hague, Mouton, 1966.

a small amount of data it is not always clear which way the rules will work best: here, for instance, do we want a rule to lengthen some vowels before -s or to shorten some (or all?) before -t and -ō? In spite of many hedges and complexities which we cannot treat here, we can end up with a form of (b) like the following:

porta:-o:	mone:-o:	rege-o:
-s	-s	-s
-t	-t	-t,

in which both stems and suffixes are uniform, and add the following (ordered) rules:

(12-1) e, a (:) +o: →o:, i.e. short e or a or long a drops before -o:.

(12-2) -:t→-t, i.e. length drops (long vowels shorten) before final t.

(12-3) -:V→-V, i.e. length drops (long vowels shorten) before any following vowel.

Rule 1 has to precede 3 in order to prevent *moneo:* from becoming **mono:*.

(12-4) -eC→-iC / not in env.____-C, i.e. short e changes to i before a single consonant. (It must either be specified that r is not a C, or else the reverse change must take place later before -r-.)

This is by no means the only set of rules that will work and permit perfect underlying regularity; in particular two or three alternate spellings and rules can be defended for the third column. As it happens, almost everything in these rules corresponds closely to one line of assumed historical development from Indo-European. For another possibility we might have this:

porta:-o:	mone:-o:	reg-o:
-es	-es	-es
-et	-et	-et

and rules:

(12-11) a(:) +o: →o:.

(12-12) V(:) +e→V(:), i.e. -e drops after a short or long vowel.

(12-13) same as 12-(3).

(12-14) same as 12-(2).

(12-15) same as 12-(4).

This, too, corresponds with historical developments. Because of the differential effects of leveling, quite incompatible solutions may be, not only equally economical, but equally historical. It is a merit, I think, of recent linguistics to claim that similarity with historical developments is not a defect in a set of rules. However, this similarity cannot be made a primary criterion, particularly for the description of isolated languages whose history is totally unknown.

What principle of morpheme splitting have we been exemplifying here? One certainly adhered to in the practice of virtually every linguist of the thirties and forties:

(12-21)   "A cut such that the alternations both before and after it can be described in regular phonological terms is always to be preferred to one in which the alternations on one side or the other must be suppletive (morphologically conditioned)."

It makes no difference if a cut gives absolute invariability of form on one side unless the situation is equally ducky on the other side – or can be made to seem so.

Besides segmentation and morphophonemics, what are the basic concerns of morphemic analysis? Third place in importance should very likely go to the semantic and functional analysis of paradigmatic sets – verb categories and case systems. Here the earliest and boldest attempts (even more so than in the case of phonology) were due to Roman Jakobson,[1] but the much simpler and rather confused treatment of Nida (in his sixth chapter) represents the more usual practice of the late forties and early fifties. And quite important also (and of some relation to semantic theory) were Nida's Principles 3 (2.23) and 5 (2.25), which attempt to specify when phonologically unrelated forms are (suppletive) allomorphs of the same morpheme and when phonologically identical forms are allomorphs of different morphemes, mere homophones. The principles are not worded in such a way as to lend themselves to the ready writing of algorithms, but we may at least try to explain them. The main trouble in the suppletive case is that if the data is looked upon as a collection of strings of morphs (morphs being identified at the outset solely by phonological shape), then nearly every morph is in complementary distribution with every other, so that any two morphs of similar meaning might very well turn out to be allomorphs of the same mor-

---

[1] *Zur Struktur des russischen Verbums*, originally published in a Festschrift called *Charisteria V. Mathesio oblata* (1932), pp. 74–83, and *Beitrag zur allgemeinen Kasuslehre* in *TCLP* 6 (1936), pp. 240–88, both now reprinted in *Readings in Linguistics II* (Chicago, University of Chicago Press, 1966), pp. 22–30 and 51–89.

pheme (unless, by a fluke, they did happen to occur in the same context). For instance *lamp* and *bright* have an obvious semantic similarity, and almost never occur in the same environments (*lamplight* and *bright light* differ in tone-and-juncture environments). Are they suppletive allomorphs? Nida's answer is that if you can find one form X which behaves in many environments like *lamp*, and in others like *bright*, and if the semantic relation between the uses of X in the two environments resembles that between *bright* and *lamp*, then they *may* be allomorphs. (Most of what Nida says is more directly concerned with minor morphemes, inflectional affixes principally, but he does not exclude application to stem morphs.) If you cannot find any such X, then *bright* and *lamp* must be or belong to different morphemes. This test would seem to be complicated a bit by the homophone possibility, but let us for now ignore that risk. The first difficulty here is how to measure degrees of semantic similarity. Would it be enough to find a word whose two environmental values were 'concrete count noun' and 'descriptive adjective'? Would *iron* do? Does its use in such sentences as "I brought a(n) iron/lamp", "Turn on the electric iron/lamp", etc., on the one hand, and "That's a bright/iron horseshoe", "His helmet was bright/iron" etc., on the other, constitute a sufficient degree of parallelism or not? Should one further insist that the adjectives must be members of the same positional class, i.e. not capable of co-occurring, mutually exclusive? In that case *iron* is not parallel, since one can say "a bright iron horseshoe". Should one insist that *all* uses must be parallel? If so, *iron* will not do, since it is also a 'mass noun of material' which is not the case with *lamp*, and *lamp* is also an antique slang verb of perception, as in "Lamp them sparklers, 'Arry", while *iron* as a verb is something quite different. Nida gives us little help; he opened a number of these unpleasant doors by allowing that a verb and a noun may be the same morpheme completely, i.e. class-membership is irrelevant. Many other linguists reject this principle, saying that a verb and a noun must always differ by at least one morpheme (which may be zero), so that *iron*, the adjective, cannot be the same morpheme as the count-noun *iron* – or even as the mass-noun *iron*.

This last refusal bothers some linguists, who note the interesting syntax of colors and materials. For instance, one can say "This green is very bright", "That car is very bright green", "He owns a very bright green car", or "That floor is cement", "That cement is red", "That's a red cement floor", or "That wall is pine", "That pine is knotty",

"That's a knotty pine wall". Of course, all these sentences can be dealt with satisfactorily under either assumption, but it is clear that both colors and materials are odd, and that colors are more completely adjectival (one can say, for instance, "My car is greener than yours", but not "My house is *bricker than yours"). So, in spite of colors and materials, if one says that when a noun and a verb are homophonous and very close in meaning, either the noun must be a zero nominalization of the verb or the verb consists of noun plus some verb-making zero affix, then many difficulties are avoided. And, though Nida is not alone in this (similar views were held by Harris, Voegelin and Hockett, for example), the tendency has been to maintain that two morphs cannot belong *wholly* to the same morpheme if they belong to different major mor- pheme-classes. This increases the number of homophones as well as the number of zero morphs, but it also eliminates some of the headaches.

Nida's Principle 5 is designed to solve the homophone problem where (e.g.) English *down* as in "The pillow is stuffed with down", "QHS downed their old rivals 47-23", "Walk down the road a ways". "Walk down to the corner" cannot be simplified by first breaking into parts of speech, but must be dealt with on a semantic basis. This principle is worth quoting in full:

1. Homophonous forms with distinctly different meanings constitute different morphemes.
2. Homophonous forms with related meanings constitute a single morpheme if the meaning classes are paralleled by distributional differences, but they constitute multiple morphemes if the meaning classes are not paralleled by distributional differences.

Condition 2 here seems to be an odd (or perhaps a careful?) way of say- ing that if one homophone is a verb and the other is a noun, then relatedness of meaning is enough to make them the same morpheme, but that if both are nouns then this is not the case. And yet Nida can't really mean that, since he requires only a very slight degree of similarity to make one polysemous morpheme, and tries, in general, to reduce the number of homophonous morphemes (as some later linguists also like to do).

After a few lines of discussion, Nida proposes the following definition:

Homophonous forms have related meanings when they identify regularly associated aspects of the same objects, process or state.

He then exemplifies "associated aspects" with eight pairs, of which six may be summed up as follows: process and result, object, agent, instrument, state and causative (he omits to mention state and process or process and causative); object and characteristic. Two more are either badly described or badly exemplified: 'form and function' is illustrated with two senses of *horn*, which seem rather to have similarity of form but *difference* of function, and the example given for 'form and process' (*cross*, n. and v.) seems rather to be 'form and causative' to use the term he selected earlier.

Nida seems nowhere to consider the possible function of his morphemes after they are found and classified to the utmost (and indeed no one else in the forties ever says much about this), even though without a consideration of this kind (which scarcely deserves the name of '[meta]theory') all decisions – about homophones or suppletion or synonyms or anything else for which Nida seeks principles – must turn out to be arbitrary. If we grant that subconsciously he must have had the same purpose in mind as other linguists have, namely to write syntactical rules (or tagmemic formulas, if you like), then there is a possibility of preferring one solution over another with some reason. And, indeed, I think most of us would agree that, however confused Nida's thinking may have been, his instincts led him mainly in proper directions, but not quite far enough. Certainly one does not want to regard "He's gone *fish*ing" and "He caught some *fish*" as not sharing a morpheme {fish}; so far Nida is right. But does one then want merely to label {fish} in the lexicon as NV or n., v. or 'noun or verb' or [+noun, +verb]? To do so would be to fail to note the existence of a pattern: "He went berrying and got some berries to eat", "He went crabbing and got some crabs to eat", "He went nutting and got some nuts to eat", "The cat went mousing and caught some mice to eat", etc.; contrasted with "He went deer-hunting (or -*shooting*) and got some venison to eat", "He went duck-hunting and got some ducks to eat", "He went mushroom-hunting (or -picking) and got some mushrooms to eat", etc., in which there is a separate verbal morpheme 'hunt' or 'pick' or 'gather'. Obviously any linguist with Nida's instincts would want to write a rule of some kind converting *fish-gathering* or *fish-hunting* into *fishing* (obligatorily) and *berry-picking* (optionally) into *berrying*. And similarly with his examples *man* n. and v., *spear* n. and v., and in part *run* n. and v. The case of *foul* adj. and *foul up* v. is different, since *up* seems to be an overt marker of the verbal category here. Two others are still problems today, at least for most of us: *horn* and *pill*. In both cases the original shift may be described as metaphorical: "This musical instrument is like a horn" (forgetting for a moment the historical fact mentioned in the footnote, that at first the musical instrument was a real animal's horn), and "This person is like a pill (*or* skunk, *or* rat, *or* wet blanket)." But it is probably not enough to yield a formula for metaphor:

(12-22) $X \rightarrow Y/Q$—R, provided that a sentence of the form "X is like (a) Y" is attested (?) or semantically well-formed (?); or perhaps "X and Y are both Z".

In this case the full details of the metaphorical use cannot all be predicted, nor can a word's (e.g. *skunk's*) automatic exclusion from all other metaphorical uses.

Once *skunk* is established as a word for an unprincipled, treacherous, unpleasant person, the word cannot then be used in the sense "person who smells bad", even though this might seem semantically perfectly reasonable. It seems probable to me that all such metaphorical items (ones that are firmly established even if not quite 'dead' to native speakers) *must* be treated as homophones, i.e. have separate entries in the lexicon. The original link can then be indicated in various ways, most simply by a (non-binary) feature saying "vague semantic link to $skunk_1$" or "metaphor from $skunk_1$" or such. Similar non-binary associational features are probably also needed for synonyms and antonyms, although it is possible that one might wish to derive antonyms by rules: *good* +opp. →*bad*. This is of course only notationally different.

Should we now try to restate Nida's rule for suppletion (Principle 3)?[1] It might go like this: If morph X (e.g. *go*) occurs in environment A (e.g. present) while dissimilar morph Y (e.g. *went* minus its suffix, if

---

[1] Forms which have a common semantic distinctiveness but which differ in phonemic form in such a way that their distribution cannot be phonologically defined constitute a single morpheme if the forms are in complementary distribution in accordance with the following restrictions:

1. Occurrence in the same structural series has precedence over occurrence in different structural series in the determination of morphemic status.

2. Complementary distribution in different structural series constitutes a basis for combining possible allomorphs into one morpheme only if there also occurs in these different structural series a morpheme which belongs to the same distribution class as the allomorphic series in question and which itself has only one allomorph or phonologically defined allomorphs.

3. Immediate tactical environments have precedence over nonimmediate tactica environments in determining morphemic status.

4. Contrast in identical distributional environments may be treated as submorphemic if the difference in meaning of the allomorphs reflects the distribution of these forms.

any) occurs in environment B (e.g. past), and they can be shown to fit semantically and syntactically into classes x (e.g. present stem) and y (past stem) such that in general x = y or x + q = y (where q represents some sort of regular phonological change), then Y + B (*went*) may be regarded as a suppletive replacement for *X + B (*goed*). Go ahead and laugh, if you think this is no clearer than Nida, but first give it a little effort. Maybe it does make sense.

The second important rule of morphemic analysis is generally associated with the name of Rulon Wells, who formulated it in his *Language* article of 1947 (23: 81–117) on 'Immediate Constituents'; but it appears in Nida (p. 91, 4.43.2) as Principle 2 of Immediate Constituent Analysis.

Divisions are made on the basis of substitutability of larger units by smaller units belonging to the same or a different external distribution class.

'External distribution class' is approximately equivalent to Bloomfield's '(major) form class', or other grammarians' 'part of speech'. Again this is not as felicitous as we might like, but it is easy to show what is meant. If we have a sentence of five words (say), and it is possible to replace the first four by a single word without changing the grammatical character of the sentence, *and there is no set of two, three or four which includes the last word, of which the same is true*, then the first four constitute a single construction (i.e. depend from a single node, in tree terminology). This is a very good principle, and works well much of the time. It will not provide every possible IC cut, however. The condition "without changing the grammatical character of the string" is an awkward one, of course, and may perhaps seem question-begging (though it is merely an appeal to speaker's intuition), while the italicized restriction is designed to exclude ambiguity. Are there really such ambiguous cases? Not many, perhaps, but there are a few, even if we exclude the uncertainty which often arises when we consider simple omissions (i.e. if "all the day long" is equivalent to "all day", is this because "all the" is replaceable by "all" or because "the day" is replaced by "day", etc.?). Consider the expressions "He came from under the house" and "He came from there", which equates "under the house" with "there". Now compare it with "He came off the house", in which it looks as if "off" replaces "from under". Which cut tells the truth? Even puzzles like this are quite often soluble without the addition of clumsy codicils to the basic rule. Nida proposes the rule first in a context of single-word constituency: does "ungentlemanly" consist of "ungentle" plus "manly" or of "ungentleman" plus "-ly"? No, on the basis of "unkind", it consists of "un-" plus "gentlemanly", and so on.

Some years after his *Morphology* Nida attempted a Bloomfieldian syntax, which had two SIL competitors within a few years (based on the linguistic ideas of K. Pike, expressed in his *Language I* and *II*),[1] one by Velma Pickett, the other by Ben Elson.[2] Pike's theory went for a while by the name of *grammemics* (or *gramemics*) but was later changed to *tagmemics*, with a basic 'unit' called the *tagmeme*. For discovery procedure, however, the most important point was the assumption and listing of universal 'slots' or 'spots' or functional parts of a sentence: Subject, Predicate (in the narrowest possible sense), Object, Indirect Object, Location, Manner, Time (and others). This ran counter to the counsel of caution so often preached in the forties, "Do not assume that the next language you come to will have any structural similarity to any other language known", and obviously helped investigators very much, even though it is hard to say what is novel about it. As expounded by Pickett, it was harmonized with successive IC dichotomies (much like typical early Chomsky trees); as later developed by Longacre[3] under the name of string constituent analysis, these spots are all equal and on the same level, so the trees are more like a 1966-type Fillmore tree, or perhaps a 1962-type M. A. K. Halliday tree. But as an aid to syntactic analysis this makes little difference. Pickett (and later Longacre) makes use of this device right at the outset, both pedagogically and in the field; i.e. she starts with the sentence and works gradually down through clauses, phrases, words, etc. ('levels' in the tagmemic sense, not in the sense discussed in ch. 8). The Elson–Pickett manual reverses this order – at least for pedagogical purposes. In the field, of course, nothing prevents a linguist from working on several different levels simultaneously, but in many cases it does seem to be helpful to start at the top (as generative grammars do), and for presentation it is probably more communicable.

Much of Longacre's book, in spite of its title, is concerned with pro-

---

[1] *Language in Relation to a Unified Theory of the Structure of Human Behavior* (Glendale, Summer Institute of Linguistics, pt. 1, 1954; pt. 2, 1955).
[2] V. Pickett, *An Introduction to the Study of Grammatical Structure* (Glendale, SIL, 1956), and B. Elson, *Beginning Morphology–Syntax*, (Glendale, SIL, 1957); later the two merged, and recent manuals are called *An Introduction to Morphology and Syntax* by B. Elson and V. Pickett, with the problems bound separately as *Laboratory Manual for Morphology and Syntax* by Merrifield, Naish, Rensch and Story.
[3] R. E. Longacre, *Grammar Discovery Procedures* (The Hague, Mouton, 1964).

cedures in a very elementary sense (and I do not mean to suggest that this is contemptible), such as advice on what to write in which corner of a given 3 × 5 slip, but one of his principles is sometimes cited as a substantial contribution. It occurs on p. 18 first (again on pp. 56–7, 89–90, 114–5, 134–5), in the following form:

For two patterns (syntagmemes) to be in contrast they must have more than one structural difference between them; at least one of these differences must involve the nuclei of the syntagmemes.

It is not easy to make out exactly what all this means; 'structural difference', 'nucleus' and 'in contrast' are perhaps the main stumbling-blocks. (1) A 'nucleus' or 'nuclear' item in a tagmemic formula is equivalent to an obligatory item in a phrase-structure rule, *whether or not it may be deleted later* (if it is deletable in generative terms, it is optional *and* nuclear in tagmemic terms); other items which are optional from the outset, i.e. are merely extras that may be added to a construction without altering it, are called peripheral (by Pickett and Longacre). (2) 'Structural difference' is harder. Study of the examples shows that (a) the distribution-class of a spotfiller is structural (a Predicate Noun differs from an Intransitive Verbal Predicate); (b) a difference in transformational possibility is structural; (c) deletability or non-deletability ('optional nuclear' vs. 'obligatory nuclear') of a term is structural; (d) number of nuclear elements is structural; (e) apparently (though this is not clear) meaning of some elements, at least, is structural. (3) 'In contrast' is the real sticker; from the early days of Prague linguistics this has been taken by many to be the one reliable datum elicitable from a native speaker, and as such provides the most important and adaptable tool of discovery in syntax as much as phonology. The difficulty that leads Longacre to propose arbitrary legislation (at least he seems to offer no reasons other than hunches or empirical effectiveness for preferring two to one or three as the number of differences needed to establish a contrast) is not, of course, directly known to me, but I am willing to make a guess. In phonology it is often quite easy to run down truly minimal pairs – even if you demand that they be embedded in identical sentence-contexts. But in the case of meaningful stretches of speech, except for single words (or stems) belonging to the same substitution class and fairly similar in meaning, direct simple contrasts are very rare indeed. As I once remarked in another context,[1] everything is in complementary distribution with everything else (or nearly so).

[1] *Language* 30:393 (1954).

But let us return to the one reliable criterion for discovery,[1] contrast (or opposition), with a brief glance at Jakobson's noun and verb articles. Unfortunately he never gave a full exposition of his procedures so that (as in the case of his phonological analyses) it is difficult for another linguist to duplicate his results. But we can easily see a number of them. The first step is always the same: collect as many minimal contrasts as you can find, pairs which exemplify the same contrast (as far as you can tell). This means, if possible, whole sentences (many elicited rather than found in a corpus, since no manipulable corpus of naturally occurring utterances is likely to have many minimal pairs) which differ in only one point (barring evident cases of solidarity or discontinuous morphemes). The formal differences can easily be specified in terms of morphemes or in terms of phonology; what you wish to pin down as clearly as possible are the semantic-and-distributional differences. Suppose you were concerned with the contrast between *of* and *for* in English. Start grinding out the pairs, e.g.:

(12-24)   (a) It had a series of diphthongs.
           (b) It had a series for diphthongs.

(In (a), no doubt "it" is a language; in (b) "it" must be a linguistic publisher. Hence the pair is not quite minimal, and (b) a bit improbable.)

(12-25)   (a) This symbol is used of the back vowels.
           (b) This symbol is used for the back vowels.

(Here it is (a) which seems implausible, but might mean "used to describe the back vowels.")

(12-26)   (a) This is the form of a report.
           (b) This is the form for a report.

(Both plausible enough, though "form" in (a) must be abstract; in (b) it can be a concrete piece of paper.)

(12-27)   (a) This is the basis of my report.
           (b) This is the basis for my report.

(This pair is nearly synonymous, although in (b) "my report" may still be in the future, whereas in (a) it must be past.)

---

[1] Simple introspection and asking-the-native-speaker are so hideously unsuccessful in semantic analysis that many linguists have grasped what may seem like inadequate heuristic procedures. No high claims are made for the methods which follow, only that they have been used and have seemed (subjectively) to be helpful – as well as to model or parallel (to some extent) the way we learn 'correct usage'.

(12-28)   (a) What is the justification of this?
         (b) What is the justification for this?

(Again almost synonymous, with the same possible tense distinction. Note that I can replace "this" by a verbal embedding in (b) only – "What is the justification for mixing olives with cherries?".)

(12-29)   (a) My explanation of this phenomenon is simple.
         (b) My explanation for this phenomenon is simple.

(Similar in type to (12-28).)

(12-30)   (a) John spoke of his family.
         (b) John spoke for his family.

(Here there's a conspicuous difference in meaning: "about" vs. "on behalf of".)

(12-31)   (a) His idea of a campaign is clear.
         (b) His idea for a campaign is clear.

(Somewhat like (12-27).)

(12-32)   (a) These are the men of the posse.
         (b) These are the men for the posse.

(Again like (12-27), but even more specifically future in the case of (b), where there is no possibility that the posse is already in existence.)

(12-33)   (a) There's no time of relaxation.
         (b) There's no time for relaxation.

(Again the contrast is not strictly minimal because of the differences in IC structure: *time-of-relaxation* in (a) is a single nominal expression, whereas in (b) *There's-no-time* is a verbal expression. If you try to convert the negatives into positives, you see that for (a) you will have "a time" but in (b) simply "time", uncountable.)

(12-34)   (a) He was making a bowl of salad.
         (b) He was making a bowl for salad.

(Here in (a) we have a cook, but in (b) a wood-carver or potter.)

(12-35)   (a) He needs correction of his vision.
         (b) He needs correction for his vision.

(Both sentences are too brief, but will sound O.K. with enough context. In (a) "of his vision" looks like a simple direct object of "correction"; in (b) the *for*-phrase seems adverbially bound to "needs".)

(12-36)   (a) He accepted the keys of the school.
         (b) He accepted the keys for the school.

(Not really minimal either; as in (12-33), the *of*-phrase is adjectival, the *for*-phrase adverbial; or else, if adjectival, modifies "he" – "he, on behalf of the school" or "he, representing the school"; ambiguously, it might also mean "keys designed or intended for the school".)

(12-37)   (a) He used to sit out here of an evening.
         (b) He used to sit out here for an evening.

(With time nouns *for* marks duration, *of* in a few rare expressions indicates time when in sentences of habit or repetition.)

This is only a rough and random sample of minimal or apparently minimal pairs; thorough search would certainly reveal other examples not quite identical with any of these. It is often helpful also to look at a sample of non-contrastive instances, to see where *for* is possible, but not *of* or where *of* is possible, but not *for*. First *of*:

(12-38)   He did it in the hope of finding the truth.

("Hope", like many other verbal nouns, requires *of*, though here the basic verb would take an infinitive – "he hopes to find".)

(12-39)   He has a mental image of the scene.

(*For* might be barely possible, similar to (12-24) or (12-25), but would require an odd ambiguity of "mental image".)

(12-40)   What good will come of it?

(If "good" could function as an animate noun, *for* would be possible.)

(12-41)   He was driving through the edge of town.

(Many partitive expressions occur with *of*; for *for* to be possible here – with different structure again – "town" would have to be a man's name, although with "heading" instead of "driving" *for* could indicate destination.)

(12-42)   He came from the direction of the pool.

("Direction" is one of those nouns which cannot occur unmodified, and changing *of* to *for* here would require linking the phrase directly to "came". One might say "the right direction for the pool", in which it would depend upon "right".)

(12-43)   What crime is he guilty of?

(Many adjectives take complements with *of*: cf. *worthy, proud, fond, jealous,* etc. Sometimes a context may be created where *for* is possible: e.g. "He was found guilty for telling the truth", where *for* gives a cause or reason. See (12-48).)

(12-44) It was because of his clothes.

(There are many two-word or three-word prepositions ending in *of* either always or optionally: *outside, on account, in front, instead, on top, out,* etc. There are also some in *for* – see below (12-52).)

(12-45) He enjoyed the touch of the ice cubes against his lips.

(A transformed subject nearly always takes *of*, almost never *for*. If it's an object, it's like (12-38) and (12-39).)

(12-46) Why didn't we hear of it?

(*Of* equivalent to *about* occurs with verbs of expressing, perceiving, thinking and the like, with some of which – like *hear* and *know* – a *for*-phrase is ruled out because it almost invariably implies *intention*.)

(12-47) Of course they like him.

(A few fixed phrases begin with *of*; cf. also *of set purpose, of all things*.)
    Now let's look at a few sentences in which *for* cannot be replaced by *of*.

(12-48) This is fit for a king.

(Adjectives which take *for* complements include *fit, suitable,* and various others implying destination or purpose.)

(12-49) Let's make him pay for it.

(In general few verbs may be followed directly by *of* other than those mentioned in (12-46); note also colloquial "I go for that".)

(12-50) We'll stop for gas in the next town.

(Again adverbial, equal to "in order to get gas".)

(12-51) For a moment I thought you were serious.

(Cf. (12-37); though *of a morning* or *of an evening* are possible, *of a* with units of duration like moment, second, minute, hour, day, week, month, year, etc. is not.)

(12-52) I would have got here on time, except for the traffic.

(Cf. (12-44). Other phrasal prepositions ending in *for* are *but for* and *as for*. Not as common as *of* in this use.)

(12-53) The place for him is with the family.

(Note that in certain combinations *of him* is simply ungrammatical, and must be replaced either by *his* before the noun – as here – or by *of his*, as in "This is a place of his".)

(12-54) He'd foisted himself on them for lunch.

(Again strictly adverbial, something like (12-50).)

(12-55) We've built up a demand for deep-fried spinach.

(A case of an object noun with *for* instead of *of*; cf. (12-35) (b), (12-39). Other words of similar meaning also take *for* (though a few may equally well have *of*): desire, longing, hankering, pining, honing, fondness, wish, love, liking, etc. Some such meaning as "object of purpose or wish" seems to link them all.)

(12-56) I asked him for an appointment.

(Something like (12-49), though *ask for* is even more unitary than *pay for*. It is possible also to *ask of* something as in (12-46), and to *ask something of* someone, approximately as in (12-40), but these won't fit in this frame. Other verbs of this sort are *account for*, *look for*, *wait for*, etc.)

(12-57) English has *a score* for twenty.

(Although in some contexts where 'meaning' is the meaning *of* may be substituted for *for* – cf. above (12-35) – there are a few cases like this one with *have*. The use is closely related to the *on behalf of*, *instead of* or *in exchange for* uses of (12-49), (12-30) (b), etc.)

The above sample is certainly not enough; I hope I do not mislead anyone on this point. But I think we must admit that a certain sharpening of our notions about the opposition between *of* and *for* has come. We can easily go on in either of two ways, which we might describe as the Jakobsonian or unitary way and the Stratificational or polyhomophone way. To take the last first we would say that 'for' has fifteen (more or less) meanings, and consists of the same number of homophonic morphs: (1) 'on behalf of', (2) 'in exchange for', (3) 'instead of', (4) 'to mean', (5) 'direct object', (6) 'during the extent of', (7) 'when referred to', ...etc. and that some of these represent sememes which may also be represented by other words, including *of* in certain cases.

One difficulty with this procedure is that it leaves unanswered the quite reasonable question "Why should just these fifteen distinct meanings be represented by this particular word?" implying, in fact, that it might just as well have been any other random set of prepositional meanings. This view, however, can be shown to be incorrect by comparing similar words or affixes in other, quite unrelated languages (e.g. Azerbaijani); it turns out that a high number of these meanings are represented homonymously there too. Chance, except in a small way, must then be ruled out, and an explanation is in order.

The Jakobsonian way is to find the common element in all these examples. If we are concerned with *for*, of course, we do not stop with examples contrasting *for* and *of*; we also collect examples contrasting *for* and *to*, *for* and *with*, *for* and *at*, *for* and *from*, and so on until we can pin down for each sentence containing *for* a set of three, four or some small number of reasons which are sufficient to require *for* rather than anything else, or to allow either *for* or *of*; or some other alternative. And these reasons must be short and simple. Jakobson spoke of the *terms* or *members* of an opposition here just as he did in the case of phonemes, but we may, here too, use the term 'features'. What features we could now specify for *for* and *of* it would be impossible to determine without a complete analysis and comparison of these and the other seven or eight primary prepositions of English: by, with, at, to, from, in, on and probably into. But it would have to account for many facts about both words: (1) *of* is especially common when dependence is from a preceding noun (verbal or not), while *for* depends mainly on verbs and verbal nouns; (2) *for* often has implications of futurity and intention, which *of* generally lacks; (3) a noun modified by an *of*-phrase tends to be definite, while with *for*-phrases this is less often so – indeed there are rather complex interrelationships between definiteness of the preceding and the following noun phrases which cannot be shown in a few examples; (4) the phrase bound by *of* is usually more closely knit than with *for*, i.e. NP + of + NP is generally itself an NP, while NP + for + NP is often not one; (5) whole-part or universe-scope relations and constituency relations (*consisting of*, *made of*) are regular with *of*, impossible with *for* (12-24), (12-32), (12-34), (12-41); (6) direct object relationship is regular with *of*, restricted to certain special verbal nouns with *for* (12-25), (12-27), (12-28), (12-29), (12-31), (12-35), (12-36) – probably, (12-38), (12-39), (12-55); (7) *of* is also regular for the subject relationship when the subject is not a personal pronoun or name, whereas *for* is rare in this function (12-45); the case in which *for* introduces the subject of an infinitive – or perhaps the whole infinitive clause – is different; "For him to be here this early is an event." The use is probably an extension from the type of (12-48); (8) *for* is common in providing the restriction needed to make a statement true (12-25), (12-26), (12-30), (12-35), (12-48), (12-52), (12-54); the purest type is in sentences like "She's smart, for a girl"; ... It would be easy to list more inferences that could be drawn from these and other examples, but we are not here concerned with the definitive analysis of *of* and *for*, but only with exemplifying a method.

The availability of high-speed computers has stirred up some interest in the use of various computable measures as aids or preliminaries to 'semantic' or 'distinctive feature' analysis of small sets like cases, prepositions, sentence-particles, conjunctions, personal pronouns, determiners, etc. Some sets are so small that the use of a computer would be extravagant, though their analysis by manual or cut-and-try methods may provide suggestions for algorithms suitable for programming. Other sets are so large that only the vaguest ideas are current about where to begin and what to do next. Completely programmed procedures have also been explored by a number of investigators,[1] but require such an enormous corpus and so much machine time before significant output can be had on any but the most common words that they must be considered pilot studies.

The completely mechanized procedures search for two things: different words occurring in the same frame (e.g. *apple, pear, banana, orange, mango*, etc. might all be found in several identical frames) and pairs of words occurring near each other in many contexts (such that if either one is considered the test word, the other is a common frame word), most often of different word-classes or at least different subclasses (e.g. *dozen* and *eggs, scramble* and *eggs, ham* and *eggs, poach* and *eggs, hatch* and *eggs*, or *dozen* and *oranges, dozen* and *cookies, dozen* and *doughnuts, dozen* and *rolls, give me* and *dozen, I'll take* and *dozen, let me have* and *dozen, half* and *dozen, two* and *dozen*, etc.). Having traced a whole set of pairs co-occurring with *eggs*, for instance, one could then go on to *oranges* and see how many recur, then to *cookies* and so on. Here we run into the frequent phenomenon of unique pairs: practically nothing is

---

[1] See, for instance, the Final Report to the National Science Foundation (GS 108) of the Indiana University Linguistics Research Project, *Linguistic Analysis of English*, CFSTI, PB 167 950 (February 1965), ch. 3 and 4, by Erik Fudge.

ever *poached, soft-boiled, hard-boiled, fried hard, fried sunny-side up,* *scrambled* or compounded with *-nog* except *egg(s)*. But, in any case, for each pair of words which share any contexts at all (same frame) or co-occur in context (like *fried* and *eggs*) some numerical index of strength of association or similarity of context can be computed, so that eventually one is able to describe an n-dimensional semantic space, studded with words (or morphemes) like raisins in a fruit-cake, words which are so placed that the distance between any two words is an exact index of the semantic kinship. Further (possibly by applying some such programs as those for Factor Analysis to the same sort of data), one might come up with a set of n *labeled* dimensions (e.g. ' Size, 'Sex', Emotional interest', 'Relative power' or what not)[1] such that by allowing some small number of values for each dimension one can completely specify every word by giving the values. If the number of values allowed is only two, we have the familiar binary feature system whose possible applications to a whole lexicon are still being explored. In principle, if one is willing to make careful use of the 'complementary distribution' notion, one should be able to specify a very large vocabulary (a million or more morphemes, say) with a very small inventory of binary features (25 or less). Naturally, no one believes that anything like this economy can be achieved without a great deal of arbitrariness, and if the human brain does anything at all like this in its unexplored depths, it may well use more like 1,000 binary features than 25.

Let us now examine one or two samples of mental and manual rather than computer-aided research in this direction.

(a) The sorting of verbs or adjectives or adverbs into a small number of subclasses by trying out the way they sound in an equal or slightly greater (if two or more frames conjointly specify one subclass) number of simple frame sentences is a fascinating occupation. It is also useful sometimes to submit test sentences to a series of transformations (embedding, imperativizations, questions, pro-element substitutions, paraphrase, etc.) or translation into one or two other languages. It is interesting how much variation there is between informants set to this task, and how much inconsistency even in the decisions of a single informant. Nevertheless some clearly legitimate classifications do emerge.[2]

---

[1] Cf. C. E. Osgood, G. J. Suci, P. H. Tannenbaum, *The Measurement of Meaning*, Urbana, University of Illinois Press, 1957.
[2] For examples see the following reports issued by the Indiana University Linguistics Research Project from 1963 to 1965: Alexander and Kunz, *Some Classes of Verbs in English*, June, 1964; Alexander and Matthews, *Adjectives Before That-Clauses in*

(b) A closely similar technique involves finding every occurrence of some fairly common item specified in advance as belonging to a certain class, and testing the substitutability of every other member of the class in each of these contexts. I recently tried this procedure on two classes, (1) the nine basic English prepositions as listed above, but excluding *into*: of, for, with, at, in, on (= upon), by, from, to; (2) the basic or minimal English postverbs (equivalent to the preverbs of other IE languages, but generally occurring in English after the verb), more loosely defined at the start of the investigation, but eventually narrowed down (partly on grounds of frequency) from twenty-one to eleven: down, up, out, off, away, back, in, on, over, around, about (the last two treated as partly equivalent; *into* was analyzed as containing an instance of the postverb *in* followed by the preposition *to*). The other postverbs examined for inclusion (and considered throughout as possible substitutes) were: along, across, forward, through, home, forth, ahead, together, apart, aside.

The criteria differed slightly in the two cases. In the first test I counted preposition x as substitutable for y if, in the given sentence, replacement of y by x did not destroy the acceptability of the sentence as English. For example, if the text sentence was:

(12-58)   She held the pointed knife *to* her heaving bosom,
the following prepositions would be considered substitutable for *to*: in, on, from, by, at. The substitution of *of* gives an implausible possessor; *with* depicts an unlikely contortion; *for* implies a personification of the bosom. I also tested the substitutability of a short list of less frequent prepositions: about, toward, through, during, over, along, under, among, into and inside. (The text occurrences of these words, however, were not tested.) In (12-58) the following were adjudged to have passed the test: toward, over, under.

The corpus used was approximately the same in the two experiments, somewhat larger for the less frequent items, the goal being (for the prepositions) to test exactly 70 instances of each item, and (for the postverbs) 100. Ngaio Marsh's *Death at the Bar* was the first text; Edgar Rice Burroughs' *Tarzan of the Apes* was second; another Ngaio Marsh, *Dead Water*, was third; John Muir's *Mountains of California* was used only for the prepositions.

English, September 1964; Bridgeman *et al.*, *Nouns Before That-Clauses in English*, June 1965; Wölck and Matthews, *A Preliminary Classification of Adverbs in English*, August 1965.

The test criterion for the postverbs was preservation of meaning. Given a text sentence:

(12-59)   A language is handed *down* from one generation to another, the following postverbs would pass the test: on, over, along, forward. Near misses are perhaps *across, through* and *ahead*, all of which seem to me to lead to possible misunderstandings. Most of the others would not even make acceptable sentences, except possibly for *up, out,* and *back.*

The tighter criterion used here does not have as much effect as one

Table 12.1   *Prepositions*

	of	in	to	with	on	for	from	by	at
of	(12)	12	10	7	6	19	16	9	3
in	35	(10)	15	37	21	25	28	36	14
to	9	4	(6)	10	10	13	17	4	7
with	20	24	23	(8)	12	16	14	32	7
on	25	23	23	6	(8)	21	21	15	25
for	42	20	35	18	16	(17)	25	22	9
from	33	8	20	10	14	11	(7)	24	8
by	9	23	20	27	18	13	24	(3)	17
at	15	9	5	5	18	3	10	7	(20)
about	26	9	7	6	26	12	12	3	16
toward	7	2	29	2	10	6	17	8	19
through	2	16	5	10	2	6	6	30	3
during	1	17	2	4	7	9	4	8	6
over	2	6	8	0	16	2	7	2	6
along	1	2	4	0	16	0	6	2	6
under	0	5	2	1	4	1	5	9	3
among	16	3	5	7	3	0	3	11	0
into	2	3	10	4	5	3	6	0	5
inside	11	16	3	2	7	0	6	5	6

might think; it is rare to find no acceptable substitute – *out* was the worst in this respect, with 26 cases – just as it was with the other criterion (where *at* showed 20 such occurrences out of 70, or about 29%), and even rarer to find only one synonym. In most cases there are two or three from the test group and another three or four from the supplementary group. The raw results may be shown in matrix form (tables 12.1 and 12.2) where the words listed across the top are the text items being tested, those down the side the substitutes. Figures on the diagonal (*of–of, in–in,* etc.) number cases where nothing else will do.

The data so far can, in essence, be collected only by using a live informant: increasing a given corpus by random accretion so that it includes every possible synonymous sentence of each one containing items to be tested in the initial corpus is very nearly equivalent to producing the complete text of Shakespeare by a random sentence-generating program, that is to say that for every page of the initial corpus something on the order of a billion pages must be added. With an informant, on the other hand, one adds only as many new sentences as there are passable equivalents. No machine program can be substituted

Table 12.2   *Postverbs*

Zero means "postverb may be deleted without change of meaning". For testing purposes *about* and *around* were counted together: The 100 cases here included 57 of *around*, 43 of *about*.

	down	up	out	off	away	back	in	on	over	about/ around
down	(4)	46	44	27	32	46	22	40	35	13
up	40	(9)	52	26	32	58	30	50	47	16
out	41	48	(26)	70	54	47	57	37	31	30
off	33	38	59	(14)	80	56	12	13	24	20
away	19	14	19	53	(4)	53	21	18	17	26
back	58	37	42	27	66	(3)	38	21	31	19
in	59	56	24	43	26	59	(17)	30	16	12
on	12	25	20	38	34	38	42	(13)	19	3
over	44	37	25	13	20	53	46	33	(9)	23
around	31	23	21	12	19	48	36	23	51	43/(0)
about	10	3	9	10	6	16	7	7	11	24/(9)
[zero]	66	63	50	36	53	70	48	51	58	51
along	37	29	23	28	52	53	44	73	56	47
across	27	23	29	18	24	42	41	25	55	11
forward	36	21	25	14	16	28	23	39	38	15
through	17	22	33	16	11	21	46	21	35	10
home	15	11	18	17	32	42	20	11	9	7
forth	13	11	20	12	19	13	10	13	5	8
ahead	7	6	9	9	19	14	16	38	7	3
together	7	19	9	3	10	17	12	13	9	20
aside	6	3	5	12	32	21	5	5	12	9
apart	7	6	8	12	14	11	4	7	1	5

for this step, then, until we have one which can perfectly duplicate the judgement of a native speaker – and this is still a long way off.

But the next step, manipulating and interpreting the data to yield patterns of similarity, placements in semantic space, or plausible binary feature analyses, can easily be done by various types of program which are already available.[1] For such small amounts of data, only a little time

---

[1] In general these form the class of taxonomic programs; people interested in such things issue a periodical called *Taxometrics*. The copy I have was dated from the Progetto Sistematica Actinomiceti, L.I.G.B., Via Marconi 10, Naples, Italy. A recent textbook (showing many parallels to linguistic problems) is *Principles of Numerical Taxonomy* by R. R. Sokal and P. H. A. Sneath, San Francisco and London, W. H. Freeman, 1963.

and patience is required to reach similar results by a simple cut-and-try procedure.

Let us first add the two half-matrices (i.e. add the number of cases where *with* can be replaced by *in* – 37 – to those in which *in* can be replaced by *with* – 24 – yielding 61 total cases of *in–with* equivalence) and present the resulting half-matrix so arranged as to make the numbers on the diagonal as large as possible (tables 12.1.1 and 12.1.2). As you

Table 12.1.1   *Prepositions*

	on	in	with	by	from	of	for	to
at	43	23	12	24	18	18	12	12
on		44	18	33	35	31	37	33
in			61	59	36	47	45	19
with				59	24	27	34	33
by					48	18	35	24
from						49	36	37
of							61	19
for								48

Table 12.1.2   *Postverbs*

	up	out	off	away	back	in	on
down	86	85	60	51	104	81	52
up		100	64	46	95	86	75
out			129	73	89	81	57
off				133	83	55	51
away					119	47	52
back						97	59
in							72

will notice, the goal has not been perfectly achieved: in the preposition half-matrix (table 12.1.1) the only flaw is the presence of two 59's in the *by*-column, but in the postverb half-matrix (table 12.1.2) the *down–back* value (104) is greater than *down–up* on the same horizontal while the *up–on* figure is slightly more than the *in–on*. And in both of them there are many biggish numbers which are too far away from the diagonal. (The ideal is to have the smallest value in the upper right-hand corner, with gradually increasing numbers from there out to the diagonal.)

The next step is to attempt a two-dimensional plot such that each item's distance from each other is inversely related to the substitutability figure, i.e. (on the prepositional plot) the closest pairs are *in–with* and *of–for*, the most distant *at–with*, *at–for*, and *at–to*, or (on the postverb plot) the closest is *away–off* and the furthest apart *up–away*. As I mentioned above, there are computer programs that can do this in two, three or any number of dimensions, and infallibly come up with the best possible fit, but even the crude approximation we arrive at by testing

Table 12.2.1   *Prepositions*

							with	
	to				by			
						in		
			from					
	for							
	of		on					
		at						

Table 12.2.2   *Postverbs*

		away				
	off			back		
	out					
			down	in		
					on	
			up			

several schemes is of some illustrative interest. One way to start is to consider the ordering in the half-matrix as a string of beads, and then introduce loops and coils in various ways. In any case, a pair of such maps are shown in tables 12.2.1 and 12.2.2. A little experimentation will convince you that you can do better, I'm sure, but one feels cramped in two dimensions. If you move one pair closer together, you may be automatically moving another pair too far apart. But there's no harm done; it's only a heuristic device, not an ultimate truth.

The next step, as I remarked earlier, might be the discovery of a minimal set of binary features which would account (in some way) for the observed similarities and differences; the substitution possibilities of the other words (*about, toward, during* etc. for the prepositions, and *along, across, forward*, etc. for the postverbs) may also be a help here.

With a two-dimensional plot one usually starts by drawing a minimal set of (more-or-less) straight lines sufficient to isolate each word. To be optimal, each cut should nearly divide the group in half; for instance, to separate *at* from all other prepositions, or *on* from all other postverbs by a single line would be easy and tempting, but uneconomical.

Three vertical cuts suggest themselves in the preposition plot (table 12.2.1): two would set *to, for, of* or *by, with, in* against the rest, the third cuts off *with, in, on* and *at*. Since the latter divides the group 4 and 5 (rather than 3 and 6), it is better. One can even suggest a meaning: 'relational' vs. 'locational' or the like. A good diagonal slice set off *to, for, of, at* against the rest (just adding *at* to the obvious three), though a meaning is not obvious; let us call *by, with, in, from* and *on* 'definite'. Cutting off both top and bottom we could get a group in the middle, more or less – *to, for, from, on* – which might be characterized as 'directional' (though *on* seems less obviously so). Since we have nine, three features are not enough: one more is needed to distinguish *in* from *with* and *to* from *for*, even though we cannot put such a line on our two-dimensional plot. Let us say that *with* and *for* are more 'personal' or more 'intimate'. In the conventional plus–minus array, the picture looks like this (the prepositions are arranged in rank-order of frequency from left to right, with *of* the most frequent):

	of	in	to	with	on	for	from	by	at
Relational	+	−	+	−	−	+	+	+	−
Definite	−	+	−	+	+	−	+	+	−
Directional	−	−	+	−	+	+	+	−	−
Intimate		−	−	+		+			

The most disappointing feature of this chart is that *at* has three minuses, which is appropriate for high frequency, not for low. If we reverse all the signs in the first row, calling it 'Location', perhaps, then *of* would have three minuses, and *at* would have one plus, but *for, from* and *by* would each have one less plus, while *in, with* and *on* would each have one more. I am sure that taxonomies of this sort (or 'feature analyses') can be devised which are better in every way than this one; however, I am also sure that the same thing is true here as we saw before in the case of phonological features: the goals or criteria are not mutually consistent, so that if the relation of markedness to relative frequency is optimized, the relation to distribution in semantic space will be off, while if that can be optimized, intuitive notions of meaning will be jolted. Consequently, the investigator must see clearly what he wants to use his features *for* before he opts for one analysis over another.

Let's look now at two similar analyses for the postverbs, one in which intuitive semantic ideas are accorded more importance, and one in which economy and distribution are the principal considerations. Once again frequency rank goes from left to right.

	out	in	up	down	on	away	back	off
Speaker	−	+	−	−	−	+	+	+
Continue	−	−	−	+	+	+	−	+
Home	−	−	+	−	+	−	+	+

The first cut (in table 12.2.2) goes from NW to SE, with a few curves; the second is O.K. except for *down*, which can't be reached; the third contains two pairs which can be separately cut out, but *away* prevents any simple slicing.

	out	in	up	down	on	away	back	off
Limit	+	−	−	−	−	+	+	+
Definite	−	+	−	−	+	+	+	−
Marginal	−	−	−	+	+	+	−	+

Here the first two cuts are excellent, one being almost horizontal, the other from upper left to lower right, but the third is impossible. Markedness and frequency are fairly well correlated in both.

We might set up a universal set of 'directionals' or 'directional features' in terms of which other systems as well as the Indo-European one (of which English is a special development) could be represented. One should not forget, however, that the carriers of this system may, in other languages, be verbs or nouns with special privileges or restrictions, as well as prefixes, suffixes, infixes or adverb-like particles as in English. And for prepositions (which cannot be distinguished on a universal scale from cases) there have already been attempts, like those of Sebeok and Fillmore.[1] Fillmore's treatment would seem to imply a two-level system, one basic set of five or six universal case or prepositional relations, and dependent on two or three of these (perhaps mainly those

[1] T. A. Sebeok, 'Finnish and Hungarian Case Systems: Their Form and Function', *Acta Instituti Hungarici Universitatis Holmiensis*, Series B, *Linguistica*, 3, 1946. C. Fillmore, 'Toward a Modern Theory of Case' in POLA Report No. 13, Ohio State University Research Foundation, August 1966; revised from 'A Proposal Concerning English Prepositions' in *Report of the 17th Annual Round Table Meeting* (Georgetown, Georgetown University Press, 1966). An enlarged version called 'The Case for Case' appears in *Universals of Language*, ed. by E. Bach and R. Harms, New York, Holt, Rhinehart and Winston, 1968.

concerned with Place and Time) one or more subclasses. Fillmore's basic cases bear a strong family resemblance to the tagmemicist's basic spots or slots. The system of Proto-Indo-European has a small number of cases (seven or eight) as the first level and a somewhat larger number of adverbial particles (from which the later IE languages derived both their prepositions, their verbal prefixes, and such sets as the English postverbs), but the cases do not correspond to slots in any simple direct way, with two or three exceptions.

We have, in this chapter, considered only a few of the many principles or procedures which have been proposed as aids in the analysis of semantic, syntactic or morphological structure.[1] Most of these seem to be helpful, and there must be others just as good which have not been mentioned here.

[1] We might mention here Martin Joos' scheme (SIL 13, 1958; Bobbs–Merrill *Language Reprint* 54) for graduated sorting of different occurrences (or senses) of, e.g., the English word *code*. Using a concordance program, one could extract all the occurrences of the given word in some large corpus. Slice up the print-out and start discarding duplicates and sorting semantically. Of course, the unintended implication of Joos that such a sort will always yield a single closed curve should not be accepted; there may be lines with two ends or with branches, double curves, two or more disconnected or unlinked piles, and so on.

I

13   The primacy of writing

To many people nowadays Tarzan is vaguely associated with old television shows or old movies, or else with comic books; but originally he was introduced in a book, a romance, at least, if not quite a novel, called *Tarzan of the Apes*.[1] And the story related in that book is one that should fascinate all linguists. Tarzan is adopted by an ape mother when only a few months old, and grows to be some ten or twelve years old before he discovers English. Now we are not to suppose that the little lad was a complete mute (as some movie versions portrayed him); Burroughs may not have been aware of the best psychological opinion, that if the language-learning ability is not used early it is either lost or greatly reduced, but the apes who brought Tarzan up were a very special kind of ape, and had a language (his name Tarzan is a compound word of that language) which Tarzan spoke fluently (as, indeed, he did the 'languages' of most of the mammals of the jungle). But I think you will appreciate Tarzan's educational feat better if you read Burroughs' own account:

Among the other books found by Tarzan in his parents' cabin were a primer, some child's readers, numerous picture books, and a great dictionary. All of these he examined, but the pictures caught his fancy most, though the strange little bugs which covered the pages where there were no pictures excited his wonder and deepest thought.

Squatting upon his haunches on the table top in the cabin his father had built – his smooth, brown, naked little body bent over the book which rested in his strong slender hands, and his great shock of long, black hair falling about his well-shaped head and bright, intelligent eyes – Tarzan of the apes, little primitive man, presented a picture filled, at once, with pathos and with promise – an allegorical figure of the primordial groping through the black night of ignorance toward the light of learning.

His little face was tense in study, for he had partially grasped, in a hazy, nebulous way, the rudiments of a thought which was destined to prove the key and the solution to the puzzling problem of the strange little bugs.

[1] Edgar Rice Burroughs, *Tarzan of the Apes*. Originally copyrighted in 1912 and renewed in 1939; reissued in paperback by Ballantine Books Inc., New York, in 1963 (U2001). Page numbers will refer to this edition.

In his hands was a primer opened at a picture of a little ape similar to himself, but covered, except for hands and face, with strange, colored fur, for such he thought the jacket and trousers to be. Beneath the picture were three little bugs –

BOY

And now he had discovered in the text upon the page that these three were repeated many times in the same sentence.

Another fact he learned – that there were comparatively few individual bugs; but these were repeated many times, occasionally alone, but more often in company with others.

Slowly he turned the pages, scanning the pictures and the text for a repetition of the combination b-o-y. Presently he found it beneath a picture of another little ape and a strange animal which went upon four legs like the jackal and resembled him not a little. Beneath this picture the bugs appeared as:

A BOY AND A DOG

There they were, the three little bugs which always accompanied the little ape.

And so he progressed very, very slowly, for it was a hard and laborious task which he had set himself without knowing it – a task which might seem to you or me impossible – learning to read without having the slightest knowledge of letters or written language, or the faintest idea that such things existed.

He did not accomplish it in a day, or in a week, or in a month, or in a year; but slowly, very slowly, he learned after he had grasped the possibilities which lay in those little bugs, so that by the time he was fifteen he knew the various combinations of letters which stood for every pictured figure in the little primer and in one or two of the picture books.

Of the meaning and use of the articles and conjunctions, verbs and adverbs and pronouns he had but the faintest and haziest conception.

One day when he was about twelve he found a number of lead pencils in a hitherto undiscovered drawer beneath the table, and in scratching upon the table top with one of them he was delighted to discover the black line it left behind it.

He worked so assiduously with this new toy that the table top was soon a mass of scrawly loops and irregular lines and his pencil-point worn down to the wood. Then he took another pencil, but this time he had a definite object in view.

He would attempt to reproduce some of the little bugs that scrambled over the pages of his books.

It was a difficult task, for he held the pencil as one would grasp the hilt of a dagger, which does not add greatly to ease in writing nor to the legibility of the results.

But he persevered for months, at such times as he was able to come to the cabin, until at last by repeated experimenting he found a position in which to hold the pencil that best permitted him to guide and control it, so that at last he could roughly reproduce any of the little bugs.

Thus he made a beginning at writing.

Copying the bugs taught him another thing, their number; and though he could not count as we understand it yet he had an idea of quantity, the base of his calculations being the number of fingers upon one of his hands.

His search through the various books convinced him that he had discovered all the different kinds of bugs most often repeated in combination, and these he arranged in proper order with great ease because of the frequency with which he had perused the fascinating alphabet picture book.

His education progressed; but his greatest finds were in the inexhaustible storehouse of the huge illustrated dictionary, for he learned more through the medium of pictures than text, even after he had grasped the significance of the bugs.

When he discovered the arrangement of words in alphabetical order he delighted in searching for and finding the combinations with which he was familiar, and the words which followed them, their definitions, led him still further into the mazes of erudition.

By the time he was seventeen he had learned to read the simple, child's primer and had dully realized the true and wonderful purpose of the little bugs.

No longer did he feel shame for his hairless body or his human features, for now his reason told him that he was of a different race from his wild and hairy companions. He was a M-A-N, they were A-P-E-S, and the little apes which scurried through the forest top were M-O-N-K-E-Y-S. He knew, too, that old Sabor was a L-I-O-N-E-S-S, and Histaha a S-N-A-K-E, and Tantor an E-L-E-P-H-A-N-T. And so he learned to read.

From then on his progress was rapid. With the help of the great dictionary and the active intelligence of a healthy mind endowed by inheritance with more than ordinary reasoning powers he shrewdly guessed at much which he could not really understand, and more often than not his guesses were close to the mark of truth.

There were many breaks in his education, caused by the migratory habits of his tribe, but even when removed from recourse to his books his active brain continued to search out the mysteries of his fascinating avocation.

(*Tarzan of the Apes*, ch. VII, pp. 48–50)

Many days during these years he spent in the cabin of his father, where still lay, untouched, the bones of his parents and the little skeleton of Kala's baby. At eighteen he read fluently and understood nearly all he read in the many and varied volumes on the shelves.

Also could he write, with printed letters rapidly and plainly, but script he had not mastered, for though there were several copy books among his treasure, there was so little written English in the cabin that he saw no use for bothering with this other form of writing, though he could read it, laboriously.

(ch. IX, p. 61)

Here we have a truly remarkable feat, of course, beside which the decipherment of Egyptian, Old Persian, Sumerian, Hieroglyphic Hittite and Linear B must be considered child's play, even unworthy of Mensa children. Tarzan reads (and writes) purely by eye, without any associated sounds or sound-images, except perhaps (Burroughs never tells us this, even though, on p. 95 (ch. 13), we learn that Tarzan spells his ape-language name in capital letters, TARZAN) for some ape-language equivalents. But the way Tarzan makes the transition from writing to non-ape speech is quite as remarkable.

They sat beneath the shade of a great tree, and Tarzan found some smooth bark that they might converse.

D'Arnot wrote the first message:

What can I do to repay you for all that you have done for me?

And Tarzan, in reply:

Teach me to speak the language of men.

And so D'Arnot commenced at once, pointing out familiar objects and repeating their names in French, for he thought that it would be easier to teach this man his own language, since he understood it himself best of all.

It meant nothing to Tarzan, of course, for he could not tell one language from another, so when he pointed to the word man which he had printed upon a piece of bark he learned from D'Arnot that it was pronounced *homme*, and in the same way he was taught to pronounce ape, *singe*, and tree, *arbre*.

He was a most eager student, and in two more days had mastered so much French that he could speak little sentences such as: "That is a tree," "This is grass," "I am hungry," and the like, but D'Arnot found that it was difficult to teach him the French construction upon a foundation of English.

The Frenchman wrote little lessons for him in English and had Tarzan repeat them in French, but as a literal translation was usually very poor French Tarzan was often confused.

D'Arnot realized now that he had made a mistake, but it seemed too late to go back and do it all over again and force Tarzan to unlearn all that he had learned, especially as they were rapidly approaching a point where they would be able to converse.

(*Tarzan of the Apes*, ch. XXIII, pp. 173–4)

But of course Tarzan eventually learns to speak English:

"You are quite right, Monsieur Clayton," he said, in French. "You will pardon me if I do not speak to you in English. I am just learning it, and while I understand it fairly well I speak it very poorly."

(ch. XXVIII, p. 212)

Now the order in which Tarzan does things is not to be attributed to Burroughs' desire to impress us by making the feat as difficult as imaginable, it is the order that, then and now, appeals to the naive mind as intuitively, logically right. He has merely represented this logical order as a temporal order, correcting the usual state of affairs. Even the fact that he proceeds from reading English to speaking French may be considered symbolical of the abnormality of the usual arrangement: we learn first to speak, and then to read and write, *after which we must go back and correct all the errors we made by learning to speak first.* Some of you may doubt that such an intuitive view really exists, but I think that vestiges of this view can be found in some very sophisticated people. And from very early times students of language have found it necessary to attack this notion (that writing is logically prior and speech is a way of performing written materials) with vigor and enthusiasm. I will quote here a few representative remarks.[1]

Aristotle (IV–III B.C.), *De interpretatione* 1, 16A

Spoken words are symbols of mental events, and written of spoken.

Meigret (1550), p. 4

Car come l'ecriture ne soęt qe la vray' imaje de la parolle, a bone ręzon on l' estimera faos' ę abuzive, si elle ne luy ęt conforme.

De Saussure (1906–15), p. 15

Language is a storehouse of sound-images, and writing is the tangible form of those images.   pp. 23–4 .Language and writing are two distinct systems of signs; the second exists for the sole purpose of representing the first. The object of linguistic study is not the written and spoken forms of words; the spoken forms alone constitute the object, but the spoken word is so intimately bound to its written image that the latter manages to usurp the main role. People attach even more importance to the written image of a vocal sign than to the sign itself. . . . mistake . . . illusion.

Sapir (1921), pp. 19–20

The most important of all visual speech symbolisms is, of course, that of the written or printed word . . . . Each element (letter or written word) in the system corresponds to a specific element (sound or sound-group or spoken word) in the *primary* system . . . . Even those who read and think without the slightest use of sound imagery are, at last analysis, dependent on it.

Bloomfield (1933), p. 21

---

1 The editions used are as follows: Ferdinand de Saussure, *Course in General Linguistics*, ed. Charles Bally and Albert Sechehaye, in collaboration with A. Reidlinger, tr. from the French by Wade Baskin, New York, Philosophical Library, 1959. Edward Sapir, *Language*, New York, Harcourt, Brace, 1939. Leonard Bloomfield, *Language*, New York, Holt, Rinehart and Winston, 1965 (reprinted from 1933). Robert A. Hall, Jr., *Leave Your Language Alone*, Ithaca, New York, Linguistica, 1950 [Revised as *Linguistics and Your Language*, New York, Doubleday, 1960]. Robert A. Hall, Jr., *Introductory Linguistics*, Philadelphia, Chilton Books, 1964. Louis Meigret, *Trettè de la Grammęre françoeze*, ed. by Wendelin Foerster, Heilbronn, Gebr. Henninger 1888. Paul Postal, review of R. M. W. Dixon 'Linguistic Science and Logic' in *Language* XLII (1966), 84–93.

Writing is not language, but merely a way of recording language. p. 40. Drawing a particular set of lines becomes attached, as an accompaniment or substitute, to the utterance of a particular linguistic form. p. 144. Apparent exceptions, such as ... the use of writing ... turn out, upon inspection, to be mere derivatives of language. p. 282. We are so used to reading and writing that we often confuse these activities with language itself .... Writing is ... merely an external device like the use of the phonograph.

Hall (1950), p. 31

Almost all of us tend to think of language in terms of writing and spelling and only secondarily, if at all, in terms of sounds; and we usually consider sounds subordinate to and determined by letters. p. 32. Writing is essentially a way of representing speech, almost always an imperfect and inaccurate way. p. 35. Writing is a derivative of speech.

Hall (1964) pp. 8–9

... it is easy to derive the idea that writing is more important than speech, that writing is 'primary' and speech only 'secondary' .... In fact, however, the spelling of a word is never more than a reflection (in English ortho-graphy often a very imperfect reflection) of the way it is pronounced; chang-ing the spelling of a word does not change the word itself, any more than photographing someone from a new angle changes the person photo-graphed .... Once we have made the effort required to turn our attitude right side out, and realize that, in language, speech is fundamental and writing ... only a secondary derivative and representation of speech, then whole new vistas are opened up to us.

Postal (1966), p. 91, n. 20

... the enormous body of literature concerned with showing how and in what respects language is basic and writing secondary, i.e. showing that writing is a crude way of representing linguistic structure rather than a sign system with a direct relation to the world.

A few of these people have reservations (though Hall, for instance, has none). Here are samples from the later chapters of Bloomfield's *Language*.

Bloomfield (1933), p. 448

The influence of literate persons works against a faithful rendering (sc. of loan words). p. 286. The decisive events occur in the spoken language yet the written style, once it has seized upon a form, retains it more exclusively, and may then weight the scales in its favor. p. 487. The spoken standard is there (sc. in Germany and similar places) largely derived from the written. p. 488. Purely graphic devices lead to novel speech-forms. pp. 492–3. The number of learned and semi-learned forms in the Western Romance languages is very large. p. 495. These formations (sc. *tatsama*) show us written nota-tion exercising an influence upon language. p. 501. To be sure, the ortho-graphy does cause some linguistic alterations.

Linguists of other schools (especially Prague, Glossematics and Firthianism) have expressed slightly different views; e.g. from a glossematist:

We can invent new pronunciations, or new orthographies, or new systems of expression manifested in any other way, ... and they will all be adequate, if they fulfill the single condition of providing a sufficient number of units to express the units of content.[1]

By this view speech and writing are in principle two mutually independent expressions. The Prague view is a bit different:

It is often overlooked ... that speech utterances are of two different kinds, i.e. spoken and written utterances. The latter cannot be simply regarded as optical projections of the former.... Whereas a transcribed [sc. phonetically or phonemically] text is to be regarded as a sign of the second order [i.e. the sign of a sign ...], the text recorded in writing is to be taken, at least in advanced cultural communities, as a sign of the first order.[2]

This view does not go quite as far as Uldall's in implying total independence, but clearly states that there are two kinds of texts, those which are basically written but may be pronounced, and those which are basically spoken but may be noted down, and indicates that there are also structural differences between the languages of the two kinds of texts.

In addition to the points of view represented by the above quotations, we should also consider that many linguists (e.g. Zellig Harris) imply, by their total silence, that writing and written materials (other than linguist's transcriptions, of course) are of no concern to the linguist, that his description of a language is complete if it correctly accounts for every possible spoken utterance. I think it is worth our while to ask some of these questions here again, and look at one or two plausible answers to them.

(13-1) Are texts in conventional orthography, printed books, periodicals, and written or typed manuscripts within the province of the linguist? Must a grammar of English correctly account for these materials? In particular, must it account for the spelling?

In spite of the minority 'No' answer alluded to above, surely we must admit that it is a queer division of responsibility that assigns everything

---

[1] H. J. Uldall, 'Speech and Writing', *Acta Linguistica* (Copenhagen) IV (1944), 11–16; reprinted in *Reading in Linguistics II*, p. 150.
[2] Josef Vachek, 'Some Remarks on Writing and Phonetic Transcription', *Acta Linguistica* (Copenhagen) V (1949), 86–93; reprinted in *Readings in Linguistics II*, 153 and 155.

recoverable from a text by reading it aloud to the grammarian's province, but excludes the form in which it is written, which must then belong to a distinct science (no doubt 'orthographics' or something of that sort). If we allow the answer to (13-1) to be 'Yes', then we have a second question.

(13-2) What is the relation of orthographic shape to phonological shape?

Do we first specify phonology (in the lexical 'matrices') and then derive orthography from it by rules and lists? Or do we specify both phonology and orthography side by side in the lexicon? Or do we join the ranks of the naive Tarzans and specify the orthography in the lexicon and derive phonology from it by rules and lists? Our choice, even if based primarily on considerations of economy, will necessarily also commit us to some kind of view on mutual independence and on relative logical priority.

Now let us get clear at once that logical priority has nothing to do with temporal priority, whether in ontogeny or phylogeny. Obviously children speak long before they read and write (though sometimes it is true that they cannot as adults remember when they could not read), and obviously our human ancestors spoke for millions of years (on some estimates, at any rate; over a hundred thousand by anyone's view) before the first crude systems of writing were devised. But this is not the question. The question is this: in literate communities, by and large, does orthography influence pronunciation or does phonology influence spelling?

I submit that when one looks at the matter in this way it is hard to be hesitant. One can think, naturally, of cases where individuals misspell certain words, cases in which this misspelling is influenced by the pronunciation, but how often has this error become the rule? There are a handful of words (at best) which exemplify this, and in most of them acceptance is by no means complete. In recent years a spelling *sherbert* for *sherbet* has become so widespread in the United States that it will have to be officially recognized in time; but in most of the country the new spelling is accompanied by a new pronunciation as well (both being mysteriously influenced by the name Herbert as well as assimilation of the unstressed to the stressed syllable). In all my other examples the new spelling does not begin merely as an error of orthography, but as a conscious attempt at cuteness. Up and down the land, the word *barbecue* occurs correctly spelt only once in a thousand times on signs and menus (or in advertisements); most of the time it is **barbeque** and much of the time it is **bar-B-Q**. Words like *nite* are also in many cases influenced by public campaigns for reformed spelling, occasionally pushed hard by large newspapers (so also *tho, thru,* and a dozen more of the same sort).

But what about the converse situation, referred to by linguists as spelling-pronunciations? Here recent examples are so numerous that I can only offer a small sample; since many of you have never heard anything but the spelling-pronunciation, I will indicate by phonemic transcription what the earlier 'correct' pronunciation was (which can in many cases be traced continuously back for 300 years or more). Those few of you who know only the 'correct' pronunciation can easily guess what the spelling-pronunciation is

Orthography	*Pronunciation*
palm, balm, psalm, etc.	/-aːm/
yesterday, Sunday, Saturday, etc.	/-dy/
Wednesday	/wenzdy/
diphth-eria, -ong	/-pθ-/
forehead	/'fɔrid/
harass	/'haeris/
Xavier	/zeːvyr/
kiln	/kil/
victuals	/vitlz/
conch	/-ŋk/
draught	/-aft/

These are all words in which the older pronunciation still survives among some speakers or in some areas. Also numerous are the cases in which the spelling-pronunciation has triumphed completely and finally everywhere (except occasionally for some backwoods dialect). Here are a few of this type.

certain	/sartin/

(and many other -er- words, of which only *sergeant* now survives in the U.S., *clerk* and one or two more in England)

author (etc.)	/-t-/
yes	/yis/
housewife	/hozwif/
gold, Rome (etc.)	/guːld/,/ruːm/
bomb	/bom/ [bʌm]
jaunt, laundry (etc.)	/-aː-/ or [-æ-]
sewer	/šoːr/

For a great many words, the influence of spelling on pronunciation has been continuous for so long that it is impossible to document any striking changes. It is only the most common and frequent words which seem to be in some measure exempt from this influence: few persons ever attempt to pronounce l's in *could, would* or *should* or to make *have* rhyme with *cave* or *says* rhyme with *raise* (though the archaic *saith* is often rendered as *sayeth*). In some measure these may be the words which are learned or perhaps *thoroughly* learned before the child begins to read. Even so, a few fairly common words can be cited: *cannot* (for spoken *can't*) has its own special pronunciation; the forms /e:/ for *a* and /ði:/ for *the* (preconsonantal) can often be heard in spoken use; *again* as /əge:n/ is not as widespread as it once was, but can still be heard, while /oftn/ with a *t* in it is almost the norm in some areas. And I could easily double this list. (Incidentally, it is entirely possible that a few of these pronunciations are in fact dialect preservations of very old variants, at least in some instances; and in other cases speakers now using them may be unaware that twenty or fifty or a hundred years ago they were always and only spelling-pronunciations.)

The point is clear, I think. Consider also the attitude of the law. If I change the pronunciation of my name, the law does not care (nor, indeed, is anyone bound by my decision); but if I change the spelling, if, for instance, my name is Kerr /ka:r/ and I respell it as Carr, pronounced the same way, then I must go to court to make it legitimate. And public sentiment is behind the lawyers one hundred per cent. A few years ago as I came out of a movie theatre in Pennsylvania I overheard a couple discussing an actress; they were arguing that anyone whose name was Kerr had no right to pronounce it /ka:r/. In China, too, it is the character that is your name, and the same pronunciation may be represented by two or several different characters.[1]

Are we ready to answer (13-2)? Certainly all this tends to show that naive speakers (of English; I have been assured that the same is also true for French and Chinese and have observed it on a small scale for Modern Greek and for Persian) intuitively feel that speech is a rendition of writing, not vice versa. What about economy? Is it more economical to specify phonology first and derive orthography from it, or the other way round? Let us consider a few simple cases.

Suppose we started with the pronunciation specified /-šn/ [šn] as

---

[1] On Chinese intuitions about character and sound, see also Y. R. Chao, *Language and Symbolic Systems*, New York, Cambridge University Press, 1968, pp. 103–7, 120–1.

at the end of 'pronunciation' itself.[1] How complex would it be to go from there to the various spellings? We would need first a series of residue rules and exceptional forms:

(13-01) /gro:šn/→Groschen /fašn/, /kušn/→fashion, cushion
/tišn/, /dayə-tišn/→Titian, dietician
          dietitian
/ptrišn/, /mɔr-tišn/, /byu:-tišn/→patrician, mortician, beautician

/sspišn/→suspicion	/o:šn/→ocean
/ko:oršn/→coersion	/θre:šn/→Thracian
/spɔnšn/→sponsion	/gri:šn/→Grecian
	/kdu:šn/→Caducean

/fikšn/→fiction after #
/toršn/→tertian after #
/l-soršn/, /n-moršn/→Lacertian, Nemertian.

(13-02) /šn/→-shen if there is a corresponding monosyllable ending in /š/ = -sh. Or else list ashen, freshen, harshen. (The monosyllabic limitation excludes words like demolish, abolish, admonish.)

(13-03) /išn/→-ician if there is a corresponding word in /ik/ = -ic or /-iks/ = -ics. (Alternatively, list about 40 words.)

(13-04) /išn/→-ission if preceded by /s/, /f/, /m/ (/s/ = *sc*).

(13-05) /-lšn/→-lsion.

(13-06) /-anšn/→-ansion.

(13-07) (a) /tenšn/→-tention if preceded by *in* or *dis*, or if there is a corresponding word in /te:n/ = tain
(b) →tension if preceded by zero or /haypo:/, /haypr/ (= hypo, hyper) or if there is a corresponding word in /tend/ = tend (note that this includes *in* and *dis* again).

(13-08) (a) /fikšn/→-fixion except after # (fiction)
/flokšn/→fluxion

1 The phonemic transcription used here for English is the same one we use throughout the book, most fully exemplified near the end of ch. 11. A very similar scheme is described by W. Nelson Francis in *Papers in Linguistics in Honor of Léon Dostert*, The Hague, Mouton, 1967, pp. 37–45.

(b) optionally:
/flekšn/→flexion
/nekšn/→-nexion
/kmplekšn/→complexion.

(13-09) (a) /tɔ:ršn/→torsion after #, /r/ (re-), /in/ (in-)
(b) /oršn/→-ersion after m, st
(c) /aršn/→-artian
(d) /e:šn/→-acean.

(13-10) /-šn/→-ssion if preceded by a lax vowel (or by the features [−tense, −consonant] or some equivalent). Actually only /a, e, o/ occur, represented by a, e, u respectively, which is the usual representation and would be part of some more general rule.

(13-11) /šn/→-tion.

Here rule (13-11) is the general rule (covering 2,500 or so words) for which all the others have been clearing the way. The rules are ordered, except for the two halves of rule (13-08), although the only important ordering is that (13-11) must be last. With a little care I am quite sure several more economies could be effected, but roughly this is the order of messiness required for rules going from phonemic shape (or phonetic shape, if you like, but not morphophonemic shape, which we will consider below) to correct orthography, on the assumption that it is only the ultimate output of the grammar that is converted into written form.

Suppose we take the opposite assumption, that (in the main, anyway) the immediate output of the lexicon is correct orthography, subject to minor morphographemic adjustments, and that it is the final adjusted spelling which is input to the phonological component. Consider the same case in reverse, i.e. instead of all the ways of spelling /šn/, let's generate all the ways of pronouncing -tion.

(13-21) -stion→/sčn/ or /ščn/.

(13-22) cation ⎱ →/katayen/.
　　　　 kation ⎰

(13-23) himation→/hay-matyn/ or /hay-me:šn/.

(And although the first pronunciation is indicated in my dictionary, I have always heard the second from my fellow Hellenists.)

(13-24) equation→/i:-kwe:žn/, /əkwe:žn/.

(13-25) -tion→/-šn/.

That is surely a good deal simpler. Even if we choose to take care of several other spellings, the economy is considerable. First, modify (13-21):

(13-21) (a) -stio/an→/sčn/ or /ščn/.

Then add, before (13-25), several new rules:

$$(13\text{-}24)\ (a)\ \begin{bmatrix} \text{-mersion} \\ \text{abstersion} \end{bmatrix} \rightarrow \begin{bmatrix} \text{/moršn/} \\ \text{/ab-storšn/} \end{bmatrix}$$

(Judging by the dictionaries, there are some dialects – including RP – in which the rule is simpler: -(V)rsion→/ršn/, but in my own dialect most words of this sort have /ržn/ with voicing.)

$$(13\text{-}24)\ (b)\ \text{-\,-\,-}\begin{bmatrix} \text{-l} \\ \text{n} \end{bmatrix} \text{sion}\rightarrow\begin{bmatrix} \text{/l} \\ \text{n} \end{bmatrix} \text{šn/.}$$

(13-24) (c) - - -xion - - - -→/kšn/.

$$(13\text{-}25)\ (a)\ \left.\begin{matrix} \text{-sh} \\ \text{-c} \\ \text{-ss} \\ \text{-t} \\ \\ \text{-s(c)hen} \\ \text{-cean} \end{matrix}\right\} \begin{matrix} \text{i} \left\{\begin{matrix}\text{an}\\\text{on}\end{matrix}\right\} \end{matrix} \right\} \rightarrow/\text{-šn/.}$$

$$(13\text{-}26)\ \text{-si}\left\{\begin{matrix}\text{on}\\\text{an}\end{matrix}\right\}\text{-\,-\,-}\rightarrow/\text{-žn/.}$$

Even with this extension of coverage, the rules are simpler and more general, the exceptions or rules of narrow scope very few (25 words or bases must be specified the first way, only 5 the second). Clearly if there are only these two alternatives, we must prefer the second. But are there really only two?

As is commonly known nowadays, Chomsky and Halle[1] posit for their deep or 'systematic phonemic' representation of lexical items a 'distinctive feature matrix' which, for words of Latin origin such as these, corresponds roughly to the surface or 'systematic phonetic' representation which would match this spelling in classical Latin, i.e. they specify

[1] Their recent book *Sound Patterns of English* (New York, Harper and Row, 1968) should be consulted for further information.

nation as if it consisted of a Latin sequence n + a (Latin tense long a, like British a in *alms*, more or less) +t (a real voiceless apical stop) +i +ō (long tense o) +n, and then subject the matrix to alterations which eventually yield current pronunciation. Since this deep representation is clearly based on the orthography, it would obviously be rather easy to derive the orthography from it directly. But why is it needed? If we are required to provide the orthography anyway, and if we can reach the phonology from it without an intervening deep feature specification, Ockham's razor would suggest that we dispense with this 'systematic phonemic' level entirely, replacing it by the orthography, at least for words of this class. It may be argued that if we specify *t* as [+anterior, +coronal, −continuant] and *c* as [−anterior, −coronal, −continuant], we can write a rule changing both at once to /s/, [−anterior, +coronal, +continuant] or something of the sort, and maybe even include the rendition of *g* as /j/ – though *-di-* as /j/ is now substandard or British – in the same rule. In a sense this is true enough, but will there be any net gain in economy? And how about generality? Rule (13-25) (a) can easily (and surely would, in a complete grammar) be decomposed into subrules or sequences of rules which would achieve the same measure of generality, perhaps by adding features on the right one or two at a time. How then can one count features for comparing economy? Most simply by allowing written strings to consist of sequences of the same (non-binary) feature [letter] with 26 values [a letter], [b letter], [c letter] etc. up to [z letter].

But it does seem reasonable to suppose that two series of rules may be called for, one to manipulate letters, and the second to map letters into sounds. For instance, for a large segment of the vocabulary, a graphic rule of the form

(13-27) *y* → *i*

would simplify matters, since every later rule that affects i affects y in exactly the same way. (It is true that there is now a tendency at work whose ultimate effect would be to specialize y for the value /ay/ everywhere except finally, but at present this has merely led to a number of variant pronunciations, e.g. of *cyclical*, *gynecology*, or *synod*.) Deletion rules might also apply more economically at the spelling level, e.g.

(13-28) *ed* → *d* before juncture and after a morph-boundary except in *naked*, *dogged*, *beloved*, etc.

The cases of *fitted* and *breaded* are better regarded as having later insertion of subphonemic vowels than as continuing the e of -ed, but both ways are economical. Certainly the e comes in handy to explain the singer's /di:-fi:ted/ for *defeated*. Stylistic alternatives to some rules must obviously be provided. In the /šn/ and /žn/ words we have been examining, exceptions like *equation* could be handled by a respelling rule

(13-29)   **equation** → **equasion**,

which brings it under the general rule. Similarly **cation** → **cat-ion**, **himation** → **himattion** (for the older dictionary pronunciation), **-mersion** → **-mercion** (or **-mertion**). And one wants a general rule

(13-30)   **x** → **ks**,

after which we could have

(13-31)   **-sion** → **-cion** /n, l, k ____,

while still at the orthographic level.

It may be argued that this is all very well for literary or rare words, but that certainly for the basic 500 most frequent or earliest learned it is against nature to have the rules lead from spelling to sound. For a long time I was inclined to the same view myself, but the arguments against it proved irresistible (for me). In the first place, this portion of the vocabulary is full of irregularity,[1] so that whichever direction one chooses to go in, the economy is low. A rule for pronouncing *could*, *would* and *should* is quite efficient:

(13-32)   **-ould** → /-ud/ before #,

but a rule to spell these words (and *good, hood, stood,* etc.) will have to use labeled bracketing:

(13-33)   /-ud/ → { **-ould**/ if modal
                   { **-ood.**

Of course **-oo-** itself is one of the ambiguous spellings which will cause more trouble in the spelling-to-sound direction than vice versa.

---

[1] Axel Wijk, for instance, in his useful book *Rules of Pronunciation for the English Language* (New York, Oxford University Press, 1966) on p. 9 says, "Among the first thousand of the commonest words...no less than 160, i.e. 16 per cent, must be considered irregular." For a less ambitious attempt at rules leading from spelling to pronunciation, see R. L. Venezky 'The basis of English orthography' in *Acta Linguistica Hafniensia* 10:145–59 (1967). The same issue contains (217–40) a more rigorous scheme for French proposed by B. W. Christensen, 'Phonème et graphème en Français moderne'.

But even so it's not too hard, and there are far more ambiguously pronounced words than ambiguously spelt ones. Let us just list 100 or so of the most common English words (by various counts).[1]

a, about, air, all, also, an, and, any, are, as, at, be, because, been, before, being, but, by, can, could, day, do, does, done, down, each, earth, either, even, every, first, for, four, from, go, gone, good, had, has, have, he, her, here, him, his, how, I, if, in, into, is, it, its, just, know, last, light, like, look, love, made, make, man, many, may, me, mean, more, most, much, must, my, new, no, not, nothing, now, of, on, one, only, or, other, our, out, over, own, people, pretty, said, say, says, she, should, since, so, some, state, still, such, than, that, the, their, them, then, there, these, they, this, those, three, through, time, to, too, two, under, up, us, use, used to, very, was, way, we, well, were, what, when, where, which, who, will, with, work, world, would, year, yes, yet, you, your. (143)

If we had counts derived from spoken English data in which contractions were counted as single words, some of those would probably also appear in the top 200: won't, don't, can't, doesn't, didn't, haven't, hasn't, isn't, aren't, wasn't, weren't, I'm, you're, we're, he's, they're, I've, she's, and maybe a few more. Because of the obligatory apostrophe, it should be no trouble at all to write pronunciation rules for these; in fact, one can delete the apostrophe and bring under more general rules such forms as won't, don't (provided 'font' is taken as exceptional), can't, we're, they're, I've. Nearly all of them except *won't* and *don't* can also be treated as having the pronunciation of the first part (*does, has,* etc.) with the second part simply spliced on (n't, 'm, 're, 's, 've), where only the 's needs a semi-special rule. The converse direction can be handled in an analogous way, but not without labeled bracketing. In most varieties of English *their, there* and *they're* are homonyms, as are *your* and *you're, we're,* and *weir, can't,* and *cant, won't* and *wont.* But these are minor issues. Let us return to our 143 basic words and see what problems they offer.

First, let us note that many (about 40%) of these words have reduced forms, which may be manufactured in most cases by simply deleting the written vowel (and some initial th's, w's, and h's). These offer about the same degree of difficulty for both directions of rule-writing.

a, an, and, any, are, as, at, but, by (perhaps not in all dialects), can, could, do, does, for, from, good (in certain fixed phases only), had, has, have, he, her,

---

[1] Particularly useful is the list given by H. Kucera and W. N. Francis in their book *Computational Analysis of Present-Day American English* (Providence, Brown University Press, 1967).

him, his, if, in, into, is, it, its, just, must, my (in some dialects), not, nothing, of, or, pretty, should, so, some, such, than, that, the, their, them, there, to, us, very, was, were, will, with, would, you, your. (57)

Some of them have spellings for the reduced forms, but most of them do not (except in idiosyncratic notations used by writers attempting to convey a folksy or dialect flavor). But let us now consider only the full-grade variants. How many of them go along with general rules?

about, air, all, also, an, and, at, be, because, before, being, but, by, can, day, down, each, earth, even, first, for, go, had, he, her, here, him, how, I, if, in, it, its, just, last, light, like, look, made, make, man, may, me, mean, more, most, much, must, my, new, no, not, now, on, or, other, our, out, over, say, she, since, so, state, still, such, three, time, too, under, up, us, very, way, we, well, when, which, will, with, year, yes, yet. (83)

This is more than half (*c.* 60%); and several words could be added to the list by adding some less general rules: e.g. *-ould-* → /ud/ if final or before n't, which covers the three words *would*, *should* and *could*.

If we attempt to work out ways for handling the other 40%, we find that it can be done with about 30 special rules and a certain number of underlying spellings – protographemic representations – such as representing words like *gas* as *gass* and then deleting one s in word-final position, eventually, but not till after the pronunciation /gæs/ had been assured. This allows *has* to be *has* and yield /hæz/.

Are these easier if we go the opposite way? Two cases are simpler:

$$/ð, \theta/ \rightarrow \text{th}$$
$$/u(:)/ \rightarrow \text{oo}$$

in certain environments (but here you must also account for *u* and *ou* as well, which may mean no net gain). Suppose we write the same words out 'phonemically' and derive the orthography.

First let us list (out of the whole set of 143) the ones which can best be brought under general rules.

about, all, an, and, as, at, because, before, but, by, can, day, down, each, even, every, for, good, had, has, have, her, here, him, his, how, I, in, is, it, its, just, last, like, look, love, made, make, man, may, mean, more, must, my, new, not, now, on, or, other, our, out, over, say, state, still, than, that, them, then, these, those, three, time, too, under, up, use, used to, way, well, when, will, with, work, world, year, yet. (77)

This is slightly less than the number (83) which we found to be regular in the opposite direction. Different assumptions could alter the list only a little without increasing the cost paid (in complexity) elsewhere in the grammar.

To deal with the remainder of the words in this direction will require about 40 *ad hoc* rules or exceptional listings, though several items can be handled by utilizing a special feature [+function word] or the like, which prevents the doubling of some final vowels (*e, o*) and consonants (*s, f*) which would be so doubled in other words.

This may suggest what the problems are and how one might attempt to cope with them. The number of phonemes here used for English is 30 (and in any system will not greatly exceed 40); the number of graphs which correlate with phonemes is (in Wijk's lists) 109. Though many of these graphs are ambiguous, there are few phonemic oppositions which fail entirely to be represented (voiced vs. voiceless th is almost the only case). Obviously rules leading from 109 to 30 have a much better chance of simplicity and exceptionlessness than rules going from 30 to 109.

Suppose then we adopt the dodge of variant precursors in the lexicon for the same phonemes when spelled in different ways; how difficult will this be? If no tests of plausibility or speciousness are required, since the number of unused sequences of two and three phonemes or unused combinations of five or six features is enormous, it should be easy in some *ad hoc* way to supply a perfectly unambiguous deep structure notation for every phone-graph correlation pair. There must be well over 200 of these couples, but I have not attempted an exact count; for instance, *ei*–/e:/ is one couple, *ei*–/ay/ another, *ai*–/e:/ another, *a-e*–/e:/ another, and so on. I do not believe there is a single closed couple, i.e. one such that neither term appears in any other couple, but a few come fairly close: *th*–/θ/ is probably the only couple containing /θ/, though *th* appears in at least three others: *th*–/ð/, *th*–/t/ (as in Thomas, etc.), *th*–zero (as in *asthma, isthmus,* /azmə/, /isməs/).

However, if the protophonologist chooses to store a different sequence or feature representation for every distinct phone–graph couple, then we must have interlocking order of graphemic rules and phonological rules. The chain of steps which leads from the stored form to the printed shape must come *before* the rules which eliminate the multiplicity of apparent phonological shapes, which must, in their turn, be earlier than the majority of phonological rules. Hence, even if you reject the lexical storing of pure orthography only, and store instead some precursor notation which will yield both orthography and phonology, the written shape must be generationally earlier, prior to the phonological shape.

And where should features go? In such a precursor system phonological features would be extravagant (unless one chooses to specify the alphabet as a 26-valued feature 'letter', as has been suggested, and add a similar phonological feature 'phoneme' to every matrix of binary features). How would features be introduced, then, and when? Most plausibly in the series of rules which have letters on the left and phonemes on the right:

instead of *b*→/b/, one would then have

$$*b* \rightarrow \begin{bmatrix} +\text{stop} \\ +\text{labial} \\ +\text{voiced} \end{bmatrix} \quad \text{or} \quad \begin{bmatrix} +\text{anterior} \\ -\text{coronal} \\ +\text{voiced} \\ -\text{continuant} \end{bmatrix}.$$

Or else, if we keep the first rule, or modify it slightly to

$$*b* \rightarrow [\text{b segment}],$$

then in the next following set of rules, e.g.:

$$[\text{b segment}] \rightarrow \begin{bmatrix} +\text{stop} \\ +\text{labial} \\ +\text{voiced} \\ \text{b segment} \end{bmatrix}.$$

This means that the rules cannot be used to generate phonologically correct non-occurrent strings from random input, at least not without first discarding information and then recovering it, which seems an implausible procedure.

So both from the point of view of the naive speaker (Tarzan's intuition), and from that of economy and plausibility of rule construction we must allow that writing is prior.[1]

But what about non-literate languages? Do they perhaps have something which functions as orthography does for us? There are many hints that some of them (evidently not all) do, as a distinct oral style which is carefully taught, assigned prestige and used as a standard of reference. In different areas the cultural expression of this style may differ: in

---

[1] Specialists in various types of aphasia and alexia can contribute other kinds of suggestive evidence (e.g. the patient who can say words only after he has traced the spelling in the air with his hand). See, for instance, H. Hecaen 'Aspects des troubles de la lecture (alexies) au cours des lésions cérébrales en foyer', *Word* 23: 265–87 (1967). For a somewhat different but related criticism of the doctrines of *SPE*, see J. P. Maher, 'The Paradox of Creation and Tradition in Grammar', *Language Sciences* No. 7 (October 1969), 15–24.

one South American area (reported by E. Migliazza) it functions as a standard language of intercommunication (not a 'lingua franca', which generally carries no such prestige) among tribes whose dialects have diverged considerably from each other, though each can be related by simple rules to the 'standard language'. In some North American cultures (Florence M. Voegelin's Mother Language) it functions as the first form of speech taught to children, representing as it were the output of a grammar before any but the most necessary of the morphophonemic rules have applied. In other cultures a special style is used for religious purposes, for memorizing and narrating the historical traditions or the laws or the myths of the group. (In some cases, of course, such a language loses contact with ordinary speech and ceases to function as its basis; so Latin split off from the Romance languages in the early Middle Ages. But a new standard often develops quite rapidly to fill the gap.) Or it may be a special style used for improvising epic poems or songs of insult. But, whatever its uses, there is often a variety of the language which is formally taught, highly respected, referred to as an arbiter in disputes, and which has a different (in detail, at least) phonological structure, but one from which the phonology of the spoken language can easily be derived (though the converse is not possible). Such a style does not appear to be attested for every language which has been investigated, but it is a phenomenon which occurs in all parts of the world; one may even say that some tribes have a counterpart to the French Academy. It is for languages spoken in such non-literate cultures that we must postulate base forms in something related to Chomsky and Halle's systematic phonemic shape. What we literates have instead (i.e. truly stored in our brains) is generally a complete double specification, 'systematic phonemic' or 'morphophonemic' and orthographic (possibly in part morphographemic, i.e. a form containing anticipations of later spelling rules).

In an economical *description* of such a language, however, the stored form must be primarily graphic, but suitably modified to serve as a convenient precursor for both the ultimate graphic shape (derived by a short set of rules applied early) and the ultimate phonemic (and allophonic or broad phonetic) shape. There will presumably be a series of transitional rules, simplifying and regularizing the orthographic shape leading to the first bridge rules, which map letters of the alphabet into phonemes and distinctive features.

So Tarzan is vindicated, except that the insertion of French phonology into the bridge is discarded. The chain envisaged leads like this:

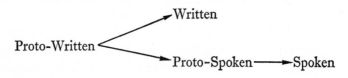

Or, alternatively:

Written → Respelled → Proto-Spoken → Spoken

in which the 'Respelled' shape is very close to the supposed Proto-Written form. Illiterates are presumed to have only two stages, P-S→S. New words which are seen first in writing, are immediately (if regular) supplied with the appropriate Proto-Spoken form; if ambiguous, they may be temporarily stored with no Proto-Spoken or with two alternative Proto-Spoken shapes. Every one of us has a well-used (even if not consciously formulable) set of rules for pronouncing new words, and it is interesting to note that some easily pronounceable (i.e. English-sounding) strings are difficult or quite impossible to spell[1] – and not merely because of the *th* and *oo* problems. We also have rules for spelling newly heard words, but these rules are full of multiple choices. New words first heard are often held in suspense for some time, or the spelling may be directly elicited: "How do you spell that?" The same question serves also to verify the Proto-Spoken form, as when I am uncertain whether you said "Sterling" or "Sturley". And there is no excuse for leaving orthography out of our grammars.

[1] Try /giːsčr/ or /uːprnayšn/, for instance.

14 *Accent, stress, prosodies, and tonal features*

In chapters 4 and 9 we considered the phonetics and phonemics of segments, merely noting that there were also such things as quantity oppositions (long vs. short), pitch, and other similar phenomena that could not *always* be treated as segments (and, of course are not 'really' segments, anyhow). But this is obviously not enough. We must also ask, in the languages of the world, how do these phenomena differ from segmental features, and why? How many uses do they have? Are any of them purely natural, and not at all arbitrary?

Quantity is perhaps the easiest one of these to dispose of. Many languages have a straightforward binary quantitative opposition which serves to distinguish one word from another exactly as segments do, e.g. Latin *ma:lum* 'apple', *malum* 'evil'. Quantity may also serve, like a segment, as an affix, e.g. Latin *tuba* 'a trumpet' (nominative), *tuba:* 'with a trumpet' (ablative). Roughly this state of affairs is found in many languages all over the world. But prolongation of a phoneme or syllable as an expressive device (in English more or less wheedling in tone, in other languages amazed or incredulous, and simply emphatic in still others) is also very widespread both in languages which have binary, 'segmental' quantity and in languages which do not. It is often linear in nature rather than binary: the more you prolong the sound, the more incredulity you express. And, finally in many cases extra length is a partially automatic consequence of something else, either segmental (e.g. tenseness, openness, voicing, friction, nasality) or expressive (extra high or extra low pitch, extra loud stress). This is length of a single segment or a few adjacent segments. Length may also be alleged of whole utterances or styles of speech, but here the term more generally used is tempo: if I say a given sentence once in one second and again in three seconds, the first utterance of it is perhaps 'fast' or 'rapid' or 'allegro', the second 'slow' or 'drawled'. But the phenomenon is obviously very much like quantity in physical expression. Such tempo variations never express distinctions between single words – or indeed distinctions in ordinary lexical meaning at all. And here, too, the differences are scalar rather than binary.

In an earlier chapter we mentioned the uncertainty with which analysts face length in answering the question 'segment or feature?' It resembles a feature in being applied to a segment in a uniform manner; the long vowel is presumably physically the same from start to finish, as can in particular cases be noted by recording a sample and playing it backwards (which also shows retroflexion of some English vowels as uniform). But it resembles a segment in that a given segment with length may well occupy a similar length of time to the same segment plus another segment. And, structurally, it often behaves like a segment in many rules. In Latin, for example, a medial vowel is weakened regularly to -i- before a single consonant other than r or l, but not before two consonants or *length* – i.e. length plus consonant, in this respect, resembles consonant plus consonant. In Greek verse and in the ordinary Latin verse based on Greek models a sequence of vowel-consonant-consonant or vowel-length-consonant counts as 'long' for the meter. And examples can be multiplied. It is never quite true that length is *exactly* like a consonant; for one thing it is commonly thought of as following a segment, whereas consonants frequently begin syllables. But there are, in fact, languages in which certain phonemes which we would regard as consonants *cannot* begin syllables, but must always be preceded by something: [l] is often of this nature, [ŋ] also, and [r] sometimes; in such languages length falls naturally into the same class of syllable-closers. As a result of all this, many linguists like to retain the option of treating length as either feature or segment depending on the circumstances. However, if we must legislate for them, I think there can scarcely be any doubt of our choice; against those many cases where the rules are eased by treating length as a segment, there are very few cases where it is easier to treat length as a feature. Consequently, binary length belongs above, in chapter 9, in the company of w and y or h and ?. They, too, can jump either way.

Word-accent is probably best treated from the viewpoint of function rather than phonetic nature. It may sometimes be represented by length (of vowels or consonants) but more often the two chief elements to the ear are raised or changing pitch and increased loudness. From the viewpoint of the speaker's proprioceptive sense, it often corresponds to sharp contractions of the muscles in chest and abdomen.

Well, what is its function? First, and chiefly, to unify the word, and occasionally to help mark its boundaries; second, occasionally in some languages and fairly often in others, to distinguish one word from another. Since it is the rule that only one syllable in any word may be so marked (with exceptions; if for many words two or more syllables are marked it is a tone language, not a word-accent language), we can see two possibilities. Either this syllable is a predictable one – the first (as in Hungarian, for example), the last (as in many Turkic languages), the penult (as in Polish, or, somewhat differently, in many Oceanic languages), etc., and hence serves in part to mark the beginning or end of the word – or it must be learned for each word, so that two words may be identical except for the position of the word-accent. There are two possibilities (at least) here, as well: either the two words are generally unrelated and semantically dissimilar (as in Balangao *'bukal* 'seed', *bu'kal* 'wild pig') or they are related, and the accent shift has grammatical significance (as is the case with most English examples, e.g. *'pervert* n., *per'vert* v.). It might be interesting to pause for a moment and inspect a listing of such words (with two syllables orthographically as well as phonetically, excluding, e.g., those in – Cle) in five classes: (1) words which exist in pairs with the accent variation as shown; (2) words which are always penult-accented in both verbal and nominal value; (3) words which are always accented on the ultima, in both values; (4) words which occur in only one of the values, but (n.) with recessive accent if nouns, and (v.) with ultima accent if verbs; (5) (v.) verbs with recessive accent and (n.) nouns with ultima accent; (6) adjectives (a) with ultima stress, (b) with penult stress. The lists can be taken to be representative of the current state of English in this respect.

List 14-1, words which occur as nouns with penult accentuation and as verbs with ultima accentuation. Of course, in most cases, there will also be considerable differences of vowel quality, but if we take the conventional spelling as our basic lexical form in these instances, we can consider the accent shift as brought about by a fairly early rule and the vowel quality changes as due to later rules. This is entirely reasonable. Rules 14-C and 14-D (pp. 272, 274) would correctly predict many of these; violations of 14-A and 14-B (p. 269) are marked -A, -B. Note that in many cases there is fluctuation; most often (27 times noted with a parenthetical 2) the alternative pronunciation is to accent both noun and verb on the penult. In other cases (25 times, marked 3), both noun and verb may be stressed on the last syllable. Other speakers might add a few words to the list or delete a few, but these are approximately all.[1] (S) means specialization of meaning of the noun.

LIST 14-1

abstract (-B)
accent (2) (-B)
addict (-B)
address (3,2) (-B)
affect (S) (-B)
affix (2) (-A)
ally (3,2) (-B)
alloy (2) (-B)
annex (2,3,S) (-A)
assay (2) (-B)
augment (S)
colleague (S)
collect (S)
combat (2)
combine (S)
commerce
commune (S)
complot
comport
compound (2,S)
compress (S)
concert (S)
concord
conduct
confine (S,3)
congee (-B2)
congress
conscript
conserve (S,3)
console (S)
consort (S)
construct (S)

contact (2)
content (S,3)
contest (2)
contract (S)
contrast (2)
converse (S)
convert
convict
convoy (2)
defect (S,3) (-B)
descant (-B)
detail (2,3) (-B)
digest (S) (-B)
discard (3) (-B)
discharge (3) (-B)
discount (2) (-B)
discourse (3) (-B)
eject
entrance (S) (-B)
escort (2)
essay (2,S)
exploit (2,S)
export (2)
extract
ferment
forecast
foredoom
fragment
impact
import
impress
imprint

incense (S,2)
incline (3)
increase
incurve (S)
infix (S) (-A)
inflow
ingrain
ingress
inlaw (S)
inlay
inrush
inseam (S)
insert
inset
instinct
insult
intern (S,3)
invert
invite
inwall
misdeal
mismatch
misplay
object (S)
outcrop
outgo
outrage (2)
outwork (S)
perfume (3,2)
permit (3)
pervert (S)
prefix (2) (-A)

[1] The list was prepared from a scan of all the solid entries (i.e. single words as opposed to idioms or phrases) in the *Normal and Reverse English Word List* compiled (by computer) under the direction of A. F. Brown at the University of Pennsylvania. I scanned all the entries in the three volumes (2685 pages) of the *Normal* (i.e. initially alphabetized) list, and long sequences in the *Reverse* (i.e. alphabetized by end letters) list. All two-syllable words listed by B. Trnka in his useful little book *A Phonological Analysis of Present-day Standard English* (Prague, vol. V of *Studies in English by Members of the English Seminar of the Charles University*, 1935) were also checked. See also K. Kohler, 'Modern English phonology' in *Lingua* 19:145–76 (1967).

present (s,3)	record (-b)	retail (-b; 2,3)
proceed (s)	recount (-b)	retread (-b)
produce (s)	refill (-b)	rewrite
progress	refund (-b)	segment
project (s)	refuse (s) (-b)	subject (s)
protest	regress (-b)	surbase (s)
purport	rehash (-b; 2)	survey (3)
rebate (3) (-b)	reject (-b)	torment
rebel (-b)	relapse (-b; 3)	transfer (-a)
rebound (-b; also 3)	relay (-b; 3)	transform
recap (s,2) (-b)	replay (-b)	transplant
recess (2,3,s) (-b)	reprint	transport
recoil (3) (-b)	research (-b; 3)	traverse (s)

Note the frequency of specialization; generally it is the noun that has a more specialized meaning. Occasionally a new verb, with penult accent, may be derived from the noun – e.g. *to combine* meaning to harvest grain with a combine, and a few of the words marked s and 2 may be of that type.

List 14-1 includes *all* the words (135) I could find which satisfied the criteria. Notice that all those which do not (at least historically, like *essay* or *escort*) begin with a prefix, end in *-ment*. The remaining lists will contain only those words whose accent is not predictable from orthography alone by one of the following three sets of rules: (a) rules of penult accent which resist shift; (b) rules of ultima accent (1) by prefix, (2) by ending; (c) the general rule of penult accent.

(14-A): Regardless of prefix, dissyllabic words with the following orthographic endings take penult accent, with the exceptions which appear in lists 14-1, 14-3, 14-4v., 14-5n. and 14-6a.

-ed (if syllabic)
-Vx/s (V means a, e, i, o, u, eu, ie, ou, or y)
-V₁ (V₁ means a, i, u, ae)
-er -or -ic -ish -th
-on (except -oon, rule B₂) -ture -sive/-tive

(14-B1): Words whose accents have not been determined by A (with the listed exceptions) take accent on the ultima if they begin with one of the following letter-combinations and contain at least two more letters. (If these are labeled as 'prefixes' and the rule stated accordingly, so that not every instance of the letters un- is a case of the prefix un-, exceptions are fewer.) Exceptions are listed in 14-1, 14-2, 14-4n., 14-5v. and 14-6b.

a- (if followed by one or more consonants (not x or a non-geminate cluster beginning with l, r, m, n); this includes various distinct prefixes

be- (followed by permitted initial consonant or cluster)

de- (followed by any permitted initial)

diff-, dig(r)-, dir-, dil-, div- (followed by vowel); dis- (followed by permitted initial)

eff-, eg(r)-, ej-, el-, em-, er-, ev- (followed by vowel); ex- (followed by permitted initial)

emm-, emb-, emp- (followed by vowel or r, l); en- (followed by permitted initial)

mis- (followed by permitted initial)

re- (followed by permitted initial)

un- (followed by permitted initial)/Many words, e.g. *undue*, have rather even stress, so that immediately before a main stress, -due is weaker: undue influence.

For all of these it is the case that verbs obey the rule more perfectly than nouns; but, for all but one, nouns obey more than half the time.

Some figures are shown in table 14.1.

The verbs are remarkably consistent, not only for these 'prefixes' but for a number of others which are not included in this count, but appear on p. 275 with list 14-4v. The exceptions are most often denominative verbs which retain the accent of the noun for one or another reason, and include some (naturally) where the 'prefix' is not historically a prefix at all. Adjectives are somewhat less consistent. The purely English prefixes un-, be- and mis- are virtually never stressed; adjectives in de-, e-/ex-, em-/en- are endstressed with more regularity than those with a number of other prefixes of similar origin (Latin or French), for no obvious reason. In the case of de- and e-/ex- this is true of nouns as well, where re- (and un-) also show high percentages. Re- includes two distinct prefixes; the purely Latin prefix (generally weakened to /rə-/) in borrowed words, and the productive English prefix (always /ri:-/). Much the same thing is true of de:- /də-/ is Latin, /di:-/ is productive 'remove' or 'undo'. Many of the penult-stressed words in all columns, especially with the 'prefixes' be-, de-, mis- and un-, do not in historical (or descriptive) reality contain any such prefix.

(14-B2): Apply ultima accent to words with the following endings:

-que -eau -eur -oo -é
-gue (with silent e) -ee (or -ée)
-oon -ign -euse -C_1C_1e (i.e. any doubled consonant followed by -e)
-een -eer -ade -oose -ese

Table 14.1

	Verbs		Nouns		Adjectives		Total	
	◡́	́◡	◡́	́◡	◡́	́◡	◡́	́◡
a-	189	2	95 (54%)	81 (46%)	54 (67·5%)	26 (32·5%)	338 (75·6%)	109 (24·4%)
be-	184	0	16 (59%)	11 (41%)	12	0	212 (95·1%)	11 (4·9%)
de-	136	5	71 (83·5%)	14 (16·5%)	18 (90%)	2 (10%)	225 (91·5%)	21 (8·5%)
di-, etc.	132	3	36 (69·2%)	16 (30·8%)	17 (70·8%)	7 (29·2%)	185 (87·7%)	26 (12·3%)
e-, etc.	103	3	26 (63·4%)	15 (36·6%)	19 (90·5%)	2 (9·5%)	148 (88·1%)	20 (11·9%)
em-, en-	104	2	15 (45%)	18 (55%)	8 (88·9%)	1 (11·1%)	127 (85·8%)	21 (14·2%)
mis-	75	1	20 (59%)	14 (41%)	3	0	98 (86·7%)	15 (13·3%)
re-	273	3	104 (77%)	31 (23%)	19 (57·6%)	14 (42·4%)	396 (89·2%)	48 (10·8%)
un-	210	0	10 (66·7%)	5 (33·3%)	226 (98·6%)	3 (1·4%)	446 (98·2%)	8 (1·8%)
Totals	1,406	19	393	205	376	55	2,175	279
Per cent	98·6	1·4	65·7	34·3	87·2	12·8	88·6	11·4

(14-C): Apply penult accent to all unlisted words not covered by rules 14-B1 and 14-B2.

List 14-2, words with accent on penult both as nouns and as verbs. Rule 14-C covers most of these; if they are exceptions to 14-B, they are labeled (-B).

LIST 14-2

ablaut (-B)	decoy (-B; 1,3)	prelude (1)
accent (-B; also 1)	deluge (-B)	premise (1)
address (-B; also 1)	detail (-B; 1,3)	presage (1)
alloy (-B; also 1)	detour (-B; 3)	probate
alum (-B)	devil (-B)	process
ambush	discount (1)	profile
asphalt (B-)	distance (-B)	profit
assay (-B; also 1)	district (-B)	program
audit	engine (-B)	promise
azure (-B)	envy (-B)	prospect
ballast	escort (1)	provost
banquet	essay (1)	purchase
bargain	excerpt (-B; 1)	purpose
bevel (-B)	excise (-B; 1)	rampage (also 1)
boycott	exile (-B)	recess (also 3, -B)
bypass	exit (-B)	rescue (-B)
captain	flimflam	respite (-B)
challenge	forfeit	revel (-B)
chelate	forward	rollick
chirrup	gossip	romance (also 3)
combat (also 1)	hiccup	second (also 1)
comfort	hoodoo (-B)	segue (-B, -D)
comment	incense (also 1)	sequence (-D)
compass	injure	sojourn
complot	input	solace
compo	instance	squeejee
compost	issue	sublease (also 1)
compound (also 1)	mildew	surcharge (also 1)
conjure (also 1)	mischief (-B)	surface
construe (also 1,3)	outfit	surfeit
contact (also 1)	outlaw	surname (1)
contour	outline	surtax (1)
convoy	outrage (also 1)	tiptoe
costar (also 1)	parlay	trespass
costume	postmark	value
curtain	powwow	voodoo (-B)
debit (-B)	preface	worship

(111 words listed; there may be a few more. Note that some 15 of the words marked (1) here were not actually included in list 14-1.)

List 14-3, words with final accent used both as nouns and verbs, provided they are *not* covered by rule 14-B or *are* exceptions to 14-A.

LIST 14-3

canoe	finance (also 2)	permit (1)
caress	garage	police
cement (also 1,2)	grimace (also 2)	salaam
collapse	guffaw	salute
command	incline (also 1)	stampede
commend	indent	sublime
compare	inspect	support
compute	intrigue	suppose
concern	lament	surcease
confine (also 1)	lassoo (1)	surmise
consent	machine	surprise
consult	manure	surround
content	marcel	survey (also 1)
contour (also 2)	massage	suspect (also 1)
control	parole	suspire
corral	patrol	sustain
crochet	perfume (2)	travail

(51 words listed; rule 14-B accounts for at least 100 more. The list is longer than 14-1.)

List 14-4n. Nouns only, stressed on penult but exceptions to B and not specified by A.

LIST 14-4n

abbess	adnoun	anise
abby	adscript	annal
abbot	advent	annate
abnet	adverb	anode
abscess	agate	aphid
absence	agent	apod
absinthe	aglet	April
access (also 1)	agnail	apron
acid	agnate	Arab
acme	ague	arak
acne	alcove	arrow
acorn	alien	arum
adage	alley	aspect
adept (also 5n)	aloe	asset
adit	alum	atoll
adjunct	ament	atom
adman	amide	attar
adnate	amyl	azote

LIST 14-4n (*cont.*)

banshee (5)	effort	misprint (also 5)
bebop	egress	missal
becard	egret	missile
bedlam	eland	misstep (5)
bedrail	elute	mistral (also 5)
bedrock	emblem	mistress
bedroll	empire	mongoose
bedroom	empress	ogee
beryl	enclave (5)	peewee
besom	encore (5)	puggree
betel	endive	rebec(k)
bethel	engine	rebirth (also 5)
bezel	engram	recipe
buckshee	ensign	recluse
bureau	entrails	recourse
chauffeur (5)	entree (also 5)	redeye
coffee	entry	refuge
colleen (also 5)	envoy	regent
comrade	enzyme	reindeer
cuckoo	evil	relict
decade	exarch	resale (5)
decane	excess (also 5)	rescript
decare	exode	resource (5)
decyl	expert	resin
depot	extern (also 5)	seesee
despot	geegee	spondee
dibase	grandeur	subclique (also 5)
digit	igloo	teaspoon
diglot	kil(l)dee(r)	tepee
diglyph	koodoo	toffee
digram	levee (5)	towhee
digraph	melee (5)	trochee
discord	miscue (also B, reg.)	unguent
distaff	misdeed (also B, reg.)	unit
distich	misfit (also 5)	unode
distyle	mishap (also 5)	yahoo
divot	miskal	yankee

(165 listed; the number of this type by rule 14-c is over 500)

List 14-4v. Verbs, first by rule D:

(14-D): All verbs beginning with one of the following combinations (followed by at least two letters):

coll-, corr- (followed by a vowel), com- (followed by m,p,b), con- (followed by a permitted initial consonant). [See also 14-D′ below] for(e)- (followed by a permitted initial)

ill-, irr- (followed by vowel), im- (m,p,b), in- (permitted initial vowel or consonant). [See also 14-D′, below]

occ-, off-, opp- (followed by vowel, l, r); ob- (followed by a permitted initial)

out- (followed by a permitted initial)

per- (followed by a permitted initial)

pre- (followed by a permitted initial)

pro- (followed by a permitted initial)

se- (followed by a permitted initial)

su- (followed by two consonants, the first of which is not n or l), sub- (followed by a permitted initial) [See also 14-D′ below]

trans- (followed by a permitted initial); tra- (followed by d, j, v)

up- (followed by a permitted initial).

LIST 14-4V

abhor (-A)	inter (-A)	postpone
admix (-A)	kowtow (also 5)	postpose
aver (-A)	liquesce	postscribe
baptize (also 5)	locate (also 5)	prefer (-A)
blaspheme (sometimes 5)	maintain	pursue
	maltreat	purvey
bombard	maraud	ransack
cajole	mature (-A; 6a)	recon (-A)
capsize (also 5)	molest	refer (-A)
carouse	negate (also 5)	relax (-A)
commix (-A)	omit	rewax (-A)
confer (-A)	opine	rewish (-A)
confix (-A)	ordain	rotate (also 5)
defer (-A)	osmose	sashay
deter (-A)	outfish (-A)	trepan
embed (-A)	outwish (-A)	trephine
foment	phonate (also 5)	undon (-A)
gainsay	pollute	unite
gyrate (also 5)	portend	unson (-A)
harass (5)	portray	usurp
imbed (-A)	possess	vacate
immix (-A)	postdate (also 5)	vouchsafe
infer (-A)	postfix (-A; also 5)	

(67 listed; rules 14-B and 14-D yield about 400 more.)

14-5V. Verbs with penult accent but not covered by rule 14-A or rule 14-C (i.e. they are exceptions to 14-B or 14-C).

K

LIST 14-5v

collate (also 4)	ingrow	perjure
connote (also 4)	injure	pronate
destine	inspan	prostrate (4)
exhale (also 4)	instance	update (4)
indwell	perfect (archaic; now 4)	

(14 listed; the rules account for about 30.)

14-5n. Nouns, not covered by rules 14-B1 and 14-B2, or else specified by rule 14-A, and accented on the ultima.

LIST 14-5n

babu (also 4)	chiffon (-A)	gestalt
Bahai	cigar	gourmand
ballet	clavier	gourmet
backwoods (4)	cocaine	guignol
batiste	commis (-A)	gravure
baton (-A)	commode (also 4)	guitar
bazaar	complaint	gyrene
berlin	conceit	hachure
bijou (also 4)	concent	hakim, hakeem
bopeep	concrete (also 4)	hotel
bougie	confrère (also 4)	infill
bouquet	conjoint	inane
bourgeois	conjunct (also 4)	incog
brassiere	consols (also 4)	indult
brazil	constraint	infarct
brevet	contempt	inside (4)
brunet	cornet (also 4)	intent
burnous (-A; 4)	corsage	intern (4)
cabal	cortège	Koran
cachet	cravat	lapel
cadet	croquet	latrine
cahoots	croquis (-A)	latrobe
camass	crouton (-A)	legume
canal	curie (also 4)	levant
caprice	debris (-A)	locale
carafe	decor (-A)	lucern(e)
cartouche	dessert	madame
catarrh	domain	mahout
Cathay	estate	mankind (also 4)
champagne	galoot	marine
chemise	galosh	marquis (4)
cheroot	gangrene (also 4)	mirage
chicane	gemel	misbirth (-A)

misfaith (-A)

misgrowth (-A)

montage

mustache (also 4)

oblate

octet

offence, offense

ondine

orang

ordeal (also 4)

outrance

pastiche

pavane

percent

perdu (-A)

peruke

petard

pilau

piquet

plantain (also 4)

pogrom

prestige

provost (4)

pursuit

quartet

quintet

raceme

raki (-A)

rapport

rattan

ravine

rebirth (-A)

sabot

salon (-A)

saloop

sardine

sauterne

savant

savoy

schlemiel

secesh

sedan

septet

sestet

sextet

shadoof

shellac

simoom

sordine

stenog

subtense

success

surtout

suscept

suspense

tarboosh

terrain

tibet

tomfool (also 4)

trapeze

trombone (also 4)

ukase (also 4)

unfaith (-A)

valet (also 4)

valise

vandyke

velour

verdun

vermouth (-A)

virtu (-A)

vizier

yaoort

(171 words listed; the B rules account for another 100, at least.)

14-6a. Adjectives accented on ultima, but either not covered by B or D′ (given herewith) or in violation of A.

(14-D′): Rule D applies for only three 'prefixes': coll- etc., ill- etc., and su- etc.

LIST 14-6a

arcane

august (also B)

austere

berserk (also B)

cerise

coed (also B)

complex (B)

convex (B)

galore

germane

humane

innate (B)

jocose (B)

legit

ornate

marine

mature (-A)

minute

morose

mundane (B)

naive

oblate (B)

occult (B)

outworn

perdu (-A)

perplex (-A)

perverse

petite

polite

postpaid (B)

precise

prepense

prescript

pristine (B)

profane

profound

profuse

prolix (-A)

propense

LIST 14-6a (*cont.*)

robust	select	tiptop
rotund (B)	serene	upright (B)
secluse	sincere	upset (B)
secure	snafu (-A)	upstage
sedate	supreme	

(53 words listed; the rules account for about 75 more.)

14-6b. Adjectives accented on penult, in violation of B or D′ but not by A.

ablate	dedal	incut
absent	dement (also A)	ingrain
acrid	difform	ingrate
acid	discal	inmost
adjunct	discoid	innate (A)
adnate	dismal	inshore
adverse	distal	inside
agile	distant	instant
agnate	divers	inverse (A)
alate	docile	misty
alien	empire	recent
anal	enate	regal
arid	ensate	regent
arrant	even	regnal
azure	expert (also A)	restant
complex (also A)	extant (also A)	serene (A)
compound (also A)	falcate	subtile
concave (also A)	foreign	subject
concrete (also A)	inboard	subscript
condign (also A)	inbond	substant
contrite (also A)	inborn (A)	surplus
converse (also A)	inbred (A)	surgy
decent	inburnt	suspect (also A)

(69 listed; rules account for about 50 others.)

Naturally this is not sufficient data for a complete grammar of English (note, for instance, that no distinction is here made between neutral or zero vowels and full vowels); however, it does give a fair idea of the actual distribution of accent in words of two syllables. Words of three syllables which are otherwise like the ultima-accented verbs are generally antepenult-accented with a full vowel preserved in the ultima (like *dedicate, abdicate*) though many words covered by rules B1 (unstressed prefixes) and B2 (stressed Frenchy suffixes) still have end stress (like absolute, misbehave, understand, octoroon, Japanese, silhouette), whereas a few (cigarette, amateur, etc.) have shifted stress to the antepenult, or developed so-called even stress (i.e. stress conditioned by what follows:

'It's rèd hót'   vs.   'a réd hòt póker').

How do you write a rule to shift accent or place it? The notation which corresponds most closely to such statements as "Accent verbs on the ultima" is one which regards accent as a feature of the whole word, a word-prosody in the Firthian sense,[1] with as many values as there are possible positions for the accent (or, if you choose to treat one position as neutral, 'unmarked', one value less). So, for English, one possible way of formulating the given rule might be:

$$[\text{u accent}] \rightarrow [\text{1 accent}] / [\overline{+\text{Verb}}]$$

Where u means 'unmarked' (as opposed to m 'marked') and 1 means 'ultima', 2 'penult', 3 'antepenult', i means 'first syllable', etc. A system of this sort would make it fairly easy to write rules shifting the accent a uniform number of steps to right or left, e.g.:

$$[\text{n accent}] \rightarrow [\text{n}+\text{1 accent}]$$

says change all oxytones (i.e. words accented on last syllable) to paroxytones (next-to-last), all paroxytones to proparoxytones (antepenult), and so on for any number of syllables. I have never heard of a language or language-family in which such a rule would be useful, but I hesitate to claim that there are none. The English verb case which we have been glancing at may look superficially like a shift one step to the right, but when all the evidence is inspected, it seems rather like a shift from non-last (perhaps recessive) to last, which might be written

$$[\text{K accent}] \rightarrow [\text{1 accent}]$$

(where $K > 1$). But such a rule is no simpler in this notation than in a dozen others.

In languages like Azerbaijani, where the *normal* position of the accent is fully predictable (on ultima) in terms of junctures (i.e. What comes next?), only one shift rule is needed (to the initial syllable for vocatives and some imperatives) and this could be well handled by a binary prosody rule:

$$[-\text{Accent (or u Accent)}] \rightarrow [+\text{Accent (or m Accent)}]$$

[1] See, e.g., John Lyons, 'Phonemic and Non-Phonemic Phonology: Some Typological Reflections', *IJAL* XXVIII (1962), 127–34.

where [+Accent] is a word-feature or prosody which means "Put high falling pitch on first vowel of word".

One traditional type of feature-rule is based on the principled exclusion of features with scope greater than the single segment. In such a system every syllabic segment must be labeled either [+stress] or [−stress] (or whatever the accentuation feature may be) and a stress-shift rule necessarily has two parts: (1) change [−accent] to [+accent] on the syllable which is to receive the new accent, and (2) change [+accent] to [−accent] on the syllable which is losing it. The two parts might go best in this order in case it is possible and desirable to have a general rule "If any word has two (or n) stressed vowels, delete the stress on the first" (or "on the second" or "all but the last", etc.). The other order (deletion of accent before insertion of accent) might also be desirable just in case there is independent need for a rule which says "If any word has no accented vowel, add an accent to the last" (or "the first" or "the next-to-last" or whatever is required). This style of rule-writing relegates the fact that each word has one and only one accented vowel to a late rule, more or less implying that, except for the peculiarities of individual languages, one might just as well have any pattern of accented and unaccented vowels. This looks like an undesirable implication (or 'claim', as young people say).

Paul Kiparsky has recently proposed[1] a slightly different scheme. Instead of marking only one vowel [+Accent] and all the rest, whether before or after, [−Accent], he would mark all vowels *after the accent* also as [+Accent]. Thus a shift one step to the right is immediately accomplished by a rule [+Accent]→[−Accent] (in the desired environment). He makes a half-hearted and unconvincing attempt to justify this decision on phonetic grounds, but in fact it amounts to using a new feature which might be better called 'Nonpretonic'; i.e. the vowel labeled [+Nonpretonic] is either the accented vowel or any later one, [−Nonpretonic] is any earlier one. An equally good case could be made for the opposite sort of feature (either [Pretonic] or [Nonposttonic], whichever works best). Some of the disadvantages are avoided by specifying the value of this feature for only one syllable in each word at the outset, then having an automatic copying rule which extends it to the boundary. This is especially convenient in languages where the proper-

---

[1] 'On the History of Greek Accentuation', *Langages*, vol. I (1967). Compare W. S. Allen's *Contonation* notion in *In Memory of J. R. Firth*, London, Longmans, Green and Co., 1966, pp. 8–14.

ties of pretonic vowels are different from those of tonic and posttonic vowels (or the converse), and such languages probably do exist (English may be one, at least in some measure).

Are there ways of writing binary word-prosodies for the position of the accent? Of course there are, several. Given a language in which the accent may stand on any one of the last three vowels, more or less as in Greek, one could have two binary features [proparoxytone] and [oxytone], so linked that the value [+proparoxytone] entails [−oxytone]. This would make antepenult accent cost one ' + ', ultima accent one ' + ' but penult accent only minuses (or, if you prefer, use m's for pluses and u's for minuses).

In this scheme a rule shifting accent from antepenult to penult would go:

$$[+\text{proparoxy}]\rightarrow[-\text{proparoxy}]$$

in one step, a rule from penult to ultima:

$$[-\text{oxytone}]\rightarrow[+\text{oxytone}] \text{ in the environment } \overline{[-\text{proparoxy}]},$$

and one from the ultima to the antepenult would be:

$$[+\text{oxytone}, -\text{propar.}]\rightarrow[-\text{oxytone}, +\text{propar.}],$$

part of which could be made automatic. Variants of this could choose one of the other accent positions as the unmarked or double-minus position.

Sometimes our rules suggest other types of features. In Greek it is common to distinguish between 'recessive' accent and 'fixed' accent, although the difference between 'recessive' accent and accent 'fixed' on the antepenult is non-existent. Customarily one talks of antepenult accent when some form chosen as the basis of the paradigm (nominative singular masculine, for instance) actually has the accent on the antepenult, but of recessive accent when some other form or forms have accent on the antepenult, but the base form (if one is recognized) has it on the penult because the ultima is long. If we choose to regard accent on the ultima as neutral (whether 'unmarked' or 'irrelevant') we could define [+accent] as recessive, and [−accent] as paroxytone. (Or, if it proved more advantageous, make recessive accent neutral, [+accent] penult accent and [−accent] oxytone.) Either system makes it easy to write rules shifting the accent – indeed it is obvious that this is notationally equivalent to our first method, with the values [i] = 1, [+] = 3 and $[-] = 2$, without the possibility of writing rules of addition and subtraction.

Is there any argument to help us decide whether to mark accent as a feature of the word (analogous to T. M. Lightner's markers)[1] or as a feature of every segment (or every syllabic segment)? Jakobson's argument that accent (stress or tone) is a contrastive feature, requiring reference to preceding or following syllables, is not sufficient, since this is also true of quantity which often seems to get along fine as segmental. The existence of uncertainty about the cost of such features in an evaluation procedure (i.e. a system for comparing the simplicity or economy of different descriptions of the same language) is no argument, since surely this uncertainty can be removed. If we consider arguments based upon speakers' intuitions, we would be inclined to favor features extending over the whole word rather than attached to each segment. On the other hand, it is clearly *possible* to get along without 'marker features' or 'word prosodies', and so Ockham's Razor seems to favor operating with only segmental features.

Another way of handling the problem is suggested by IPA notation, in which accent marks are placed *before a syllable* rather than *over a vowel*. This makes the accent itself a segment. Rules to shift accent then becomes rules of metathesis. Unfortunately such rules, though needed, are difficult to write. Furthermore, if accent is a segment, what kind of segment is it? It would seem rather odd to specify it (even with redundancy rules) for all the features of ordinary segments, though one could start with a base form represented as one of the unused combinations of features (e.g. [+strident, +vocalic] or the like) which would ultimately vanish after affecting the next following vowel. This would resemble the historical situation in some East Asian languages, where the loss[2] of a given initial segment or feature is accompanied by certain tonal consequences for the remainder of the syllable. Placing the accent segment in IPA manner just before the onset consonant(s) (if any) raises difficulties for formulating transposition rules; considerably easier would be to place it immediately before the vowel (after the onset, if any), and write rules to shift it to the environment just before the next syllabic segment. Of course, this rule, like other metathesis rules, could be eased by planting dummy segments between each pair of consecutive segments.

[1] 'On the Description of Vowel and Consonant Harmony', *Word* xxi (1965), 244–50.
[2] Tonal change is not always accompanied by loss.

A quite different kind of rule and a different kind of feature is required for handling tones in languages like Chinese.[1] Here traditional terms already imply a kind of feature analysis: a tone described as High Level as opposed to High Falling and Low Level suggests two binary features [±high] (or low) and [±falling] (or level). In fact Wang's proposed features are only slightly elaborated from that base: *contour, high, central, mid, rising, falling,* and *convex.* Of these *contour* is simply a cover feature for all non-level tones (i.e. falling, rising, or both); *central* is neither high nor low, while *mid* is exactly half-way between high and low, and *convex* means Rising-Falling. This system is much richer than any existing tone system (7 features fully utilized could generate 128 distinct tones, whereas few languages have even as many as 7). Note that glottalization (and by implication 'register' or 'phonation type' in general) and length, which are sometimes treated as tonal features (this seems to be always so in languages reported to have 8 tones or more), are here excluded (and attached to the vocalic segment). In reducing this excessive richness, Wang makes use of redundancy conventions by which the 128 possibilities may be cut to 13 (5 level and 8 non-level, 'contour' tones). No language is alleged to have all 13, or even 10 tones. Some of the redundancy conventions are an inevitable consequence of the secondary nature of such features as contour (which is wholly defined in terms of other features 'either rising or falling or both'), but others appear to be empirical, such as the limitation of [central] to [−contour] tones, which is equivalent to an assertion that no language has three distinct rising tones or three distinct falling tones (distinct in respect to pitch level, high, low, etc.). But there seem to be other such empirical propositions which are not implicit in the features or the redundancy rules: "Languages in which each syllable independently may have any one of four or more tones, including at least two (rather frequent) contour tones, will have many monosyllabic morphemes and many closed syllables." "Languages with four or more level tones (and few and infrequent contour tones), allowing maximum contrast only on some syllables, will have many words of two or more syllables and have many open syllables." Furthermore, one kind of language is found predominantly in Eastern and Southeastern Asia, the other kind in Central

---

[1] See especially the article by William S-Y. Wang, 'Phonological Features of Tone', *IJAL* xxxiii (1967), 93–105. See also the criticisms in Peter Ladefoged, *Linguistic Phonetics (Working Papers in Phonetics 6)*, U.C.L.A., 1967, pp. 70 and 87. For another type of tone problem, see P. Schachter, 'Phonetic Similarity in Tonemic Analysis', *Language* xxxvii (1961), 231–8.

America, Africa and perhaps New Guinea. The geographical fact can be regarded as purely accidental, i.e. due to historical causes, but the structural facts have at least the air of being organic. If an attempt were made to make the theory account for the facts (assuming for the moment that they are facts), it would surely entail deriving all or most contour tones by deletion (which accords with known history only partially). If this is true, then contour features would not appear at the 'systematic phonemic' or morphophonemic (lexical) level, but only after the operation of certain rules. Quite possibly some of the features used for level tones, too, might be secondary, appearing only after some phonological rules have operated.[1]

A second interesting device adopted by Wang (as by others before him) is the use of m(arked) and u(nmarked) values for certain features (+ and − for others), stipulating that a u marking does not count as contributing to the complexity of analysis, whereas m, + and − all do. Most features allow only m and u or only + and −, but the features [rising] and [falling] have the value u for non-contour tones, + or − for all contour tones (with the restriction that both cannot simultaneously be −). Wang's justification (p. 103) is that "there is no empirical ground for favoring either +HIGH or −HIGH, or RISING or FALLING". This seems to be an error; at least there is a distinct statistical excess of non-High over High, of non-Rising over Rising and of non-Falling over Falling in the collection of 630-odd tone systems which he made use of. In short, all the +'s again might be made m's. This would then conform to Jakobson's use of + (always marked) rather than Trubetzkoy's notion that only *some* binary oppositions are privative (see ch. 11 above); and the remaining u's which might be distinguished from −'s would be equivalent to the i's (*irrelevant*) which we have suggested. Even in the chart (table II, p. 103) offered by Wang, it is clear that there is a difference in the value of u's for three features, CENTRAL, MID and CONVEX, between irrelevant non-contrastive u's and relevant, contrastive u's which should rather be called minuses. That is, [u CENTRAL] or [u MID] for CONTOUR tones is ruled out in principle, but for level

---

[1] My own feeling after spending many hours studying the data collected by Wang is that fewer features differently defined will need fewer redundancy rules. E.g., a low rising tone is scarcely possible without at least a short initial fall; nearly all 'level' tones tend to fall at least a little; high, sharply falling tones will inevitably have a little rise. All these facts can be planted in a proper set of features directly, so that they need not be handled by rule until the lowest level. A long popular device for eliminating rising and falling tones is to resolve them into sequences of level tones. This is often a historical fact, though not in all cases.

tones it is contrastive (for [−CENTRAL] ones only, in the case of MID), and [u CONVEX] for level tones is meaningless, for RISING only or FALLING only impossible, but for [+RISING, +FALLING] it is significant. But in a general way Wang's system satisfies our criterion that the number of marked features must vary with scarcity.

The cutest thing in Wang's article is the rule for Amoy Hokkien tonal sandhi with which he closes:

$$
\begin{bmatrix} \alpha \text{ HIGH} \\ \beta \text{ FALLING} \end{bmatrix} \rightarrow \begin{bmatrix} \beta \text{ HIGH} \\ -\alpha \text{ FALLING} \end{bmatrix}
$$

which says that a High tone becomes non-Falling (i.e. level), a non-High tone becomes Falling, a Falling tone becomes High, and a non-Falling tone becomes non-High. (Read "becomes or remains" throughout for "becomes".) The rule works beautifully, but, like other such cross-feature alpha-rules, it raises a question about the theory which permits them. Why should this be so? What logic links HIGH with NON-FALLING, or FALLING with HIGH? Perhaps we can say that Falling means changing from relatively higher to relatively lower. This might be expressed in a numerical notation, in which the tones are

	+H	−H
+F	53	31
−F	55	33

(given obligatory rules automatically changing $11 \rightarrow 31$, $75 \rightarrow 55$) by the formulation: "subtract 22 if the digits are equal, add 22 if they are unequal". Maybe there is a little rationale here, but the theory (as of 1966, anyway) allows such rules to be written quite without restraint, e.g.

$$[\alpha \text{ VOICED}] \rightarrow [-\alpha \text{ DIFFUSE}],$$

which says that (e.g.) in some language b, d, g might be converted to e or o, but p, t, k to i or u, or

$$[\alpha \text{ STRIDENT}] \rightarrow [\alpha \text{ NASAL}],$$

or any random pair you like. It certainly looks as if a restraint should be placed upon such rules to eliminate the ones which make phonetic nonsense and allow those which make phonetic sense.

Grammars in general either give procedures which can be used as devices for producing sentences from scratch or ways of decomposing, analyzing or parsing any given sentence. In ordinary life we certainly do things analogous to both of these acts, at least occasionally, but we also perform a variety of operations which take a sentence as input and (without a total parsing operation) make various alterations in it to yield a different sentence as output. The range of such operations is considerable, and, since many of them are under conscious control, they are somewhat more accessible to study (via introspection or otherwise) than the more radical operations of spontaneous speaking and understanding.[1] It is particularly easy to observe them if you, like myself, have the habit of editing your own manuscripts. There seem to be five basic sorts of alteration, although one of the five has a number of subtypes.

(15-1) Deletion. This is not like the deletion of a transformational (competence) grammar, since it is normally irrecoverable; perhaps one ought to give it a special name for better understanding. 'Excision' would not be bad, suggesting as it does the cutting out of diseased or undesirable elements. The most common excised elements are intensifiers (anyone may betray his enthusiasm or his prejudices by too many *very*'s or other judgemental words), but various qualifying adjectives and sentence modifiers (things like *in general, of course, clearly, for example*) may also need the knife, as well as repetitions and redundancies of many kinds and sizes (even paragraphs). The reasons for excision are generally to improve clarity and public relations – i.e. to avoid giving the reader a bad impression of yourself (as gushy, excitable, incoherent,

---

[1] Our concern here with writing does not mean that we ignore or consider unimportant the parallel operations of self-editing in speech, surely one of the most conspicuous and studiable of the phases of performance. Two types may be noted: (1) rapid mental revision of a sentence or some part of it before it is uttered; (2) revision of a sentence or part of it after it has come out. The first can only be studied by introspection, but cases of the second are usually easy to identify, frequently marked by introducers like "or rather", "I should say", "I mean", "what I'm trying to say is", etc. Cf. the discussion by C. F. Hockett in *The State of the Art* (The Hague, Mouton, 1968), ch. 6, especially 6.1, pp. 89–99.

fragmentary, boring, etc.), though occasionally an item may be deleted from a list because it is found not to belong on that list. But correction of errors more often involves the other devices, not excision.

(15-2) Expansion. Again, I do not mean the generative expansion in which A is replaced by B +C, but rather the simple addition or insertion of words or phrases (i.e. A→A +B or A→B +A, most nearly) – perhaps *adjunction* comes closer than any other traditional term. This may be done to correct an error of omission, to restrict a generalization which is too broad as it stands, to specify an assertion with regard to time and place, to improve a description, and for various other reasons. The insertion is generally adverbial or adjectival; often also parenthetical, and without syntactic ties (at least on the surface) to the sentence in which it is placed.

(15-3) Substitution. This cannot be compared very closely either to P-rule expansion, where a more generic label is continued by a more specific one (e.g. NP→N, or N→N^hum or N^hum→Henry), or to transformational replacement, where one item is deleted and a different one put in its place, though it bears a little resemblance to both of these. At any rate editorial substitution cannot, as a rule, be derived in two steps by an excision and an adjunction, since those two can be applied only to optional items in the string, while substitution is most commonly applied to things like noun-phrase and verb-phrase heads, including non-deletable elements. It *is* like excision-cum-adjunction, however, in that the bracketing usually remains the same; i.e. if the word replaced happened to be a noun head of a subject expression, then the replacing word will also be the noun head of what is (in some sense) the *same* subject expression. Occasional cases will turn up, of course, where an actual editorial substitution violates this rule; all such cases must be considered due to two (or more) operations rather than one, normally a transformational change followed by a substitution or an adjunction followed by an excision. However, the usual thing is the replacement of one word by another of closely similar meaning either in the interests of accuracy (the new word is a little closer to the truth, somehow) or of esthetics (the new word avoids a close repetition or improves the rhythm).

(15-4) Reordering or transposition. This is such a simple operation that I nearly forgot to mention it. In some languages almost every element is likely to be shifted (Plato is said to have tried every possible permutation of the first three or four nodes of the *Republic* – "Yesterday

I went down to the Piraeus, etc". – before settling on one), but in English it is most often adverbial elements (like *always, certainly*). This operation cannot invariably be resolved into an excision from one spot followed (or preceded) by an adjunction at another, for the same reasons as in the case of substitution. But here it is more often the case that we are dealing with optional elements, though occasionally a substantial constituent may be shifted, whether for contrast ('emphasis') as when objects are put first ("*This* I've got to see") or when long expressions (relative clauses, infinitives, etc.) are shifted after their heads[1] to make the sentences terminable at an earlier point. (Unlike Latin or Turkish, English does not take kindly to long-delayed dropping of the second shoe, so that most sentences may be grammatically and sensibly stopped at several points before the end.) The reasons for transposition are nearly always stylistic, except where an outright mistake has somehow been found in the first draft, a thing which does happen. Once in a while ambiguity may be prevented by transposition, but I am not yet sure whether the avoidance of ambiguity is narrowly linguistic or stylistic. If we change "Well cared-for lady's bicycle" to "Lady's bicycle, well cared-for" in a classified ad, can this be other than stylistic?

(15-5) Sweeping revisions. Here we are not concerned with the utter expunction of one sentence or paragraph and the insertion of a quite different one; this would surely be a case of procedures 1 and 2 or perhaps of 3. What is involved here is the reframing of a sentence or two, keeping the general tenor unchanged and using mostly the same words, but in a rather different syntactical arrangement. In practice, of course, some part of such changes may be attributed to repeated applications of 1, 2, 3 and 4, but there will remain a residue which is closely analogous to the transformations of an earlier day (the emphasis shift mentioned under 4 might well be a case), whereby passives are made active, for instance, or one form of embedding is changed into another, or a co-ordinate construction is made subordinate (or the converse), or one pattern of nominal and prepositional complements is replaced by another (e.g. one might change "Substitute money for brains" into "Replace brains by money" – here with a vocabulary substitution which my foreign students often forget to make (and even Eugene Nida, sometimes) – or change "Shower them with gifts" into "Shower gifts upon them"), and so on. In other words, deep structure (or semantic structure) re-

[1] V. Yngve, 'A model and an hypothesis for language structure', *Proceedings of the American Philosophical Society* 104:440 (1960).

mains substantially unaltered, but the surface is restructured. Examples of changed form of embedding are, for instance, switches within the following sets: "He needs a scolding" – "He needs to be scolded"; "He bought it to get ahead" – "He bought it so he could get ahead"; "He thought about going" – "He thought he might go"; "This may cause loss of time" – "This may cause us to lose time" – "This may cause some time to be lost."

All five of these devices are motivated in much the same ways. One motive we haven't mentioned is the simple desire to change the length, either to cut a thousand-word paper down to five hundred words (where obviously device no. 1 will be heavily used) or to expand a paper into a monograph, which will lead to heavy use of no. 2.

It should also be quite obvious that these devices may easily be formulated as rules (given an adequate semantic notation, which we may have some day); indeed most of these rules will look quite like one type or another of transformational rules, although the semantic restrictions on applicability will be a bit novel. The substitution rule will read something like: "Replace A by B provided B shares n features with A" or perhaps "all feature-values except x." An alternative possibility (and a more attractive one) is to suppose that each word or lexeme includes among its features a list of synonyms with indications of restrictions on their substitutability. One of the things we (at least some of us) do know automatically for almost any word is such a list (as well as lists of antonyms, co-hyponyms and generic names), and a reasonable theory of a language must account for this.

Editing, whether for simple improvement or adjustment of length, isn't the only activity which makes use of these rules. But before we mention others, we might first describe one or two other sorts of editing. Consider the case of a man preparing offset copy on an ordinary typewriter; he wants his lines to be justified (that is, have a straight right-hand margin) so he wants each line to contain exactly (say) 48 letters and spaces. By first typing out what he has to say, regardless of length of line but in such a manner that line-breaks come somewhere between the 40th and 55th letter, and then carefully revising (all 5 operations may be relevant: transposition, for instance, is useful to shift a short word into the next line in exchange for a long one), he can achieve his desired goal.

Consider also the case of the undergraduate student who wants to turn in a plagiarized paper without getting caught. One obvious protective device is the application of our rules in such a manner as to produce notable infelicities of style (which the professor can gleefully correct and so fail to notice the plagiary). Of course, a student clever enough to do this well would really not need to do it; but this is not a sufficient cause for his not doing it.

The same rules may be used jointly with a phonological screening rule or rules (to count syllables, determine metrical length, space stresses, test for rhymes or alliterations, etc.) to make a versification device. Suppose, for instance, that you are writing a version of the *Psalms* in heroic couplets using some standard translation as input. Step one might be to measure off two stretches of 8 to 12 syllables each followed by a suitable break (e.g. the last syllable could not be all or part of a proclitic – article, preposition, conjunction – or – in most styles – of an attributive adjective; for a Popean couplet the second line should end at a major syntactic break). If this is impossible, apply any rules necessary – substitution, deletion and transposition especially, but sometimes also adjunction – to make it so. Search the two proto-verses (or versoids) for suitable rhyme words that can be shifted to the end. If there are none, substitute synonyms in one or both lines until a rhyme-pair is found. Shift these to the ends. Now apply the rules again until the lines satisfy the metrical requirements. Resort to rule 5 only when other methods fail.

This may not be the way great poets work (still, preserved samples of successive revisions by a number of famous poets show that they do make use of all our procedures, though sometimes *they* will make substitutions which cause substantial semantic changes), but it is a feasible procedure which could be converted into an algorithm for programming on a computer.

So far we have spoken only of application of the 5 procedures *salva significatione*, i.e. with a proviso that the meaning must be changed less than some predetermined amount. If, now, we relax this restriction, we immediately broaden the scope of application of the rules considerably. The first place I remember encountering the use of such broader rules, and one where they are still used, is in the language class. This is the exercise in which the students in turn make slight alterations in a given sentence in rapid oral drill. The conditions on excision and adjunction are not much different, since *they* almost invariably do alter the meaning, but the new condition on the substitution process is that the result must be (while syntactically unaltered) semantically merely non-deviant, i.e. a sentence which can be (as the British say) contextualized, imagined as really being uttered under such-and-such conditions. By this means one can derive sentences of wholly incompatible meaning from the same input or base sentence. Process 5, transformational alteration, and 4, transposition, will not usually have great effects on the meaning, but whatever restrictions were needed before are now removed. Like all the other processes except 5, 4 is understood as not altering the syntactic structure; any change which does this is, by definition, an instance of 5 or of some combination which includes 5. If I change "John saw Bill" into "Bill saw John", for instance, this is not a transposition or a transformation, but a double substitution (process 3). The structure is not altered, but merely two of the exponents of points in the structure, fillers of unchanged slots. If I change "John saw Bill" into "Bill John saw [but not Bill's wife]", this is an instance of 4, and maybe of 5 (since a new contrastive structure has been introduced).

At any rate, with the restrictions as stated for language-learning drills, it is clear that (with exceptions) any sentence of a language can be converted, in a finite number of steps, into any other given sentence. Let us exemplify by choosing two reasonably short English sentences at random and tracing one possible route (out of many) leading from one to the other (excluding the trivial route of substituting the whole sentence in one step). Suppose our first sentence is:

(15-01) Your period of suffering is coming to an end this summer.

And our second is:

(15-02) I am a leper if there is a lie in anything I say.

First delete "to an end":

(15-11) Your period of suffering is coming this summer.

Then substitute "I" for "Your period of suffering", making the obligatory change of *is* to *am*:

(15-12) I am coming this summer.

Now insert:

(15-13) I am coming if there is any trouble this summer.

Substitute "a leper" for "coming" (if you reject structural equivalence here, other routes are open):

(15-14) I am a leper if there is any trouble this summer.

Finally, delete "this summer" and replace "any trouble" by "a lie in anything I say" and get the desired result:

(15-02) I am a leper if there is a lie in anything I say.

Cases like this where virtually nothing is retained except an NP+VP frame, are not especially practical (although they may be amusing). If the two sentences are similar at a somewhat lower level, the process is more significant. Look at these:

(15-03) The situation seems to be analogous on both levels of analysis.

(15-04) This is very different from the successivity of pieces in a time sequence.

Let's see if we can proceed here one word at a time (not counting articles and prepositions, of course).

(15-31) *This* situation seem to be, etc.

(15-32) *This seems* to be, etc.

(15-33) This *is* analogous on both levels of analysis.

(15-34) This is *different* on both, etc.

(15-35) This is *very* different on both, etc.

(15-36) This is very different *from the successivity* on both levels of analysis.

(15-37) This is very different from the successivity *of pieces* on both levels of analysis.

(15-38) This is very different from the successivity of pieces on *the level* of analysis.

(15-39) This is very different from the successivity of pieces on the *analysis level.*

(15-310) This is very different from the successivity of pieces on the *time* level.

(15-311) This is very different from the successivity of pieces *in a* time level.

(15-04) This is very different from the successivity of pieces in a time *sequence.*

The phenomenon that shows up in the last few steps, namely the preference of *level* for *on* but of *sequence* for *in*, is a kind of agreement phenomenon, though the difference elsewhere may be significant (as in the three-way contrast "He's in Washington", "He's at Washington", "He's on Washington", i.e. state or city, university, mountain or street – or horse). Agreement phenomena and other formal adjustments are more noticeable in languages like Latin than in English.

These examples should suffice to show the nature of the game; I think if you experiment with it a few times you will begin discovering structural and semantic facts which you hadn't thought of before.

One further class of activities makes use of rules of the same kind (indeed pretty much the same rules, but with different restrictions): the stylistic exercises known as parody and pastiche. There are several subtypes. I will describe first a form of pastiche or cento[1] which has been a traditional feature of education in the classical languages for centuries – I first met it in Latin, then in Greek – and it seems especially important for languages whose cultures are remote in time or space or both, since it involves not only how you express what you think but also how and what you are likely to think in the first place. The assignment is to translate a passage (e.g. from the *New York Times*, or from Emerson, or from *Punch*, etc.) into Latin or Greek prose (the same exercise is also done in verse, but I have had more experience with prose). Correctness is demonstrated not by proof that you have violated no rules of grammar and that your product means the same as the original, but by showing that every individual collocation, including whole phrases here and there, can be found in a good classical author. The goal is to write a discourse such that an expert would find no internal evidence to suggest that it was not written by an ancient Roman. (We ignore here the probability that a truly qualified expert would have read every word ever written by an ancient Roman and should be able to identify most of the tags.) At the beginning any author will do, i.e. you may combine pieces from Tacitus, Livy, Caesar, Cicero and Sallust all in one composition. As your skill and experience develop, though, you are expected to stay as close as

---

[1] Typical centos (for those who find the word strange) are the *Christus Patiens*, a crucifixion play made up entirely of bits – generally half-lines or whole lines – from Euripides, and many medieval poems constructed from Vergil, e.g., Ausonius' *Cento Nuptialis* or Pomponius' *Tityrus*. I know of no good example in English, though some burlesques or parodies make partial use of the technique, as in A. E. Housman's *Fragment of a Greek Tragedy*.

possible to some one author; Cicero is the favorite, since we have ten or fifteen volumes of his works. A small part of this is grammatical in the narrower sense; one must know that Cicero always prefers such-and-such a form, that Sallust likes certain archaic endings, that Tacitus never uses construction X, and so on. And some of it is vocabulary control; of various synonyms, be sure to avoid the ones avoided by your model, and use his favorites. Some of it has to do with details like word-order and rhythm, particularly that of the last words before a sentence-end (clausulae). But if you can lift a whole sentence from your model, you *know* the word-order will be right and the clausula right, the vocabulary correct and the morphology and syntax true. So you generally end up with several longish phrases lifted outright (and, of course, slightly modified to fit) connected by bridges studded with shorter phrases taken from your author.

This is an extremely valuable exercise; it forces you, in the first place, to make a deep and searching semantic analysis of your English original noting what parts are meaningless embroidery, what the author was *really* trying to say, what devices he was using to achieve his effects, and so on. Then you must also study many different passages from your Latin (or Greek) model looking for ones with usable phrases which mean the same thing as your English source (even though superficially they may appear different). You begin to discover constant characteristics of English style (even in simple narrative) which are rare in antiquity – a tendency never to say directly what you mean, for instance (as the Greek or Roman frequently does), a generosity with metaphorical language, the effect of unnoticed echoes of Biblical or Shakespearean language. Greek indeed shows some echoes of Homer, but classical Latin apparently has nothing similar, and even in Greek the effect does not seem as great, particularly in prose. But all this is by the way.

What are possible steps in writing such a prose composition? (1) Select a number of key words in each sentence. Determine as many potential Latin or Greek equivalents for each one as you can. Look these words up in such places as *Harper's Latin Dictionary* (also known as *Lewis and Short* or *Andrews' Freund*), the great *Thesaurus Linguae Latinae* (which is not a thesaurus in the ordinary English sense but a very large monolingual dictionary with copious illustrative sentences from the whole range of Latin literature) and in the various Concordances, Indices Verborum and Special Lexica to individual authors (here you can do well with most prose authors, although for Livy you have almost nothing, and in Greek there is no really good Index or Lexicon to Plato). What you're looking for is passages which approximate the ideas and expressions of your given English text. (2) Look the more promising of these up in editions of the authors concerned to get a view of surrounding context. Very often you'll find other usable phrases nearby and perhaps get a plan for revising the architecture of the passage in hand. (3) Make necessary modifications to fit the piece into your puzzle; sometimes you will merely have to blend or fuse two source sentences to get an excellent equivalent for your test sentence; more often you have to put together and rearrange bits from several sources. (4) Having finished the first draft in this manner, go through the whole thing for consistency, concinnity, connexity, stylistic correctness and general smoothness. Here you may change a conjunction; there select a different pronoun; invert the order of clauses down below; choose a different variant of the infinitive suffix or the accusative plural or the perfect stem or what not. (5) Copy it off neatly and hand it in. It comes back to you with red marks all over it, pointing out that this phrase is purely Apuleian, or that expression mingles archaism with Medieval Latin, or objecting (rarely) to too great a departure from the sense of the original, or to too faithful a retention of purely modern ways of thinking. Do a hundred or more exercises of this sort, and you'll learn a good bit about lots of things, including English, semantics, stylistics, psychology and the ancient world.

In monolingual composition similar exercises can be found, with two principal sub-types: (1) stylistic imitation (whether as an exercise or as a means of achieving a certain kind of style); and (2) parody, in which the imitation is distorted (a) by increasing the frequency of certain (already frequent) tricks of vocabulary or syntax, and (b) by burlesque, i.e. changing some elements of subject matter so as to make the style incongruous (e.g. applying a solemn, religious style to a discussion of some frivolity, or less often, a light, slangy style to some deep philosophical discussion). The joke may be even better if the attitude expressed or implied toward this new and incongruous subject matter is known to be quite different from the parodee's own attitude, e.g. an oracular treatise in the style of Bertrand Russell written in praise of certain trivial aspects of warfare (e.g. medals and ribbons). Of course there is always the danger, in this case, that the work will be interpreted ironically (i.e. expressions implying praise are adjudged to convey condemnation, while hostile criticism means enthusiastic endorsement). As we remarked in ch. 6, one of the necessary ingredients of irony is that the reader should not be able to demonstrate its presence conclusively; if it's unambiguous, it's no longer ironical. And parody is often used as a vehicle for irony.

One example of recent origin (more often discussed than produced) is the mechanically generated style imitation. Two quite different versions of this have been mentioned (and in part executed), the nth order Markov approximation and the small grammar with random choice programming.

The outputs of the two methods are not strikingly different. How do they work? An nth order approximation is made in the following way. Take some basic text (Goethe's *Faust*, in an experiment once discussed by Martin Joos), and compute for each string of n words occurring in it the most probable n + 1st word. In order to get started, select also the most probable opening strings of n words (or of 1, 2, 3, etc. up to n) from beginnings of Acts or Scenes or Books or Chapters. Now write a program which will make a random choice among various probabilities; first picking an opening sequence of (for example) five words, then a probable sixth word to follow those five, then a probable seventh word to follow words 2–6, then a probable eighth word to follow 3–7, and so on until a specified limit has been reached. One difficulty with even a fifth order approximation is that the grammar frequently requires knowledge of words which are ten, twenty or even thirty words back; hence many of the output sentences will not parse. However, a stochastic method which will generally parse is easily devised with the aid of a push-down store. That is, each word in the basic text is given a grammatical mark of what is expected to follow, and this mark is carried along until the requirement is satisfied. But parsing has more commonly been achieved by building a grammar and lexicon to fit the given text (e.g. Lois Lenski's *The Little Train*), and then writing a stochastic program to generate a sentence frame first, then fill its slots with appropriate vocabulary items. Even with a very simple grammar and a small lexicon it is possible to get some interesting results: one German program using a single sentence pattern (roughly "The [Noun] is [Adjective]" with one or two additions) and a vocabulary of words like *snow, fir-tree, star, bright, cold, clear, white*, etc., generated a Christmas poem which is said to have won a prize in a children's magazine. In this case any sentence follows well after any other sentence, but this is not so when vocabulary is less restricted. Sheldon Klein[1] has tried introducing a device to insure some continuity from sentence to sentence (as well as the more easily achieved relevance to a common topic or plot), and sophisticated schemes might use semantic tags and identity numbers. Without such controls, a random Markov approximation or set of randomly generated sentences will really be random – anything may follow anything.

In writing centos or parodies, however, and certainly in making paraphrases or translations, we do not want complete randomness. On the contrary, we usually have a very good idea what we want to say, and how we want our topics linked up and the argument organized. How is this accomplished? In the case of such modified centos as are represented by the Latin or Greek compositions already discussed, the basis is provided by the given English text, and the search for usable phrases proceeds side by side with syntactical and stylistic smoothing and linking operations. It would, however, be quite possible to proceed in a different manner (as indeed I and my fellow-students occasionally did); first make a complete word-by-word translation, leaving multiple Latin equivalents at crucial points (much in the manner of the early King-style IBM Russian–English MT output), then fit the stolen phrases into this matrix until there are no uncertainties left. A procedure of this sort could be programmed (at very great expense, of course) provided one had a semantically marked text of enormous size (best restricted to one or two narrow fields) and a method of searching rapidly for the longest match. A computer-aided human project would be easier to achieve. Somewhere in this direction lies the only likelihood of true HQFA ("high quality fully automatic") machine translation, a goal which (fortunately or unfortunately) no longer interests many governments.

What of our five types of rule? The one primarily used in this sort of program would be substitution, very often of stretches which are not whole single structures, but bits of two or three adjacent structures. Fitting the bits in will often require operations of excision and adjunction, as well as transposition. Transformations may have to be applied to the purloined patch before it can be inserted, and occasionally also one may want to transform a stretch of basic neutral text before making a substitution. So, though substitution is the main operation (indeed multiple substitution), the other procedures are also needed.

[1] S. Klein and R. F. Simmons, 'Syntactic dependence and the computer generation of coherent discourse', *Mechanical Translation* 7:2, 50–61 (1963); S. Klein, 'Control of style with a generative grammar', *Language* 41:619–31 (1965); 'Automatic paraphrasing in essay format', *Mechanical Translation* 8:68–83 (1965).

One rather inartistic method of writing a parody or forgery is just like the Latin prose method described above except that (1) only a single language is involved, so the basic text is invented rather than translated, (2) in the case of parody an element of exaggeration is needed, so that frequent repetition of vocabulary or syntactical tricks is not avoided (as it would be in forgery or Greek composition) but sometimes aimed at. Another style of parody or forgery, however, closely resembles the sort of literary improvisation practiced by guslars[1] and Homers (and no doubt many other literary and musical improvisers as well), in having a Markovian element. Instead of starting with a complete and explicit base text (as in the style we have just spoken of) we start now with only a general notion of theme, plot, and ultimate outcome, and allow each ready-made phrase to give its hint to us of where to go next, so that the choice of each new phrase is partly conditioned by our vague underlying theme and partly by the last phrase (and the next-to-last, and the one before that – and so on – with decreasing force). This is (I believe) essentially the way we talk at length and write anyway, except that here we are restricting our source material or our metrical pattern (or both) much more. It is true that we restrict ourselves in some measure in ordinary speech or writing, but that is mainly done by choosing a level of style or a degree of formality and sticking to it, avoiding obvious puns, rhymes and repetitions as well as we can at the rate we're going. In formal parody or heroic improvisation, however, we are limiting ourselves drastically. Can these kinds of composition without an explicit base text be formalized in terms of the rule-types we have been considering? Only, it seems, by adding a device for selecting the next point to be added, the next thing to be said, that somehow incorporates (a) general semantic field and (b) a measure of consecutiveness in relation to what precedes.

In particular we need, for improvisational composition, rules of consecutiveness, rules limiting the free choice of sentence topics to those which may appropriately follow our last sentences. With a suitable notation it should be possible to compute semantic transitional probabilities for sentences, quite like those for letters, phonemes and words which we mentioned earlier: "Given that the semantic value of the last sentence was S' and of the one before it S'', the most probable choices

---

[1] The Yugoslav improvisers of heroic poems who accompany themselves on the gusle, a sort of single-string violin. Their art was extensively studied by the late Milman Parry and by Albert Lord.

for this sentence are S³, S⁴ and S⁵, and we will (randomly or for irrelevant reasons) choose S⁴." In order to gain some understanding of the problems involved, an interesting experiment can be performed with a pair of scissors. Ask a friend to select a paragraph from a book, magazine or paper and type each sentence as a separate paragraph, so that the page can be cut apart, leaving one sentence on each piece. Then try to restore the original order. You will soon note that there are two kinds of clues, which we might call grammatical and logical: (1) grammatical clues are provided by certain conjunctions and by pronouns (and the definite article) which regularly refer back, not forward; (2) logical clues are somewhat vaguer, but include (for instance) the fact that a narrative of events follows the order of events (with rare exceptions). In improvising, links of the first type can be introduced by algorithm (at least this seems feasible now), but we do not yet know enough to write algorithms for the second type. The one difficulty with the first type is itself semantic; pronominal substitution, deletion, and various similar operations depend not upon grammatical or lexical identity, but on identity of reference. To use a hoary example, "The author of *Waverley*" and "Sir Walter Scott" refer to the same individual, and this fact must be known before certain grammatical rules can be applied. Mechanically we can achieve some success by adding (as has often been proposed) an index or identification number to each definite reference, whether name or description, so that (for instance) human^male^adult^past^125 might mean Sir Walter Scott while book^fiction^23 (or whatever features may prove necessary to replace [book]) could be *Waverley*, in a particular passage or article. Indexes would not (presumably) be permanently assigned, but given only for the needs of a particular discourse. Though persons, places and other 'proper name' entities would be the most usual recipients of indexes, it is possible that, in a particular passage, windows or chairs or pencils or predicates might have to be numbered briefly as well. Though our brain does not attach numbers, it has to perform the equivalent feat of keeping distinct all the men or race-horses or railroad trains or events involved in a given discussion.

Since, in certain types of paraphrase (like the Greek or Latin composition described above) it is only identity of reference, not semantic identity that is required, it would seem that some universal index numbering system would be needed, so that an expression like "Pompey's opponent" might be rendered as "Cleopatra's lover" in some contexts. Note that such descriptions need not be unambiguous (in most cases);

"Cleopatra's lover" in another passage could easily be "Octavian's rival", if that were appropriate. Something of the same freedom has to be allowed for the Homeric type of improvisation, but most of the other kinds of paraphrase or epitome discussed here use semantic identity more than referential identity. So it might be of interest to digress briefly on some of the problems which must be solved before we can have a complete universal system of sememes or semantic features.

The lexicon of any language contains items of several quite different semantic types, even if we exclude for the moment all question of differences in emotional or connotational coloring and in style or level or dialect.

(15-001) Some words are fully reducible, i.e. may be perfectly and unambiguously replaced by other words or phrases.

And all speakers (in general) will agree that the replacement is correct. The manner of reduction is not the same for all such words; let us examine a few types. (a) As has long been known to logicians and mathematicians, all natural numbers can be derived from the notions of *one* and *one more* or *and*. That is "Three dollars" is exactly equivalent to "A dollar and another dollar and another dollar" or "One and one and one dollar". The reduction of amounts like $217,000,000,000 (American etc. 217 billion, British 217 thousand million) becomes infinitely tedious, of course, though it could easily be performed by modern computers in a reasonable time. It is convenient, therefore, to make reductions by steps, so that *billion* (U.S.) is first reduced to *cube of a thousand, cube of X* to *X times X times X, thousand* to *ten cubed, N times X* to the *sum of N X's*, and so on. But this does not change the essential fact. Notice that there is no way this can be represented naturally by features. *Five* might be represented as five occurrences of the feature one (one^one^one^one^one), but any economical representation of large numbers is bound to be arbitrary; the least arbitrary are no doubt those which reflect in some way (for any given language) the linguistic structure of the number system. It seems chauvinistic to prefer a ten-hundred-thousand-thousand^n system to a ten-hundred-thousand-myriad-myriad^n system (like Chinese) or a ten-hundred-thousand-(ten-hundred)thousand-million-million^n system (British) let alone the dozen-gross-12^3 – etc. system so loved by puzzlers and amateur mathematicians.

Somewhat similar are kinship systems. In English, for instance, all relationships may be expressed by iteration of 'child of' and 'parent of' plus 'male vs. female'. Male vs. female is no doubt a semantic feature, but the others are not. ('X's wife' incidentally is assumed to be 'female parent of X's child', implying that a childless couple are not related; if allowance is to be made for this and for a distinction between legitimate and illegitimate relationships, other primitives must be used. 'X's brother' is 'male child of X's parents', assuming that relation to oneself is excluded.) Of a somewhat simpler type are many terms which depend upon the number system, e.g. weights and measures: so a 'week' is always and only 'seven days', an 'ounce' (Avoirdupois) is one-sixteenth of a pound, a 'yard' is three feet. In most of these systems, any unit at random may be chosen as base and the others are then reducible to it; time, however, in our culture has three partially independent (once entirely so) units – the day, the month and the year. Based on *day* are *hour, minute, second* (in one direction) and *week, fortnight* (in the other); from *year* we have *decade, century* and *millennium* (and nowadays perhaps *semester*, though that was originally a *six-month* period). All personal pronouns (in most languages, at any rate) can be defined in terms of *I, thou, not,* or *other than,* and *and.* For convenience we might add *one vs. two or more,* i.e. 'plural', which can be derived from *and* and some rule for indefinite iteration. English *we* is 'I and one-or-more others' except in *let's,* which must be inclusive 'I and thou or you-all' where *you-all* is taken to mean 'thou and thou etc.' or 'thou and one or more other than thou or I', and so on. Clumsy but undoubtedly correct and clear (if not, it's my fault and can be made clear).

Every language has reducible words like these; it's hard to guess how frequent they are, but some small inspections I have made suggest that less than 10% (probably much less) of consecutive speech consists of items of this kind. And some of these lexical items are reducible, but with a residue which requires ostensive definition (so, e.g. weights and measures).

(b) Many other words are in part reducible by features (most of them by nature binary, all easily treated as binary) such as male-female-(castrated)-generic, big-small, human, animal, mineral, etc. So bull-cow-steer-calf-cattle, stallion-mare-gelding-foal/colt-horse, etc., can be reduced to one base 'morpheme' (itself only ostensive) each by the use of one or two of these features. A 'female horse' is unambiguously a mare. Some other sets are less certain. Physical color is a continuum (in at least three dimensions) which is variously chopped up by various languages. How many primitive terms are required for English? How reducible are they? Many color names are somewhat like proper names or species names: 'the same color as this item or this sample', some may include a feature 'pale' (e.g. *pink*) or 'dark', or 'metallic' or the like. But most will be described in terms of the set black, white, brown, red, orange, yellow, green, blue and purple (possibly violet or mauve may be basic for some speakers instead of purple). Nearly all speakers of western culture languages, at any rate, will resolve *orange* into red^yellow, green into blue^yellow and purple into red^blue, suggesting the use of red, yellow and blue as three binary features. *Brown* may then be red^yellow^blue with all three plus-values, while *black* and *white* are either primitive, or consist of features 'dark' and 'light' with three minus-values. Here we do not have the same kind of unanimity as with kin, measures or numbers. And yet everyone could get along quite well with the six or seven binary color features suggested here, and errors would be very low. Other cases of the arbitrary dissection of a natural continuum are not numerous. Sound shows continua in pitch (frequency) and in loudness (amplitude), but the number of people who have or develop anything like absolute pitch (i.e. can say of any given note that it is – let's suppose – a B natural above middle C, slightly flat by the international concert standard) has evidently always been too small to influence the development of language, and I've never even heard anecdotes of an absolute loudness sense. Qualitative (i.e. spectral) differences in sound can cause violent arguments among professional musicians; the best one can say is that a few terms are used with some degree of consistency, mostly terms which imply something about pitch or volume, as well – *shrill, squeaky, harsh, brassy, mellow, full, thin, nasal, reedy, pure*, and a number of others, most of which resemble special color names as requiring ostensive definition and in not being fully understood by ordinary people.

(15-002) The great majority of nouns, verbs and adjectives correspond in some way to discontinuous entities in the real world.

This portion of the vocabulary must always be learned ostensively; contextual clues alone are never enough. So an arbitrary discrimination between chairs and tables is not needed because in ordinary life chairs do not imperceptibly shade off toward tables; most of the time there are many differences and possible confusion is very rare. A word like *table* or *pine-tree*, even though there are clearly genera ('furniture', 'trees') to which they belong, is not uniquely reducible any more than proper names are. The way to get precise definitions of such words is like the way to get precise identification of a person. Once the range of application in the world is clearly established (by introspection or informant interviews or questionnaires), the rest of the job consists in a careful examination of *things*, with only an occasional check to make sure that the thing you're looking at is really called by the name you're interested in. And, of course, informants may disagree; my pine may not always be your pine or the botanist's pine. Considerations like this very possibly led Bloomfield to make his strange remarks about semantics.[1]

As has often been pointed out, folk taxonomies[2] are not always directly convertible into scientific taxonomies; nevertheless, their procedures and methods are essentially the same.

Although I have spoken of discontinuous *entities*, it must not be supposed that all words of this class are nouns. Many verbs specify states, events or forms of behavior that happen to exist in nature and are not analyzed out of a continuum: *sleep, walk, breathe, die, eat, burn, fall,* etc. However, almost all non-scalar adjectives of this sort are, even superficially, denominative or deverbal (like *alive, rotten, hairy,* etc.).

For any given speaker, then words of this class may be perfectly defined, but not uniquely; nor will the average speaker agree that *table* is merely a short expression for 'a piece of furniture with a flat upper surface for putting things on' in the same way as *uncle* is a short expression for 'parent's brother-in-law'. In this case you're describing a class of *objects* as well as specifying the applicability of a *word*.

(15-003) Words which name the features or the operators for reducing class one words, and high-level generic names of class two words may be regarded as primary words.

Obviously there are at least two, probably three or more kinds of primary words: (a) primary words of ordinary speech, like *father* and *mother, tree* and *berry*; (b) primary words of more learned character (often of Latin origin in English), like *parent, male, seedling* and *vegetation*; (c) some primary words belonging to specific sciences, like *sepal* and *stamen, sibling* and *integer*. The lines are not firm, and class (c) words easily shift to (b), and (b) words to (a), among primary words as among reducible words (since this division goes through the whole lexicon). What is irreducible at one level may be reducible at another.

---

[1] P. 139 of the American edition.
[2] E.g. H. Conklin, in *Problems in Lexicography* (Bloomington, 1962), pp. 119–41.

Some primary words may be ambiguous because of different uses on two levels, leading to futile arguments about whether or not the tomato is a fruit (levels (a) and (c)), or a fish is an animal ((a) and (c), or perhaps all three: $animal_a$ = 4-limbed vertebrate, $animal_b$ = any vertebrate, $animal_c$ = whatever the biologists say, but certainly including insects, spiders, shellfish, etc., excluded on the lower levels).

(15-004) Many words enter into a variety of phrases but have little productive life of their own.

Some of these are hard to classify as reducible or primary, though the whole phrase in which they occur may be clearly reducible. *Civil* is (for most people) one thing in *civil war*, another in *civil law* and a third in *civil answer*; only in the third use can it be marginally productive and function as a predicate ("His behavior was barely civil"). Besides *civil war* one may speak of *civil strife* and *civil conflict*, but not of a *civil battle* or *contest* or *hostilities* or *shooting* or *bombing*. Beside *civil law* stand *civil suit* and possibly one or two other legal terms. A civil war is opposed to a foreign or external war, hence is domestic or internal; civil law is opposed to criminal law, and the two terms resemble proper names in their irreducibility, even though the generic term 'law' clearly covers both.

Phrases of this sort (you may say) form a separate class merely because of our own deficiencies; a better analyst could fit them all into one of the other classes. This is probably true, but languages are loaded with difficulties like this.

(15-005) Purely relational words, like common prepositions and conjunctions, seem to be primary at level (a), though analyzable into features of some sort in a higher style (by no means unambiguously).

But there are also many words which make a very slight contribution – often none at all – to the meaning, but do complete the grammatical structure and convey some sort of emotional tone. In the *Gettysburg Address*, for instance, the contribution of *dedicated* in the phrase "dedicated to the proposition, etc." is mainly to give support to the *to*; similarly, further on, with *engaged* supporting *in*. Both words sound like important words, but contribute very little to the sense. Every language has verbs of this sort (nouns do not seem to be so numerous in this function), some big ones, like these, others smaller, like *do, make, get, take, have, put,* and so on. Some seem to correspond simply to [+verb] or the like, others have one or two more features (transitivity, motion, direction, etc.). But it is hard to say that they are fully reducible, except for the linguist, who is not here functioning like the biologist mentioned above. Indeed some linguists use some of these *instead* of features, so that *I bid you* or something of the sort replaces [+Imperative], *make* replaces [+Causative], and so on. This is quite as feasible here as reducing *ram* (say) to 'adult male sheep' in words instead of having [adult^ male] – and maybe even [sheep] – as semantic features or sememes. Basic English (as originally proposed by Ogden and Richards) was a kind of effort to carry reduction of this sort out to the utmost.

This chapter, like most of our others, must end inconclusively. We can see the need for some way of specifying degree and kind of similarity of meaning between pairs of phrases or sentences, as well as the location and relevance of semantic discrepancies. This need exists not only for the specification of the editing rules of various sorts which make up an important portion of our linguistic performance (what might be called performance-competence, i.e. competence at performing, rather than pure performance, if such a thing exists), but also for specialized studies in bilingualism, memory, originality, scientific discovery and other similar philosophical-psycho-linguistic problems.

16   *Idiolect, dialect, linguistic change and the neogrammarian principle*

The notion that languages are inherently stable and all change must be due to weakening of the moral fiber (or perhaps malevolent conspiracy) has been around for a long, long time and is not likely to vanish overnight. And yet it has co-existed in many places and times with an acute, even formalized awareness of dialect differences and linguistic multiplicity. The prevalence of mutually incomprehensible languages can be reconciled with a belief in linguistic permanence by some form of Babel myth – a miracle, divine intervention. But the existence of minor or major dialect diversity does not seem to have struck men of any era or culture as being inconsistent with linguistic immutability. At least I know of no Babel-type explanations; there is in various places some attempt to associate character with dialect, but this is hard to separate from an association of character with geography and climate. Do the Arcadians speak their simple rustic dialect because they are simple rustic people, and are they so pure and noble because they live in a lonely mountainous region, or does the causation go some other way? Whatever the answer, it was somehow felt that it was appropriate for Arcadians to speak Arcadian, for Dorians to speak Doric, and for sophisticated Ionians to use Ionic. So some Americans have felt that Negroes, Jews and Italians should talk like Negroes, Jews and Italians, and that it is deceitful and immoral (or, from the other side, disloyal and treacherous) if they don't.

We know that variation in speech is universal, that different variations are associated not merely with differences in time and place but also with social level, age, occupation, and many other factors as well. In this chapter let us concentrate on only three of these factors (geography, age and time), and see if we can construct a simplified model (not a mathematical model, but merely a thought model) that will help us to understand linguistic variation. Let us start with the communication net.

L

Imagine[1] a uniform population over a closed area, such that each individual has the same amount of communication with the same number of other individuals, and that there are not only no dialect differences but no social levels,[2] no significant age differences, and no occupational jargons or styles. We can map this as a set of points connected by lines, such that the length of the line varies inversely with the frequency of communication along it (assumed to be equal in the two directions). Now how do linguistic changes start? The first time a speaker repeats or imitates a (to him) novel item (whether form, accent, sound, word, construction or what not) which he has heard (either from another speaker or himself), we have a potential change beginning. It is not the first *occurrence* of the novel item which is relevant, but the first *repetition-imitation* (and the second, third . . ., etc., etc.).[3] Edgar Sturtevant devoted a great deal of study to slips of the tongue, which he thought might provide the initial step in phonetic change, but with mostly negative results. Extremely common types of *lapsus* are never attested as linguistic changes, and most common change-types are rare as lapses. The item imitated may have originally been a slip, in some cases, but mishearing, misinterpretation and deliberate innovation are far more common. However, we won't worry at the moment about this question, but merely note that we must add two features to our model before any linguistic change is possible: (1) some or all speakers must have a tendency to innovate (however slight, and by whatever mechanism) and (2) some or all speakers must have a tendency to imitate what they hear. (We assume for the moment that both hearing and imitation are errorless.) Note that (2) would be indetectable without (1) (since all speakers are given an identical initial dialect), unless perhaps we bring in frequency figures for different items.

Now can we assign both of these tendencies in the same strength to

---

[1] For a somewhat similar experiment, see Sheldon Klein, 'Historical Change in Language Using Monte Carlo Techniques', *Mechanical Translation* 9:67–82 (1966). Also S. Klein, M. A. Kuppin and K. A. Meives 'Monte Carlo Simulation of Language Change in Tikopia and Maori', Preprint No. 21 of the International Conference on Computational Linguistics (Stockholm, 1969).

[2] Adding two levels or styles might simplify some points. See U. Weinreich, W. Labov and M. L. Herzog, 'Empirical Foundations for a Theory of Language Change' in *Directions for Historical Linguistics: A Symposium*, Austin, University of Texas Press, 1968. A landmark. See also below, pp. 315, 318, 326.

[3] A still later first may sometimes be important, the first speaker whose grammar has been somehow reshaped by the change (not just added to), the first *mutation* speaker, to use Elizabeth Closs's term (*Language* 41:402–15 (1965)). In a two-style model, a shift from style A to style B is another important first.

all speakers? Let us examine two types of innovation and see what would happen to each under this assumption. Type (1) is a substitution, modification or alteration of an item already present in the dialect: e.g. of a word, as saying *'shmig' in place of 'boy', or of an affix, as saying *'ba-like' for 'unlike', or of a segment, as saying *'vable' instead of 'table', or of an embedding pattern, as saying *'I want from going' in place of 'I want to go', or of pronunciation (subphonemically), as saying all initial b's and d's implosively (i.e. with larynx-lowering before release), or pronouncing all back vowels with more lip-rounding than is usual. These are all common kinds; there may well be others. Type (2) is the addition of an item or pattern which does not really replace anything pre-existing: in the main this means new words for new things, e.g. 'sputnik' for Russian artificial satellites (there might be other less novel-sounding names proposed at the same time, and there could also be periphrastic descriptions – like 'Russian artificial satellite' – but the new name does not drive out a pre-established old name). An out-and-out addition of this sort in phonology seems possible only if a number of simultaneously introduced new names contain the same new phone-type, which can be successfully imitated by a significant number of speakers, as is the case with some speakers of English and the velar fricative /x/ as it is reproduced in *Bach, ach, loch, Rachmaninoff* and a half-dozen or so other loans from German or Scottish or Yiddish or Russian. In syntax it seems quite impossible in the strict sense if we accept the axiom that everything which can be said in one language can be said in any other language (even if somewhat long-windedly). A totally new affix (usually) implies a new embedding or abbreviation, and hence merely a syntactical or superficial modification, as if one were to introduce an augmentative suffix into English, so that (e.g.) where 'Johnny' means 'little or friendly John', *'Johnno' /jɔnoː/ would mean 'big, disagreeable John', or the like. But, in many cases, such introduced affixes are used far more frequently than their vaguely possible paraphrases were before; hence, we may allow the possibility of some non-competitive affixes.

Now how would a competitive innovation fare in our model situation, given universality and equality of the imitative tendency? Note that the tendency we postulate is not restricted to imitating novelty; these hearers simply pattern their speech on *everything* they hear, old or new. First, it is clear that innovations can never drive out the pre-existing pattern under these conditions, unless we make two new and rather unlikely assumptions: (1) that the speakers who have heard the innovation immediately adopt it to the total exclusion of the earlier competitor, and (2) that speakers who have not heard it never, by accident, make use of the earlier competitor in speaking to those who *have* heard it (since that would make it an innovation – a sort of counter-revolutionary one – to adopt). The most we could expect is a very slow spread of the innovation, which would always remain less frequent than the earlier form, since, if speaker B heard the innovation all the time from A and the earlier form all the time from nine other equal-time speakers, he would then use it one-tenth of the time. Then each of these speakers hears it used by B one-tenth of the time, and never by each of nine other speakers, so that they will each use it one-hundredth of the time; and so on. Cross-influence (among 100 speakers, e.g., who each use it one hundredth of the time) is capable of slowing down the convergence of this series, but cannot ever make it divergent. Some fraction can be chosen which is equivalent to extinction; if a form has only one-millionth as much chance of being used as its competitor, and if an ordinary person is likely to use either one only (say) 500 times in his life, the odds are very much against any other speaker ever hearing it from him.

What can we do to improve the mechanism for spread? Alter the absolute equality condition. Let's try a situation in which 1% of the nodes, evenly scattered in the net, are given preferential *imitability* (*their* innovations are always picked up at once), while the others are given preferential *suggestibility* (they immediately imitate whatever they hear). Clearly each leader-type will soon become the center of a small dialect area. The borders of these areas will be formed of schizophrenics who switch dialects several times a day, and movement of innovations across borders can occur only in the absence of competition. Suppose we add a factor of *loyalty*: each speaker knows his own group (i.e. the 99 who are closest to one leader) and imitates other group members but consciously avoids imitating members of other groups. In this situation there can be *no* spread across borders at all, and eventually the dialects would become mutually unintelligible. This is obviously extreme, but bears a distinct relationship to what is known to happen.

What will make it more realistic? We have already relaxed our original condition of speaker uniformity at one point (leader-follower), but we still have our starting uniformity of language control and of age. In real life speakers for part of their lives have no language and imitate (in our sense) everything they hear almost indiscriminately, while they have virtually no linguistic influence on others, but as time passes they gradually improve their control of language, become less easily influenced and begin to influence others. Finally, some speakers die. Let us try to incorporate these factors in our model, and see what happens. Assume that the net remains uniform in *size*, but that at certain moments individual nodes may switch abruptly from being preferential models (leaders) to being total imitators. This would correspond to a death and a birth (or rather an arrival at the age of learning to speak). At other moments a certain percentage of the total imitator nodes shift to being preferential models, and another (larger) percentage to being partial models and partial imitators. Let the distribution of all types remain even throughout the area during these changes.

The effect of this alteration in the model is immediately to prevent the direct development of mutually unintelligible hundred-man languages. Centers of imitation and group boundaries are constantly shifting about; the loyalty effect may still operate, but the object of loyalty is no longer permanent. A second result is that we may now have phonological change as easily as lexical and grammatical change. The only mechanisms in a uniform community of perfect speakers of a single dialect by which one could introduce phonetic or phonemic change were the imitated slip of the tongue (if allowed) and the deliberate innovation, both of which are known to be rare in real life. In fact, we seem to have a built-in mechanism for ignoring slips unless they destroy communication, and we imitate them under such circumstances only for ridicule. The deliberate innovation or affectation seems to be often limited to clique situations, where the innovation is used within the group, but not with outsiders. Children, however, sometimes make errors of imitation which pass undetected by themselves and uncorrected by adults until after a habit has been fixed. This certainly seems to be one source of the individual (i.e. idiolectal) phonological differences between one speaker and the next, the other important one being deliberate imitation of different models. It is interesting to note that in many cultures there are particular childish errors that rarely go undetected and uncorrected; among us the lisp ($s \rightarrow \theta$) – much more prominent in fiction than real life – and the labial r or l ($r \rightarrow w$, $l \rightarrow w$) are especially open to ridicule and criticism. Nevertheless, I have known several adults with quite conspicuous labial l's. (Note that imitation – good or bad – of a *foreign* word is excluded from our model by the assumption of complete homogeneity and isolation.) Certain other childish errors seem to be in some measure against the grain (the substitution of a more complex or more difficult or more ambiguous sound for a simpler, clearer one), and hence almost never appear as attested changes in languages. The lisp may be an example; if a language has a fricative (other than aspiration, h), it is almost universally a sibilant, not θ. Similarly interchange of p, t and k is rare, and k < t is particularly uncommon, but such interchanges are quite usual among children (often only in certain positions). The model as now presented would seem to yield a kind of fluctuating multi-dialect area in which some areas might, by chance, grow more diverse from their neighbors, but not easily bigger than their neighbors. Clearly we have not yet reached the real-life situation; something still needs to be added to our model.

As it stands, all language-style-leaders are rated equal in strength, all adult partial imitators equal, and all children equal. If we allow this equality of the *leaders* to be upset temporarily now and again, so that one leader is more influential than his neighbors, we get a mechanism for differential growth. If we now alter our original equal interaction rate (by which A spoke to B exactly as much as B to A, and all speakers had a certain number of others with whom they interacted at high rate, another fixed number at a slightly lower rate, and so on down) in various ways, particularly to allow strong leaders to speak to many more imitators, and if we also improve the in-group loyalty factor, we can get a fair approximation of the known situation. We must, however, not forget to mention three other factors of some influence: (1) mobility or lack of it, including communication at a distance in space or time; (2) geography as influencing mobility (an uncrossable river is likely to be a major language boundary); (3) a strong traditional educational system which exposes many successive generations to a large amount of unchanged linguistic material (i.e. perpetual and universal leaders to be imitated). Factors (1) and (2) are illustrated in the great uniformity of language in the plains of Central Asia, for instance, as contrasted with the great diversity in isolated mountain valleys of New Guinea, the Caucasus, or California. The first and third factors are active in the domains of the prosperous modern languages such as English, French, Russian and others.

Let us consider our two types of innovation (displacement and addition) and see how frequent they must be in everyday life in order to yield attested rates of change. We probably have more information on lexical change than any other type, and here we should not be surprised to find, in a given language, that 20% of the vocabulary items (in running text, not lexicon) now used were not known 500 years ago, and 20% of the items used then have vanished. Pure vocabulary loss, which we have not yet mentioned, occurs most commonly when an article (natural or manufactured) or a custom disappears from use and knowledge, taking its name with it. So words like *patten* or *cuirass* or *scot* or *feoff* or *snuffbox* are nowadays quite rare in ordinary discourse. If such a word (shape only) is used in a new sense, as often happens (e.g. with *car* or with various plant and animal names), we will regard this as a loss and an addition, not a 'change of meaning'. However, it is sometimes difficult to draw a sharp line (familiar examples in linguistic literature are the gradual shift of 'meat' from *food* to *flesh*, or that of 'hound' from *dog* to *hunting dog*) between what is still the same word (semantically speaking) and what is not. But, ignoring these difficulties, how fast must change be to yield a 20% replacement in 500 years? Let's make some gross simplifications. Assume that total vocabulary remains constant at 50,000, so that 20% change means that 10,000 words go out and 10,000 new ones come in. This would average out to 20 words per year. This may seem high but is probably not far out of line for the growth rate in current English. Suppose we allow 20,000 imitable innovators (in a population of 100,000,000 or so); then if each one generates 100 innovations a year (the implied total of 2,000,000 should be reduced because of duplications), only 1 out of every 100,000 would have to achieve acceptance in order to account for the assumed rate. One interesting result is obvious; given modern rates of intercommunication over large territories, the rate of change is bound to be faster than in languages spoken by small groups. The forces that, in earlier conditions (little travel, no radio or movies) would tend to introduce dialect diversity, are nowadays replaced by forces which tend to produce more rapid uniform change over the whole area. A language spoken by an isolated group stabilized at 1,000 should change much more slowly than our 100,000,000 group, even if education is more intensively developed in the large group; the conservative models provided in the educational system are simply overwhelmed by the great number and force of the living anticonservative models. If this is so, English must be changing much more rapidly today than it was a century ago. It does not seem easy, but it should be possible to devise a means of verifying this conclusion.

We have not yet reflected enough about the rise of dialect diversity. Our model starting from original total uniformity, with stable and non-mobile population, could develop a kind of dialect diversity on the assumption of a small number of speech leaders and a strong group loyalty co-extensive with the sphere of influence of each leader. Indeed, if the loyalty were absolute, we could expect complete divergence to mutual incomprehensibility. This never occurs in real situations like this. In part loyalties are weaker than this and intercommunication more extensive, and in part we do not find real leaders of speech influence so few and so monopolistic. No historical situation quite resembles the assumed case, either, in starting from a widely-spoken wholly uniform language. Suppose that we alter our model so that, at the outset, only one-thousandth of the potential nodes are occupied (and those closely grouped), and then allow for population growth and expansion to fill the empty nodes. This does not seem too different from the prehistoric settlement of Australia by the aborigines (the coming of the Indians to America is generally believed to have been more complex than this), and it may be that the expansion of the speakers of Indo-European was something on the same style. The model should allow for something analogous to cell-growth; as a group grows, it sooner or later reaches a critical size at which it splits into two. These, in their turn, grow and split, and so on until the available space is filled.[1] Suppose we give the imitable innovator one or more sub-leaders, whose function at first is to transmit innovations from the leader to the followers. Assume that each of these sub-leaders has an obligatory rate of N innovations per week. At the beginning he is close enough to the leader to receive the whole number from him; as the group grows, however, his distance from the leader (i.e. his interaction rate) drops to the point where he is receiving only part of this total. The remainder he must supply himself. As this happens, various parts of the area will begin to diverge linguistically. When the distance reaches the point where less than half of the innovations are coming from the original leader, the sub-leader's group begins to be more and more his, less and less a sub-group of the great Speech Father; loyalties shift, and the whole sub-group moves further away (leaving some empty space between it and the remainder of the original group). The two groups may now spread toward each other, but by the time contact is again made, they have diverged too much to unite.

In real life, of course, many men are in some measure leaders of

[1] For a discussion of the analogous problem of speciation in biology, see *Science* 159:1065–70 (1968), 'Models of Speciation' by M. J. D. White. The parallel is remarkably close; in both cases some limitation on changes is exercised by survival value, with the extreme cases of lethality of mutation paralleled by communication suicide as the effect of a language change. See also R. D. Stevick, 'The biological model and historical linguistics', *Language* 39:159 (1963).

linguistic innovation (unconsciously, for the most part), and nearly everyone is in some measure an imitator. The way in which this model concentrates the innovating force at one node (or a few nodes) does not, however, seem to lead to any counter-intuitive results. Consider also the knowledge built up by a century or two of research in dialect geography. This shows that many individual changes are propagated independently and at different rates, that there are some centers whose innovations have a powerful force which will carry them relatively quickly over much of the area, while others propagate innovations that fade and falter within a day's journey. The first of these types of center corresponds to a node with a very high degree of imitability (and we have already seen reasons for believing that each interaction pair – and hence each node – has some internally unpredictable index of imitability), the second to one with a lower index.

But even the highest index rating must not be assumed to mark influence as proceeding in one direction alone. Many facts require the assumption of cross-dialect influences ("There are no *pure* dialects; all dialects are mixed"), particularly the occasional occurrence of flip-flop changes, i.e. mutual interchange, of which two types are particularly entertaining.

(1) The reversal in preference for competing variant forms or lexical items in two dialect areas is difficult to demonstrate, but does sometimes occur. For instance, let us suppose that (say in 1930) it was stylish in England to pronounce 'again' /əge:n/ and unstylish to say /əgen/, while at the same time in the U.S. /əgen/ was stylish and /əge:n/ substandard. Now let us suppose that in 1970 the situation is exactly reversed (this is not a true account, but there is some relationship to truth here). How could this come about? The question becomes even more nagging if we omit to report the unstylish variants. The answer is, of course, that dialect loyalty is not absolute, and that sometimes it is even possible to develop a belief that a borrowed form is not borrowed at all, but pure native talk, so that loyalty may actually contribute to the spread of a loan.

(2) The other type appears in the phonology sections of historical grammars, and an imaginary instance might look like this: between the Old Low Slobbovian Period and the Middle Low Slobbovian, the following vowel shifts occurred . . .

(16-1) OLS a→MLS e

....

....

....

(16-2) OLS e→MLS a

Usually there are paragraphs of distraction in between, so that the contradiction doesn't leap to the eye as it does here, but shifts something like this can be found in many different handbooks. They have bothered linguists, of course, and at least one other hypothesis besides the dialect-crossing hypothesis has some measure of prestige, the intermediate-states explanation. Assume that the *full* changes are as follows:

(16-11) OLS a→Late OLS a^e→Early MLS æ→MLS e

(16-21) OLS e→Late OLS $æ^i$→Early MLS a^e→MLS a

(Indeed four or five intermediate stages may be inserted, all showing that while a went to e by way of Chicago, e went to a via New Orleans, and they couldn't have met on the way.) In very many cases something like this is correct, or at least partially correct, but there are others where the dialect crossing hypothesis is conceivable, e.g. in this case:

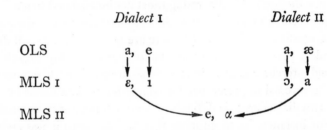

This is most plausible when only a small group of words is involved (say for the words with OLS e, MLS II α), and some additional factors can be cited. Note that the diagram assumes that the standard dialect of OLS is I, whereas in MLS II it is (as far as we can tell) neither I nor II. 'Pure' Dialects I and II might survive alongside the new hybrid standard, or it might (in other respects) be a simple continuation of Dialect I (or Dialect II). The speakers who first used e and a together, however, had to make an abrupt shift, either saying e where they had previously said ɔ (if they were II-speakers) or else α where they had once said i. Abrupt shifts as great as this are probably unattested, except for single words or a handful of words, so the example is unrealistic to that extent, but smaller shifts of a similar sort are not unknown.

What about a third alternative, simultaneous double abrupt shift so that speakers suddenly start saying a where they had said e and e where they had said a? The usual case described in these terms is that of the foreigner who (it is believed) replaces all v's by w's and all w's by v's, or all b's by p's and p's by b's. However, when these cases are examined, it generally turns out that the foreigner is in fact using an intermediate sound for both, which differs enough from each of the two native sounds for the native to assume reversal. (Here perhaps a weak fricative [β] would account for the first case, a lenis, unaspirated and unvoiced [p] for the second.) It is an instructive and amusing game to attempt such a switch of only two phonemes (or of a single feature-value, for that matter) in free conversation without written notes. The effort is enormous, and mistakes are frequent. Even reciting a bit from memory (try the *Gettysburg Address* or Hamlet's soliloquy, just for fun) is an imposing task. Much easier is simply canceling an opposition, i.e. cutting out all devoicing ("Vour zgore and zeven years ago, etc.") or keeping the velum wide open throughout, or pre-stopping all fricatives ("Pfour tscore and dzeven yeards ago, etc."). Various deliberate changes are used around the world for so-called 'secret' languages,[1] but no systematic interchanges of segments or segmental features seem to have been reported, though distortions of pitch and stress occur. Probably the only way a speaker could really master phoneme-reversal or feature-reversal would be by assiduously memorizing every word which would be affected by the rule ([α Feature]→[-α Feature] or Original X→Y, Original Y→X). And yet some secret languages seem to require just about as much effort and practice as this, particularly those of the metathesis types (reversing the order of pairs of syllables systematically, for instance, in languages where monosyllables are rare).

The existence of both abrupt (hence largely conscious) and gradual (mainly imperceptible) change is perhaps even more obvious in the lexicon and morphology (semantics?) than in phonology. Both types are easily illustrated from dialect geography. It is a striking characteristic of closely similar dialects spoken in adjacent territories that word (or affix) X in dialect A is an absolutely perfect synonym of word (or affix) Y in dialect B, even though the meanings and distribution involved are complicated. In Ancient Greek, for instance, Attic and some other dialects have a particle *an* which has a variety of modal functions in conjunction with optatives, subjunctives and indicatives, and has complex restrictions on relative order in the company of other particles, pronouns, etc. In other dialects there is an exactly equivalent particle *ke* (or *ka*, in some), with the same functions and the same positional restrictions (with, at most, minor differences). We cannot here say with assurance

---

[1] The Indiana University dissertation (1963) of Glen Pound collects a large number of examples.

that this situation did not arise by imperceptible gradual changes (e.g. from an original **kean*[1] which has undergone a variety of shortenings), but in other cases we can. Consider, for instance, the British *drawing pin* and the American *thumbtack*, or the Hoosier *mango* and the general *green pepper*. Here we have names for artifacts or natural species which are identical. The case of the American *sycamore* and the British *plane tree* (as opposed to the British *sycamore*, a kind of maple tree) is one of close similarity and generic rather than specific identity, so we cannot really assert synonymy. In the Turkish-Azerbaijani dialect continuum there are somewhere speakers who use the form /sæksæn/ for the number 80 and are neighbors to others who use the form /hæšdad/ (a loan from Persian). At one time in the English-speaking world there were some vessels on which the word for 'left' was *larboard* and others on which it was *port*. The abruptness in such cases cannot be mitigated by phonological intermediate stages. It *can* be made more gradual, however, by areas (or periods) within which the two competing terms are both in use, but with different frequency, different affective value, different style level, different contextual restrictions. Sometimes the transitional area (or period) is attested or present, sometimes not; it can safely be postulated for all cases.

In the case of phonology we considered the possible mechanisms whereby a perfect flip-flop could appear (e.g. all p's become b's while simultaneously all b's become p's). The equivalent case in lexicon (or semantics) is the case where, in neighboring (or successive) dialects, *black* (e.g.) corresponds to *white*, and *white* to *black*. The first question we might ask, is "Is this possible?" Well-attested cases are not easy to find, but at least three possible mechanisms suggest themselves. (1) The use of semantic reversal as a device for secret language is only sporadically attested. Still, it is at least imaginable, in a small community, that something which started as a coded form might end up as the normal form. This device is much easier to operate here than in the domain of phonology, but it requires the existence of a particular set of lexical pairs which are conventionally accepted by all speakers as antonyms. In English there is certainly a fairly large set of adjectives: black-white, hot-cold, thick-thin, big-little, large-small, long-short, dark-light, tall-short, heavy-light, strong-weak, warm-cool, and many more. Among nouns and verbs, aside from those directly related to

---

[1] Almost this explanation has, in fact, been proposed. Compare also Meillet's remarks on IE conjunctions (*Ling. hist. et ling. gén.*, 159–74)

adjectival pairs (blacken-whiten, blackness-whiteness, heat-cool/chill, etc.) there arises an uncertainty as to which feature should properly be reversed. In cases of an asymmetrical binary action or relation, this is usually accepted: teach-learn, buy-sell, give-take, and so on – English has perhaps a dozen such pairs that everyone would agree to. Verbs which indicate the reversal of action of other verbs are also well agreed on: live-die, marry-divorce, sink-swim/float, bind-loose (literary), tie-untie (usual), open-close, lift-drop, and in general pairs formed with the verbal prefix un-, like do-undo, button-unbutton, etc. (although the adjectival prefix un- is not so consistently acceptable: *common* may be the opposite of *uncommon*, but *unfunny* is not the opposite of *funny*). Names, naturally, have no opposites: chair, elm, George, etc.; and relational terms may sometimes have too many. Reversal of sex is dubious: *boy* may be the opposite of *girl* for some, but not for others. What about *father*? is the proper opposite *mother*, *son*, or *daughter*? In general this whole class is regarded as having no true antonyms (by unsophisticated speakers of English, that is), though in many languages there are kin-terms of reciprocal application, such that if A calls B 'cousin' B also calls A 'cousin', even when A is several generations above B (i.e. 'grandparent' may be identical with 'grandchild').

So in a few cases secret language reversal might conceivably account for a flip-flop. (2) Irony, whether for critical, humorous or superstitious effect, may easily be misinterpreted by young language-learners. Critical irony (when words of praise are used to convey dispraise) has had some effect upon a few words in English already – 'fine' in emphatic attributive use, 'a *fine* friend' or 'great' in the predicate 'that's just *great*' – but not enough to effect a complete reversal. Nor do I know of any attested case in the literature. However, given favorable conditions, this would seem possible. Humorous irony (as in calling a tall man 'Shorty', a skinny boy 'Fatso' or a slow one 'Genius') likewise seems to be without permanent effect and in English is virtually limited to the naming situation. Superstitious irony (one variety of euphemism) is designed to propitiate mysterious hostile forces, and is a small aspect of verbal taboo, of which other aspects are frequently cited as contributing permanent alterations to the lexicon (e.g. the words for 'bear' in several branches of IE). Here the context restrictions would generally be too great to permit a complete flip-flop; one might speak of one especially ugly idol as beautiful on certain ceremonial occasions, but that would not be likely to lead to calling all ugly things beautiful at all times. Some words, however, might be already limited to ceremonial contexts and hence open to change.

(3) Finally, as in the case of phonology, one can imagine a dialect borrowing route, though the steps may seem implausible, as noted above. In this case the flip-flop involves a gradual flip, an innovation and two losses in each dialect followed by mutual borrowing of the survivors. Keeping the two gradual shifts in separate dialects avoids the difficulty of having them reach a point of perfect synonymy, at which one would be expected to drop.

But all this is straying from our topic and our model. Let's get back to the dialect-borrowing situation. The most frequent mention of the term is by historical linguists who are explaining deviations from complete regularity, according to the neogrammarian principle that statements of sound change must be general, and all exceptions must be covered by other general rules, *either for the same or a neighboring dialect.* So in Latin the general rule states that initial Indo-European g^w becomes /w/ (written V in Latin), as in *venio* (come), *vivus* (alive), and so on. As exceptions to this appear a few words like *bos* (cow, ox) with initial b; but we know that there were dialects spoken near Rome in which the rule was initial g^w→b, and assume that *bos* is borrowed from such a dialect (a dialect spoken by farmers who would use such a word more often than city people). Dialect geographers have also shown that the limit of spread of a sound change may vary for different sets of words and even for individual words. Why doesn't this make more trouble for historical linguists than it does? One might think there would be so much uncertainty and need to assume 'dialect mixture' that the neogrammarian principle would have to be utterly abandoned (and indeed some linguists, particularly in Italy, have argued that it should be). The reason is not far to seek; in most cases historical linguists are studying forms of a standard language, the literary style level of the dialect of the capital city (Rome, Paris, Athens, etc.) in which innovations begin and spread to the rest of the country. Most of the isoglosses are miles away; only a few are inside the city itself. In other parts of the world linguists deal with the speech of small isolated communities – islands, rugged mountain valleys, etc. – where isoglosses again are few because the speakers are few. Changes can rapidly spread over the entire community. It is very rare for a historical comparativist to deal with a dialect spoken in a community without prestige, where influences come from one or several more distant centers of innovation at varying rates. This could conceivably be the case with Gothic (known mainly from a single document) or with some Medieval Germanic dialects, or some documents in various Romance languages before the rise of the modern standard; but it rarely happens that a weak and inconsistent local dialect suddenly becomes the high prestige standard. When Athens became the capital of independent Greece, it was a small, low-prestige village; but it rapidly filled up with settlers from other parts of Greece (particularly the Peloponnese), and it was *their* dialect which ultimately provided the basis for the standard dialect. Standard languages which have been created more or less artificially, like Nynorsk or Bahasa Indonesia, naturally raise a different problem (though Nynorsk, at least, was designed to be consistent and coherent from a comparative point of view).

Still there are occasional bits of evidence which give comfort to the opponents of neogrammarianism. In the Turkic languages, for instance, there seems to have been a pretty firm opposition of fortis-lenis stops in initial position (at least for p-b, t-d and the front-palatal k-g) for a long time. And yet in standard Turkish and standard Azer-baijani there are inconsistencies (not to mention other Turkic languages); in one word T may have d where A has t, and in the next T may have t, but A d. Even here, though, the majority of forms are consistent (and both languages have t, or both have d).

In recent years an attack has been launched on the neogrammarian hypothesis from another angle, though in this case the hypothesis can still be saved by rewording. From a morphophonemic point of view some words belong to families (involving inflection, derivation, com-pounding, slow vs. allegro forms, etc.), while others (e.g. many proper names, a few nouns and adjectives, several particles) are completely isolated. What is alleged is that a change which operates without excep-tion on the isolated forms may not apply at all or only partially or temporarily to forms which have a family of relatives. (A cruder variant of this was sometimes maintained even in the nineteenth century, but not as well argued.) In the new language this is stated as follows: "Changes in isolated words affect the representation in the lexicon, while changes in other words may alter only one or two low-level rules." Low-level rules are assumed to be inherently less stable than high-level ones (and lexical spelling). As a consequence phonemic mergers, which used to be considered permanent and irreversible, are now some-times thought to be partly reversible. Suppose, for instance, that a merger of i with e has been completely carried out at the surface level, so that the actual speech forms now contain only /i/ in all cases, never /e/. But some of the words are like English *hit* (let us say), without any relatives containing any qualitatively different segment between the h and the t, while others are like *dig*, which has a related form *dug*, and still others (some of them derived from earlier /e/) are like *sit*, which has related forms *set*, *sat* and *seat*. According to the theory, although all three of these classes may behave alike, they may also behave in two or in three different ways, and one of the possible ways could be a complete reversal of the change in the third class.

This is a very interesting theory, and cannot easily be disproved (or proved either, for that matter). It cannot be disproved, since cases where all occurrences of the same sound are changed in the same way are not counterexamples, and it cannot be proved (at least not for a century or two) since the earlier state of affairs (and sometimes the later, as well) is known only from written evidence, which is open to more than one interpretation, and (in more modern times) the place of an unchanged basic phonological form can more easily be played by the traditional orthographic form. Spelling pronunciations can always reverse a change.

This also has a lexico-semantic analog. An example would be my interpretation of certain facts of case-syncretism in Greek.[1] It was long ago observed that some prepositions which (in other Greek dialects) take the genitive, are found in Arcadian and Cypriote with the dative instead. The traditional explanation is 'by analogy'. Since some prepositions take only the dative, those which formerly took only the genitive might as well shift to the dative. I examined every use of the dative and every use of the genitive in the extant Arcadian and Cyprian inscriptions, and discovered an interesting fact; nearly *all* the genitives were true genitives (continuing Indo-European genitive uses), few were ablatival. The datives, on the other hand, exhibited other ablatival uses. I regarded this as ironclad evidence that Proto-Greek had a distinct ablative, and that the fusion of this case with the dative in the common ancestor of Arcadian and Cypriote, with the genitive in the other dialects, took place after this period and probably after the Mycenean period, on the ground that *if* the ablatives had first all become *genitives*, it would be psychologically impossible for a later generation to select precisely those genitives which had once been ablatives and convert all of them (and **no** others)

---

[1] 'Pa-ro and Mycenean Cases' in *Glotta* 38:1–10 (1959). See also A. Morpurgo Davis in *Mycenean Studies* (edited by L. R. Palmer and J. Chadwick), Cambridge University Press, 1969, for a skeptical view.

into datives. I still think this argument is very strong, and believe my conclusions were correct, but see that an alternative explanation is possible, namely the survival of a grammatical feature of ablativity (say) in the subconscious operations of speakers even after the form had vanished.

The influence of the written form (or forms) of a language upon its spoken form, whether of orthography upon phonology or of literary upon spoken vocabulary is, in principle, simply another class of dialect borrowing. The nodes in the written dialect net no longer represent individual speakers, as a rule, but more likely individual books or periodicals or perhaps literary genres, in some cases. And influence is much stronger (as well as more durable) in one direction (print to reader), though, since authors and editors are also people who fill nodes in the speech communication network, there is some current flowing the other way. The use of printing and of libraries (and more recently of recording-and-playback devices) has made the task of the historical linguist more complicated, since besides the possibility of words being either inherited (i.e. borrowed from other speakers of the same dialect) or borrowed from other languages, he must also consider the chance of a loan from an earlier printed form of the same language. This is in general what spelling pronunciations are. The word *falcon*, for instance, was originally borrowed (from France) in a form which would lead to the modern form /fɔ:kn/, crudely rhyming with *walkin'*, and this is, in fact, the form handed down among those few rare individuals with a continuous oral use for the word. But when the word was introduced as a brand name some years ago,[1] it inevitably took the form /falkn/, by the application of the simplest pronunciation rules (1. recessive stress on nouns, 2. zero the unstressed vowel before final n, 3. give the letter a the value [æ] ('short') before two or more consonants). There are exceptions to rule 3 that might have been applied had the word been spelt with a k (*falkon), since the letter l is not always pronounced in the sequences -alk- and -olk-, but no such inhibitions apply to the -lc- sequence. Since there had never been an /l/ in the word in spoken English or French (the loss having taken place in the transition from Latin to French), it would be very difficult indeed to find a reasonable dialect source for the word. With allowance for the interposition of pronunciation rules, any such case is identical

---

[1] I do not mean to imply that this spelling pronunciation was new; it had surely occurred thousands of times independently during the preceding century or two.

with ordinary interdialectal borrowing. In the modern situation of nearly complete literacy this leads to a complex situation in which words are repeatedly taken from the same and from different sources. For such innovations there is not just one center of spread, but often hundreds of centers.

To return once more to the neogrammarian principle, and at the same time cast a glance at the quarrel over the use of family trees for languages. First, what modifications in our model (if any) would be needed to make the family tree reasonable? (1) Suppose we start with a small number of strong centers of influence which spread many innovations very far, leading to a breakup into several large dialect areas. This will account for the first branching. (2) Then suppose the rise of high barriers between areas – either by migration (so that distance makes the barrier) which may also leave behind, perhaps, two newly adjacent areas whose difference in speech may be great enough to offer another kind of barrier, or invasion, thrusting an alien speech group between two dialect areas, or natural catastrophe of some kind (plague, volcanic action, flooding by the sea, etc.). (3) Then we will have in each of the now separated areas another period of dialect diversification; this makes the second branching. (4) Repeat as needed.

Given a situation corresponding to this model, the family tree is by no means an unreasonable hypothesis.[1] It *is* unreasonable for the desscription of a sedentary rustic population occupying a large area without strong centers of prestige or modern means of travel and communication. In such an area innovations may start almost anywhere and spread at varying rates in different directions, thus failing to generate boundaries. In-group loyalties may also operate only in extremely small groups (families or villages, perhaps), and even there they need not be very strong. Such a situation seems to have existed in several European dialect areas in the nineteenth century and must also have existed in many parts of China until quite recently. But the situation in prehistoric Europe was surely nothing like this. There we have all kinds of evidence for emigrations and sudden movements, for conquests and complete changes of language.

Then is there any excuse for abandoning the neogrammarian principle?[2] Obviously we cannot hope to do historical linguistics if this

[1] See also the article by F. C. Southworth, 'Family Tree Diagrams', *Language* 40:557 (1964). Distinct non-interbreeding species may arise under similar conditions.

[2] The principle as stated by the neogrammarians (Hermann Osthoff and Karl Brugmann, *Morphological Investigations*, as translated in W. P. Lehmann's *A Reader in*

abandonment means that some 10% of all changes may be completely irregular and unmotivated, since a few centuries of such change would quite destroy all chance of discovering regularities. The fact that historical reconstruction works so well (in spite of some doubts[1]) over periods of 2000 years or more is excellent proof that the neogrammarian principle (with proper qualifications) is sound.

One of the basic arguments for the principle, used by nineteenth century comparativists and by twentieth century phonemicists alike, was that phonological change is *gradual* and *unconscious*. Both of these characteristics have been denied at various times. As in many such cases, a great deal depends upon your definitions: what do you mean by phonological change? unconscious for whom? how gradual is gradual enough? Perhaps a brief examination of a simplified situation might not hurt.

The argument for gradual change usually concerns itself with vowels; when, in Greek, an earlier -k^w- became -p- under certain conditions, obviously some step in the process was abrupt, namely the transition from an articulation with lips partially open, to one with lips closed. And many (not all, or even most) consonant shifts involve such a step. But vowels form an articulatory and acoustic continuum: between any pair of distinguishable vowels it is always possible to insert another – distinguishable at least by instrumental means. Even if we limit our attention to distinctions which human beings can be trained to hear, we find far more distinguishable vowels than any one language ever uses. And if the shift is unconscious anyway, why worry about discriminability? This brings us to an important definitional refinement, the difference

---

Nineteenth Century Historical Indo-European Linguistics [Bloomington, Indiana University Press, 1967] p. 204), reads as follows: "Every sound change, inasmuch as it occurs mechanically, takes place according to laws that admit no exception. That is, the direction of the sound shift is always the same for all the members of a linguistic community except where a split into dialects occurs; and all words in which the sound subjected to the change appears in the same relationship are affected by the change without exception." The term "mechanically" here means (for Osthoff and Brugmann, at least) almost the same thing as "without exception"; it does *not* contain an implied theory of the causation of change. The term "in the same relationship" means, primarily, "in the same phonological environment", but does not exclude the possibility of considering alternations within paradigms. Nothing whatsoever is said about the factors which affect change. Osthoff and Brugmann's *second* neogrammarian principle enunciates the permanent relevance of analogy to all linguistic change; this does not concern us here.

[1] J. Gonda, 'The Comparative Method as applied to Indonesian Languages', *Lingua* 1:86 (1952), and W. S. Allen, 'Relationship in Comparative Linguistics', *Transactions of the Philological Society* (London), 52 (1953). For a recent look at some of the causes of difficulty, see F. B. J. Kuiper, 'Consonant Variation in Munda', *Lingua* 14:54–87 (1965).

between variation or change in absolute quality of a segment or feature (which we may term 'phonetic variation'), and change in the specification of a feature, i.e. the way in which a given segment-type is distinguished from other segment-types. Clearly one can change a vowel (for instance) very much, or even shift one's whole vowel system a long way without altering the relation of one vowel to another within the system. If only one vowel is shifted, there may be no influence upon communication with users of the unshifted vowel; the shift may pass unnoticed. If the whole system is shifted, however, or some substantial part of it, though the shift may be imperceptible as long as the in-group is isolated, contact with the out-group will lead to problems. If one dialect of English (say) shifts its front-gliding diphthongs up and forward, so that *fate* is closer to *feet* and *fight* is more like (the old) *fate*, while another shifts them down and back, so that *fate* is more like *fight* and *fight* almost rhymes with *Hoyt* (and *feet*, perhaps, is closer to *fate*), then communication between the two dialects is going to be impaired, even though within each dialect all relations are the same. Within the group all is gradual; at the boundary we have abruptness.

A second important distinction has to do with the contrast between childish and adult imitation. If a change, unconsciously initiated, is spread solely through new speakers (children learning to talk), and the in-group remains isolated, no one may know there has been a change. But if a change is spread through adult speakers, then there is competition between the old and the new which cannot well pass unnoticed. The first case involves an area in which there is only one imitable adult speaker at the outset – say a sailor shipwrecked on a desert island with a mute wife. Exactly this situation rarely occurs in nature, but various approximations certainly do. Adult imitators regularly use competing forms or variants which exist side by side, at least for a time, and it is rarely the case that they are completely unaware of this. Occasionally examples are cited of speakers who use unconsciously and indiscriminately two vowels which differ by a fully distinctive feature (i.e. one which is distinctive elsewhere in the system), but many of these reports may be due to what we will here call differential digitalization.

Even the most skilled phonetician classifies vowel sounds on a grid containing a small number of compartments (30, at most, although more symbols may be used), and each compartment has a certain area and more or less firm boundaries. Furthermore, these compartments rest more or less definitely upon a smaller set (of about 10 for English

speakers, fewer for many others, at most perhaps 12 or 15) of larger
compartments corresponding to the contrastive vowels of the speaker's
native language. Phoneticians trained in the London tradition may have
a partially independent set derived from careful study of the Jones
Cardinal Vowels. But, no matter what the basis is, there are a few
vowels for which the listener will say "That's an [x]", considerably
more for which he will say "That's a sort of an [x]" or, more precisely,
"a fronted (raised, lowered, backed, rounded, etc.) [x]", and a very
few for which he will say "That's half-way between an [x] and a [y]".
Self-consistency is a fair test of this; there may be recorded vowels
which I will hear on Tuesday as "definitely [ʌ]" or at least as "a kind
of [ʌ]", but on Saturday as "a kind of [æ]" or even "clearly [æ]". And
whichever way I hear it on a given day, it is only with the greatest
difficulty that I can force myself to imagine hearing it in the other way.

Now the point of all this is that I believe that in many cases where
investigators say, e.g. that speakers of Dialect A fluctuate in a completely random way between a clear [i] and a clear [ɯ] without being
aware of it, although their neighbours to the north (Dialect B) have a
sharp distinction between these sounds, I think the true situation may be
simply that speakers of Dialect A use a large and quite continuous
portion of the vowel space which happens to overlap both the investigator's areas for [i] and [ɯ] and the dialect B areas for [i] and [ɯ] but
in different ways.

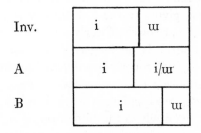

As this diagram is drawn, it might also be the case that the investigator
will report that Dialect B's use of [ɯ] in most words is very consistent,
but there are some cases in which, although [i] is normal, [ɯ] occurs
sporadically. It is now quite possible to correct for this source of error,
if you suspect it, by making a number of sound spectrograms (or other
similar analyses), but it was not always so, and it is not easy even now,
for a variety of reasons (some psychological, some statistical).

A small number of distinctive vowels means an even smaller number of vowel features. (All that follows applies equally to phonemes in general, not merely to vowels.) There seem to be several possibilities of change which affect this system, all of which are necessarily leaps from the system's point of view, though they may take place very gradually in a fine phonetic sense. (1) A distinction ceases to be made (i.e. a distinctive feature becomes redundant) at some point in the system: merger of phonemes. (2) A distinction ceases to apply anywhere (becomes redundant everywhere) in the system: loss of a feature or perhaps merger of features. Both of these types reduce the number of distinctive vowels (or other phonemes). (3) A formerly redundant feature becomes distinctive and an associated distinctive feature becomes redundant. The redundant feature might have come in recently (fine phonetic change) or been around for a long while. This need not affect either the number or the interrelations of the vowels in the system at all. Some variant of this type of change may have been present in the Germanic consonant shift (Grimm's law). (4) A redundant feature becomes distinctive without any accompanying change. This is necessarily a case where the redundant feature is only sometimes present, i.e. allophonic, and the result is a split, of one phoneme or class of phonemes into two. This is the sort of thing which is supposed to happen in cases of umlaut, for instance, where at one stage fronting of back rounded vowels (or, in other cases, rounding of front vowels) is predictable from the environment (and hence redundant), but at a later stage the conditioning environment is lost, giving rise to a distinctive series of fronted back vowels or rounded front vowels. Clearly a change of this sort cannot be fully established until it is no longer possible to regard the feature in question as belonging properly to a *different* segment (the conditioning one). If, for instance, we have a second-syllable /i/ segment fronting a first-syllable back vowel and then being itself phonetically lost, we cannot say it is phonemically lost until new second-syllable /i/ segments arise which are phonetically present in an unpredictable way (without, we should hope, any fronting effect on first-syllable vowels). Some generative phonologists (rejecting all or most principles of phonemics) may require more than this before shifting a change from low-level rules to lexical specification, though it is not clear exactly how much is required. The reason for this uncertainty is the fact that there seems to be no direct constraint on the localization of distinctiveness in the lexicon, so that it is always possible to have an additional distinctive segment there which exerts certain influences on other segments and is then deleted. An indirect constraint is provided by the agreement that all features must come from a predetermined inventory (and since this may include as many as 20 features, the constraint is slight), and that the features used in the lexicon should not include any which are completely absent at the phonetic level. All rules should also be phonetically plausible, but this condition is somewhat more difficult to make objective.

To return to our umlaut case, then in addition to the disappearance of [i] from the final phonetic string, it must also disappear from the basic lexical string. This presumably means that the total description can be somehow shown to be more economical and revealing without the retention of this conditioning /i/ than with it.

To revert for a moment to Grimm's law, presumably there is no advantage (in a description of modern English) to specifying the initial segment of *brother* as [+aspirated] or of *father* as [+interrupted] or of *ten* as [+voiced]. But when did this state of affairs come about? Would it be equally true of Gothic?

Though there are many cases in which phonological change takes place unnoticed by all the speakers, and is phonetically quite gradual, there are also cases of which at least some speakers are vividly aware, including some where the phonetic difference is great. But it can never be great enough (as far as has yet been attested) to involve a double change in distinctive features at one moment in time.[1] Nor is it possible to deny the neogrammarian principle entirely, and say that phonological changes ordinarily proceed in a random way.

[1] See William Austin's article 'Criteria for Phonetic Similarity', *Language* 33:544 (1957).

Bibliography

Abercrombie, David, *Elements of General Phonetics*, Edinburgh, Edinburgh University Press, 1967.

Alexander, D., and Matthews, P. H., *Adjectives Before That Clauses in English*, Indiana University Linguistics Research Project, September 1964.

Alexander, D., and Kunz, W., *Some Classes of Verbs in English*, Indiana University Linguistics Research Project, June 1964.

Allen, W. S., 'Relationship in comparative linguistics', *Transactions of the Philological Society* (London), 52 (1953).

'A Problem of Greek Accentuation', *In Memory of J. R. Firth*, London, Longmans, Green and Co., 1966, pp. 8–14.

Austin, J. L., *How To Do Things With Words*, New York, Oxford University Press, 1965 (GB 132).

Austin, William, 'Criteria for phonetic similarity', *Language* 33 (1957), 538–44.

Bazell, C. E. (ed.), *In Memory of J. R. Firth*, London, Longmans, 1966.

Bloch, B., 'A set of postulates for phonemic analysis', *Language* 24 (1948), 3–46.

'Studies in colloquial Japanese IV', *Language* 26 (1950), 86–125.

Bloomfield, Leonard, *Language*, New York, Holt, Rinehart, and Winston, 1965 (reprinted from 1933).

Bolinger, D. L., 'Identity, similarity, and difference', *Litera* 1 (1954), 5–16.

Forms of English (edited by J. Abe and J. Kanekigo), Harvard University Press, 1965.

Aspects of Language, New York, Harcourt, Brace and World, 1968.

Bréal, M., *Semantics*, New York, Henry Holt, 1900 (New York, Dover Publications, 1964).

Bridgeman, L., *et al.*, *Nouns Before That Clauses in English*, Indiana University Linguistics Project, June 1965.

Brown, A. F., *Normal and Reverse English Word List*, University of Pennsylvania, 1963.

Brown, R., and McNeil, D., 'The tip of the tongue phenomenon', *Journal of Verbal Learning and Verbal Behavior*, 5 (1966), 335–7.

Burroughs, Edgar Rice, *Tarzan of the Apes*, Ballantine Books, Inc., New York, 1963 (U2001).

Caws, P., 'The structure of discovery', *Science* 166 (1969), 1375–80.

Chafe, W. L., 'The ordering of phonological rules', *POLA Reports* 2nd Series No. 2, October 1967.

Chayaratana, Chalao, *A Comparative Study of English and Thai Syntax*, Indiana University, 1961.

Chao, Y. R., 'The non-uniqueness of phonemic solutions of phonetic systems', *Bulletin of the Institute of History and Philology* (Academia Sinica) 4 (1933), 363–97; reprinted in Joos's *Readings*, 38–54.

Language and Symbolic Systems, New York, Cambridge University Press, 1968.

Chomsky, N., *Syntactic Structures*, The Hague, Mouton, 1957.

'The logical basis of linguistic theory', *Proceedings of the 9th International Congress of Linguists* (ed. H. G. Lunt), The Hague, Mouton, 1964.

Aspects of the Theory of Syntax, Cambridge, Mass, M.I.T. Press, 1965.

Chomsky, N., Halle, M., and Lukoff, F., 'On accent and juncture in English', *For Roman Jakobson*, The Hague, Mouton, 1965, 65–80.

Chomsky, N., and Halle, M., 'On some disputed questions in phonological theory', *Journal of Linguistics* 1.2 (1965), 97–138.

Sound Pattern of English, New York, Harper and Row, 1968.

Christensen, R. W., 'Phonème et graphème en Français moderne', *Acta Linguistica Hafniensia* 10 (1967), 217–40.

Closs, Elizabeth, 'Diachronic syntax and generative grammar', *Language* 41 (1965), 402–15.

Conklin, H., 'Lexicographical treatment of folk taxonomies', *Problems in Lexicography* (ed. Householder and Saporta; Publication 21, I.U. Research Center in Anthropology, Folklore and Linguistics, Bloomington, 1962), pp. 119–41.

Contreras, H., 'Simplicity, descriptive adequacy and binary features', *Language* 45 (1969), 1–8.

Corstius, H. Brandt, 'Automatic translation of numbers in Dutch', *Foundations of Language* 1 (1965), 59–62.

Denes, P. B., and Pinson, E. N., *The Speech Chain*, Baltimore, Maryland, Bell Telephone Laboratories, 1963.

Elson, B., *Beginning Morphology-Syntax*, Glendale, SIL 1957.

Elson, B., and Pickett, V., *Beginning Morphology-Syntax*, Santa Ana, SIL 1960.

Esper, Erwin A., 'Social transmission of an artificial language', *Language* 42 (1966), 575–80.

Fant, Gunnar, 'Sound spectrography', *Sovijärvi and Aalto* 14–33.

Fillmore, C., 'A proposal concerning English prepositions', *Report of the 17th Annual Round Table Meeting*, Georgetown, Georgetown University Press, 1966.

'The case for case', *Universals of Language*, ed. by E. Bach and R. Harms, New York, Holt, Rinehart, and Winston, 1968, 1–88.

Fischer-Jørgensen, E., 'Form and substance in Glossematics', *Acta Linguistica Holmiensia* 10 (1966), 1–33.

Francis, W. Nelson, 'A modified system of phonetic transcription for one idiolect of English', *Papers in Linguistics in Honor of Léon Dostert*, The Hague, Mouton, 1967, 37–45.

Fromkin, V. A., 'Speculations on performance models', *Journal of Linguistics* 4 (1968), 47–68.

'Tips of the slung – or – to err is human', U.C.L.A. *Working Papers in Phonetics* No. 14 (1970), 40–79.

Fudge, Erik, *Linguistic Analysis of English*, NTIS PB 167 950 (February 1965) ch. 2 and 3.

Greenberg, Joseph, *Universals of Language*, Cambridge, Mass; M.I.T. Press, 1963.

Gonda, J., 'The comparative method as applied to Indonesian languages', *Lingua* 1 (1952), 86–101.

Gudschinsky, Sarah C., Popovich, H., and Popovich, Frances, 'Native reaction and phonetic similarity in Maxakali phonology', *Language* 46 (1970), 77–88.

Hall, Robert A., Jr., *Leave Your Language Alone*, Ithaca, New York, Linguistica, 1950, (revised as *Linguistics and Your Language*, New York, Doubleday, 1960).

Introductory Linguistics, Philadelphia, Chilton Books, 1964.

Halliday, M. A. K., 'Categories of the theory of grammar', *Word* 17 (1961), 241–92.

Hamp, E. P., Householder, F. W., and Austerlitz, R., *Readings in Linguistics II*, Chicago, University of Chicago Press, 1966.

Hare, R. M., *The Language of Morals*, New York, Oxford University Press, 1964 (GB 111).

Harms, R. T., 'The measurement of phonological economy', *Language* 42 (1966), 602–11.

Harris, Z., *Methods in Structural Linguistics*, Chicago, University of Chicago Press, 1951.

'Co-occurrence and transformation in linguistic structure', *Language* 33 (1957), 283–340.

Hattori, Shiro, 'The principle of assimilation in phonetics', *Word* 23 (1967), 257–64.

Haugen, Einar, *The First Grammatical Treatise*, Language Monograph No. 25, 1950.

Hecaen, H., 'Aspects des troubles de la lecture (alexies) au cours des lésions cérebrales en foyer', *Word* 23 (1967), 265–87.

Henderson, E. J. A., 'The topography of certain phonetic and morphological characteristics of South East Asian languages', *Lingua* 15 (1965), 400–34.

Heny, F. W., 'Non-binary phonological features', U.C.L.A. *Working Papers in Phonetics* No. 7, November 1967.

'Toward the separation of classificatory and phonetic features', U.C.L.A. *Working Papers in Phonetics* No. 7, November 1967.

Hockett, C. F., 'A system of descriptive phonology', *Language* 18 (1942), 3–21; in Joos's *Readings* 97–108.

Course in Modern Linguistics, New York, Macmillan, 1958.

'The problem of universals in language', *Universals of Language* (ed. Greenberg), Cambridge, Mass., M.I.T. Press, 1966.

The State of the Art, The Hague, Mouton, 1968.
'The origin of speech', *Scientific American* 203 (1960), 88–96.
Hockett, C. F., and Ascher, R., 'The human revolution', *Current Anthropology* 5 (1964), 135–47.
Householder, F. W.,'Review of E. Adelaide Hahn's *Subjunctive and Optative*', *Language* 30 (1954), 389–99.
'Unreleased ptk', *For Roman Jakobson*, The Hague, Mouton, 1957, pp. 253–44.
'Pa-ro and Mycenean cases', *Glotta* 38 (1959), 1–10.
'The distributional determination of English phonemes', *Lingua* 11 (1962), 186–91.
'On some recent claims in phonological theory', *Journal of Linguistics* 1 (1965), 13–34.
Householder, F. W., *et al.*, *Linguistic Analysis of English*, Final Report to the National Science Foundation under Grant GS-108 (1964), available from NTIS as PB 167 950.
Jackendoff, R., 'Speculations on presentences and determiners', 1968 (unpublished).
Jakobson, R., *Beitrag zur allgemeinen Kasuslehre* in *TCLP* 6 (1936), 240–88; *Readings in Linguistics* 11, 51–89.
Selected Writings, vol. 1, The Hague, Mouton, 1962.
Jakobson, R., and Lotz, J., 'Notes on the French phonemic pattern', *Word* 5 (1949), 151–8.
Jakobson, R., Fant, C. G. M., and Halle, M., *Preliminaries to Speech Analysis*, M.I.T., 1952.
Jaquith, J. R., 'Toward a typology of formal communicative behaviors: Glossolalia', *Anthropological Linguistics* 9, 8 (1967) 1–8.
Joos, M., *Acoustic Phonetics*, Linguistic Society of America, Language Monograph No. 23, 1948.
'Semology: a linguistic theory of meaning', *Studies in Linguistics*, 13 (1958), 53–70, Bobbs-Merrill *Language Reprint* 54.
(ed.), *Readings in Linguistics* 1, Chicago, University of Chicago Press, 4th ed., 1966.
Katwijk, A. Van, 'A grammar of Dutch number names', *Foundations of Language* 1 (1965), 51–8.
Katz, J., and Fodor, J., 'The structure of a semantic theory', *Language* 39 (1963), 170–210.
Kim, Chin-W., 'On the autonomy of the tensity feature in stop classification', *Word* 21 (1965), 339–59.
Kiparsky, P., 'A propos de l'histoire de l'accentuation grecque', *Langages* 8 (1967), 73–93.
Klein, S., 'Automatic paraphrasing in essay format', *Mechanical Translation* 8 (1965), 68–83.
'Control of style with a generative grammar', *Language* 41 (1965), 619–31.
'Historical change in language using Monte Carlo techniques', *Mechanical Translation* 9 (1966), 67–82.

Klein, S., Kuppin, M. A., and Meives, K. A., 'Monte Carlo simulation of language change in Tikopia and Maori', Preprint No. 21 of the International Conference on Computational Linguistics (Stockholm, 1969).

Klein, S., and Simmons, R. F., 'Syntactic dependence and the computer generation of coherent discourse', *Mechanical Translation* 7:2 (1963), 50–61.

Klima, E., 'Relatedness between grammatical systems', *Language* 40 (1964), 1–20.

Kohler, K., 'Modern English phonology', *Lingua* 19 (1967), 145–76.

Koutsoudas, Andreas, 'The A over A convention', *Linguistics* 46 (1968), 11–20.

Kucera, H., and Francis, W. N., *Computational Analysis of Present-Day American English*, Providence, Brown University Press, 1967.

Kuiper, F. B. J., 'Consonant variation in Munda', *Lingua* 14 (1965), 54–87.

Ladefoged, P., *Elements of Acoustic Phonetics*, University of Chicago Press, 1962.

A Phonetic Study of West African Language, Cambridge, Cambridge University Press, 1964.

Linguistic Phonetics (Working Papers in Phonetics 6, U.C.L.A., 1967).

Lakoff, George, 'Empiricism without facts', *Foundations of Language* 5 (1969), 118–27.

Lamb, S., 'Epilegomena to a theory of language', *Romance Philology* 19 (1966), 531–72.

Langendoen, D. T., *The Study of Syntax*, New York, Holt, Rinehart, and Winston, 1969.

Lanham, L. W., 'Generative phonology of Nguni consonants', *Lingua* 244 (1969), 155–62.

Lees, R. B., *The Grammar of English Nominalizations*, I.U. Research Center in Anthropology, Folklore and Linguistics, Bloomington, Indiana, 1960.

Lehiste, I., and Peterson, G., 'Some basic consideration in the analysis of intonation', *JASA* 33 (1961), 419–25.

Lehiste, Ilse (ed.), *Readings in Acoustic Phonetics*, Cambridge, Mass., M.I.T. Press, 1967.

Lieberman, P., *Intonation, Perception and Language* (Research monograph No. 38) Cambridge, Mass., M.I.T. Press, 1967.

Lightner, T. M., 'On the description of vowel and consonant harmony', *Word* 21 (1965), 244–50.

Lindblom, B., 'Accuracy and limitations of sona-graph measurements', *Sovijärvi and Aalto*, 188–202.

Lisker, Leigh, and Abramson, A. S., 'A cross language study of voicing in initial stops: acoustical measurements', *Word* 20: (1964), 384–433.

Longacre, R. E., *Grammar Discovery Procedures*, The Hague, Mouton, 1964.

Lyons, John, 'Phonemic and non-phonemic phonology: some typological reflections', *IJAL* 28 (1962), 127–34.

Structural Semantics, Oxford, Basil Blackwell, 1963.

'Comments on McNeill', *Psycholinguistics Papers*, edited by John Lyons and R. J. Wales, Edinburgh, Edinburgh University Press, 1966, pp. 129–32.

Maher, J. P., 'The paradox of creation and tradition in grammar', *Language Sciences* No. 7 (October, 1969), 15–24.

Malmberg, B., *Phonetics*, New York, Dover, 1963.

Marler, Peter, 'Animal communication signals', *Science* 157 (1967), 769–74.

McCawley, J. D., 'La rôle d'un système de traits phonologiques dans une théorie du langage', *Langage* 8:112–23 (December 1967).

'Concerning the base component of a transformational grammar', *Foundations of Language* 4 (1968), 243–69.

Meigret, Louis, *Trette de la Grammere françoeze*, ed. by Wendelin Foerster, Heilbronn, Gebr. Henninger, 1888.

Merrifield, W. R., Naish, C. M., Rensch, C. R., and Story, G., *Laboratory Manual for Morphology and Syntax*, Santa Ana, SIL, 1965.

Mohr, B., and Wang, W. S.-Y., 'Perceptual distance and the specification of phonological features', *POLA Reports*, 2nd series No. 1, September, 1967.

Moravcsik, J. M. E., 'Linguistic theory and the philosophy of language', *Foundations of Language*, 3 (1967), 209–33.

Morpurgo Davis, A., 'An instrumental-ablative in Mycenean?' *Mycenean Studies* (edited by L. R. Palmer and J. Chadwick), Cambridge University Press, 1969, pp. 191–202.

Nida, E. A., *Morphology, The Descriptive Analysis of Words*, Ann Arbor, University of Michigan Press, 1966, etc.

Osgood, C. E., Suci, G. J., and Tannenbaum, P. H., *The Measurement of Meaning*, Urbana, University of Illinois Press, 1957.

Osthoff, Herman, and Brugmann, Karl, 'Morphological Investigations', translated in W. P. Lehmann's *A Reader in Nineteenth Century Historical Indo-European Linguistics*, Bloomington, Indiana University Press, 1967, pp. 197–209.

Palmer, F. R., 'Bilin [Word Classes]', *Lingua* 17 (1966), 200–9.

Pickett, V., *An Introduction to the Study of Grammatical Structure*, Glendale, SIL 1956.

Pike, K., *Phonetics*, Ann Arbor, University of Michigan Press, 1944.

'Grammatical prerequisites to phonemic analysis', *Word* 3 (1947), 155–72.

Language in Relation to a Unified Theory of the Structure of Human Behavior, Glendale, Summer Institute of Linguistics, Part One 1954, Part Two 1955.

Postal, Paul, 'Review of M. W. Dixon, *Linguistic Science and Logic*', in *Language* 43 (1966), 84–93.

Aspects of Phonological Theory, New York, Harper and Row, 1968.

Pound, Glen, *Phonological Distortion in Spoken Secret Languages*, Indiana University Dissertation, 1963.

Quirk, R., and Svartvik, J., *Investigating Linguistic Acceptability*, The Hague, Mouton, 1966.

Rischel, Jørgen, *Phoneme, Grapheme, and the 'Importance' of Distinctions,*

Interim Report No. 1 of the Research Group for Quantitative Linguistics (KVAL PM 260), 1967.

Roberts, A. H., *A Statistical Analysis of American English*, The Hague, Mouton, 1965.

Sapir, Edward, 'Sound patterns in language', *Language* 1 (1925), 37–51; Joos's *Readings in Linguistics* 1, 19–25.

Language, New York, Harcourt, Brace and Co., 1939.

Saussure, Ferdinand de, *Course in General Linguistics*, edited by Charles Bally and Albert Sechehaye, in collaboration with A. Reidlinger, translated from the French by Wade Baskin, New York, Philosophical Library, 1959.

Schachter, P., 'Phonetic similarity in tonemic analysis', *Language* 37 (1961), 231–8.

Scholes, Robert J., *Categorical Responses to Synthetic Vocalic Stimuli by Native Speakers of Various Foreign Languages*, Indiana Language Program Grant, 1965.

Searle, J. R., *Speech Acts*, Cambridge University Press, 1969.

Sebeok, T. A., 'Finnish and Hungarian case systems: their form and function', *Acta Instituti Hungarici Universitatis Holmiensis*, Series B, *Linguistics* 3, 1946.

Seuren, P. A. M., *Operators and Nucleus*, Cambridge University Press, 1969.

Sigurd, B., *Phonotactic Structures in Swedish*, Lund, Uniskol, 1965.

Sokal, R. R., and Sneath, P. H. A., *Principles of Numerical Taxonomy*, San Francisco and London, W. H. Freeman and Co., 1963.

Southworth, F. C., 'Family tree diagrams', *Language* 40 (1964), 557.

Sovijärvi, A., and Aalto, P. (eds.), *The Proceedings of the Fourth International Congress of Phonetic Sciences*, The Hague, Mouton, 1962.

Stevick, R. D., 'The biological model and historical linguistics', *Language* 39 (1963), 159–69.

Sturtevant, E., *Introduction to Linguistic Science*, New Haven, Yale University Press, 1947.

Trnka, B., *A Phonological Analysis of Present-day Standard English* (Prague, vol. V of 'Studies in English by members of the English Seminar of the Charles University', 1935).

Trubetzkoy, N. S., *Grundzüge der Phonologie* (TCLP 7), Prague, 1939; Vandenhoek and Ruprecht, Göttingen, 1958, French version (tr. J. Cantineau), Klincksieck (Paris), 1949; English, translated by C. A. M. Baltaxe, Berkeley, University of California Press, 1969.

Twaddell, W. F., 'On defining the phoneme', *Language* Monograph No. 16, 1935, reprinted in Joos's *Readings*, 55–80.

Uldall, H. J., 'Speech and writing', *Acta Linguistica* (Copenhagen) 4 (1964), 11–16; *Readings in Linguistics* II, 147–51.

Vachek, Josef, 'Some remarks on writing and phonetic transcription', *Acta Linguistica* (Copenhagen) 5 (1949), 86–93; *Readings in Linguistics* II, 152–57.

Vasiliu, E., 'The phonemic status of Rumanian affricates', *Proceedings of the*

9th International Congress of Linguists (ed. H. Lunt), The Hague, Mouton (1964), 589–92.

Venezky, R. L., 'The basis of English orthography', *Acta Linguistica Hafniensia* 10 (1967), 145–59.

Voegelin, C. F., 'Linear phonemes and additive components', *Word* 12 (1956), 429–43.

Voegelin, C. F. and F. M., 'Guide for transcribing languages in fieldwork', *Anthropological Linguistics* 1, No. 6 (1959).

Wang, W. S.-Y., 'Competing changes as a cause of residue', *POLA Reports* 2nd Series, No. 2, October 1967.

'Phonological features of tone', *IJAL* 33 (1967), 93–105.

Weinberg, A. M., 'In defense of science', *Science* 167 (1970), 141–5.

Weinreich, U., Labov, W., and Herzog, M. L., 'Empirical foundation for a theory of language change' in *Directions for Historical Linguistics: A Symposium*, Austin, University of Texas Press, 1968, pp. 97–145.

Whitaker, H. A., 'On the representation of language in the human brain', U.C.L.A. *Working Papers in Phonetics* No. 12, September 1969.

White, M. J. D., 'Models of speciation', *Science* 159 (1968), 1065–70.

Wijk, Axel, *Rules of Pronunciation for the English Language*, New York, Oxford University Press, 1966.

Wölck, W., and Matthews, P. H., *A Preliminary Classification of Adverbs in English*, Indiana University Linguistics Research Project, August 1965.

Yasui, M., *Consonant Patterning in English*, Tokyo, 1963.

Yngve, V., 'A model and an hypothesis for language structure', *Proceedings of the American Philosophical Society*, 104 (1960), 444–66.

Index—Glossary[1]

---

[1] Technical terms not glossed here are explained in the text. Several people helped in the preparation of this index – especially my wife, Clarice Householder.

M